STRATEGIES FOR CHANGE

Jack Lindquist

Pacific Soundings Press

Strategies for Change
Jack Lindquist

WILLIAM BERGQUIST *Publisher*
STEVEN R. PHILLIPS *General Editor*
JENNIFER GRIMES *Editor*
KITTY R. ANDERSON *Designer*
EMILY J. BEEBEE *Associate Designer*
TYPESETTER *Thompson Type*

Printed by
Perfector Web Printing
Santee, California

ii

Table of Contents

iii

Foreword

The origins of this book and my baptism in strategies for change occurred in 1958 when the president of a rapidly growing private college recruited me to head a new department of teacher education. He enticed me not with money (I took a salary cut) but with his avowed concern to create "an innovative top quality program that would lead the way to improved practices throughout the state." Six months later I was suing him for breach of contract. So was a colleague in my department. The local and national AAUP was actively involved and provided financial support. In September the following year twelve other department heads offered their resignations, and by January the President was Emeritus. I was gone. A traditional teacher education program was getting underway. But my education in planned change had begun.

I'll not detail those experiences here. "You could look it up," as Damon Runyon used to say—in the AAUP Bulletins of that period. But there is no question that knowledge of the institutional change model presented in this book would have stopped much bloodshed and helped both the faculty and the administration during that very difficult time.

My interest in, and appetite for, planned change in higher education, was further whetted when I joined President Tim Pitkin, George Beecher, Forest Davis and other members of the Goddard College faculty and administration in carrying forward a six-year "Experiment in College Curriculum Organization." From 1959-1965 that experiment developed "contract learning" and "group independents," a learning resources center using programmed learning materials, (I still remember my introductory psychology students fighting their way through Skinner's programmed textbook), "experiential learning" through work and volunteer activities in the local communities and on campus, and "living and learning centers" in wood frame sixteen-person houses. We didn't use today's fashionable labels, but it was exciting to translate those early ideas into operating policies and practices.

As Coordinator of Evaluation, my main responsibility was to generate empirical evidence for use by the faculty and administration in program development and change. I learned how hard it is to get useful evidence pertinent to live problems and how difficult it can be to face that evidence. I learned that faculty members and students can and will contribute very effectively to such a research enterprise—if the research coordinator will take periodic doses of hostility and frustration. And I learned that such evidence, properly gathered and shared, can be a powerful stimulus for change even when it addresses complex goals for student development like "Venturesomeness," "Interdependence, Resourcefulness and Organization" and "Personal Stability and Integration." (See "Institutional Objectives and Student Development in College" in volume three of the Journal of Applied Behavioral Sciences *for details concerning this particular faculty research project.)*

The Project on Student Development in Small Colleges, carried on from 1965-1970, grew directly from those experiences. That project was conceived by Tim Pitkin and Ernest Boyer (then Dean of Upland College) to test one basic premise: planned change will occur if a college examines data concerning its objectives, the educational experiences of its students, factors responsible for attrition and changes which do or do not occur among those who graduate. Thirteen small colleges across the country joined that effort, which was coordinated through the Council for the Advancement of Small Colleges. They dutifully collected the questionnaire data and arranged on-campus visits and interviews for project staff. But somehow serious examination of results and efforts to change did not go quite so handily. The project staff members wrote pithy, punchy reports. They even went to campuses for workshops. But when we arrived no bands played. There were no wild hat-tossing celebrations. After we left, thank-you notes came, rather like those a grandmother might write to a grandson who gave her a catcher's mit for Christmas. Although the project produced generally useful research and theory concerning college impacts on student development, with only occasional exceptions it did not have much consequence for the participating institutions. Somehow pithy, punchy reports and persuasive on-campus presentations were not enough. Effective knowledge utilization and planned change require more.

To this end, my colleagues and I launched a four-year follow-up project, Strategies for Change and Knowledge Utilization, funded by the Applied Research Branch of the National

Institute for Mental Health, to address the problem more directly. It still had data collection and feedback at its core, but it was able to build on a developing body of research and theory concerning innovation diffusion, adoption and adaptation. Havelock's major synthesis of the literature, Planning for Innovation, *appeared just in time to provide a solid conceptual framework with which to begin the project. While we were just beginning the Strategies project, I assumed the position of Vice-President for Academic Affairs of Empire State College, a new experimenting unit of the State University of New York. The challenges of helping get that innovative effort underway left project leadership largely to its Executive Director, a position first held by William Hannah and then assumed by Jack Lindquist.*

Under their leadership, the project has been highly productive for most of the participating colleges and for our understanding of planned change in higher education in general. As Section I of this book makes clear, the adaptive development theory that Lindquist has developed extends the earlier work of Havelock and others in concrete ways helpful to faculty members and administrators. The detailed cases in Section II describe explicit conditions in widely different colleges and universities that will be familiar to those in similar institutions. The general principles and specific recommendations in Section III provide a useful guide to any person or group that would undertake institutional change making use of research, theory and the pertinent experiences of others.

The knowledge and insights presented here are especially significant now. Higher education faces financial, demographic and social forces which will require major changes during the next decade. There are two handy responses: inter- and intra-institutional cannabalism resulting from unfettered power politics based on vested interests, or slow bleeding and general anemia resulting from weakness of will and back-scratching compromises.

The results also have major implications for philanthropic foundations and federal funding agencies. Since the early 1960's the government and major foundations have invested millions of dollars supporting hundreds of projects designed to make education more effective, from pre-school through post-secondary. Yet at a recent Strategies Workshop, when Alden Dunham asked, "How many significant and successful innovations have occurred during the last 15 years?", our count still left fingers on the first hand. This sad state of affairs may result from funding patterns which have not required early collaborative planning to create broad-

based "ownership" of a project as it is getting underway and which have not required dissemination and planned change activities once projects have been completed. The principle outcomes from most projects is a paper or a book. If it sells well and receives recognition the project is presumed successful; if it drops out of sight perhaps the project was not. But surely our experience of the apparently limited impact of the wide ranging and diverse Carnegie Commission reports and of numerous other commissions and task forces now makes it clear that simply pushing paper is not going to do the job.

For this reason, this present volume is only one of a number of products resulting from the Strategies for Change and Knowledge Utilization project—although it has the potential of being a highly significant resource. It offers no panaceas for the ills of higher education. It will not make today's difficult realities more benign, nor the problems flying toward us from the future less challenging. If higher education is to change effectively in response to the shifting social forces and new conditions it faces, systematic action soundly supported will be required. Those actions require will and courage, adventurousness and tolerance for ambiguity, openness and objectivity, perspective and persistence. No book can increase the total supply of those qualities currently available from faculty members and administrators. This report, however, can help persons and institutions with such qualities achieve change more effectively. As such it can contribute materially to the work facing higher education in the next decade.

viii

Arthur W. Chickering

Preface

The demand for change is constantly with us. Yesterday's answers will not cure today's cancers. Our old ways of consuming natural resources and multiplying populations will not sustain this planet very long. Education for yesterday's elite (whether social or meritocratic) is an ill-fit for today's wide diversity of learners. The solutions of affluence hardly apply to a period of retrenchment and constraint. And whether we lick today's problems or not, tomorrow is sure to bring new ones.

What can be done? Two alternatives present themselves. One is our old standby: defensive, belated, groping, wasteful reaction when the demand gets too great to ignore. The other is to plan for change, to be intentional about it. This book is about the second alternative.

Section I summarizes existing research and theory related to planned change in complex organizations. Section II then relates this prior theory to detailed case histories of seven change attempts in seven organizations, recorded as they happened. Such pictures of planned change in process are frequently extolled as necessary to understand that process, but they are rarely done because of the time, cost and complex methodology involved. The book synthesizes from prior research and the cases a model for organizational change called "adaptive development," a general strategy quite consistent with recent theory but not yet implemented. The last section presents practical strategies and tactics for carrying out intentional change.

The focus of the research is change in American college teaching, curriculum and evaluation. Six liberal arts colleges and two universities across the country participated from 1971 to 1975 in an action-research project called Strategies for Change and Knowledge Utilization. Although this focus makes the book particularly relevant to students and practitioners of collegiate reform and innovation, the theory base and resulting synthesis have much broader application. I have found "adaptive development" useful in understanding and aiding planned change in organizations as varied as primary schools, mental health agencies and architectural firms.

There are many people to thank for such an ambitious undertaking. First is Arthur Chickering, who originated the project and provided perceptive advice as well as warm support throughout those four years. Next come core action-research staff—William Hannah, Lois Bovee, Robert Guerrin, Charles Stannard, Susan Koffman-Plante, Judy McCormack, Diana Keller and Fay Spargo. Their diversity of research backgrounds and views toward academic change checked the bias of narrow perspectives; their ability to endure the sheer drudgery, complicated methodology and difficult action demands helped make the project a success. On-campus project leaders such as psychologists Richard Kasschau, Edith Daly, Harold Yuker and James Hart; economists Herman Berliner and William Wesson; mathematician Wayne Cassel; historian Michael Reynolds; English professor Lewis Marcuson; and biologist Amy Harvey coordinated both the action and the research on each campus. Institutional presidents Adolph Anderson, Tom Jones, Ray Hostader, Sister Patricia Jean Manion, Robert Hinshaw, Rembert Stokes, Seymour Smith and James Marshall gave the project solid backing and, often, active leadership. Other administrative and faculty leaders will see themselves in the cases and deserve thanks both for their tolerance of our scrutiny and for their skillful efforts to improve their institutions. The project's national advisory board was not some distant panel of dignitaries. Goodwin Watson, Harold Hodgkinson, Ronald Havelock, Warren Bryan Martin, David Bushnell, Royce Pitkin, Benjamin Barger, Roger Voskuyl and Gary Quehl rolled up their sleeves to provide active help to staff and institutions throughout those years. Less active but equally supportive were Samuel Baskin and Edwin Hallenbeck of the project's sponsor, the Union for

x

Experimenting Colleges and Universities. Finally, a debt is owed leaders of the National Institute for Mental Health for the original three-year grant and a fourth year extension.

All these friends and others have influenced the success of the project and the substance of this book. But, in the end, you are stuck with me. I have sought through methodological checks and a conservative posture toward the data to approach objectivity. But no social scientist entirely escapes bias. I'm sure you will detect mine. Ultimately, this book is a conversation between you and me, a search for understanding within our experiences. I hope you enjoy it and find it useful as you try to be intentional about change.

Jack Lindquist

Ann Arbor, Michigan
December, 1976

Section I

Planned Change Theory and Research

A logical first step toward understanding how to go about changing attitudes and behaviors in organizations is to synthesize prior theory and research. What has been learned so far? Chapter One presents five major assumptions about change, each of which has attendant tactics and roles. Chapter Two then focuses upon a specific context in which such strategies are applied, the American college and university. Chapter Three takes another step into these settings by reporting diagnostic information regarding the educational and organizational "health" of five liberal arts colleges and two universities in the academic year 1971-72.

Together, these chapters provide the background needed to analyze the case histories presented in Section II. This section is also a good place to check your own assumptions and strategies against existent theory. Are people in organizations most influenced by reason and evidence, by social needs or by power? What makes change in colleges and universities so difficult? What needs to be changed in such organizations anyway? These are the questions addressed in Section I.

1 Strategies for Change

We carry in our heads, and lower, basic notions about how to bring about change.* Some of these "models," or "strategies," are rather simple-minded, such as those based on carrot and stick assumptions: threaten to take away some source of security or status, or promise to provide more of what the target of your change efforts wants. Some are elaborate. Planning Programing Budget Systems (PPBS) and Gestalt Therapy take extensive understanding and skill to pull off.

Basically, however, four very different assumptions about what leads people or organizations to change are represented by four rather different change strategies. I call them the Rational Planning, Social Interaction, Human Problem-Solving and Political approaches to planned change. The first three emerge from the seminal scholarship of Ronald Havelock and his associates at the University of Michigan's Center for Research on the Utilization of Scientific Knowledge.[1] They observe that all change strategies emphasize one of three particular aspects of the basic communication act: I create a message which I deliver in such a way that the receiver (myself, someone else or a whole organization) accepts it and acts on it. One set of strategies, which Havelock calls Research, Development and Diffusion (R&D), and which I call Rational Planning, concentrates mainly on developing a terrific message. Another set, called Social Interaction or Communication of Innovations, emphasizes the process and factors by which the change message gains the attention and acceptance of the receiver. It focuses on the social act of communicating new notions. A third group of studies and attendent theory, called Problem-Solver by Havelock, focuses upon how the receiver comes to feel the need and then the willingness to change. The Political model dwells on this same part of the communication act, but with quite different assumptions about how to generate change than those of the Problem-Solving model.

Figure 1 depicts the communication act and the major focus of each general strategy. It is an oversimplification. Havelock and later theorists see effective planned change as a combination of these approaches. But the separate models are well worth elaborating, for they represent strong differences in the ways academic and other changes are undertaken.

1

---

*"Change" is here defined as the modification of, deletion of, or addition to attitudes and behaviors existing in a person, group, organization or larger system. "Innovation" is defined as an idea, practice or object new to the potential user of it, not necessarily new to the world outside that person, group or organization.

THE ASSUMPTION OF RATIONALITY

Since we change on the basis of reason and evidence, the best way to obtain alterations in attitudes and behavior is to invest in systematic research and development of new knowledge, new practices, new products. Apply a rational process to attain a rational end. If the research is correct and the development sound, the proposed change will sell itself. That is the assumption which leads to heavy investment in basic and applied research and to considerable investment in the formulation, testing and packaging of innovations based on research. Havelock and Benne find these assumptions at work in the R&D efforts of American Telephone and Telegraph.[2] Clark and Guba find a similar rational sequence at work in the development and diffusion of educational innovations.[3] Guba particularly stresses development, "which is at the heart of change, for while research may make change possible, it is development that actually produces an innovation that may be adopted."[4]

Havelock identifies five basic assumptions about change which underly the Research and Development strategy:

> *First of all, the R&D model suggests that dissemination and utilization should be a rational sequence of activities which moves from research to development to packaging before dissemination takes place. Secondly, this model assumes that there has to be planning, and planning really on a massive scale. It is not enough that we simply have all these activities of research and development; they have to be coordinated; there has to be a relationship between them; and they have to make sense in a logical sequence that may go back years in the evolution of one particular message to be disseminated. Thirdly, there has to be a division of labor and a separation of roles and functions, an obvious prerequisite in all complex activities of modern society, but one that we sometimes slur over. Fourth, it assumes a more or less clearly defined target audience, a specified passive consumer, who will accept the innovation if it is delivered on the right channel, in the right way, and at the right time. The particular process which is supposed to assure this happening is scientific evaluation, evaluation at every stage of development and dissemination. Fifth, and finally, this perspective accepts the fact of high initial development cost prior to any dissemination activity, because it forsees an even higher gain in the long run, in terms of efficiency, quality, and capacity to reach a mass audience.[5]*

We can see around us plenty of examples of the rational change model. Cars and planes and other material "products" are made and sold that way. In post-secondary education, the Personalized System of Instruction is a rationally designed and packaged set of teaching methods based on Fred Keller's application of learning theory and research, which is being disseminated on a national scale from its Georgetown University Center. PLATO, the computer-assisted instruction system developed and tested at the University of Illinois, is another example of the rational change strategy at work on a grand scale. The National Institute for Education and the U.S. Office of Education have employed R&D assump-

"While research may make change possible, it is development that actually produces an innovation that may be adopted."

2

tions in supporting the research and development of educational innovations. Most foundations take Guba's advice and invest mainly in the development of model programs.

Local schools, colleges and social agencies also use the rational model, although high investment in R&D is usually not part of the scheme. Change in such organizations is often supported by encouraging individuals or committees to formulate proposals based on the best reason and evidence available. Review bodies, whether collegial governance or administrative heads, then judge these proposals and decide for or against ostensibly on the basis of rational considerations. Although we all know too well that good reason and sound evidence are not the only grounds on which decisions to change are made, the formal system, the one we put on organization charts and admit in public, stresses the rational model. We formally act *as if* we all approach change rationally. Especially in universities, which Parsons and Platt[6] claim are the fiduciary institutions for "cognitive rationality," it is hard to admit other approaches. Indeed, recent formulations for improving administration and managing academic change fit the rational model more than any other.[7] These books claim that administrators need to establish more rational research and planning sequences, whether the sequence is MBO or PPBS or some other series of capitals. Certainly, there should be participation by those whose attitudes and behaviors are supposed to change, namely faculty and students in colleges. But the emphasis in time and dollars will be on generating an impressive change message.

Although we all know too well that good reason and sound evidence are not the only grounds on which decisions to change are made, the formal system, the one we put on organization charts and admit in public, stresses the rational model.

3

FIGURE 1
MAJOR EMPHASES
IN PLANNED CHANGE STRATEGIES

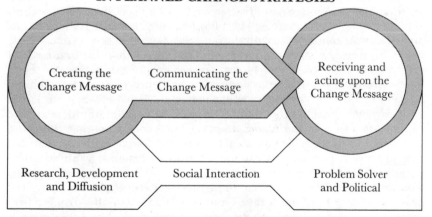

Creating the Change Message

Communicating the Change Message

Receiving and acting upon the Change Message

Research, Development and Diffusion

Social Interaction

Problem Solver and Political

Recent research and theory, however, have found the rational model inadequate in several respects as a way to go about the introduction of change in human attitudes and behaviors, the changes which are at the heart of academic innovations. In the main, criticism has focused on the isolation of R&D from its audience, the people who supposedly are going to use these new fangled ideas or behaviors. Rational systems may be good ways to research and develop change, but they do not explain all the motivations and activities by which those new things get used.[8]

The dynamics of local implementation are especially critical to the actual use of planned change.[9] Organizations, like the individuals and groups in them, do not operate simply as rational systems thoughtfully buying the latest innovations. If a change proposal threatens individual or group security and status, it is in trouble no matter how elegant its reason. If faculty and students cannot do the new behavior, or are not committed to it, watch out. Informal systems of communications and social status may be far more potent than formal communications in persuading members whether or not to do the new thing. Certainly reason and evidence are part of the change equation. You will not get very far on lousy evidence and flimsy reason. But an adequate strategy for change must include much more than clear and compelling reason.

An adequate strategy for change must include much more than clear and compelling reason.

SOCIAL INTERACTION

We live in social networks. One connects us to professional colleagues; another unites us with family and friends. Through these connections we get news and views about what's happening in the world around us. We can gain security, status and esteem from these informal systems, just as we can from formal organizations. Some researchers maintain that these contacts are essential to change, for new ideas get communicated and validated through social networks; Everett Rogers is most frequently identified with this school of thought. Agricultural extension agencies are the change agent units which best represent this approach in contrast with research and development centers.

Rogers and Shoemaker find that most empirical studies of innovation identify a few consistent types of "potential adopters" and a few specific stages in the adoption of new ideas, practices or objects.[10] In every organization or community, there will be a few *Innovators*, eager to try new things and usually uncomfortable with the *status quo* (which in turn is uncomfortable with them). A second group, somewhat larger than the first but still rarely more than twelve to fifteen percent of the outfit, are the *Early Adopters*, usually cosmopolitan in contacts and open to new ideas, though not as eager as the *Innovators*. Following in sequence of adoption is the *Early Majority*, making up perhaps a third of the population; these are the cautious followers of the *Earlier Adopters*. Then comes another third, the skeptical *Late Majority*, which wants pretty impressive evidence that this new practice is possible, effective and rewarded before it ventures a try. Finally, about fifteen percent of most systems will be made up of *Laggards*, who probably will resist change until everyone else is already doing the next new thing. Each successive group needs substantially stronger persuasion in order to change. Researchers also find that while change messages delivered through impersonal channels (books, articles, formal addresses, memoranda, written proposals) can persuade Innovators and Early Adopters, as well as increase awareness generally, later adopters need more personal communication and contact in order to be willing to change. Although it can take a short time for a change to move from one category of adopters to another, several years is more common for new

4

educational behaviors and several decades for new ideas such as progressive education. Clearly, the change advocate who thinks she can gain acceptance and use of new human behaviors or ideas by impersonal communication over a short period of time to a whole organization is in for bitter disappointment unless the group can be coerced and carefully controlled. College authorities just do not have that leverage over their semi-autonomous professors. Frankly, Ford doesn't have that kind of leverage over assembly line workers either.

Innovation diffusion researchers find that the best route into an organization or community is through *Opinion Leaders*, those persons (or institutions) to whom others turn for advice. As Hovland and Weiss summarize, "The most consistent finding so far is that the most persuasive communicator is one whose expertise, experience, or social role establishes him as a credible source of the information presented."[11] Harvard is an institutional opinion-leader on almost anything. I found in a state university that a few professors and administrators rated high by their colleagues in academic expertise and experience and often placed on key academic committees were most frequently asked their opinions on current proposals for academic change. In fact, I saw Faculty Senate meetings turned toward a decision by the remarks of key opinion leaders.[12] Effective change strategists find out who the opinion leaders are, then seek to persuade them to persuade others.

Social interaction researchers also find that certain attributes of innovations besides impressive reason and evidence influence their adoption. Does the innovation have clear *relative advantages* for our particular situation, whether those advantages are better ability to meet institutional objectives, reduced costs, higher status or greater enjoyment? Is the innovation *compatible* with our values, our structure, our skills and styles? Is the innovation *divisible* so that we can adopt only the parts we like, or adopt in some easy sequence, rather than buying the whole change at once? Is the new thing *simple* to understand and do? Does it involve *low risk and low uncertainty*? Can we *observe* it and *try it out* so we know better what we're getting into? Whether it is a professor's lecture or a proposal to change the whole curriculum, these ingredients will be important. Yet it is difficult to assess the relative advantages of academic innovations. They often clash with traditional academic values and structures. Professors and students rarely are trained to use them. Often, a whole, complex curricular reform package is laid on the faculty at once, with little promise that it will reap positive rewards. And such proposals are usually paper descriptions, not visible experiences which faculty can see and try before accepting. Small wonder significant academic change is such a rare occurrence.

RESOLUTION OF HUMAN PROBLEMS

Parsons has noted that "institutionalization [of a change] is imbedded in the non-rational layers of motivational organization. It is not accessible to change simply through the presentation to an actor of rational advantages in the external definition of the situation."[13] Hagen adds that as social change theory matures, "the units of analysis of society will not be roles,

The change advocate who thinks she can gain acceptance and use of new human behaviors or ideas by impersonal communication over a short period of time to a whole organization is in for bitter disappointment.

Effective change strategists find out who the opinion leaders are, then seek to persuade them to persuade others.

5

or persons, or social units. These are useful concepts only in the presentation of a descriptive framework. Rather, the units will be, within personality, such qualities as need for dependence, need for autonomy, and intensity of anxiety."[14] There is, in short, a psychological dimension to change to which neither the Rational nor Social models do justice. Rational planning and social interaction do form part of the equation, but, as Watson observes, underlying interests, habits, fears and prejudices compose the bulk of the iceberg.[15] We often pretend that the essential aspects of planned change are out in the open, in our plans and public discussions. We know better. And if we seek a strategy for intentional change which will work, we need to get at these hidden sources of resistance. Human Problem-Solving approaches offer some assistance.

The general strategy is familiar enough to most people: change is a process of solving problems. Something is not going right, so we diagnose the problem, set some objectives, find a solution, make a decision, implement it and evaluate its worth. Simple. It really is the Rational approach. But not if the problem is my need to have control, your fear of a change which may endanger your security, or our general distrust of one another. Then, say advocates of Human Problem-Solving strategies, we need skilled "intervention." We need someone or some process which can help us confront and reduce these hidden obstacles to change. Intervention may come in the form of leadership training.[16] It may involve building an effective problem-solving team.[17] It may focus on the department[18] or on the relationship of the whole organization to its environment.[19] Some intervention tactics, such as "sensitivity groups" or "T-Groups," are quite psychological in their focus.[20] Others, such as survey feedback, are more sociological.[21] But all aim to help us deal with the human resistances to change which we may otherwise avoid.

The Human Relations school of business administration, from Elton Mayo and Chester Barnard in the thirties to Rensis Likert and Chris Argyris today, has used this strategy extensively in efforts to improve the functioning of businesses and industry. Such persons as Ronald Boyer and Walter Sikes have applied this general notion, called "applied behavioral science," to college and university change. Havelock, in his synthesis of the literature in this field, identifies five basic tenets of this approach:

> *(1) that the* users *world (the person who is to adopt a new idea or practice) is the only sensible place from which to begin to consider utilization; (2) that knowledge utilization must include a* diagnostic *phase where user need is considered and translated into a problem statement; (3) that the role of the outsider is primarily to serve as* catalyst, collaborator, or consultant *on how to plan change and bring about his solution; (4) that* internal *knowledge retrieval and the marshalling of internal resources should be given at least equal emphasis with external retrieval; and (5) that* self-initiation *by the user or client system creates the best motivational climate for lasting change.*[22]

There frequently also is an assumption that *collaboration* and *openness*, rather than competition and closedness, are preferred ways to behave. *Consensus* is sought over majority rule or authoritative decree. Those who must carry out the charge need to *own* it as their solution to their concerns. *Trust* between the persons attempting change and the people to be changed is deemed crucial to genuine change. In all these assumptions, you can see the influence of humanistic psychology. Essentially, applied behavioral science takes a clinical model and applies it to groups and organizations.

This strategy for change is far more controversial in colleges and universities than R&D or Social Interaction, if for no other reason than that it probes sources of resistance we prefer to leave buried. Also, because it focuses at least part of its attention on our emotional needs, it conflicts with the claim that academicians are the protectors of cognitive rationality. We would like to think we are "above all that." Even if we are rather irrational at times, we dare not admit it. Do bankers admit they sometimes lose things? Still, applied behavioral science is beginning to be used in post-secondary education. If Parsons and Hagan are right, we will not get very far toward effective strategies for change unless we face the human barriers to change which human problem-solving interventions confront.

THE POLITICAL APPROACH

If we follow the Rational model, the route to change is to build and argue an impressive case. The Social strategy takes that case, puts it on terms attractive to its audience, personally introduces it to Innovators and Opinion Leaders, then through them to their various reference groups. The Human Problem-Solving path releases the resistance to change within us and makes change our solution to our concerns. All well and good. There is much to learn from the experts in these three general schools of thought. But what if Laggards block the road, blind to our eloquent presentations and determined to let no "touchy-feely" interventionist get into their locked closet of fears, prejudices and selfish desires? Not a few deans or chairpersons of curriculum committees have been characterized as such obstructionists by those who want to turn their heads in a new direction.

The most common answer is political power. Build coalitions among influential persons and groups, then seek an authoritative decision which requires others to comply with the new idea, employ the new behavior, use the innovative product. Easton gives us a picture of the political process which depicts the course of intentional change in political systems,[23] and organizations such as colleges certainly do have political systems. First, some range of gnawing concerns, some "wants," arise. Things are not as they should be for some persons in a community or with influence over it. Unless these various wants are felt strongly by influential people, and the people who hold them bring together various subgroups, no change is likely. People are usually upset about something or other but not sufficiently so to press authorities into a decision. But if the income/expenditure gap widens alarmingly, or if students become agitated not only over indifferent teaching but over Vietnam and social inequality, a "demand" may well be in the offing. Then, if those concerned feel they can make authorities take notice and have "confidence in the possibility of a more

Those who must carry out the change need to own it as their solution to their concerns.

7

If those concerned feel they can make authorities take notice and have "confidence in the possibility of a more desirable state of affairs," they may take action.

desirable state of affairs,"[24] they may take action. A high administrator probably has such a "sense of efficacy,"[25] as did student activists for a few years after the initial success of the Free Speech Movement at Berkeley and blacks for a few years after the initial successes of the Civil Rights Movement.

Once a demand is made, it must gain access to the formal decision-making system if it is to become a change in policy or program. Key here is a sympathetic "gatekeeper," a person or group who can put the demand on the authorities' agenda. Without a supportive gatekeeper, demanders must be powerful enough to break the gate down and be willing to take that risk. Faculty committee chairpersons and deans can play gatekeeping roles concerning demands for academic policy change. Once on the agenda, the demand gets deliberated. It is studied and debated, often modified or changed, usually in some committee. If it survives this buffeting, it emerges as a formulated proposal for change which then gets reviewed, modified, revised, reduced and in general worked over by all the persons or groups concerned about its potential impact on their vested interests. Will this new academic program give our department more students and faculty or less, more status or less, more autonomy or less? Usually, coalitions of interest form pro and con. Compromises are made to get some decision through. Much of the debate may focus on the proposal's soundness of reason and evidence, but savvy observers know that the issue is who gets what coveted "goodies." Important to the survival of change proposals in this river of nibbling piranhas are the persistent efforts of highly influential "issues sponsors" who are determined to carry the change through. Without such determined advocates, the *status quo* powers will defeat any change attempt.

In organizations such as colleges and universities, academic change proposals can take the short route if the demander is a president who goes ahead and exercises formal authority to set policy, or it may take the long route through layer upon layer of governance committees. In either case, the outcome is not yet change. It is an authoritative decision to change. Now comes the problem of making it stick. Usually, an executive instructs organizational units and individuals to carry out the new idea or behavior. Unless, however, that executive can force units and individuals to comply, identify whether or not they are complying, and get rid of noncompliants, the Political model breaks down in implementation. The formal authorities turn out not to be the real authorities. In colleges, academic departments and professors have considerable autonomy as expert professionals; if they do not like a new academic policy, they often can avoid serious implementation and, meanwhile, build a new coalition to get the policy rescinded. As Baldridge discovered in studying New York University:

> The system has a remarkable tendency to solve one set of problems only to generate another set; to give advantage to one group, but to disadvantage another; to eliminate one structural strain; but to create another. The political processes are self-generating, and there is constant feedback effect as the resolution of old conflicts creates new ones.[26]

Important to the survival of change proposals in this river of nibbling piranhas are the persistent efforts of highly influential "issue sponsors" who are determined to carry the change through.

8

The process is not one of open collaboration seeking consensus. It is instead a constant struggle for control. Losers of today's battles do not give up. They mount a new demand.

If vested interests and power were everything involved in planned change, an effective political strategy would be all one would need. But reason and evidence are sometimes heeded even by those whose vested interests are somewhat challenged and who have the power to ignore rational persuasion. Social dynamics are at work, and the more the change agent knows about how to make them work, the better. Often, it is more effective to seek to reduce resistance to change by human relations strategies than to try to overwhelm that resistance by force. If motivation researchers are correct that we all have need for achievement and affiliation as well as for power, we need a change strategy which speaks to all three motivations, not just to power.

COMBINING CHANGE STRATEGIES

Is it not possible to entertain the notion that humans are rational, social creatures who want to solve their hidden problems but also want to protect and enhance their vested interests? If we make such an assumption, we must combine our strategies for change. Rational research and planning is not enough. Nor is connecting innovations to opinion leaders in all the right ways. Nor is skilled intervention to diagnose human needs and to reduce resistance. Nor is the most effective political maneuvering. We must do it all.

Havelock was one of the first to provide a general change model which joined previously separate traditions of thinking.[27] He called his concept "linkage." Planned change starts with a "felt need" on the "potential user's part," on the part of the person, group, or organization which might change. Something is wrong; something needs improvement. A diagnosis is conducted and a problem statement emerges. Then there is a search and retrieval of alternate solutions both inside and outside the user. Some solution for the local situation then is developed and approved. Application follows. Often this implementation raises another need which starts the cycle all over again.

Meanwhile, outside the potential user of a new idea, behavior or practice is an external resource system of other persons or organizations, R&D centers, extension agents, process consultants. They may be engaged in trying to solve a similar problem, either because it is their problem too or because they have a direct relationship to the user, say as its funder or consultant. They go through a similar problem-solving process.

If the external problem-solver comes up with a solution in isolation from the potential user, that solution is apt not to fit local needs and circumstances nor to be of much interest to the user. If the internal problem-solver develops a solution without contact with external resources, that solution is apt to be as inadequate, for it does not benefit from broader expertise, experience and needs. The student can solve some problems on her own, but professors and books can help. The professor may be able to induce some change in the student without paying much

Often, it is more effective to seek to reduce resistance to change by human relations strategies than to try to overwhelm that resistance by force.

9

The professor may be able to induce some change in the student without paying much attention to her, but getting to know her needs, her ways of thinking, her background and circumstances, can help.

FIGURE 2
THE LINKAGE PROCESS

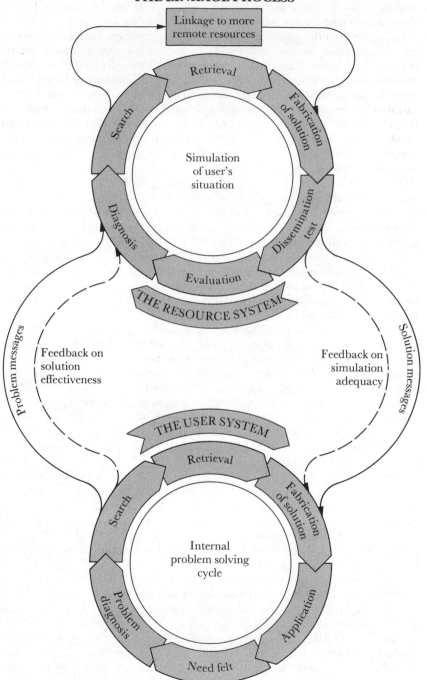

10

attention to her, but getting to know her needs, her ways of thinking, her background and circumstances, can help. Just so with the R&D center and the organization, the consultant and the client, the committee and those who might approve and implement its proposal.

Figure 2 summarizes Havelock's Linkage model. It is a representation of the basic communication act, but this time it is an interactive process, with both parties involved as sources and receivers of change messages and with both focused on solving the receiver's problem. In such a model, both the internal and external problem-solvers would employ rational planning, the R&D model, probably with the help of experts in research or development. Both would exchange messages through social networks, perhaps with the assistance of skilled linking agents. Both would confront and resolve human barriers to change, and an applied behavioral science interventionist could be of valuable assistance there. Both would use, or run against, power and authority, and a political strategist would come in handy.

Havelock's synthesis of planned change process is also a synthesis of planned change factors. Seven key ingredients in successful change efforts emerged from his and his associates' review of the literature.

Applied to academic change, these guidelines would encourage several actions. Faculty, administrators, students and relevant outsiders (like trustees and funding agencies) should be well-linked to each other and to information concerning problems and solutions. There should be an active openness, a real reaching out, to new information and new people across departmental and institutional boundaries. Change efforts should be well organized and should follow-through, perhaps by having efficient research, planning, governance and implementation structures. They should enjoy capable leadership, skilled facilitation, adequate time and materials. Useful information and other resources for change should be brought close together. Change effort, at all stages of problem-solving, should be rewarded. And change attempts should be numerous, various and redundant.

This linkage model for intentional change is very appealing in the abstract. It is far more complex than the carrot or the stick, but it has stronger evidence and logic to support it. On the rational level, it makes good sense. In the years since Havelock's snythesis, no other model for planned change has emerged which is as comprehensive and promising. It has provided a helpful way to view the academic innovation process and the faculty development process.[28] It is quite compatible with the "mutual adaptation" model which emerged from the Rand studies of major federal educational innovations, for Berman and McLaughlin find that local use of model programs occurs when the local institution and its members change to fit the innovation and when the innovation changes to fit local circumstances.[29] If proposed change and potential user do not adjust to each other, actual change is unlikely. Indeed, one investigator could not even find traces of $40,000,000 given to ten experimental schools in New York, let alone find traces of change.

But Linkage has several obstacles between theory and practice. One problem is its abstractness. Just what should we do differently than we do

11

This linkage model for intentional change is very appealing in the abstract. It is far more complex than the carrot or the stick, but it has stronger evidence and logic to support it.

now if we plan to implement this approach? Havelock provides some answers,[30] and the third section of this book addresses applications regarding academic in organizational contexts. Just how do we adapt this approach to a collegiate setting, or any other? Zaltman and others have addressed this question generally,[31] and Chapter Two of this book focuses on the collegiate organization. A third and very significant problem is that Linkage has not been tested in any multi-instructional, longitudinal study of just how intentional change does occur. A major contribution of this book is to fill that gap. Section II contains seven detailed case histories of attempts to introduce various academic changes into five liberal arts colleges and two universities. If Linkage or one of the four other basic change assumptions explains effective planned change, we can see it for ourselves in those cases.

SUMMARY

What brings about changes in attitudes and behaviors? Some believe that humans are essentially rational, so reason and evidence should do the trick. Intentional change, therefore, takes the form of a rational sequence of activities to produce a change message based in theory and research, then developed and tested empirically and logically and finally accepted because of its sound evidence and reason. Research and Development centers, institutional research and planning offices and formal governance systems are designed to operate as if change is mainly a rational process.

Others find that humans are social creatures. New attitudes and behaviors, though they may be developed by rational processes, raise awareness, interest, trial and eventual adoption through a process of social interaction and persuasion in which opinion leaders and reference groups are influences perhaps as significant as the rational soundness of the change message itself. Intentional change under these assumptions puts time and skill into linking innovative ideas, practices or products to "potential adopters" through social networks. Professional associations, information clearinghouses, learning resources centers, conferences, workshops and extension agencies use this strategy.

Still others feel that the main obstacles to change are not impressive messages nor social influences. Psychological barriers are the problem. What is needed is the skilled intervention of human relations consultation in order to diagnose and facilitate the reduction of those barriers. Leadership training, clinical counseling, T-Groups and Organization Development are examples of this assumption at work.

Yet another group maintains we are political animals at base, busy protecting and strengthening our vested interests. In order to accomplish change, we need to build powerful coalitions among interests and obtain authoritative decisions which will be enforced by requiring people to change their attitudes and behaviors. That strategy is visible in the *informal* governance process and in such administrative controls as policies on program and personnel.

Recent theorists find that all these assumptions hold, probably in varying degrees depending on the issue, the situation and the people involved. Havelock's "Linkage" theory was an early attempt to combine change assumptions. More recent planned change theories confirm his general model. It is, however, abstract and relatively untested. It needs close examination in specific change attempts over time. The remainder of this book seeks to meet that need.

2 Up in the Ivory Tower

Life isn't getting any easier, except for a fortunate few. We have for ourselves an increasingly crowded planet with dwindling natural resources. We must become more sophisticated in our knowledge concerning how to live well on such a planet, and we must become more humane in our application of that knowledge. Competitive getting and spending may work when there are few people and abundant resources, but those times and places are past. We must change our ways.

But how? Colleges and universities may hold a good piece of the answer. They can help us learn the knowledge and skills needed to cope with new social, economic and environmental conditions. Moreover, they can help us cope humanely and aesthetically, so that our lives are enriched even though we have fewer material resources for more people. Furthermore, responding to the intellectual, ethical and aesthetic needs of the future, colleges and universities may model ways by which complex organizations with highly trained and rather independent work-forces tackling complex functions (perhaps the typical organization of the future) can change. This chapter will examine, therefore, factors affecting change in American colleges and universities.

ROUGH GO

Despite the importance of colleges and universities, there has been little systematic study regarding how they change.[1] The studies which do exist mostly conclude that colleges resist changing academic practices; what little change does happen occurs more by external pressure than internal plan. Martin's study of institutional character discovered so much resistance to change that he called his final report "Conformity."[2] Hefferlin examined *The Dynamics of Academic Reform* in one hundred and ten colleges and universities and concluded there are few such dynamics within colleges and universities. External stimulus and demand brought change.[3] Ladd examined eleven self-study and planning efforts in prestigious colleges and universities and found that such "Blue Ribbon" efforts result in minor reform at best.[4] Evans found great resistance in the arts and sciences to the adoption of instructional television,[5] just as House found the adoption of computer-assisted instruction frought with obstacles.[6] I traced seventy years of decision-making in one midwestern university and found that stability, not change, was its hallmark.[7] Harmon followed one small college's attempt at academic reform and discovered that a major self-study and a highly skillful dean squeaked only minor changes out of the faculty.[8]

Some recent authors are more optimistic. Sikes, Schlesinger and

The studies which do exist mostly conclude that colleges resist changing academic practices; what little change does happen occurs more by external pressure than internal plan.

Seashore believe that applied behavioral science can help bring about academic change, but their own research does not offer much substantiation.[9] Martorana and Kuhn, Richman and Farmer, Lahti and Balderston all offer rational formulas for conducting academic improvement and reform.[10] Their strategies may work. But they offer little more than anecdotal evidence or one-person (often one heavily involved person) case reports that their approaches actually bring about academic change. Rather, we must trust that strategies developed in business management and organizational development work in higher education despite debatable evidence that they have much effect on change anywhere. Levine and Weingart, Riesman and Stadtman, and Riesman, Gusfield and Gamson offer useful descriptions of innovative program implementation in colleges and universities, plus helpful tips,[11] but these case studies do not examine cases in the light of prior change theory nor do they result in coherent models for planning and implementing organizational change.

Yet academic innovation does occur. Changes in graduation requirements, individualized and adult degree programs, independent and field studies, competency-based education, interdisciplinary studies, basic skills programs, freshman seminars, Black studies and Women's studies, computer assisted and personalized instruction, learning resources and faculty development centers, modular and 4-1-4 calendars, narrative evaluation: this is just a partial list of the academic innovations which have been introduced into many colleges and universities in the past decade. Things have been happening. A major aim of this book is to follow such changes to learn just how they do happen. But, in the main, such innovations remain minor "add-ons." The primary bill of fare remains a supermarket of three to four month courses taught in large classes on formal campuses, often by lecture following textbook, focused on disseminating knowledge, organized by academic disciplines, evaluated on the normal curve, with little contact between a faculty not trained to teach and a student body for whom this formula is no longer effective (if it ever was). It is a curious system, weakly supported by educational philosophy[12] or evidence of substantial impact on student development.[13] But there it is, still solid as a rock after all the pummeling of recent years. Why?

THE PERFORMANCE GAP

What makes change in the teaching-learning functions of colleges and universities so difficult? Several organizational theorists provide possible enlightenment. March and Simon, for instance, emphasize the need for a "performance gap."[14] Unless organizational members, leaders or external supporters perceive a wide gap between what they think the organization should be doing and what they believe it is doing, they are not likely to bother changing it. In colleges and other organizations, a gap between low income and high expenditures can be readily perceived by financial officers, although it may take some time for the bad news to hit salaried professors. Gaps in educational performance, like performance gaps in social services organizations, are far less easy to perceive.

Education is internal. Some of its effects translate into external evi-

Unless organizational members, leaders or external supporters perceive a wide gap between what they think the organization should be doing and what they believe it is doing, they are not likely to bother changing it.

dence such as jobs, income and acceptance into prestigious graduate schools, but even these effects may be more the consequence of social class, basic intellect and personality and excellent pre-college preparation than they are influenced by the college. Our ability to measure the "value-added" by a college education remains too primitive to impress very many people that a serious educational performance gap exists. In addition, colleges have complex goals, not mere profit, and often have internal dispute about just what those goals should be. It is hard to reach consensus about what we should be doing, let alone how.

Certainly, as educational and cost research becomes more sophisticated and as goal-setting procedures improve, rational means for identifying performance gaps (and successes) also will improve. Indeed, this ability is a major reason that rational models for institutional research, planning and budgeting such as MBO and PPBS have been developing rapidly in postsecondary institutions. One component in organizations able to innovate and reform, according to March and Simon's rational view, would be mechanisms to determine the organization's performance gap. For all their limitations, information systems are sorely needed.

ORGANIC AND MECHANISTIC ORGANIZATIONS

Burns and Stalker, in their study of innovation in several Scottish industries, found that organizations which function well in stable situations have the "mechanistic" ingredients represented on Figure 3.[15] When times are changing and the organization must respond to an unstable environment, those with "organic" ways of operating tend to be more successful. They are less rigid and can process new information regarding changing conditions more rapidly than the more traditionally bureaucratic outfit. Likert and others in the human problem-solving tradition regard the organic organization as the healthy one.[16] Palola and Padgett find that academic planning works best the organic way.[17] Hage and Aiken support Burns and Stalker in their hypothesis that the more complex an organization in roles and the skills needed to perform them, the less centralized the power, the less formally codified the tasks, the less hierarchically stratified the rewards, the more the stress on quality instead of quantity of production, and the higher the job satisfaction, the more innovative the organization.[18] Of course, colleges and universities seem to fit this formula for innovation; yet changes in teaching and learning practices have been found to be sluggish at best.

Zaltman and his colleagues offer a partial solution to this apparent contradiction.[19] They hypothesize that organizations need "organic" components of the kinds outlined by Hage and Aiken, and Burns and Stalker in order to get new ideas initiated within an organization. More organization members are freer and more capable of being aware of innovations and initiating change in organizations with high complexity, low formalization and low centrality than in mechanistic organizations. On the other hand, effective implementation of innovations requires more channeled and formalized tasks under greater control in order to focus time, materials and talent on carrying out a program instead of doing some other thing.

When times are changing and the organization must respond to an unstable environment, those with "organic" ways of operating tend to be more successful.

17

Figure 3 Mechanistic and Organic Organizational Forms

Mechanistic	Organic
1. Tasks are broken into very specialized abstract units	1. Tasks are broken down into subunits, but relation to total task of organization is much more clear
2. Tasks remain rigidly defined	2. There is adjustment and continued redefinition of tasks through interaction of organizational members
3. Specific definition of responsibility that is attached to individual's functional role only	3. Broader acceptance of responsibility and commitment to organization that goes beyond individual's functional role
4. Strict hierarchy of control and authority	4. Less hierarchy of control and authority sanctions derive more from presumed community of interest
5. Formal leader assumed to be omniscient in knowledge concerning all matters	5. Formal leader not assumed to be omniscient in knowledge concerning all matters
6. Communication is mainly vertical between superiors and subordinates	6. Communication is lateral, between people of different ranks and resembles consultation rather than command
7. Content of communication is instructions and decisions issued by superiors	7. Content of communication is information and advice
8. Loyalty and obedience to organization and superiors is highly valued	8. Commitment to tasks and progress and expansion of the firm is highly valued
9. Importance and prestige attached to identification with organization itself	9. Importance and prestige attached to affiliations and expertise in larger environment

18

Whether the institution be a "model" or a "maverick," it develops its version of the status quo *and then sticks to it, not for lack of new ideas but for lack of the consensus and control needed to implement changes or because an "institutional saga" has defined the organization's identity.*

Colleges and universities may be great places to get all kinds of new ideas initiated, but terrible places to get them implemented. Professors, as other professionals, are hard to channel and control. In consequence, colleges and universities end up no different from other organizations; once a program does get implemented, it turns to granite. Whether the institution be a "model" or a "maverick," it develops its version of the *status quo* and then sticks to it, not for lack of new ideas but for lack of the consensus and control needed to implement changes or because an "institutional saga" has defined the organization's identity.[20]

If we are to follow Zaltman's suggestion, organizations must be both organic and mechanistic in order that innovations become not only initiated but also implemented. At either extreme is the inability to renew. Zaltman and his associates add another ingredient as well. They agree with the human problem-solvers that strong interpersonal relations and the ability to confront and resolve conflicts openly are critical to the innovative organizations, if for no other reason than that organic and mechanistic folks will get in each other's way. A "mechanistic" dean trying to implement a program will have a hard time appreciating an "organic" professor who chooses not only noncooperation but also a new, competing initiative; and *vice versa*. As Figure 4 indicates, Zaltman's full formula includes skilled attention to interpersonal relations and conflict management.

Figure 4 Ingredients in Innovative Organizations

Initiation Stage	Mediators	Implementation Stage
Higher Complexity		Lower Complexity
	High capability for effective interpersonal relations	
Lower Formalization		Higher Formalization
	Higher capability for dealing with conflict	
Lower Centrality		Higher Centrality

Harvey and Mills are two theorists who apply a political perspective to organizational innovation.[21] They agree with Baldridge that a major dynamic is the constant concern by various groups in and related to the organization to protect and enhance their own interests. Bargaining is the major innovation process under such conditions. They also hypothesize that when a problem arises, "routine" solutions (those the organization has used before) are likely to be imposed unless the pressure to change is very great. They find that relatively old, relatively large organizations with little technological change and relatively uncompetitive markets are most likely to impose routine solutions. Prestigious universities certainly fit this definition. Relatively small, relatively competitive, relatively young organizations undergoing rapid technological obsolescence are most likely to impose innovative solutions ("innovative" meaning solutions new to that organization). Small colleges without the security of high prestige and impressive endowments fit most aspects of this formula. Martin, Hefferlin, and Ladd each found that academic reform and innovation occurs more readily in small colleges than in large universities.[22] Universities may be full of new ideas and rich resources, but they are too decentralized and too complex to be able to mount any concerted reform effort even in one department (with its many sub-specialties and considerable individual autonomy), let alone in a school or in the university as a whole.

What are the chief components in organizational complexity, formalization and centralization as they relate to the politics of initiating and implementing innovations? Easton delineates five factors that are helpful in understanding what it takes to introduce change into organizations such as colleges and universities: political norms, values, decision structure, political community and authority.[23] Each is worth considering in some depth.

19

Martin, Hefferlin, and Ladd each found that academic reform and innovation occurs more readily in small colleges than in large universities.

THE RULES OF THE GAME

Whereas most organizations are dominated by bureaucratic rules, post-secondary institutions have strong currents of collegiality and democracy as well.

What is the "proper" way to go about change attempts in colleges and universities? That question immediately thrusts an innovator into complexity, for whereas most organizations are dominated by bureaucratic rules, post-secondary institutions have strong currents of collegiality and democracy as well. One bureaucratic rule is that control over the formulation, decision and implementation of policies and programs should be left to those with formal administrative authority over these functions. One collegial rule is that control should go to those with the most expertise concerning the issue at hand. The democratic rule is that control should go to those affected by those policies and programs. Bureaucracies have pyramidal hierarchies based on formal responsibilities and accountability upward. Collegiums have professional hierarchies based on expertise, and accountability goes to one's expert peers. Democracies have representative or openly participative governments based on interest; accountability supposedly is directed to the body politic.

Colleges and universities have administrative bureaucracies. Everyone reports upward to someone, eventually to the president and trustees. They also have governance hierarchies in which each lower body (committee, department) is reviewed by each higher body, eventually reaching the president and board. They have senates or faculty meetings in which sub-group interests are represented. But there is dispute among researchers regarding which rules of the game dominate. Baldridge champions the representative, pluralistic model, for he saw political jockeying among vested interests as the main model at New York University in the late 1960's.[24] Eckert, McConnell, and I see in other research on university governance a power elite of a few senior faculty members and top administrators.[25] Bucher claims that interviews in a medical school reveal heavy dependency on both expertise and negotiation among interest groups.[26] Platt and Parsons maintain that collegial reason and evidence rather than high administrative position prevails in universities; they also conclude, however, that "a collegial, influence-oriented social system, under stress, tends to regress to the level of greatly enhanced emphasis on power relations."[27] Gamson draws the same conclusion: "Under conditions of university-wide conflict, the effective authority reverts to those bodies with formal authority—the office of the president and, if necessary, the boards of regents."[28]

Dykes observes that the proper political players vary depending on the subject.[29] Faculty members regard academic policy and personnel as their business, for they are the avowed experts. These issues also affect them most directly. They do not regard themselves as equally expert in finance, except for those business professors who wonder how the financial vice president ever got the job. They feel the effects of budget, however, and will unionize to protect and enhance their interests. In student services and public relations, faculty feel neither expert nor interested, so they leave those matters to administrators. I found a similar division of concern in a later study.[30]

Rules also may vary by institutional type. Harvard and Berkeley have prestigious faculties not about to let bureaucrats determine changes in academic practices and personnel, while the faculty at less prestigious institutions may not have the control which national reputations can bring. Administrators probably carry greater influence on formal bureaucratic grounds in such places.

The safest prediction seems to be that all three political norms (bureaucratic, collegial and democratic) will be present in any college or university regarding any issue; but the weight given each norm will vary by issue, by institutional type and by amount of pressure to change. The greatest danger is in oversimplification. Colleges are not simple bureaucracies, but they are bureaucracies. They are not just collegiums, but they have strong collegial elements. They are not mere collections of vested interests vying for power through representative governance, but these political dynamics are always present. College members have respect for authority, for reason and evidence and for the needs of individuals and sub-groups (especially their own). An effective strategy for change must combine rules of the decision making game.

There is a fourth rule of the game. It is not played much, but it is central to the "problem-solving" strategy for change. Several organizational theorists conclude from their research that an essential ingredient in effective organizations is open collaboration.[31] Organizational members are involved in decisions because such involvement increases commitment and responsibility while reducing resistance to change. Open, two-way communication between leaders and staff is practiced because that increases trust and reduces the contamination of rumor. Behind the scenes lobbying or string pulling therefore is avoided. Not only rational arguments and empirical evidence but emotional concerns are respected, openly confronted and resolved through joint problem-solving. Competitive tendencies to win and to defend are given over to cooperation in seeking ways everyone can win. People are not excluded from decision making because they are not of sufficiently high office or expertise but are encouraged to participate as creative and thoughtful people with useful experiences to share.

It is a grand norm, one many of us would like to believe. Argyris and Schoen find that many executives do hold it as their "theory of action" concerning their own behavior, but in practice they resort to more competitive, defensive, less respectful and open, behavior.[32] Such behavior, of course, begets response in kind. If open collaboration is such a valuable norm for planned change and is so hard to fulfill, a major training focus for leaders of organizational reform, in colleges and elsewhere, might be just this "rule of the game." In general, it may be a fair hypothesis that the rarity of academic change stems in part from the complexity of political norms in colleges and universities and inattention to training which might lead to open collaboration.

ACADEMIC VALUES
Collegial, bureaucratic, democratic and collaborative norms tell us how to go about the process of deciding what will be done. Values tell us what is worth doing. These two kinds of beliefs are "the matrix that forms the social relations among groups and individuals."[33] They are what we hold

An effective strategy for change must combine rules of the decision making game.

21

If open collaboration is such a valuable norm for planned change and is so hard to fulfill, a major training focus for leaders of organizational reform, in colleges and elsewhere, might be just this "rule of the game."

in common. Colleges and universities all have formal values, stated in timeless prose at the front of college catalogs. Yet these statements are taken with more than a few grains of salt by college members. What, then, do academics value?

The landmark book on this subject remains Jencks and Riesman's *The Academic Revolution* (1968). It is an elaboration of Riesman's earlier thesis that all of higher education is slithering in a "snake-like procession" after king cobras such as Harvard and Berkeley at the University level, Amherst and Vassar at the "university college" level.[34] Such "national" institutions enjoy the most social and academic prestige; the fattest endowments; the lion's share of federal and foundation grants; the brightest students from the "best" families; and the famous faculty who spend their days teaching apprentice scholars their disciplines, pursuing personal research interests and picking up second incomes consulting with every other American institution. The rest of us were trained and socialized to crave positions in such places, or failing that, to make our institution the Harvard or Amherst of our particular geographic area. The lighter the teaching load, the more the system supports and rewards publication of scholarly research, the more academically capable and committed the students *when they enter* college, the more disciplinary the curriculum, the tougher it is to get high grades, the more graduate school oriented the program and the more administrators, students and budgets serve the interest of independent professor-scholars, the better. So goes the academic revolution thesis. It is, of course, an elitist model. It is, of course, a collegial model. It is, of course, alive and thriving a decade after Jencks and Riesman's investigation.

Many writers who discuss institutional "quality," such as Blau and Parsons and Platt, simply define high quality according to these values.[35] A community college without productive scholars, departments highly rated by other academicians and a majority of 750 SAT students cannot be of high quality according to such standards, no matter how able it is to meet the educational needs of the students it serves. Gross and Grambsch surveyed American colleges and universities about the same time Jencks and Riesman conducted their visits across the land. They also found the elitist model everywhere: "In general, we may say that American universities emphasize the faculty's academic freedom, concern themselves primarily with goals related to pure research and with maintaining or enhancing the university's position, and manifest relatively little interest in the student beyond developing his scholarly abilities."[36] Martin, studying college and university innovation in the same mid-1960's, found this central value system a solid rock: "Beneath diverse structures and functions we found uniformity in educational assumptions and socio-political values across major interests groups and in various types of institutions. . . . For academics today the undergirding ideology is professionalism or, as it is called, the 'professional orientation,' for which the autonomous research scholar is the paradigm."[37]

Now, the mid-1960's are not the mid-1970's. More recent goals studies reveal that many colleges and universities not in the national elite increasingly have adopted (instead of just publicly espoused) more

"Beneath diverse structures and functions we found uniformity in educational assumptions and socio-political values across major interests groups and in various types of institutions."

genuinely egalitarian values, greater commitment to teaching, to local or regional service, to students less able and interested in academic disciplines and to the personal and ethical development of those students.[38] The snake-like procession is breaking up. But changes in academic values come slowly. Many "academic revolutionists" recruited into colleges in the 1960's have by now become influential full professors, department chairpersons, deans, presidents, accrediting agency leaders or government officials. They have become the "gatekeepers" by which new ideas would have to pass. Boards of trustees went to college when elitist values prevailed. As expansion of higher education slowed, persons socialized in the student and civil rights movements had greater difficulty finding jobs and achieving tenure than their older colleagues did. And the great external pressures of the final years of the 1960's abated in the early 1970's. Institutions were less pressed to change, and, as Hefferlin observed, "The personnel of any organization, including the faculty members of a college, quite rightly believe in what they are doing. Most of them are committed to activities and functions that they will not by themselves abandon or neglect except by external intervention."[39]

These studies suggest that innovations failed to infiltrate very far into colleges and universities in the 1960's in part because these organizations were not diverse but uniform in their fundamental values and faced no glaring performance gaps. Then, as external pressure mounted and values diversified, many new ideas were initiated but had to confront a political system dominated by traditional academics. That dynamic may account for the appearance between roughly 1967 and 1973 of many academic innovations designed as small "experiments" existing on the periphery of colleges and universities, experiments not intended to replace the entrenched system. The traditionalists gave a little ground but held the center. As persons and institutions espousing more diverse values gradually move into positions of influence, peripheral experiments may become genuine reforms, fully adopted innovations. Then again, inertia favors the more traditional model. The best strategy for change may be to relate a new idea as closely as possible to traditional standards *short of compromising the integrity of the innovation itself*. Thus should innovative institutions approach accrediting associations; thus should committees with innovative proposals approach faculty senates. Make the innovation as compatible as possible with existing values, Rogers would say.

POLITICAL COMMUNITY
Even if we play by the rules and appeal to *status quo* values, most colleges and universities are so vivisected into distant sub-groups that it is hard to imagine their getting together to agree on much of anything. Perhaps, as others have suggested,[40] common concerns over parking space and central heating are all that bind universities together, that bind often taking the form of a skirmish over who gets the choice parking space and what temperature campus offices should be.

Gamson cites four criteria for determining the extent of group cohesion: (1) symbolic treatment of the group as a collectivity; (2) treatment as a group by others; (3) common style of life, norms and values; and (4)

23

The traditionalists gave a little ground but held the center.

high rate of internal interaction.[41] If a bunch of people can be labeled "Faculty" or "The History Department" or "Young Turks," they are on their way toward becoming a separate entity. If other people treat them as "those historians" or "the damn administration," the gap between that bunch and others widens. If the damn administration has a style, a way of behaving and certain values which set them off from other groups (as faculty often claim and administrators usually deny), a chasm develops. Then if administrators mainly hang around one another, stay in their own administration building and social circuit, their relating to other groups is like shouting across the Grand Canyon.

It is safe to say that most colleges and universities, even small ones, have little sense of common community. I found in one midwestern university that administrators named other administrators as the group they most trusted to represent them and with whom they most identified, while faculty named their departments first, then councils of the faculty senate. Students identified first with themselves.[42] Lipsett and Ladd find that political attitudes separate faculty subgroups, with Philosophy, Sociology, English and Psychology on the left and Engineering, Nursing, Business and Physical Education on the right.[43] Gamson finds that natural scientists emphasize academic "performance" in dealing with students, while social scientists value "personalism" in their student relations.[44] Clark and Trow find quite separate student sub-groups which they label "Academics," "Collegiates," "Vocationals" and "Nonconformists."[45] Anderson and Case are two of several researchers who confirm that faculty members interact mainly with people near their own offices,[46] and institutional arrangements usually put members of the same department in the same complex of offices. Researchers of "invisible colleges" find that members of one discipline communicate mostly with others in their specialty on a national basis. Administrators, in turn, are members of quite different associations connecting them with other administrators. And rarely is there a faculty member or administrator in student government, except as an advisor.

Heirich nicely documented one consequence of the physical as well as social isolation of campus subgroups from one another.[47] During the 1964 Free Speech Movement at Berkeley, he noted the increasing isolation of those students (and faculty) whom attitudinal surveys found most prone to liberal politicization—humanities and social science apartment dwellers—into one area of the campus. Two large humanities and social science classroom buildings had been built adjacent to the main library next to a convenient apartment dweller eating spot (the student union), alongside Sproul Plaza facing the administration building and close by the Telegraph Avenue district of apartments and non-students. To get to this area, students and faculty most sympathetic to liberal causes had to walk every day by the political recruiting tables which were to become the focus of controversy. Meanwhile, people whose views would clash with the protest—engineers, athletes, fraternity and sorority members—were physically separated from the Sproul Plaza area by Berkeley's hilly terrain. The campus architects of the late Fifties did not know they were arranging the Free Speech Movement, but in a sense they were. And

24

nearly every other American college and university intentionally segregates its students and faculty in ways which reinforce the academic revolution. Furthermore, these institutions lend political "cleavage" to social separation by organizing decision making units to coincide with divisions into disciplines, schools, faculty governance and student government and administration. It is what Rossi (borrowing from Lenski) would call high "political crystallization: the extent to which the lines of political cleavage within the community coincide with the major social structural differentiations."[48]

In brief, colleges and universities are designed socially, physically academically and politically to have very little sense of a common community. In the one hundred and ten California colleges and universities which took the *Institutional Goals Inventory*, one of the greatest gaps between what *Is* emphasized and what *Should Be* emphasized is "Community," defined as "cooperation, mutual helping, respect, trust," the norms of human problem-solving.[49] Some small colleges with distinctive religious or educational missions can be expected to have greater member identity with the institution as a whole, but even in them the organization chart, curriculum and physical layout isolates department from department, faculty from administrators and everybody from students. I have led workshops in colleges of forty faculty only to discover that the first step needs to be faculty introductions to one another.

The strategist who takes a rational approach to introducing change somehow must make good sense to very different sub-groups whose members do not identify with the strategist. Good luck! The social linking agent must find ways to penetrate and connect many disparate groups, also no cinch. The politician must build coalitions among interest groups which have very few common interests, like Congressional sub-groups and the White House. The open collaborator must find ways to break down these great gaps, a task which seems at first glance pollyanish. Once again, the sophisticated leader probably is going to have to be an effective tactician in each general strategy; the absence of common political community makes this leader's predicted success rather unlikely.

THE STRUCTURE OF DECISION MAKING

What are the channels through which a change proposal must flow? A familiar answer in colleges and universities is that nobody knows. Governance is such a maze of overlapping or competing committees and administrative offices that to enter it is to quickly get hopelessly lost. In one university in this project, interviewees kept muttering about "circular decision making" and "death by terminal committee." In a project college, a couple of professors decided to make a chart showing the lines of relationship among committees. The chart looked enough like electronic circuitry that I swore it would light up a television set if plugged into an outlet.

Our experiences do tell us a few things about goverance structure besides its confusion. We know that there is one large pyramid of administrative authority from the trustees on down to the lowliest freshman. Students report to department members who report to chairpersons who

I have led workshops in colleges of forty faculty only to discover that the first step needs to be faculty introductions to one another.

25

report to deans who report to vice presidents who report to the president who reports to the trustees who are answerable to external funders. All that, despite the many levels a lowly reformist might have to pass, is only half the picture. Most colleges and universities have a second pyramid, called "governance," which has departmental committees which report to school or college committees (which report to university committees) which report to the faculty senate or faculty as a whole which reports to the president, and so on. Add to the picture the fact that committees and administrative hierarchies occur in several topic areas such as academic affairs, personnel, budget, student affairs and institutional planning and development. Keep in mind that administrators have their own committees and that standing committees often have a few sub-committees apiece. Small wonder the governance chart looks like electronic circuitry. Small wonder that reformists grow prematurely grey.

Those who do not want to spend the rest of their lives presenting one proposal to untold numbers of committees and administrators try shortcuts.

Those who do not want to spend the rest of their lives presenting one proposal to untold numbers of committees and administrators try shortcuts. High officials or committee chairpersons start proposals at their level. Lower folk who no longer can endure the run-around demand to see the dean. A major political problem with such approaches is that people who believe in "proper" channels will become irritated. A president cannot circumvent faculty committees very long and enjoy much faculty support, unless, of course, she is taking short-cuts in order to raise all faculties salaries by fifteen percent a year.

Besides its complexity, conflict and confusion, the decision structure of colleges and universities suffers by short changing planned change functions. Research and development structures, linking structures, planning structures, professional development structures, organizational development structures are necessary to stimulate and guide intentional efforts to improve and to respond to changing conditions; but they are not common and usually are understaffed and undertrained where they exist. Instead of such a focus of skill and time, the general practice is to have administrators and faculty whose main duty and skill (and therefore commitment) lies in implementing current policies and programs, not in creating new ones and certainly not in adding the burden of planned change to already hectic schedules. Planned change becomes the work of amateurs (albeit often talented ones) "after work." Weathersby observes that the likely consequence of putting self-examination and change in the hands of persons who are flat out implementing the *status quo* is that next year will resemble this year, plus or minus ten percent depending on the economy.[50] Katz and Kahn are two of many organizational theorists who regard such "adaptive subsystems" as those mentioned above crucial to the continuing health of any organization.[51] Without such structures and with such a maze of committees and offices, it is hard to imagine how colleges can reform themselves.

POWER AND AUTHORITY

Certain persons or groups in any organization are more able than others to get the organization to do their bidding. Who are the people with power in colleges and universities? Earlier information suggests part of the

26

answer. The higher the administrative or faculty position in the organizational structures, the greater the potential influence. I found in a midwestern university that the most influential persons, by various measures, were senior professors and top-ranking administrators.[52] Eckert confirmed the dominance of senior faculty over two decades of academic governance at the University of Minnesota.[53] Eighty percent of the faculty held no governance positions at all. Of those who did, 65% were full professors. On the powerful Educational Policies Council, 94% were full professors. McConnell found a similar pattern at Berkeley and at Fresno State.[54] A study of two small liberal arts colleges reveals that a small group of senior faculty regard themselves as watchdogs over the president but not as initiators of change.[55] A doctoral student under Blocker found in a four-year college that the average "influential" in college-wide decision making is forty-six years old, has spent over ten years at that institution, and has spent over nineteen years in college teaching.[56] Persons of influence, in short, tend not to be "new blood." Presidents and deans often are recruited to bring in fresh ideas, but they quickly discover that the senior oligarchy is no easy mark. Harmon, for example, observed that as college self-study moved proposals to the floor of the faculty, only the most senior influentials took the floor. Their central theme was preservation of the *status quo*. The academic dean, a new, innovative and persuasive issue sponsor, did push a few minor reforms through, but for the most part he met frustration.[57] This is a good example of the adage that one discovers where the dominant power lies only when all the marbles are on the table and the *status quo* is about to lose some.[58]

In addition to the obstacles to change found in oligarchies, there is a blockade embodied in faculty-administrative power struggles. Demerath, Stephans and Taylor were early documentors of this conflict over who decides.[59] They found in a large university that faculty controls academic policy but administration controls the purse. One needs the other, and therein lies the rub. Faculty unionization has become a major avenue for faculty to strengthen influence over their economic conditions, but that approach only cements an adversary relationship between two groups which must work together if serious academic innovation and reform is to happen.

College power which is not centralized in competing faculty and administrative oligarchies appears to be de-centralized into departmental fiefdoms and the autonomy of the individual professor. Peterson and Blau are two researchers who find much control at the departmental level.[60] I found that in seventy years of decision making in one university, few proposals threatened departmental autonomy, while presidents prided themselves on never interfering with a professor's teaching or research.[61] Because departments and professorial reward systems are organized to pursue specialized teaching and research, and because each department covets all the enrollments, faculty members and research monies it can get, any change proposal which is perceived by departments or their individual members as threatening these basic interests is in for a rough time. An innovative program which "borrows" faculty from departments, as many do, soon finds that departmental interests come first.

Faculty unionization has become a major avenue for faculty to strengthen influence over their economic conditions, but that approach only cements an adversary relationship between two groups which must work together if serious academic innovation and reform is to happen.

28

The locus of power within a college or university, in summary, will tend to lie among senior faculty leaders and high administrators who are respected and esteemed for long devotion to the *status quo* but whose influence is strongly checked by departmental and professorial control over most teaching and research functions.[62] In small liberal arts colleges and community colleges without great departmental and professorial autonomy, top administrative leaders can expect greater influence toward academic reform than in prestigious universities, but even there an entrenched faculty oligarchy often bars the way. It is not a power formula which promises much change, although most colleges are sure to have some top "influentials" and even a department or two which favor certain reforms. The change advocate will need to know and be able to persuade these exceptions to the rule.

EXTERNAL INFLUENCES

College and university members would like to be independent, but they are not. They depend on student fees, donors, foundations, city, state and federal governments. They must abide by the formal laws and informal mores of their society. To get the status and esteem they need, college members must meet the expectations of accreditors and professional associations. It is not, usually, an indecent collusion. Outside people seem to tolerate less orthodox behavior on college campuses than they do in their own organizations, and college members have ethical and moral limits to what they will agree to do in order to get external support. But collegiate organizations are vulnerable to external pressure. Students of academic reform find, in fact, that most change in colleges and universities appears to have an external stimulus behind it.

Hefferlin sums up his study this way: "In short, we conclude that while the responsiveness of an institution to change can be significantly affected by internal factors, the institution will seldom alter its functions without external influence. Outsiders initiate; institutions react."[63] Martin found most structural changes in undergraduate education in the 1960's to be the result of a specific external pressure group: students. They favored group interactions over lectures, independent study and integrative curricula relevant to their lives over drier disciplinary courses, and they got them—while the pressure lasted.[64] Riesman, Gusfield and Gamson concluded their study of the launching of two experimental colleges this way: "Given the diversity of educational settings in America, we must again insist that there are many institutions where pressures from students—and from outside critics—are the only leverage to support educational reformers surrounded by academic timeservers."[65] I found the same tendency at Middlegrove State University. The state legislature set up that institution to train teachers for one region of the state, and seventy years later, a major function of that normal school turned university was teacher training. As that work grew more complicated, academic specialists were brought in. They lobbied for the addition of departmentalized liberal education, but the teacher trainers and the president fought off their advances. It took a glut in teachers during the Depression to change things. Then the state, concerned to keep at least some potential workers out of the market, ruled that teacher training institutions now could offer liberal arts programs and degrees.[66] It was, as Hefferlin found, an external pressure which worked where internal attempts had not. Since 1935, those academic specialities have grown to the point where they now dominate undergraduate education at this university. Finally, Ladd draws the same conclusion:

> Generally speaking, the cases demonstrate that the proposals developed in the studies became less venturesome or simply disappeared as they passed through the various centers of decision-making except where some form of countervailing power was present. Daniel Bell . . . observed that "it is more the academic habit to deal with ideological questions than with organizational difficulties." The cases support Bell's conclusions quite directly, and more importantly they suggest the results of this "academic habit." The ability of our colleges and universities to respond to the need for change—except when faced with severe pressure or the threat of such pressure—is frighteningly limited.[67]

Currently, inflation soars college costs and income cannot keep pace, so greater efficiency is sought. An influx of "new learners" confronts an immobile faculty unfamiliar with ways to teach such persons, so faculty development and new curricula spring up across the land. The population bulge is getting older, so life-long learning becomes the rage. Students turn from the affluent 1960's to the job-scarce 1970's, so their demands turn from social justice and personal growth to career preparation. It would be nice to say that faculty members and administrators, after the careful study and thoughtful reflection which is their wont, concluded that improved efficiency, preparation of faculty for teaching and bridging between academe and occupation were wise changes to make. Surely, some administrators and faculty members had drawn such conclusions quite apart from external pressures. But the bulk of the musicians on these bandwagons, I suspect, got pushed.

Cohen and March suggest that the currents of external pressure run where they will, regardless of the finest leadership.[68] All leaders can do is ride those currents, using rudder and sails to adjust direction toward desired goals, however slight an adjustment is possible when winds blow strong. General strategies such as those mentioned in Chapter One can be that rudder and sails, but they cannot lead an organization where external pressures will not let it go.

The ability of our colleges and universities to respond to the need for change—except when faced with severe pressure or the threat of such pressure—is frighteningly limited.

29

SUMMARY

The American college or university is vital to our intelligent and ethical future but is largely unable to reform itself in response to the needs of that future without considerable external pressure. Studies of post-secondary institutions suggest several reasons for this consistently documented inflexibility.

College and universities combine deeply rooted norms, values, structures, sub-groups and power relations with great complexity, low formalization and de-centralization of control. Many new ideas penetrate such organizations, but very few can budge the *status quo*. Without serious investment in research on institutional effectiveness, in program planning and development, in professional development, in the strengthening of interpersonal relations, and in the resolution of internal conflict, there simply is too little positive energy and skill focused on planned change to offset contrary tendencies. Small innovations, usually the result of external pressure, dot the periphery of these institutions; rarely does reform or innovation of much magnitude get implemented.

Can some combination of the several strategies for intentional change outlined in Chapter One make a difference in such organizations? Can anything short of revolution make a difference? Such questions have stimulated speculation but little systematic study. This book is something of an exception in its reliance on four years of systematic study into planned change at several colleges and universities.

3 Starting Up: Educational and Organizational Health at the Strategies Institutions

In order to assist improvement or change in an individual, group or organization, leaders or consultants need to understand the state of health of their "clients." The Problem-Solving and Linkage strategies put major emphasis on diagnosis of need. The political perspective assumes that change begins with an articulation of wants. Social Interaction linking agents need to get to know the concerns of "potential users" as well as they know new developments. Even Research, Development and Diffusion experts, concerned as they are about getting their message right, are growing increasingly sensitive to the need to understand the persons or organizations that might "buy" their inventions.

Systematic diagnosis of educational and organizational goals and needs is not a bragging point in most colleges and universities. Some administrators have fine-tuned some informal ways to sense how things are going educationally, and hard budget figures or faculty votes of no confidence can give an administrator blunt messages about certain aspects of organizational health. Some professors are equally adept at picking up signals early in a course regarding the learning needs, styles and motivations of different students. But few professors or administrators have joined science to their diagnostic art. Institutional research on the nature of students, on educational practices and on outcomes is rare. So is the professor who engages in formal diagnosis of students *before* prescribing a course syllabus and teaching-learning methods. How well administrators and faculty members are working together to improve the institution is a major topic around campus coffee pots, but it is not usually a subject of systematic study. If doctors went at patients with as little diagnostic information as colleges have before "treating" students, the casualties would be staggering.

For all these reasons, we in the Strategies project thought it wise to collect some survey and interview data on the nature of educational and organizational practices in project colleges and universities. The information could guide us as external consultants. Its feedback could help campus members in their own diagnosis of whether or not changes were needed. And it could provide a gross pre-test and post-test by which to gauge the impact of change attempts made during the four years of the project. We found few satisfactory research instruments and methods to guide us in this inquiry. Still, the information we gathered did prove useful to campus members and to us. It at least marks a rough beginning toward assessment of educational and organizational "health." Incidentally, I mean by educational health the ability of an educational institution to achieve its learning goals and those of its students. I mean by organiza-

Systematic diagnosis of educational and organizational goals and needs is not a bragging point in most colleges and universities.

31

tional health the ability of a formally constituted group to clarify and agree upon its goals, to identify obstacles to the achievement of those goals, to discover and develop ways to reduce (or get around or overcome) those obstacles, to gain necessary commitment and material support for implementation of those ways, to implement them successfully and to return to Go (goal-setting). I mean, in short, effective planned change.

This chapter reports general diagnostic findings across all seven institutions. During the course of the project, over eight hundred questionnaires were returned from faculty members and over twenty-five hundred from students; instruments included the *College and University Environment Scales*, the *Institutional Functioning Inventory*, the *Experience of College Questionnaire*, and the *Professional Development Questionnaire*. Four hundred hours of interviews were conducted with faculty and administrative leaders. Project staff visited each campus at least once a year for direct observation, and on several campuses faculty members completed participant observer forms bi-weekly. Finally, campus documents were reviewed and analyzed to trace particular events. This rich mixture of information, rather than any single approach, accounts for the detail and completeness found in these chapters and also provides a system of checks and balances against possible distortion caused by the use of any single source of information. Some institutions have been identified by their real names, others have been changed at the request of their leaders.

Seven institutions do not, of course, make a universe. I will not claim that the kinds of organizational and educational concerns unearthed in this diagnosis generalize to American higher education in the 1970's. But I think you will find that many of the problems facing these institutions will ring bells on your campus.

32

We wanted to learn how well things were going for undergraduate students and their professors.

EDUCATIONAL HEALTH

The focus of the Strategies project was undergraduate curriculum, teaching and evaluation. We wanted to learn how well things were going for undergraduate students and their professors. A full inquiry would have sought to identify various characteristics of students and their teachers as well as evidence of educational outcomes. Partly because of limited availability of useful instruments and partly because our research concern was change in educational *practices*, we decided to take a picture of current teaching-learning activities. In many ways, this approach mirrors the way we informally assess our environment. We examine what we are doing now and then try to determine whether that is good or bad on the basis of assumptions about how well those practices should work for whom regarding what ends. It would be much more satisfactory to test those assumptions, but systematic recording of current practices is at least a start.

Three measures of educational health were used by project staff. One was a survey instrument which produces a general student perception of institutional environment, the *College and University Environment Scales*.[1] Second was a survey which obtains student descriptions of specific learning activities and their impacts, the *Experience of College Questionnaire*.[2] Third, supplementing these broad surveys were hour-long interviews with twenty-five to thirty faculty members, administrators and students on each campus. Interviewees were asked if there were parts of undergraduate education which needed "substantial improvement or change." Each of these measures had its limitations. But in concert and as validated or contradicted through later on-campus discussions, a few themes emerged.

On almost every campus in 1971, interviewees and survey respondents reported inadequate academic and intellectual challenge. Respondents consistently found teaching too uniformly didactic and learning too passive. Students reported spending considerable class time just taking notes and much study time just memorizing, rather than in such mental activities as analysis, application, synthesis and evaluation. Many faculty members and students felt there was too little informal interaction between them. Students reported that their peers were more influential than professors as sources of personal development. Let's examine the data which suggested each problem to campus members and Strategies staff.

On nearly every campus, interviewees complained that many students were not vigorously pursuing academic and intellectual goals, nor were many professors cited as particularly stimulating or challenging teachers. There were intellectually excited students and professors around, said interviewees, but they tended to be exceptions rather than the rule. The "Scholarship" scale of the *College and University Environment Scales* (CUES) brought this problem clearly home to many campus members. Table 1 indicates how students rated each of several "Scholarship" items. Consistently, students think their professors know their subject. No problem there. That, after all, is what professors are trained in and rewarded for knowing; they should appear knowledgeable to their far less trained students. But that capacity does not seem to carry over very consistently into an ability to stimulate vigorous learning. Such scale items as "There is a lot of studying here over the weekends," "Class discussions are typically vigorous and intense," "Professors really push student capacities to the limit" and "Students put a lot of energy into everything they do" were all perceived as true by less than one-third of the student respondents. Reacting to a specific, randomly selected, course on the *Experience of College Questionnaire* (ECQ), over a third of the students in most Project institutions reported that they were "rarely" interested, and nearly half in most institutions were "rarely" challenged by that course. Student interviewees could identify faculty members and courses which were invigorating, but they were quick to identify many which were soporific. They also reported that many fellow students were not particularly serious about their own academic or intellectual development.

As you can imagine, campus members had a variety of explanations for these findings. One was that lax admissions policies (or necessities) had produced students who were neither interested in nor capable of serious study. Indeed, comparison of these institutions' scores with those of national norms for highly selective colleges and universities confirms that the higher the admissions standards, the higher the "Scholarship" score on CUES. Bring in enough academically and intellectually vigorous people, and the atmosphere will be charged by their energy. As the following student quotation shows, this "solution" was proposed by students as well as faculty:

Respondents consistently found teaching too uniformly didactic and learning too passive.

33

Student interviewees could identify faculty members and courses which were invigorating, but they were quick to identify many which were soporific.

There are basically two divisions among the students, two different kinds or types of students. The one has mainly come in this year. There's a new kind who has expected a much different learning situation than they have encountered here. The other, who have maybe been here one or two years and who like the sort of lax atmosphere and, you know, not very demanding curriculum and course loads—it's pretty easy to fly through four years and get a B.A. and all that. I don't feel any kind of empathy for that kind of person at all. I've felt ever since I've been here that we've got to hike up standards. Somehow, if we did that, we might attract a different kind of student who'd be motivated to learn to do things.

Unfortunately for persons who interpreted the problem this way, droves of 700 SAT students were not begging to be accepted into these institutions. Financial exigencies were forcing admissions officers to dip lower in the high school graduate barrel (lower, that is, in terms of predictors of *academic* success such as grades and board scores). Also, most project institutions were aggressively seeking "disadvantaged" students as part of the national effort toward equality of educational opportunity, and these recruits by definition were persons who found high academic achievement difficult. Faculty members and students might grouse about admissions standards. Some maintained that a *good* admissions staff could attract plenty of top students to a college such as ours, and others said we must publicize our strengths more effectively. But admissions officers tended to say the market for top students was fiercely competitive, and they were doing the best they could with the limited reputation and program uniqueness of their institutions. In addition, some persons were not willing to put the blame entirely on students (instead of educators) for uninvigorating education.

Another "solution" quickly proposed was a toughening of grading standards. Most Strategies institutions recently had dropped flunking grades and had experimented with "Pass/No Credit" systems. Some faculty members and students regarded such policies as free rides to sloth. Surveys indicated that "B" now was the average grade. Highest standards were too easy to attain, some claimed, and lazy students were not faced with the fear of failure. Despite what the psychologists say, some faculty interviewees held high stock in negative reinforcement as an inducement to learn. Of course, they did not care for it as an administrative strategy to improve faculty performance.

A few members of each institution saw at least part of the problem in the nature of local teaching and learning practices. Some felt that professors were being asked to stimulate vigorous learning among widely diverse students without any special preparation for that extremely difficult task. Some believed that if curriculum and teaching were changed to encourage active student participation, if subject matter were related to student concerns and if faculty-student relationships were strengthened, education could become exciting for the students presently on campus. Certain other data supported this general train of thought.

McKeachie and Erickson, summarizing extensive research on teaching, indicate that course experiences which actively engage the student,

34

Some believed that if curriculum and teaching were changed to encourage active student participation, if subject matter were related to student concerns and if faculty-student relationships were strengthened, education could become exciting for the students presently on campus.

such as discussions, seminars and independent study or field work, do not yield greater or lesser test performance but often do increase learner motivation.[3] The student gets involved and thereby becomes stimulated to learn more. Dewey, of course, advocated active learning long before these studies were summarized.[4] The *Experience of College Questionnaire* measures this degree of involvement in several ways. First, students are asked what

FIGURE 5
ROLE OF THE TEACHER

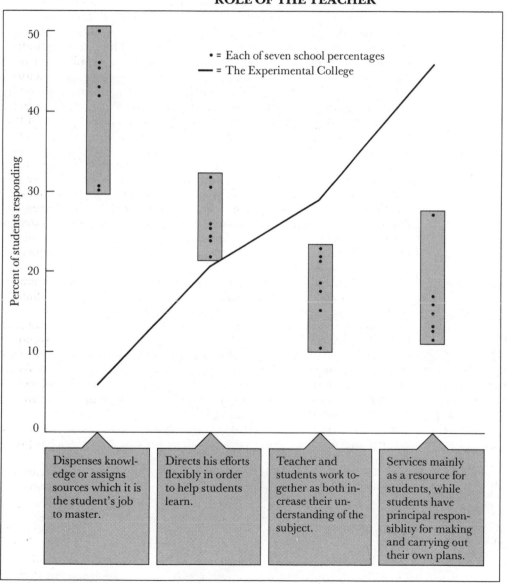

the role of the teacher was in a specific recent course: one who dispenses knowledge and leaves learning up to the students or one who operates more on the collaborative and resource models similar to those described by Axelrod and Mann.[5]

Figure 5 presents the responses of Strategies institutions in contrast to a well-known experimental college which emphasizes the principles of progressive education: building from student goals, interests and abilities; engaging students with their environment through increasingly complex problem-solving activities; and teaching based on facilitation rather than on control and expertise. Most Strategies professors were described by their students as conforming to "the teacher as expert" and "teacher as authority" models identified by Mann.[6] Very few students at the experimental college see their professors in those roles. For them, most professors are collaborators in learning ("persons with whom students work as both increase their understanding") or learning resources ("mainly a resource—students have principal responsibility for making and carrying out their own plans"). Few students in Strategies institutions felt that these roles fit their professors' behavior.

This finding in itself did not worry many faculty members. Their concern rose, however, when they saw other student responses which correlated with these teaching roles. For example, students were asked how much influence they had in setting course content and structure. Students who saw their professor as a dispensor of information tended to feel little influence themselves. As the teaching role was viewed to be more collaborative or facilitative, so student influence was rated more strongly. At the experimental school, students felt a great deal of influence in their courses. Some Strategies interviewees became concerned that students seemed too passive in courses led by dispensing and controlling teachers, although others said professors are trained to know what is best for students. A third piece of information, however, raised the concern of some of these latter persons. Student respondents were asked how they spent their time in class and in studying for this particular course. The general pattern of activities correlated with student influence and teacher role. At the experimental school, most students reported being quite active in class and frequently engaged during study in such complex mental activities as analyzing, applying, synthesizing and evaluating knowledge. Most Strategies students, in contrast, spent over half their time in class listening in order to take notes, and they spent about 45% of their study time memorizing (see Figure 6). The most information dispensing, teacher-controlled courses and institutions had the most note-taking and memorizing.

Few faculty members who saw these tables and figures wanted their institution to have a teaching-learning profile resembling the experimental college, which seemed to them to put too much control in student hands and to put too little emphasis on mastering a set of academic material. But several felt that their own institution needed to give students more practice in active thinking and learning. They saw a need to obtain a better balance of teaching approaches across the faculty and within each of them so that the next time the *Experience of College Questionnaire* were adminis-

Several felt that their own institution needed to give students more practice in active thinking and learning.

tered their institution's profile might resemble Figure 6.

A lack of meaningful relationships between individual professors and students was another possible reason for low intellectual vigor. Close to a fifth of the respondents in most Strategies institutions had not had one conversation longer than five minutes during the past semester with any member of the faculty or administration (see Figure 7). Only about a quarter of the students reported at least six such conversations. Interviewees generally confirmed that many professors and academic advisors were hard to catch (or were unsought). Again, they could cite outstanding exceptions—faculty members who, no matter how busy they were, found time to lend students a personal hand and whom students eagerly sought for help. But the rule was infrequent and brief faculty-student contact, despite the demonstrated educational importance of such interactions.[7]

The *Experience of College Questionnaire* asked students to rate the impact of contacts with faculty or administration and friends on six areas of development: (1) increasing intellectual competence, (2) increasing sense of purpose, (3) clarifying values, (4) becoming more open, (5) increasing self-awareness and (6) increasing one's range of feelings. These vectors of student development are well-explicated by Chickering.[8] At every Strategies institution, faculty or administration members were regarded as having "moderate" influence on increasing intellectual competence. The impact of close friends was rated slightly lower in that area. Regarding all other areas of personal development, faculty or administration members were perceived to have less than moderate impact; in every other area close friends were rated well-above faculty in terms of impact. Close friends of the opposite sex were especially influential.

These findings are not surprising. Faculty members and administrators generally do not perceive themselves as facilitators of student development in areas other than intellectual competence, and the infrequency of their personal contact with students cannot be expected to result in more than moderate impact even in intellectual development. Friends interact much more frequently. Also, peers tend to play a considerable role in a late adolescent's search for purpose, values, new relationships, identity. The question for academicians, of course, is "So what?" The answer some faculty members and administrators considered was that if we want to have more than moderate impact on intellectual competence, we must seek better ways to bring faculty members and students together in academic and intellectual interactions. We also might seek to strengthen peer contacts of the same kind, for they apparently can be nearly as potent as faculty in intellectual development. If we care about these other, more "affective," areas of development (and they do sound like the fancy phrases in our liberal arts goal statements), we will need to figure out ways to help faculty members and administrators make more difference in student development, and we especially will need to be creative in tapping peer influence. Such thinking, of course, has led colleges and universities to develop special advising programs, living-learning centers, contract learning, freshman seminars and peer teaching and advising. Just such innovations began to be proposed within Strategies institutions.

Regarding all other areas of personal development, faculty or administration members were perceived to have less than moderate impact; in every other area close friends were rated well-above faculty in terms of impact.

37

It would be wrong to conclude that the feedback of data such as these caused most faculty members, administrators and students to boil over with desire to overhaul undergraduate education. The Social Interactionists appear quite right that awareness of need and interest in solution

FIGURE 6
STUDENT MENTAL ACTIVITY IN CLASS
AND WHILE STUDYING

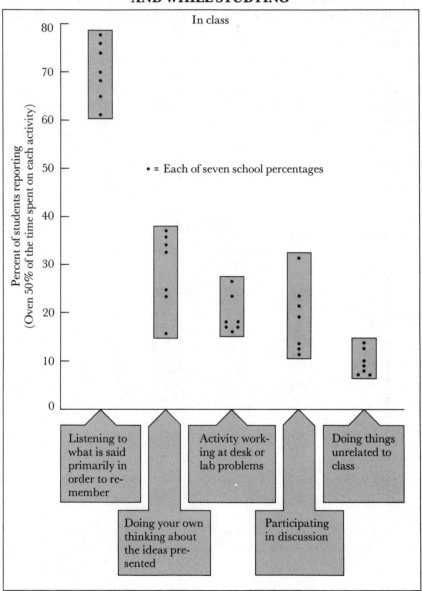

starts in only a small percentage of any system. Over 70% of the student respondents in these institutions reported they were at least fairly satisfied with their educational experience, and very few students became involved in efforts to change institutional practices. In 1972, when this evidence was reported to faculty and administration, only a handful of persons in each group took visible action to begin solving what they took to be problems clarified in the data. It was, however, a beginning, and among those who got involved, the data struck consistent chords: insufficient educational challenge and vigor, teaching-learning activities which did not involve students' minds very actively and inadequate faculty-student relationships outside the classroom. These will be central themes in later case histories.

ORGANIZATIONAL HEALTH

What are the attributes of a "healthy" organization? Miles identified ten characteristics which participants in Strategies workshops have found helpful:

1. Goal Focus

   In a healthy institution, the goals of the system would be reasonably clear to the system members and reasonably well accepted by them. They should also be achievable and appropriate.

FIGURE 6
CONTINUED

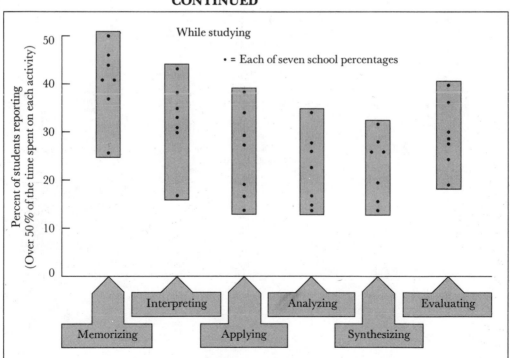

2. Communication Adequacy

The movement of information within the organization is crucial. Information should be distortion free, to and from the surrounding environment. Internal strains should be sensed and good diagnosis made possible. Information should be easily obtained.

3. Optimal Power Equalization

The distribution of influence is relatively equitable. Subordinates can influence upward. Intergroup struggles should not be bitter. Collaboration rather than coercion should exist. Interdependence should be the rule. Knowledge rather than position should influence decisions.

4. Resource Utilization

The system's inputs are used effectively. Overall coordination assures that people are neither overloaded or idling. The fit between people's own dispositions and the role demands of the system is good. A genuine sense of learning, growing and developing as persons exists.

5. Cohesiveness

The organization "knows who it is." Its members feel attracted to membership in the organization. They wish to stay with it, be influenced by it and exert their own influence in a collaborative manner.

FIGURE 7
EXTENT OF FACULTY-STUDENT CONTACT

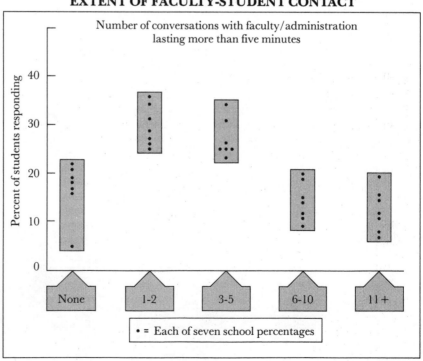

6. Morale

A sum of individual sentiments, centered around feelings of well-being, satisfaction and pleasure; as opposed to feelings of discomfort, strain and dissatisfaction.

7. Innovativeness

The tendency to invent new procedures, move toward new goals, produce new products, diversify and become more differentiated over time. A set to grow, develop and change rather than to standardize. A self-renewing organization as contrasted to "embeddedness."

8. Autonomy

An organization which responds actively, not passively, to demands from outside, acting as a tool of the environment; not responding destructively; maintaining an independence from the environment at the same time.

9. Adaptation

The organization is in realistic, effective contact with its surroundings. When environmental demands and organizational resources do not match, problem-solving and restructuring evolves so that both change in some respects. An ability to cope with change as well as stability and tolerance exists.

FIGURE 7
CONTINUED

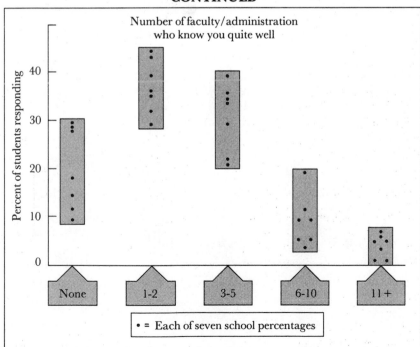

41

energy and the ability inherent in the mechanism is not weakened, but strengthened, in the process. Well developed structures and procedures exist for sensing problems; for inventing possible solutions; for selecting among solutions; for implementing solutions; and for evaluating their effectiveness. The whole operation is controllable. This includes active coping *with* rather than passive withdrawing *from* problems.[9]

Havelock and his associates culled a similar array out of four thousand planned change studies: the more the *linkage* of individual to individual, group to group, and persons to knowledge resources; the more organized and coordinated the planned change *structure*; the more actively reaching

FIGURE 8
FACULTY AND PEER INFLUENCE
ON DEVELOPMENT SELF REPORTS BY STUDENTS

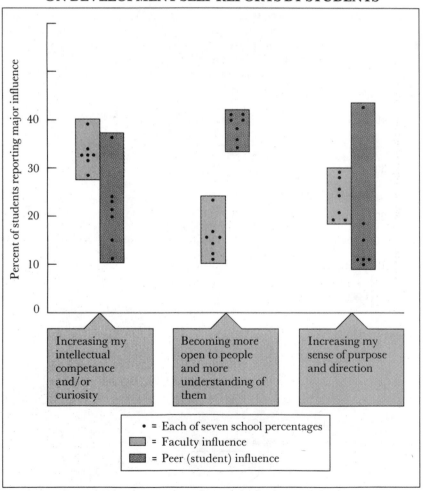

out are members in their *openness* to new information and ideas; the greater the human and material *capacity*; the closer the *proximity* of a change to the institution in values, required behaviors, and geographical distance; the greater the *rewards* for planned change; and the more frequent, various and persistent the change efforts (thereby producing *synergy*), the more likely is an individual or an institution to be able to plan and implement needed changes.[10]

A third formulation of institutional health is embodied in the scales of the *Institutional Functioning Inventory* (IFI), a survey instrument designed by the Educational Testing Service out of interviews in which college and university members were asked to describe the characteristics of "institu-

FIGURE 8
CONTINUED

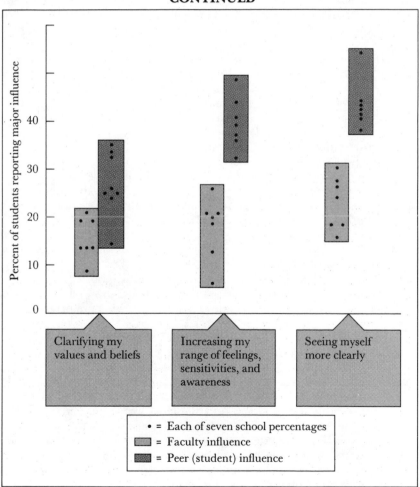

tional vitality." These scales measure degrees of "Intellectual-Aesthetic Extra-Curriculum," "Freedom," "Human Diversity," "Concern for Social Improvement," "Concern for Undergraduate Education," "Democratic Governance," "Concern for Advancing Knowledge," "Self-Study and Planning," "Meeting Local Needs," "Concern for Innovation" and "Institutional Esprit."

There are several points of agreement in these three lists of the dimensions of organizational health. Each agrees that the organization should be internally cohesive, well-connected to pertinent external information, effectively organized for self-examination and problem-solving and willing to try, as well as to reward, new practices.

We were uncomfortable, however, about laying any particular formulation of organizational health on Strategies institutions, so we took two tacks in our diagnosis. We administered the *Institutional Functioning Inventory* to faculty members and administrators. We also asked about twenty-five leaders in each institution an open-ended interview question: "What are the strengths and weaknesses of the college (or university) for diagnosing and solving such problems" (as those educational concerns just mentioned)?

Interviewees most frequently answered the open-ended question in terms of what Havelock calls "capacity," the wherewithal to manage planned change. One measure of capacity is financial resources. Three of the institutions had shrinking enrollments and mounting deficits in 1971, and three others would join that group by 1973. Some interviewees thought these stringencies decreased chances of any investment in innovation, while others felt the predicament increased local commitment for finding new ways to attract students, donors and funding agencies. On the bright side, one of the universities had a large Ford "Venture" grant for undergraduate innovation, a second had a National Endowment for the Humanities grant for an interdisciplinary freshman program, two had grant support for establishment of a University Without Walls program, another had support from several sources for its largely minority student body and yet another enjoyed the many special activities made possible by its membership in the Council for the Advancement of Small Colleges. So, although none could be said to be lavishly well-supported for planned change and almost all were under the threat of rising costs and falling enrollment, none was without some externally provided financial capacity for change.

A different measure of capacity is leadership, the ability for and commitment to reform and innovation. All Strategies institutions had at least one high-ranking administrative officer who was seriously dedicated to academic reform. After all, one does not ask to be included in a project called "Strategies for Change" if the *status quo* looks rosey. In several institutions, both the president and the chief academic officer were interested in innovation. And several of these leaders had planned change abilities as well as interests. Some were charismatic. Some were skillful entrepreneurs. Several were extremely knowledgeable about the latest developments in higher education. And all exercised their authority to gain some leverage on the change process. We will see later that each had

44

his or her liabilities as well. Several were too aggressive and too impatient for many of their faculty members. Few knew much about facilitating the planned change process beyond a couple of rough ideas gained from experience. They sometimes got in their own way. Because their roles are so important, I will describe them with some frankness in ensuing chapters. It speaks to their remarkable openness that they tolerated this kind of reporting, even under a pseudonym.

Besides these high administrators, each institution had a few faculty members who felt strongly enough about the need for reform that they actively pursued it. The number was not large anywhere. A handful of young, often student-oriented faculty members and a sprinkling of senior, highly esteemed professors were identified by institutional leaders as potential innovators and participants in undergraduate reform. Needless to say, we got to know many of these persons over the years in the institutions which stayed active in the project. Few of them had any training for the process of institutional renewal and innovation. Few were as well-connected as the administrators were to the currents in higher education or to local decision making authority. They had almost no time free from other demands to devote to academic reform. As they gained planned change skill, awareness of local needs and distant solutions, high governance positions and some spare time, however, these few committed faculty members became a vital force for the improvement of undergraduate education.

These few committed faculty members became a vital force for the improvement of undergraduate education.

How close would change in undergraduate education be to the values of these college members? The *Institutional Functioning Inventory's* "Concern for Undergraduate Learning" and "Concern for Advancing Knowledge" scores tell part of that story. As Figure 4 reveals, university faculties perceived little institutional interest in helping undergraduates develop, at least in comparison with IFI national norms. Advancing knowledge by graduate training, research and the preparation of undergraduate majors for graduate work: that is our main business. It is a portrait quite in keeping with the American university goals depicted in Chapter Two. Several of the liberal arts colleges, however, put strong stock in their primary source of income, the undergraduate. Mountain College, Hartwick and Quaker Academic all scored above the seventieth percentile nationally in their concern for undergraduate learning. Messiah was not far behind. Advancing knowledge was a strong competitor with undergraduate development in some of these institutions. Closer faculty attention to student growth would not occur without a fight. But it appeared to have a good chance in most liberal arts colleges, although little chance at the universities, if perceived emphases were accurate.

Besides general values, another measure of "proximity" and "linkage" might be the amount of "Human Diversity" in the institution. The more diverse, the greater possibility that new ideas might infiltrate the campus, but the less possibility that everyone could come to agreement on what to do next. The two universities were well over the fiftieth percentile in Human Diversity, as we would expect. At the ninety-second percentile, however, was Quaker Academic, a college of eight hundred students which had agricultural and technical programs along side the liberal arts, liberal Eastern "freaks" along side the "straights." These institutions might expect to have a lot of new ideas, most of which would get compromised or eliminated in political in-fighting among diverse interests. At Messiah, in contrast, most students and faculty came from the same religious upbringing and similar rural towns. That school registered little "Human Diversity." If a new idea fit this value commonality, it should fare well.

Geographically, even the small colleges practiced distance instead of proximity. Each institution was split into departments, and each department's faculty members were housed together. Social science faculties were in separate buildings from science faculties and humanities faculties, and on every campus the central administration was housed together. Students were separated from faculty and administration into dormitories, student centers, fraternities or commuting vehicles. There rarely were occasions when people from diverse sub-groups could come together to study educational practices, plan improvements and carry them out. Occasional faculty retreats were nice, participants said, but they were rarely followed up. Interdisciplinary programs were tried, but departmental grip on faculty kept pulling them apart. Communication across organizational sub-groups was a problem everywhere.

The IFI also includes a scale called "Institutional Esprit," which asks the "level of morale and sense of shared purposes among faculty and administrators." On this scale, Strategies institutions varied considerably. Faculty in two of them, Messiah and Quaker Academic, perceived the faculty-administrative bond as very close—at about the 90th percentile nationally. Hartwick faculty perceived fairly good relationships as well. South Carolina and Commuter Private were above only a quarter of the IFI institutions, while Mountain College and Black Cooperative were so low in perceived agreement among faculty and administration that their scale score barely registered. It would appear that only a few Strategies institutions had the closeness among faculty and administration which might be necessary to reach agreement concerning reform of undergraduate education.

How open were these institutions to change? An IFI scale called "Concern for Innovation" gives faculty perceptions of "institutional commitment to experimentation with new ideas for educational practices." Most Strategies institutions were rated at or above the fiftieth percentile nationally. These ratings may be influenced particularly by the strong orientation toward innovation among the schools' executive administrators. Interviewees consistently said that these administrators and very few others cared enough about innovation to stick their necks out for it. Yet another measure of openness, as well as "linkage," is the actual contacts between faculty members and sources of new ideas. As Table 1 showed, only about a third of the faculty and administration in these institutions were well-linked to sources of new ideas in undergraduate education. A major agendum for improving undergraduate education would appear to be strengthening the ties between faculty members and knowledge resources related to the latest teaching-learning research, theory and practice.

There rarely were occasions when people from diverse sub-groups could come together to study educational practices, plan improvements and carry them out.

46

A major agendum for improving undergraduate education would appear to be strengthening the ties between faculty members and knowledge resources related to the latest teaching-learning research, theory and practice.

Change theorists emphasize the value of systematic "Self-Study and Planning." Again, Strategies institutions showed considerable variation, with Messiah well-organized with an efficient administration, a new planning committee and involvement in the data collection and feedback of Chickering's "Project on Student Development in Small Colleges." Their rating put them at the 97th percentile nationally on this scale. Some other Strategies institutions had new planning committees and one had a recent goals survey, the results of which most interviewees could not recall; none had a great investment in systematic research, development and problem-solving. Most interviewees said the self-study and planning process was not having much influence on the organization. Research on the institution was neither regular, thorough, nor convincing. Planning was the business of only one committee, often without staff or budget resources. Follow-up on plans was at the mercy of on- and off-campus politics, as well as the deep rut of existing structures and functions. Adaptive structures such as organizational and staff development programs, teaching improvement services and innovation linking agents did not exist on Strategies campuses in 1971.

The Problem-Solving strategy stresses the importance of collaboration. "Democratic Governance" is an IFI scale which is composed of items concerning faculty-administrative-student collaboration in decision-making practices. Several Strategies institutions were perceived above the norm in governance collaboration, with the town meeting, consensus system at Quaker Academic putting it at the 95th percentile. On the other end, however, both South Carolina and Black Cooperative faculties rated their institutions below almost ninety percent of the other institutions using the IFI. Interviewees also varied from seeing their institutions as generally open to faculty and student involvement in governance to basically administrative shops. Faculty members in the latter institutions (and a few even in the most democratic places) saw increased faculty involvement in decision making as a major change need.

The collegial norm favors the freedom of professionals to do as their expertise dictates. That freedom, a primary university "goal" in America, would allow plenty of room for individual innovation but also would make it difficult, to say the least, to force autonomous professors to do something they preferred to avoid. The IFI's "Freedom" scale put Quaker Academic and the universities at the top; they were clearly richer in academic freedom than most IFI institutions. Messiah faculty members, on the other hand, saw little freedom in their religiously oriented institution. That state did not depress Messiah interviewees. They said it seemed appropriate to a religious institution, and the College's high "Institutional Esprit" score suggests that low freedom did not interfere with strong faculty-administrative rapport.

Yet another part of organizational health is the degree to which rewards match goal achievement, in our case the achievement of effective undergraduate learning. A couple of items on a 1972 Strategies survey suggests the reward structure. In the universities, the majority of faculty agreed that "In my department, it is difficult for a person to achieve tenure if he or she does not publish." Only about five percent of the small

47

TABLE 1
LINKAGE TO DISCIPLINARY vs. TEACHING-LEARNING INFORMATION

Disciplinary Linkage			Teaching-Learning Linkage		

To how many academic or professional journals do you subscribe?

	Large School	Small School
3 or more (%)*	81.1	60.4

To how many journals do you subscribe that deal primarily with teaching methods, aids, improving teaching or higher education in general?

	Large School	Small School
3 or more (%)	16.1	14.0

How many regional or national conventions of your discipline have you attended in the past two years?

	Large School	Small School
2 or more (%)*	69.3	52.6

How many regional or national conventions devoted to issues of teaching, learning or higher education have you attended in the past two years?

	Large School	Small School
2 or more (%)	33.3	28.1

How often do you read academic or professional journals in or related to your field of competence?

	Large School	Small School
Regularly (%)*	86.2	68.4

How often do you read academic or professional journals dealing with teaching, learning, or higher education?

	Large School	Small School
Regularly (%)	32.8	27.6

I am in communication with people in my academic specialty in other institutions.

	Large School	Small School
Frequently (%)*	62.3	50.4

I am in communication with colleagues in other institutions about new teaching methods, techniques and aids.

	Large School	Small School
Frequently (%)	31.6	28.3

I talk with people at my institution about developments, techniques, findings and theories in my own discipline.

	Large School	Small School
Frequently (%)*	71.2	55.7

*Differences are significant at the .05 level, symmetric test.
Large School, N = 230
Small School, N = 255

I talk with people at my institution about new teaching methods, techniques, aids and theories.

	Large School	Small School
Frequently (%)	53.5	50.4

college faculty respondents agreed with that statement. In contrast, over 80% of the small college faculty agree that "Teaching effectiveness, not publications, is the primary criterion for promotion of faculty at my institution." Less than thirty percent of the university faculty agreed. Any change which would pull faculty away from publishing would appear doomed in the universities but potentially rewarded in the small colleges. Even in the colleges, however, several interviewees said they felt pressed to publish or complete dissertations in order to secure tenure, and they felt that methods to evaluate teaching effectiveness were highly subjective.

Any change which would pull faculty away from publishing would appear doomed in the universities but potentially rewarded in the small colleges.

FIGURE 9
FACULTY CONCERN FOR UNDERGRADUATE LEARNING AND FOR ADVANCING KNOWLEDGE

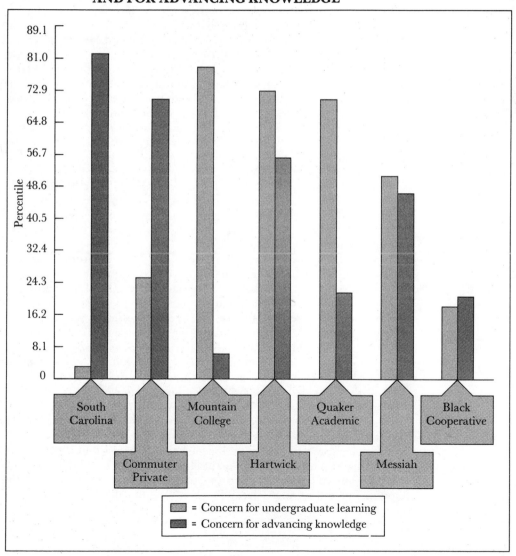

49

The final Havelock factor is "synergy," the cumulative effect of variety and redundancy of change attempts. We found it a difficult factor to judge. Some Strategies institutions had experienced several innovations in recent years and had leaders who kept pressing toward reform and improvement. They might be said to be healthily innovative. Yet faculty interviewees complained about too much change too fast. They said past changes needed to be given a good test and careful evaluation before the institution went charging into a new project. Leaders tended not to see past attempts as either too fast or too much. They seemed small, agonizingly slow starts toward substantial improvement. The two views appear to represent significantly different degrees of felt need for change. Leaders, besieged by news of decreasing student markets, rising costs and innovative developments among competitors, perhaps saw no time to waste in reforming local practices. Faculty conservatives, less responsible for enrollments or budgets, less connected to new trends, well-entrenched in local practices and committed by profession to slow and careful study, did not seem to see the hurry.

How "healthy" were the Strategies institutions as providers of effective undergraduate education? There was not one easy answer, because each institution varied from the others in relation to such general factors as diversity, academic values and faculty-administrative relations. That finding in itself serves as fair warning to reformers who would apply ready-made change strategies to any particular institution. Strategies clearly should be tailored to specific circumstances following local diagnosis. Reformer approaches for a small evangelical college low in freedom and diversity might be quite different from tactics used in a small Quaker college high in freedom and diversity. A leader in a small college which is greatly concerned about student development might have quite a different approach than a reformer in a large university which regards undergraduate students as distractions from its primary concerns.

This said, certain commonalities stood out. Each institution had only a few top administrators and a handful of faculty members who felt a strong need to try new approaches to undergraduate teaching and learning. Only a few people in each place were well-connected to news about teaching-learning research, theory and practice. Almost no one at any institution had any training in strategies for planned change. It was a field full of amateurs of varying experience, limited knowledge and only occasionally much skill. Self-study and planning were never regular, systematic or influential in major decisions. Each institution, no matter how small, was sub-divided into competitive units which rarely got together to work problems out in a collaborative fashion.

Out of these common problems, a common strategy for change was suggested: establish systematic self-study to provide an evidential basis for clarifying institutional goals and problems in achieving them; create well-organized planned change structures and activities for diagnosing problems, building solutions and persuading faculty and administrative adoption; link more and more campus members to colleagues and external resources regarding new ways to teach and learn; train leaders for the difficult art and science of reform, academic development and innovation;

Strategies clearly should be tailored to specific circumstances following local diagnosis.

50

TABLE 2
PROFESSIONAL REWARDS

"In my department, it is difficult for a person to achieve tenure if he or she does not publish."

UNIVERSITIES	AGREE
South Carolina	54%
Commuter Private	71%
LIBERAL ARTS COLLEGES	
Black Cooperative	6%
Hartwick	5%
Mountain College	5%
Quaker Academic	4%
Messiah	2%

"Teaching effectiveness, not publications, is the primary criterion for promotion of faculty at my institution."

UNIVERSITIES	AGREE
South Carolina	28%
Commuter Private	21%
LIBERAL ARTS COLLEGES	
Black Cooperative	81%
Hartwick	80%
Mountain College	85%
Quaker Academic	88%
Messiah	87%

find ways to bring together persons from campus sub-groups to study, discuss, build, decide and implement together better ways to help undergraduates learn. These were the agenda suggested by theory about organizational health, by survey evidence and by open-ended interviews. Fitted to the specific norms ("Freedom," "Democratic Governance") and values ("Concern for Undergraduate Learning," "Concern for Advancing Knowledge") of each institution, these strategies did seem to define a promising route toward organizational health.

I should correct myself. Those were the organizational change needs suggested to me and not many others in the Strategies institutions. Even on the Strategies staff, we had no neat agreement in 1971 about what the evidence suggested and what the institutions needed to become self-renewing. It was too early in research on planned change in organizations and in our acquaintance with these institutions for a leap to grand conclusions. Instead of giving pat formulas to college leaders on the basis of slim evidence, therefore, we fed back these data with limited commentary and settled in to watch each institution as undergraduate reform and innovation was attempted over the next three years. The following chapters report those cases in some detail. With these accounts, you will have much the same formal evidence as I—if not the experience of living with these institutions as a friendly observer—on which to draw more substantial conclusions than research on planned change in colleges and universities has yet provided.

Section II

Case Histories of Planned Change

Change is a process. It must be studied over time, often over several years. It should be studied by several research methods and several researchers, each approach supplementing and checking the others, for it is very easy to report the biases of the observer rather than the events themselves. Change should be studied as it occurs, for memory distorts.

Such case histories are rare. First person, retrospective "stories" are much more familiar. The following case histories are exceptions to the rule. They were built as the change attempts occurred over a period of four years. Observations, surveys, interveiws and campus documents were analyzed by several researchers and verified by on-campus participants. A conservative posture was taken toward reporting any action which was not confirmed by several sources of information. Five years' work and several hundred thousand dollars in funding resulted in the cases presented in this section.

A word of caution is appropriate. These cases are not snappy adventure yarns. They are presented as accurately as possible. In some places, they get dull and seem to go nowhere

53

for many pages because the action was dull and went no-where for many months. Real life is like that. Still, initial readers have found them compelling accounts of planned change as it actually occurs, not as it is doctored to make some point or other. My intention is to present cases of sufficient accuracy and detail that you can first determine for yourself how planned change occurs (or why it does not) in these colleges and universities and can then place your conclusions against the theory presented in Section I and against your own experiences. A useful teaching or work-shop use of these cases, without my summary perspectives, is to ask students or workshop participants to extract change strategies and factors from their own reading of this material.

54

4 Stimulating Innovation in a State University: University of South Carolina

The University of South Carolina, like many American universities, sits today on four academic traditions and philosophies. One, liberal education for the best and the brightest, is grounded in the institution's 1801 origin as the state's college for Southern gentlemen. A pre-Civil War part of the campus called the "Horseshoe" serves as a visual reminder of that tradition. A second tradition, rooted in a century's ebb and flow of programs in agriculture, law, medicine, engineering and business, is the notion of regional service through professional training. Third, the mass education movement is well-represented in the university's rapid expansion, its state-wide branch campuses and its associate degree programs. The College of General Studies, tucked beneath the huge basketball arena, symbolizes this interest to many faculty. Finally, the rapid expansion of the 1960's, still continuing at South Carolina, brought with it a boom in support for graduate training and research in the academic disciplines. Formerly, outsiders might characterize South Carolina as a sleepy Southern university or a collegiate place best known for social life and Frank McQuire's basketball teams. But in recent years, under the energetic leadership of a highly innovative president and with strong state support, first rate academic and professional programs as well as a wide range of undergraduate innovations have begun to receive notice.

Amidst these familiar university traditions and recent bustle, certain educational and organizational problems appeared. Student questionnaire respondents perceived little academic vigor in undergraduate life. Many students were not excited about academic or intellectual endeavors and many faculty were not successful in striking sparks in them. Teaching was primarily didactic and learning passive. Faculty-student contacts were infrequent. A summary report from a faculty-student retreat agreed with the survey data that the academic atmosphere

> is deficient in several respects: first, there is far too little genuine enthusiasm for learning being generated in the student community as a whole; second, there is far too little opportunity for cooperative faculty-student learning experiences; third, curricular modifications, allowing greater diversity in educational experiences for a broader variety of students, need further development and wider application; fourth, intellectual and cultural exploration need special emphasis.

On the organizational side, the major problems, according to faculty, were weak emphasis on undergraduate learning and little reward for undergraduate teaching, inadequate self study and planning, plus little democracy in governance. The latter problem was related in interviewees'

In recent years, under the energetic leadership of a highly innovative president and with strong state support, first rate academic and professional programs as well as a wide range of undergraduate innovations have begun to receive notice.

minds to the rather personal leadership style of the president. Our observations suggested that the president had pursued university development and innovation by a three-fold strategy. First, he made special efforts to be well-linked to external news of innovation, and he tried to disseminate such news within the university. Second, he attempted to identify and then encourage internal innovators. Third, he acted as an entrepreneur who found external funding and used his internal authority to establish new programs. His strong initiatives to build a modern university were appreciated by faculty, but by the advent of the Strategies project in 1971, many professors and administrators were irritated by his penchant for nontraditional education and by his unilateral decision making. One reason faculty recently had developed a faculty senate was to check the charge of their president.

What strategies for change would be appropriate under such conditions? To seek answers to that question, we followed events related to these problems over a four year period: 1971-1975.

The president, perhaps sensitized by the Student Movement of the late 1960's, had become very concerned about the responsiveness and flexibility of the undergraduate curriculum. He felt a need, then went looking for solutions. In 1969-70 he picked up the idea of a semester-long independent study program from Joe Rhodes of the Scranton Commission and volunteered South Carolina as one of three universities to implement Rhodes' "Contemporary University," a full semester's academic credit for independent study. He also had placed USC in the Union for Experimenting Colleges and Universities and, in 1971, had instituted a University Without Walls unit. The president had also approved a comprehensive preparation for university learning designed for disadvantaged students. Called Opportunity Scholars, this experiment was initiated by a special university institute for research and development on social problems. All these innovations were undertaken without faculty involvement. Each program had external funding. Each had a few internal people ready to lead it. Each enjoyed the president's ability to open the gate to decision and implementation. None had been fought through faculty governance. Each was non-traditional, taking place outside regular departments and through unorthodox teaching and evaluation. Contemporary University and University Without Walls differed from Opportunity Scholars in that they were innovations developed outside the university and brought in. Also, Opportunity Scholars meant to prepare students to succeed in the regular curriculum, not offer an alternative to it. Still, each of the programs was viewed by some faculty as part of the president's scheme to jeopardize departmental standards and controls through unilateral innovation.

THE ILL-FITTED STUDENT

Into these precedents entered a new concern. For some time, most upper division units of the university would not allow students with grade points below 2.0 to enter their programs. Yet the university allowed such students to remain. The business school had been accepting these marginal performers, but in 1970 its faculty decided to join other units in holding to

Each of the programs was viewed by some faculty as part of the president's scheme to jeopardize departmental standards and controls through unilateral innovation.

the 2.0 standard. Where would the marginal students go? A need was present, but who would articulate it as a demand for change, and what change could solve the problem? On February 11, 1970, the dean of business put the issue on the table of the deans' council. The provost, as chairperson of the council, opened the gate farther by setting up a subcommittee of deans to study the problem. Again, felt need precipitated action. The strategy here, in contrast to the president's initiatives, was to use regular administrative channels and procedures to deliberate the issue.

Members of the deans' council revealed in later interviews that they brought their own views of the need and its solutions to their deliberations. The dean of student services immediately argued that the solution to the marginal students' problem was also a solution to the problem of many students who, for one reason or another, made an ill-fit with the university's set curriculum and teaching. What was needed was a general degree with no set requirements, a degree which could be tailored to individual student needs. This individual was aware of higher educational trends and in fact taught a graduate course in higher education. The Bachelor of General Studies degree, recently adopted in some major universities, was his solution.

The provost himself agreed with the business dean's concern that there was no articulated route to a four year degree for many of the university's associate degree students. He told a Strategies interviewer that the traditional requirements were too restrictive: "an endurance contest to see whether you can follow all the little rungs of the ladder and please all the people as you go up the ladder. Therefore, you probably need an unstructured degree and a place where, to use the present day cliché, the individual can do more of his own thing." He went on to say this general degree student "in all likelihood would be a very bright fellow rather than the kind of person I was talking about before, who didn't meet our entrance requirements."

The dean of the college of general studies in turn maintained that he had argued for such an unstructured degree the last fifteen years "to take care of people who do not meet the minimum requirements for a degree, but whom, being a tax-supported university, we have to try to serve. I have asked on several occasions to get this created without any luck."

The mass education need to serve marginal students and associate degree graduates had merged quickly with more elite notions of serving bright students "turned off" by traditional structures. Two needs had combined, each supported by a different academic value. And a solution, derived through the external linkage of at least the student affairs dean, just as quickly entered the formula. The question now was how to move from this point to implementation of a polished new program. The committee of deans decided to form their own subcommittee of associate deans and faculty whose charge was "the responsibility of studying various possibilities by which the university might accommodate students eligible to continue in the university but ineligible for admission to professional schools or programs." The charge reiterated the business dean's initial demand and his associate dean was named chairperson of the new subcommittee.

57

The mass education need to serve marginal students and associate degree graduates had merged quickly with more elite notions of serving bright students "turned off" by traditional structures.

The new group sent for the Bachelor of General Studies (BGS) degree descriptions from the University of Michigan and the University of Iowa. Despite the academic respectability of these institutions, some committee members still felt uneasy about leaving curriculum up to a student and his advisor. Their report concluded:

> On the plus side, . . . [the Bachelor of General Studies] was seen as low cost, stressing student responsibility, and allowing existing programs to maintain current standards. Negatively, student freedom could result in poor programs, and students desiring traditional degree programs but "in limbo" might find the BGS a poor substitute for their original goals.

Despite their ambivalence about the solution, the group had no doubt that the problem was genuine:

> The problem will not go away and it is of such magnitude that it requires attention. While it is easy to be very critical of a General Studies degree, it seems obvious that if departments, schools, and colleges are not willing to substantially modify requirements for admissions to upper division and professional programs, then serious consideration must be given to a generalist degree. Failure to do one or the other is to ignore the problem of a large number of students and places the university in somewhat of an untenable position.

Still, they did not actually recommend either a BGS or any other solution.

The original committee, however, was more decisive. It endorsed the BGS eight months after its appearance on the agenda of the deans' council. The recommendation stressed that the new program should have a careful advisement program, an administrative structure separate from present schools and colleges, all-university support, an eight year trial with careful evaluation, student-designed programs "with minimum constraints" and the opportunity for students to re-enter other programs. Because the committee was administrative and viewed this recommendation as one needing faculty sanction, it urged appointment of a faculty committee "to develop a specific proposal." One member of the subcommittee, the dean of arts and sciences, was on leave when this action was taken. He was strongly against the establishment of a new administrative structure and felt that a new "General Major" in arts and sciences solved the problem. Were he present, he might have blocked the committee's action. He certainly tried later.

The president received the deans' proposal. Because establishment of a new degree program was an issue he thought faculty would perceive to be their business, he established an *ad hoc* committee to draft a formal proposal for submission to the faculty. He appointed several faculty members and administrators known for strong interest in undergraduate education and innovation but, for the most part, respected among more traditional faculty. He called the group the "Experimental College Committee" (ECC) and charged it to think creatively not only about the deans' proposal but also about a structural home for other experimental programs. His strategy, it appeared, was to influence the formulation stage of decision making and to expand the deans' idea into a much larger

58

agenda for innovation.

A two-day retreat at Myrtle Beach, with the president and provost present, kicked off the committee's work. One member noted that "The report was completed at the beach. The proposal presented five months later was essentially the same as the one they wrote at the beach." One sustained time together, apparently, moved them as far as many short meetings later could manage. But in those five months, committee members studied materials concerning experimental colleges such as New College, University of Alabama, the University Without Walls, Third World College and Ottawa University. The University Without Walls director was on the committee and was the university's liaison to the Union for Experimenting Colleges and Universities. He was also quite knowledgeable about the latest higher education innovations and linked the committee to several of these outside knowledge resources. There was some discussion of visits to these resources, but no such actions were taken. Besides searching out models, the committee debated whether the BGS would have adequate academic standards and whether the program should be for marginal performers, for the disadvantaged, for able students turned off by regular programs or for stimulation of additional undergraduate innovation. An attempt to devise a detailed design for an Experimental College failed, for as one member commented, one detail "just opens up more and more problems." Though it studied other experimental colleges in addition to BGS programs, the new committee resembled the earlier group in its combination of debate on internal needs or standards and search of external models. Neither group looked much at research or attempted to involve the faculty more broadly. Each operated in semi-isolation from the rest of the institution.

The Experimental College Committee reported its recommendations to the president in May of 1971. This document reiterated the proposal for a general degree, but now the phrase was "an experimental college offering a four-year degree program." The president's intervention apparently had been successful in broadening the demand to encompass experimentation in general. The proposal said the new college would be for "students who find the university unduly impersonal as well as those who feel that their curriculum is irrelevant to their needs." Student movement criticisms of traditional programs as impersonal and irrelevant, a particular concern of the University Without Walls director, thus found voice in this proposal. The report also stressed the need to aid students whose areas of study were not found in the regular curriculum and "the disadvantaged or initially ill-prepared student: clearly, the present wastage of potentially talented students held back by earlier educational deprivation cannot be tolerated." The Experimental College would not be simply a holding company for existing experimental programs and the new Bachelor of General Studies. It would serve "as an experimental unit where program concepts, examination and measurement methods, teaching modes, use of time, facilities and personnel, and the like, may be evaluated, refined and modified for application to undergraduate education." The conclusion reveals the broad innovation agenda represented on this committee:

One sustained time together, apparently, moved them as far as many short meetings later could manage.

59

It is clear to the committee that the university and higher education in general must face up to many new problems and opportunities, such things as admission of the highly motivated and not just the intellectually elite, a concept of advising which deals with the total development of the individual, the use of the educational contract, the problem-focused approach to general education through inter-disciplinary seminars, the crediting of off-campus learning experiences, the use of depth study programs involving more independent study and individualized graduation requirements. The committee recognized that the university must come to grips with these and other developments and believes that an Experimental College in which innovations in the educational process may be researched, developed and tested, is needed by the university.

The prose of the second report pays special heed to the "academic credibility" concerns expressed on the committee, especially by an associate professor of physics; since "the programs must be subject to close academic scrutiny and evaluation," the committee proposed the establishment of an advisory committee of faculty from existing colleges and schools. It urged the recruitment of "only the highest quality faculty" and a dean with "national respect." Thus its comparability with existing standards would be assured. It attempted to allay another concern, that such a college would take significant funds, numbers of students or status from existing units:

Clearly such an institution would attract only a small minority of students. Moreover, the new system must not endanger, but should serve to protect, the traditional curriculum which will continue to attract the great majority of students. Indeed, it is only with the assurance that the traditional liberal arts curriculum will remain the heart of the university that the committee advocates a new college.

Several tactics are readily apparent. First, stress the need to serve good students who find the university impersonal or irrelevant as well as the disadvantaged so that the program cannot be stigmatized as a dumping ground. Second, provide plenty of faculty safeguards to pacify academic standard-bearers. Third, assume small numbers of students so as not to threaten any existing program's enrollment. A small, respectable experiment under your critical control is all we ask, faculty.

The president accepted this report and forwarded it to the faculty's standing Committee on Curricula and New Courses (CCNC). After a year and a half's deliberation, the demand finally was moving from the administrative to faculty governance pyramid. The president was going to follow democratic governance channels all the way on this one. An immediate problem arose. Few faculty members had heard of the "Experimental College" or "BGS" proposal, according to interviewees. One CCNC member who had heard "bits and pieces" said the word was "just the general theme of our president's being hepped up on the subject of innovation, that anything which is different, anything which is new, is by definition good." Persons outside CCNC not only assumed that it was the president's idea, they confused it with two programs recently im-

60

plemented by the president without faculty review: Contemporary University and the University Without Walls. It thereby attracted guilt by association. The latter program had drawn adverse publicity in the student newspaper for granting credit for such things as growing up black in the South, while the former had become infamous for approving an independent study project which consisted in part of walking the Appalachian Trail. The 1971-72 chairperson of the Faculty Senate commented that both programs drew such faculty assessments as "Why don't we just let somebody buy a degree who sends a check for so much tuition?" As for the president's connection, the Faculty Senate chairperson observed that "the president had so consistently harped on innovation that it became past the level of marginal utility. It simply generated hostility and antagonism any time the word cropped up. It's now just a word of rebuke." One reason, the chairperson said, was that teaching innovations usually meant more work without professional rewards:

> *A faculty member says, "Great, I'd love to do that, but I'm supposed to do that on top of my nine or twelve hour teaching load? I'd be happy to teach on a one to one basis, but I've got fifty students and I've got to schedule fifty hours to see each one one hour a week and I've got to do a little lecturing and committee work on the side—then I'm not so enthusiastic about it!" So the people I ran into in these informal situations, their almost unanimous reaction was, "This is another one of those damn crackpot schemes that will either be worthless or will result in a lot of extra work without any compensation!"*

Lack of faculty awareness and involvement, suspicion of shoddy standards because of its confusion with recent and academically controversial programs implemented unilaterally by the president, expectation of added burdens: these appeared to be the conditions facing the Experimental College proposal as it was introduced to faculty governance.

The proposal was considered first in a joint Curricula Committee-Experimental College Committee meeting during the summer of 1971. Vacations left only three ECC members present. Those members introduced only the final document, not any of the information and argument generated over the past year. The provost did stop by briefly to stress the need to serve students whose grade points are not bad enough for dismissal but not good enough for admission to upper division programs or completion of them. The chairperson of CCNC recalled that his committee's concerns focused mostly on the "academic integrity of the new college." Another CCNC member remembered a second issue: "The main issue was the number of students that was likely to be involved in this." Members were assured the numbers would be small, but their fear was that many students might be attracted to the Experimental College and therefore affect allocations of funds and positions elsewhere in the university. The third CCNC concern was that experimentation would not need a special college or degree program: "As far as we could see, all this could be done now." Enthusiasm for the Experimental College did not run high in the Committee on Curricula and New Courses. The final proposal and three ECC members did not assuage their concerns.

"This is another one of those damn crackpot schemes that will either be worthless or will result in a lot of extra work without any compensation!"

After ECC members left the meeting, several hours were put into revising their proposal. The core faculty was eliminated to avoid endangerment of existing allocations. The separate college was eliminated. The Experimental College was placed in the College of General Studies because CCNC members felt the program was meant for remedial students: The chair observed, "The advocates would skirt around the words 'remedial preparation' or 'remedial courses,' but this, as far as we could tell, was what they were talking about. A fair amount of work in General Studies is remedial in nature [according to this interviewee] and [Experimental College] students would have to do a lot of remedial work. It seemed to us that many of the courses given in General Studies could serve this purpose."

Contemporary University and Opportunity Scholars were placed under the Experimental College umbrella, and the especially controversial University Without Walls would merge into the Experimental College: the new college "will fill the needs envisioned by the University Without Walls, whose mission will thereby have been accomplished." The committee finally changed the BGS stipulation that "the degree program would be determined by negotiation between a student and a faculty committee" by altering "negotiation between" to "plan with": "Negotiation involves a matter of equal bargaining which we would not accept," said the chairperson. With these revisions and without accompanying rationale, information or recommendation, CCNC forwarded the proposal to the Faculty Senate.

The Committee on Curricula and New Courses clearly did not feel much "ownership" for the Experimental College proposal. It was not their idea, and they did not become devotees in their one brief meeting with representatives of the last year and a half's work. Their strategy appeared to be to minimize the aspects of the proposal which might make the program compete for students in their own programs and to increase faculty control. No one on CCNC was ready to campaign for the proposal. In fact, advocates were hard to find. The deans were out of the picture in faculty governance, and it was an old, tired proposal to them by now. The Experimental College Committee had gone through sufficient compromises among the experimentalists and traditionalists, the meritocrats and egalitarians, that no one on that body was very enthused. As one member said, "We could all agree on it because it did not say anything. There were no real points of agreement." The one member who was committed to establishing an experimental college, the director of University Without Walls, had become ill in the controversy over his own program and had left the university. The dean of arts and sciences returned from leave to learn about the academically unorthodox things going on in that program. He called an arts and sciences faculty caucus to urge a clean-up or eradication of this program which CCNC now would merge into the Experimental College. Things looked bleak. Without active advocates, contaminated by rumors about the University Without Walls, suspected as another presidential scheme, perceived as a potential threat to academic standards and existing program enrollments, the Experimental College proposal was distributed to faculty senators for considera-

62

It was not their idea, and they did not become devotees in their one brief meeting with representatives of the last year and a half's work.

tion at their October 5, 1971, meeting.

About this time, the Strategies for Change and Knowledge Utilization project entered the life of the university, again by presidential initiative through his linkage to the project sponsor, the Union for Experimenting Colleges and Universities. The University Without Walls director was to have been the university's liaison to Strategies and the project's on-campus leader. He and the president agreed that the project's action and research focus ought to be the Experimental College. When he left the university, the president turned to a young associate professor of psychology who was just beginning his one year stint as director of Contemporary University. This person and several colleagues had recently joined the university as part of its expansion of graduate-research departments. Their initial interests were those described by Jencks and Riesman, building their departments and establishing their own academic reputations. During the Kent State-Jackson State-Cambodia crisis, however, these young scholars found themselves immersed in the concerns of undergraduate students. Several of them traced their new commitment to improving undergraduate life to that tragic week.

The first thing the new Institutional Representative did in his new Strategies for Change role was to ask around to see how faculty members felt about the Experimental College:

> I began checking around and couldn't find a single faculty member who was in favor of the University Without Walls. And likewise, I couldn't find a single faculty member who could distinguish for me successfully between that and the Experimental College. So it may have been nothing more than guilt by association. But the fact was, simply, that if Experimental College came up for a vote, it wasn't going to go through. In fact, it was going to go down in flames.

He found that his own Contemporary University board had no interest in being associated with the University Without Walls in a new proposal calling for new faculty scrutiny, for Contemporary University had just received a favorable review from a faculty senate evaluation committee. Opportunity Scholars leaders felt the same way. In consultation with Strategies staff, therefore, the psychology professor decided to try to seek a tabling motion in the senate so as to allow faculty a chance to consider the proposal on its merits. He had only one day to garner support for such a motion, and he regarded the vice provost for academic affairs as key to such support. The vice provost had been English chairman under the dean of arts and sciences. Now the bureaucratic reporting relationship was reversed; the University Without Walls was under the vice provost's office. He had quickly investigated the charges against that program by the dean of arts and sciences and had found them "90-95% incorrect." The psychology professor assumed that the vice provost was ready to do battle with the dean in the context of the Experimental College proposal. Such an altercation might leave little enthusiasm for the proposal.

After a few hours of persuasion, supported by an associate professor of biology on the board of Contemporary University, an associate vice provost for regional programs who was a developer of Opportunity Schol-

"But the fact was, simply, that if Experimental College came up for a vote, it wasn't going to go through. In fact, it was going to go down in flames."

63

ars, and an associate vice provost for academic affairs who was a member of CCNC, the vice provost finally agreed to seek a tabling motion. He went to lunch with the CCNC chairperson and faculty senate chairperson to gain their support. They agreed that the vice provost would be the first person recognized once the Experimental College proposal was introduced. And so it occurred three hours later. The vice provost requested tabling because of the confusion about University Without Walls, and such a motion was quickly made and passed. The psychology professor, himself a senator, overheard what he felt was a fair summary of faculty understanding on the matter:

> a. "What happened? What's going on? . . ."
> b. "The vice provost is in trouble, and he knows Experimental College is in trouble. They don't want to discuss it; they want to sweep it under the rug."

The strategy had been for the one person who felt obliged to save the Experimental College, the psychology professor, to persuade the key "influential" to delay action in order to save a proposal that the influential valued. Recruitment of allies with credibility to the vice provost helped. But delay was all that was gained. The obstacles to faculty support for the Experimental College remained. The proposal itself, by the tabling rule, was back in the hands of CCNC, whose members were not excited about it and had presented it to the senate "without recommendation" pro or con. Earlier advocates of the BGS and Experimental College were still not visibly seeking support or even faculty understanding of the proposal.

In the next few weeks, several activities occurred in relation to the proposal. First, CCNC formally decided to take no action on the proposal until the University Without Walls was fully investigated. The associate vice provost for academic affairs took on that investigation, which included interviews of each student in that program. Second, the dean of Arts and Sciences took the CCNC chairperson to lunch in an attempt to persuade him to get his committee to drop the proposal. The CCNC chairperson concluded, "I think the dean's fear is that he will lose a substantial number of arts and sciences students to the Experimental College if it is done." Third, the psychology professor and his group of colleague friends, most of them young faculty senators, began meeting informally to consider what could be done to save the proposal. Fourth, as part of the Strategies project, the psychology professor organized an action-research "Task Force." He sought to make it credible by balancing interests for and against the Experimental College. The dean of arts and sciences, the CCNC chairperson and the associate vice provost for academic affairs joined it along with a student selected by the dean and a student selected by the associate vice provost. This group met for the first time (without the dean) at the first Strategies workshop for campus teams, October 25-28, 1971, in Philadelphia. There a split developed which was to doom all task force attempts at action. The CCNC chairperson wanted the task force only to observe university affairs related to the proposal and to do only the research of the action-research project. The dean later joined this side. In contrast, the psychology professor, the associate vice provost and the student selected by the associate vice

"They don't want to discuss it; they want to sweep it under the rug."

64

"I think the dean's fear is that he will lose a substantial number of arts and sciences students to the Experimental College if it is done."

provost wanted to mount a campaign to inform the faculty about the issue so that when the proposal was untabled, a knowledgeable decision could be made. A chart of possible actions was made, including outside consultants, public debates, questionnaires, open meetings of CCNC, position or fact papers, contact with senators and a retreat or workshop. Despite protestations that all sides of the issue would be covered in such activities, the dean and CCNC chairperson steadfastly opposed task force action throughout the next five months.

One of the purposes of the first Strategies workshop was to begin to expose teams to planned change theory. Members of the South Carolina contingent later said that Goodwin Watson's keynote address stuck in their minds and guided later activities. Other workshop members responded similarly. Watson himself cited Gross, Giacquinta, and Bernstein's *Implementing Organizational Innovations* as a main source of some of the following points.

Fifteen Factors in Reducing Resistance to Change
Goodwin Watson

OWNERSHIP
The more an innovation is "owned" by those affected by it, the greater will be full acceptance. Innovations pushed from above or from outside the institution are less likely to succeed than those shared by college members. It is important, therefore, to be sure that a proposed innovation is a) responsive to members' needs, b) diagnosed and designed with their involvement, and c) implemented with their participation.

REDUCTION OF BURDENS
Participants in an innovation should see it as reducing their burdens, lightening their load. Adding responsibilities to already beleaguered faculty, administration and students is no way to gain acceptance.

SUPPORT AT THE TOP
Although pushing an innovation from the executive administration without sense of ownership at other levels is unwise, few innovations can succeed without firm commitment to them at the highest administrative level.

COMPATIBILITY WITH INSTITUTIONAL VALUES
Innovations whose content and purposes agree with traditional values and goals of the college are more likely to be accepted than those clashing with those values.

COMPATIBILITY WITH
ORGANIZATIONAL STRUCTURE
The innovation whose implementing structure fits into existing college or university organization has best chance of success.

DESIRE FOR NEW EXPERIENCE
Routine can grow tedious. The opportunity to do something new and exciting can go far toward gaining acceptance of a new idea. It can also, however, cause anxiety.

65

RESPECT FOR THE OPPOSITION
Those opposed to an innovation usually have sound reasons and legitimate concerns. Innovators need to sit down with the opposition and listen. Conservatives should not be forced to move until they are ready.

CLEAR GOALS
Foggy goals among innovators often lead to failure in implementation. Clear goals are prerequisite to innovation.

OPEN, TWO-WAY COMMUNICATION
Full and open two-way communication before and during the innovation is vital not only to increase participant ownership but to enhance accuracy of interpretation. Full feedback from participants and other affected parties should be carefully maintained. If the normal communication structure is top-down, hierarchical, however, and if that is the pattern to which people are accustomed, opening up communication flow may cause insecurity.

BUGS INEVITABLE
No innovation works right the first time. Bugs and disappointments should be expected.

TRAINING FOR NEW ROLES
Undertaking new roles is difficult. New skills must be learned. A training program needs to be developed.

SUITABLE MATERIALS
New approaches to curriculum, teaching and evaluation usually require appropriate materials and facilities. Success is contingent upon adequate resources of all kinds.

UNEXPECTED EFFECTS
Change in one part of an organization may have unexpected consequences, some desirable, some not, for other parts. These need to be taken into account in planning and implementation.

REWARDS
College members cannot be expected to participate in a new program without attractive compensation. Credit for students, salary incentives for faculty, recognition for everyone may be necessary. A rule of thumb is that participants should be rewarded at least as fully as are those in traditional learning, teaching and research pursuits.

CLIMATE OF READINESS
Institutional members who have an open approach to change, who are well-informed about innovations and about the impacts of their own college's educational process, and who have participated previously in successful innovations are more accepting of new ideas. It is therefore vital to keep college members well-informed about change in higher education and about the effects of teaching and learning. An office or committee for this research and informational purpose is desirable.

In closing, Watson emphasized that innovations never are as disruptive as opponents suspect nor as glittering as supporters hope.

In December, Strategies staff visited the campus and met with the president and task force. The president expressed great enthusiasm for efforts to individualize education and endorsed the Experimental College proposal. Because of faculty suspicion of his agenda, however, he had decided not to push publicly the proposal. The task force at some urging from the psychology professor did agree to split into two subgroups, one for action to inform the faculty and one for research. He argued that "I would like to see this faculty make a decision in the open on the evidence presented either beforehand or in a Senate Meeting." Still, in later task force meetings the dean and CCNC chairperson succeeded in blocking such proposed actions as inviting Neal Berte, dean of New College, University of Alabama, to come speak with faculty about the Experimental College. He said he opposed such a visit "so as not to appear to be attempting to influence the senate." Others suspected that he feared Berte would raise interest in such a college.

Over Christmas, the president and provost took action of their own to get the Experimental College proposal moving. The dean of general studies, regarded by many faculty as not sufficiently academic to be entrusted with a four year degree such as the BGS, was made Registrar. The dean of arts and sciences then drafted a new "Proposal for a Four-Year College of General Studies," which the provost presented to CCNC. This proposal placed the BGS in the College of General Studies but placed all the faculty, the new assistant dean, coordinators and student credit hours in other colleges. The potential threat to staff and enrollment in these other colleges was thus eliminated while those colleges' deans could exert control through the new assistants. The proposal made no mention of Contemporary University, University Without Walls, Opportunity Scholars or experimentation in general. In effect, the president's idea of an experimental college had been erased. The original idea of a general degree survived.

About the same time, the "Tuesday discussion group" of young faculty was meeting weekly in faculty homes to discuss a possible substitution for the Experimental College proposal. They were unaware of the president's and provost's actions until the new administrative proposal appeared. When they did sit down to study it, they decided that it was a ploy by the dean of arts and sciences to keep most BGS students and faculty in Arts and Sciences (the largest college), and they agreed it was inadequate because it ignored educational experimentation. One professor in the group did feel the whole idea of a BGS and encouragement of "experimentation" sounded like weak education for weak students—a threat to academic standards. He maintained this theme at every discussion group meeting but eventually went along with the group as it developed what he took to be adequate safeguards: careful review and control by faculty in colleges other than General Studies. His presence in the small group and participation in the deliberations may have been key to future avoidance of public attack on eventual proposals, for he had a reputation for scholarliness and outspoken insistance upon academic

67

rigor. The psychology professor and an associate professor of mathematics decided to draft an alternative to the dean's proposal, plus a second proposal for a "Division for Experimentation." In meeting with the president, they received his backing: "Let's get this Experimental College through this year. We need it. I appreciate what you're doing for it. Keep working." Mostly, however, the president talked of his keen interest in new opportunities for the freshman year, a topic about which he already had constituted another task force (including the associate professor of math). The president had been criticized by faculty for turning to new innovations before less new ones were fully implemented. That appeared to be the case concerning the Experimental College and changing the freshman year.

The Committee on Curricula and New Courses now had two advocacy groups, one administrative and one faculty, with which to contend. CCNC members regarded the administrative group, with its conservative proposal and official standing, as somewhat more legitimate than this *ad hoc* bunch of "Young Turks." One member commented,

> *The counter group seemed to be made up of the same individuals who are involved in all such activities. Privately, I and several other faculty regarded them as a self-appointed clique who have convinced themselves that they are the anointed Keepers of the Flame in the Temple of Faculty Conscience. Personally, I think they tend to be dilettantes who are seeking power.*

The Tuesday discussion group was paying the price for operating outside sanctioned governance channels. It introduced its two proposals, one for BGS and one for experimentation, at the same CCNC meeting in which the provost offered the administration's proposal. CCNC members recalled that their main reaction was confusion over this abundance of related proposals and irritation that this *ad hoc* "cabal" was interfering with CCNC work. Subsequent presentations to CCNC by the Tuesday discussion group did not help much, said CCNC members, for the self-selected spokesperson of the group tended to irritate them:

> *His general presentation had a massive indifference to anything concrete and a general belligerence to anyone who could not perceive what he was saying and the merits of what he was saying. . . . Everything was vague and general, and the few attempts by the committee to pin anything down were unsuccessful.*

Instead of seriously considering the Tuesday discussion group's proposals, CCNC modified the administrative proposal to house BGS in General Studies, establish a faculty advisory council to watchdog quality and emphasize that all BGS courses would be regular university offerings in colleges other than General Studies. The chairperson reported that there was "general agreement that much of the experimentation emphasized by the . . . *ad hoc* committee referred to non-academic affairs and could be handled by administrative action." The Experimental College notion was dropped. When the Tuesday discussion group got wind of this action, it decided to seek another delay of senate action so that it could persuade faculty to support its own proposals. It distributed these proposals to faculty senators prior to the March senate meeting as initiatives by senate

---

"Privately, I and several other faculty regarded them as a self-appointed clique who have convinced themselves that they are the annointed Keepers of the Flame in the Temple of Faculty Conscience."

68

members, an unusual but legitimate act. At the meeting, therefore, the original Experimental proposal was joined by the CCNC revision and the two Tuesday discussion group proposals. The provost urged passage of the CCNC version, but a professor of physics rose to beg that action be delayed until the faculty could openly debate this confusing array of proposals. He noted that there had not yet been any open discussion of any of these ideas. Despite a Tuesday discussion group member's contention that these notions had been in committees the last eighteen months (actually over two years), the senate agreed to refer the CCNC proposal back to committee until the next month's meeting. The chairperson of the senate concluded from the podium: "I am not sure I should say this, but I think it is quite apparent to everyone that the reason the senate is in such confusion at this point is because of the substitute motion of this *ad hoc* group."

Back in committee, CCNC did add faculty review procedures to ensure BGS quality—the Tuesday discussion group's concern. The vice provost for academic affairs then recommended an open faculty meeting to discuss the proposal, but the CCNC chairperson wouldn't have it: "Were we going to meet again and propose changes on the basis of ideas presented at this meeting? If we kept altering our proposal, we were going to look like indecisive fools."

The vice provost then argued that the committee should meet with the Tuesday discussion group. The CCNC chairperson was not interested. The Tuesday group, however, gained support of the provost for an attempt to get the two groups together under the auspices of the chairperson of the faculty senate. The provost later recalled that, "Fortunately, I had a few friends on each side." In the joint meeting, the Tuesday group agreed to endorse the CCNC proposal now that it had proper academic safeguards.

On April 5, 1972, the revised proposal for a new Bachelor of General Studies degree was presented to the faculty senate by the CCNC chairperson. A letter from the provost was read immediately. It urged passage in order to meet state needs for upper division education of associate degree students, especially those from regional and technical centers. Discussion centered on whether the program would be kept small and academically respectable. After primarily administrative assurances on these scores, the motion passed 36 to 18.

After two years of governance labor, a Bachelor of General Studies finally received faculty approval. Before continuing to trace efforts to improve undergraduate education, it might be helpful to reflect on the factors which appeared to encourage, and resist, this approval. In the beginning there were several "wants," problems and desires which did get pooled into a single demand for action. Certainly one factor supporting eventual innovation was the articulation of a need to change by someone (the dean of business) who could get his "demand" on the table of a governance group. Another supportive factor was the responsiveness to this demand by a key gatekeeper who later became a persistent "issue sponsor": the provost. The president's continued support appeared helpful, though identification of the proposal with him created obstacles as

"I am not sure I should say this, but I think it is quite apparent to everyone that the reason the senate is in such confusion at this point is because of the substitute motion of this ad hoc *group."*

69

well. Also in the innovation's favor was awareness of innovative resources by the dean of student activities, the director of the University Without Walls and a few others involved in the proposal's early stages. Yet another positive factor appeared to be the advocacy of the psychology professor and his Tuesday discussion group. They may have caused irritation by working outside governance channels and confusing the issues, but they did take up the cause when few advocates were visible, they got the tabling motion at a critical time and they did strengthen the quality safeguards of concern to meritocratic faculty. The flexibility of the innovation also seemed to help. It quickly expanded from a program for marginal academic performers to one which was responsive to the desire of students for programs relevant to their individual concerns. It could also become a vehicle to a four-year degree for associate degree recipients. It thus combined several needs and gained diverse support. By the same token, the proposal was divisible. When it became clear that the controversy over the University Without Walls would doom the Experimental College notion, that part of the proposal could be dropped. A related factor was the program's increasing ability, as group after group whittled on it, to fit into existing organizational structures instead of establishing a new competitor for existing units.

But why, with so many favorable factors, was approval so slow in coming? After all, the University Without Walls was implemented almost as soon as the president heard about it. One answer is that the proposal followed a long route through administrative channels and, because it would constitute a major new academic policy, eventually had to traverse faculty governance channels as well. With committees giving the proposal only the few hours a week their members had free from pressing duties, the journey was slow. Second, as the proposal moved from group to group, early supporters and early spade work were lost. Several committees independently and redundantly revised the BGS until it finally looked like that proposed by the first committee of deans. Such early linking agents and advocates as the dean of student activities, the director of the University Without Walls and the two business deans were not involved in later faculty discussions; nor were the University of Michigan and University of Iowa models, not to mention the several experimental colleges, visible in later deliberations. Only the submitted ECC proposal, a couple of short pleas by the provost, and one brief meeting between some members of ECC and CCNC tied a year's work in administrative committees together. The vast majority of faculty was simply not enlightened regarding the need for change or the desirability of proposed solutions. Two years after the demand and potential innovation surfaced in university governance, faculty senators still confessed ignorance of the whole matter. Third, the dean of arts and sciences and CCNC chairperson played a role in keeping faculty uninformed by their gate-closing activities on the Strategies task force and on the curriculum committee.

Fourth, the recent history of presidentially-initiated and academically unorthodox innovations to individualize education raised suspicion that here was another of his unilateral brainstorms. Placing Contemporary University, University Without Walls and Opportunity Scholars

70

As the proposal moved from group to group, early supporters and early spade work were lost.

under the Experimental College umbrella both confused the issue and confirmed suspicions. Fifth, the proposal not only seemed to deviate from accepted academic standards, it threatened to attract students away from existing programs. The dean of arts and science's actions are only the clearest example of this win/lose game: if an Experimental College attracts many students, we will lose them. Sixth, the Tuesday group did violate CCNC members' notions of proper political norms, and they did cause confusion. Perhaps as retarding, however, was the lack of advocates for the proposal in CCNC. So, a slow route, a failure to link one deliberation group's thinking to the next, key gatekeeper blockage of attempts to educate the faculty, irritation with unilateral presidential actions, suspicion of weak academic standards inflamed by recent controversy over a related program, threat to vested interests, violation of proper channels, lack of advocates in the key committee: these were among the prominent obstacles to the proposal's approval.

Was all the time and effort worth it? One answer is that the faculty senate soon thereafter voted University Without Walls out of existence, while the BGS still prospers. Without faculty sanction, credible leaders and a watch-dogging mechanism to prevent the activities which raised faculty ire, University Without Walls did not survive. By the time BGS was approved, in contrast, it had legitimate sanction from faculty and some assurance that it would not become a large scale competitor against existing programs. The new dean of General Studies maintained these advantages by keeping the BGS small and by carefully picking the initial students so that they would succeed in regular courses. He emphasized the role of faculty advisors from Arts and Sciences, Business, Engineering and other colleges. He provided detailed data on student grades (which were excellent) for the faculty senate's watchdog committee. On a couple of occasions he did try to increase General Studies autonomy in course listings and use of independent study but was quickly beaten back by CCNC and the president. In general, he did everything he could to make BGS acceptable to elitist values and interests, while leaders of University Without Walls had gone out of their way to attack such values. This strategy no doubt made the BGS a more educationally conservative program than the other, but it also permitted BGS to survive. And its survival proved a blessing to students who had felt blocked from achieving a meaningful degree. Student interviewees resoundingly praised the program for giving them an otherwise non-existent opportunity to obtain a four-year degree, develop a unique specialty or receive a broad liberal education.

71

In general, he did everything he could to make BGS acceptable to elitist values and interests, while leaders of University Without Walls had gone out of their way to attack such values.

SAME PROBLEMS, NEW ACTIONS
The new BGS would help meet several of the problems of undergraduate education at the University of South Carolina. Its flexibility enabled students to design programs about which they were enthusiastic. Its contract negotiations between the faculty team and student built in a strong faculty-student interaction, at least for the advisors who found time to meet with students. It provided greater diversity of options for a greater diversity of students. It affected, however, only a few hundred of the

University's over 15,000 undergraduates. And it had little impact on the way courses were taught. It was hardly *the* solution to the lack of vigor and responsiveness in the undergraduate learning experience. On the organizational side, it did follow a much more democratic route than previous innovations. It did not, however, help make governance efficient or effective in informing everyone involved, nor did it help improve self-study and planning.

Fortunately for undergraduates, some people saw the need for further action. One was the president. He already had established a special committee like ECC to develop a program that would make the freshman year an exciting introduction to higher learning. His acquaintance with trends in higher education again helped, for one impetus was the rash of articles and conference presentations regarding "justice for freshmen." Another committed person was the associate vice provost for academic affairs, who reported, "Most people are glad the BGS thing is 'finished.' It is not finished. We are only beginning to face the real issues of constructing a real experimental degree." A few members of the Tuesday group, including the psychology professor, meanwhile maintained interest in their "Division for Experiments in Education" proposal, which was due for senate consideration in its May, 1972, meeting. They did not campaign for it, however, because "in our various contacts we had received almost universal support for the concept behind the Division for Experiments proposal."

On the organizational side, the chairperson of the senate's Faculty Advisory Committee (FAC), a respected history professor, had become very interested in establishing a faculty-majority planning council both to help get the university looking forward and to strengthen faculty influence regarding the president's initiatives. At the May senate meeting, therefore, he moved to establish an "Academic Forward Planning Committee" (AFPC) of faculty to work with the executive administration in setting future goals and priorities. The president rose to endorse the idea, and it quickly passed. The innovation itself, a participative planning body, was hardly as foreign to senators as a BGS degree, but the Faculty Advisory Committee chairperson's action was stimulated by his own awareness of such a body at the University of Virginia. The immediate need which precipitated action was not only the faculty's desire to increase its control but also the recent deluge of change proposals which the Faculty Advisory Committee, as the senate agenda-setter, had received. A proposal from the freshman year committee, a residential college idea and the Division for Experiments plan were just three of the items which FAC members felt should be placed in the context of university goals and priorities. Once again, change occurred as a result of the relationship between a pressing need and a more general problem, support from a key gatekeeper and an issue sponsor who had credibility with the faculty (the FAC chairperson), support at the top and the availability of an innovative solution to the need. And this time there was no clash of values and interests to prolong the battle. Were the president more bureaucratically inclined and jealous of his own prerogatives, things might have been quite different.

Change in undergraduate education now had two major foci. One

"Most people are glad the BGS thing is 'finished.' It is not finished. We are only beginning to face the real issues of constructing a real experimental degree."

72

And this time there was no clash of values and interests to prolong the battle.

continued to be the president, who went ahead and hired an educational development officer to stimulate teaching innovations, recruited an innovative new dean of education and immediately persuaded AFPC to endorse the freshman year proposal which had emerged from his special committee. The second focus was the new AFPC itself. It quickly recommended establishment of the freshman program, which was a nondirective freshman seminar called "University 101," a small pilot to be financed by Ford Venture funds and staffed by faculty or administrative volunteers as a paid overload. Apparently the endorsement of this new body, made up of respected faculty selected by their peers, combined with the small pilot nature of the program, its external funding and its volunteer staffing to make it acceptable to faculty. It quickly passed CCNC and the senate. Members later said they did feel pressed by the urgency of gaining approval in time to get the program started the next fall.

After this hasty action, AFPC settled into a long, slow process of discussing the university and its goals. The associate vice-provost for academic affairs, who served as AFPC secretary because some of his administrative responsibilities lay in academic planning, advocated two particular actions. One was systematic goal-setting. He had come upon the *Institutional Goals Inventory* (IGI) from the Educational Testing Service and distributed a brochure on it to AFPC members. He had recently joined the university and had found it in need of a clear sense of mission and direction. This need and IGI combined in his mind. His other concern was to establish a residential college which would serve a cross-section of students in an intensive, intellectual atmosphere. He had experienced residential colleges elsewhere and therefore connected this potential solution to a generally perceived problem (lack of intellectual vigor in undergraduate life), just as others had connected the same problem to BGS and the Experimental College.

As AFPC got going, the psychology professor reflected on 1971-72 and drew a couple of conclusions:

> When I was writing the Annual Report for Strategies for Change and looked at what happened to the various proposals, particularly to the Tuesday discussion group, it occurred to me that, really, the conservatives or do-nothing people, had two things going for them: (a) there was a tremendous number of them and, because of that, they controlled a number of key positions on key committees; and (b) they had a coffee hour every morning in the faculty club.

He decided, therefore, to maintain the discussion group and to focus its energies on gaining some important positions in faculty governance. Membership in the group would be expanded to include older and more conservative faculty opinion leaders so that the young turks would benefit from criticism and would have influential ties to the large number of less innovative faculty. In August of 1972, a senior economics professor known to be somewhat conservative but widely respected for fair-mindedness and teaching excellence was persuaded by the group to run for chairperson of the faculty senate and to join the discussion group. He won the position and joined the group. The group managed a change in by-laws to make the senate vice-chairperson the chairperson-elect, then persuaded a popu-

"It occurred to me that, really, the conservatives or do-nothing people, had two things going for them: (a) there was a tremendous number of them and, because of that, they controlled a number of key positions on key committees; and (b) they had a coffee hour every morning in the faculty club."

the senate vice-chairperson the chairperson-elect, then persuaded a popular professor of engineering, who was "neutral" about change, to run for the office. He won and joined the group. The psychology professor himself managed to be elected chairperson of the key Senate Committee on Committees, while the associate professor of biology was elected to CCNC. The associate professor of mathematics became the director of Contemporary University. The new chairperson of CCNC and the new chairperson of AFPC, both senior faculty, widely respected, somewhat conservative academically but again noted for fair-mindedness and teaching excellence, also joined the *ad hoc* Tuesday discussion group. A new communication structure linking innovators to opinion leaders, and both to key governance channels, thus was formed.

In July of 1972, the president and the psychology professor attended the first annual review and planning workshop of the Strategies for Change and Knowledge Utilization project. Data from the first year's research were presented in loose-leaf "Self-Study Packets" to each institutional team. A national advisory board member, in this case Ronald Havelock, sat with each team as it scrutinized the evidence. The president said he was greatly concerned that South Carolina's faculty rated their university below 95% of the institutions completing the *Institutional Functioning Inventory* in "Concern for Undergraduate Learning." The psychology professor was impressed by the low "Democratic Governance" scale score. The two decided that this information should be disseminated back on campus by a re-constituted task force, one interested in making faculty better informed about problems in undergraduate education and university decision-making and one linked to key power structures. They selected the associate vice provost for academic affairs, the AFPC chairperson and the new educational development officer. Early in the fall, the president and the psychology professor shared the data with AFPC, whose chairperson commented, "I found myself seeing things about the institution that I had not previously thought through." Committee members found confirming correlations between the survey data and the report of an earlier faculty-student retreat on academic atmosphere. In response to the needs revealed in these documents and the associate vice provost's persuasion, a subcommittee to develop a residential college was formed. Also, upon the recommendation of the Strategies task force, and endorsed by the senate chairperson, AFPC decided to administer the *Institutional Goals Inventory* to the entire faculty and staff of the university. At the January, 1973, Strategies workshop, the South Carolina team drafted a step by step plan to involve faculty in ownership of the IGI administration and feedback.

The Tuesday discussion group continued to meet and provide linkage among CCNC, AFPC, the Strategies task force and senate leadership. Three members of the group—the AFPC chairperson, the CCNC chairperson and the associate professor of mathematics—were assigned by the senate chairperson to draft a proposal for a "committee on teaching." The immediate concern was CCNC's conviction that its heavy agendas permitted it to be only a reactive review body for course and program proposals rather than an active force to improve education. This new body would be a subgroup of CCNC which might take on many of the exper-

74

"I found myself seeing things about the institution that I had not previously thought through."

imentation activities envisioned by the "Division for Experiments in Education" proposal. The overlapping proposal formulation by the associate professor of mathematics tended to ensure that the new body would contain "Division for Experiments" components. A year later, the proposal for a committee on teaching passed the senate without much discussion, as did a related proposal to permit departmental approval for one semester without university review of any new course. A faculty structure and a policy to stimulate teaching experimentation thus were implemented through faculty initiative and aided by the interpersonal linkage of key leaders in the Tuesday discussion group.

It appeared by mid-1973 that several developments held promise for making a major contribution to the improvement of undergraduate education. Although University Without Walls was gone, Contemporary University and Opportunity Scholars were still prospering. The Bachelor of General Studies degree was a year old and thriving. The AFPC and the Tuesday discussion group were providing opportunities for faculty leaders to get together and seriously discuss improvement needs, not to mention their impact on democratizing governance and increasing self-study and planning. University 101 also was a year old and had stimulated several professors, they related in interviews, to re-examine their information-dispensing teaching styles and learn more about facilitating group process. A large scale goals survey was being conducted. A residential college was being developed in committee and a Committee on Teaching was being approved. Not mentioned earlier, the vice provost for academic affairs had initiated a "Center for Cultural Development" which sought by administrative act to provide the umbrella protection and encouragement for innovative programs which the Experimental College proposal described. A new freshman advising office also was underway. Momentum certainly seemed to be gathering for a major improvement in the learning experiences of undergraduate students.

THE GOALS FEEDBACK

AFPC members and the Strategies task force regarded follow-up to the IGI results as the most promising avenue toward further improvements. At the July, 1973, Strategies workshop in Saratoga, the psychology professor, the Senate chairman, the new associate provost for academic affairs (replacing the associate vice provost who had become dean of social sciences in a rapid-fire presidential reorganization of administration) and the AFPC chairperson put together a detailed plan of workshops to feed back IGI data and develop follow-up projects. The psychologist himself was about to go on leave, but the outgoing senate chairperson (the senior economics professor), agreed to take over as institutional representative duties for the Strategies project. This small group, two senior and widely process of the workshops and their follow-up. The AFPC chairperson made brief presentations to explain the IGI and put the results in the context of earlier Strategies data on student experiences and faculty perceptions of institutional functioning. Most workshop time, however, was spent in small task groups led by AFPC members. Each group was to study the material and determine its own list of goal priorities and action

The AFPC and the Tuesday discussion group were providing opportunities for faculty leaders to get together and seriously discuss improvement needs, not to mention their impact on democratizing governance and increasing self-study and planning.

75

Most workshop time, however, was spent in small task groups led by AFPC members.

process of the workshops and their follow-up. The AFPC chairman made brief presentations to explain the IGI and put the results in the context of earlier Strategies data on student experiences and faculty perceptions of institutional functioning. Most workshop time, however, was spent in small task groups led by AFPC members. Each group was to study the material and determine its own list of goal priorities and action possibilities for the university.

As groups reported back in each workshop, three concerns were reiterated and eventually reported to all faculty by the new associate provost; they were:

> *(1) a deep and widely shared concern to improve the intellectual orientation (i.e., commitment to learning as an intrinsic value) of both faculty and student; (2) a concern to improve the quality of the campus climate, including the communication among all elements, the degree of mutual trust, and the procedures for democratic governance and consultation; and (3) a concern that the university be capable of adapting to the demands for new skills, new kinds of students (older, more heterogeneous), and a greater emphasis on public service.*

The list was very similar to earlier conclusions drawn from Strategies data and the student-faculty retreat on academic atmosphere: (1) strengthen intellectual vigor; (2) increase open democracy; (3) respond to diverse new student needs. In these workshops, the very high IGI preference for the "Intellectual Orientation" and "Community" scales, and faculty perceptions of great discrepancy between what is and what should be in these areas, was observed as focusing small group attention. Corroborating Strategies data on student experiences and faculty IFI perceptions helped, participants said. The emphasis on new students emerged from Bushnell's presentation of population and occupational trends, a presentation repeated by the economics professor the second week. Participants thus were introduced both to internal and external evidence pertinent to goal setting. Faculty development, administrative development, the residential college, freshman programs, campus locations for faculty-student interaction and improved advisement were among the action possibilities listed. At the conclusion of each workshop, over half the participants submitted signed "pledges" of willingness to give time in follow-up on one issue or another. Many expressed enthusiasm for the stimulation they experienced in the workshop and said the university needs more such occasions for diverse members to study information and to talk together about serious educational and organizational matters.

I observed and consulted in these workshops. I sent back to AFPC a summary which mentioned six ingredients I thought were important to their success, according to comments I heard. First, participants were impressed that senior faculty leaders and AFPC members generally were in charge, were seriously interested in the data and intended to follow-up the workshops. Opinion leadership was at work. Second, the projections about future higher education needs and the internal data (IGI and Strategies surveys) not only catalyzed and focused discussion but appeared to open or broaden perspectives. I heard statements such as "I think we're reaching students, but a 62% student sample says not much is happening to them. Is that true? [question to a student participant]" or "I think we should just train bright students but the projections say we'll have fewer traditional students and more 'new learners.' Maybe we'd better figure out how to help them." Exposure to new information broadened the knowledge base of discussion. Third, the small groups were a big hit. Everyone could have a say, people could get to know each other and each group wanted to "come through" on its task of identifying goal priorities. Personal interaction not only helped achieve agreement but increased enjoyment. Fourth, faculty members and administrators found the student participants a rich resource in understanding what it was like to go through that university, and students were among the most effective participants in helping accomplish group tasks. Fifth, the day and a half was needed, for participants talked at each other Friday afternoon and expressed frustration at the lack of group progress; on Saturday morning they were much more visibly attempting to find agreement with one another and accomplish the goal-setting task. Consistently in the project, participants in one or two hour a week committee meetings would say that each week we start the debate all over again, while participants in extended meetings (all day, afternoon and evening, two or three days) usually were elated that so much progress had been made and that participants actually began to enjoy each other and the task. Finally, AFPC and the Strategies task force offered ongoing structures and leadership for follow-through so that the progress in the workshops would pay off.

But all was not roses. The workshops were voluntary. Leaders commented that the same people always come to such affairs, those concerned about and already involved in undergraduate improvement. Key groups underrepresented, leaders noted, were department heads, academic conservatives, executive administrators, faculty and student senators and trustees. Linkage to these groups would have to follow the workshop.

On November 9-10, 1973, the Academic Forward Planning Committee met to consider follow-up to the IGI workshops. Walter Sikes of the NTL Institute for Applied Behavioral Sciences and I were present to help consider the possibility of a specially funded project to assist that follow-up. Several topics were discussed that related to the IGI workshop conclusions; the two selected for close attention were an attempt to improve intellectual climate and skills through a residential college ("South Carolina College") and efforts to improve collaborative administrative skills in management and governance. A drafting committee including the AFPC chairperson, the new associate vice provost, the educational development officer and the economics professor was selected to develop a proposal for a joint Strategies-NTL-South Carolina project for action teams to follow-up on workshop priorities. The proposal was submitted to the Fund for the Improvement of Postsecondary Education but was not funded.

AFPC did take several concrete actions. First, it initiated a new Facilities and Grounds Committee to improve communication and democratic governance in the area of capital development and space utilization.

Exposure to new information broadened the knowledge base of discussion.

Leaders commented that the same people always come to such affairs, those concerned about and already involved in undergraduate improvement.

Second, it met with the director of Contemporary University to stimulate development of new procedures for expediting temporary courses and independent learning. Third, the provost initiated three workshops for deans and department heads to help increase interaction, understanding of enrollment and budgetary projections and skills at working with faculty in setting and implementing goal priorities. Fourth, the president helped find and develop campus spots for informal faculty-student interaction. One outdoor meeting place was established. Outside AFPC, the educational development officer was holding teaching seminars, helping a new media man develop an "instructional services center" and using Ford Venture funds to support individual teaching innovations. Still, AFPC members interviewed in November of 1973 expressed anxiety that a year and a half of role and goal clarification in the committee might not pay off unless stronger action steps were taken. In a written summary of AFPC's brief history, I recommended that the committee keep the goal priorities in mind, improve faculty-administrative openness and collaboration within AFPC, link closely to governance bodies, put financial resources into IGI follow-up, enlist the "advocates" who volunteered in the workshops, set diverse actions in motion (since a few small projects hardly would dent the problem) and develop well organized action plans and teams to structure follow-up.

AFPC members interviewed in November of 1973 expressed anxiety that a year and a half of role and goal clarification in the committee might not pay off unless stronger action steps were taken.

78

NEW LEADERSHIP, NEW DIRECTION?

Several shifts in the campus leadership regarding undergraduate improvement already had occurred. The associate vice provost had become a dean consumed with the business of running a college. The new associate provost picked up his place in the Strategies task force and became a major force in the IGI follow-through, but he had witnessed an insulated "we-they" syndrome and burning out of faculty in his former institution (a residential college), so he did not encourage the residential college idea in AFPC. The psychology professor was on leave and, although the economics professor became a major force in the IGI workshops, he did not keep the Tuesday discussion group intact. Perhaps as a consequence, a conservative professor was selected senate chairperson-elect and the current senate chairperson would later reflect that "I'd be hard pressed to identify an accomplishment of any sort" in the 1973-74 senate. Finally, the AFPC chairperson, who had guided the committee from its inception and was heavily involved in the IGI workshops, went on sabbatical in 1974-75 to study organizational development.

The primary leadership shift, however, was in the presidency. Early in 1974, the president resigned amidst considerable controversy. The provost became acting and then permanent president. Several differences in the two men struck observers at the university. The former president was perceived to be extremely interested in educational innovation, especially concerning individualizing education, assisting effective development and meeting the needs of a wide variety of students. He had a strong drive to make undergraduate education a lively and rewarding experience for as many students as could be reached. Certainly the rich array of small-scale innovations he had either initiated or supported in recent years had made a promising beginning on the concerns, and he left behind both organizational structures and leaders committed to sustaining this thrust. At the same time he was attempting to invigorate undergraduate education, he was guiding the development of a modern university plant and graduate-research program, and this thrust competed with more student-centered efforts. In personal style, he was regarded as an entrepreneur and a dominating figure who focused on new ideas rather than maintaining old ones, a charistmatic approach which both won followers and aroused irritation.

The provost was seen as much different. His educational values were regarded as more traditional. Familiar teaching roles and curricular models as well as meritocratic emphases were viewed as his kind of education. Where the former president irritated state political forces, the provost was regarded as more responsive. He was concerned, people felt, about the details of running an efficient university. His personal style was viewed as much more quiet, responsive rather than aggressive, reserved rather than outgoing. While both presidents supported faculty involvement in governance, he was viewed as more oriented toward democratic procedures than was the former president. The change in presidency, therefore, appeared to many interviewees to be a shift from entrepreneurial innovation to democratic stabilization.

During the remainder of 1974, much of the university-wide action to improve undergraduate innovation slowed while energy turned to the selection of new leaders and to lame duck maintenance. The associate provost was interrupted in his leadership of the IGI follow-up by a nine-month stint as acting provost, after which he was selected provost. The former provost himself became acting president. When he was selected full president, he did select a vice president for instruction to assume the key role in developing and monitoring instructional effectiveness, but before this officer got far in what others saw to be promising attempts to foster teaching excellence and experimental programs, he died. The economics professor, respected by the new president as an old line but highly capable teacher and faculty leader, then was selected as the vice president for instruction and took several months to get acclimated. These events were costly to innovation, for the energies he had wanted to put into re-constituting the Tuesday discussion group and holding a faculty-student workshop to kick off efforts to improve faculty-student relationships had to be delayed. The educational development officer became associate provost in charge of learning resources. He reported that these line responsiblities and the organization of a new office delayed efforts to encourage teaching innovations. The teaching improvement seminars languished.

EDUCATIONAL AND ORGANIZATIONAL HEALTH, 1971-74
In 1974, the *Experience of College Questionnaire* (including the CUES "Scholarship" scale) and the *Institutional Functioning Inventory* were re-administered to see if any changes in educational or organizational health had taken place among Strategies institutions. The two years since the ECQ, CUES and IFI were first administered had seen a variety of efforts

The change in presidency, therefore, appeared to many interviewees to be a shift from entrepreneurial innovation to democratic stabilization.

79

to make undergraduate education more involving and stimulating at the University of South Carolina and to make the organization more democratic and more systematic in self-study and planning. Those two years also marked the time in which project participants and others across education noted a reduction in student demands for social reform and personal freedom but a rise in student concern for "proper" preparation to succeed in a tightening future job market.

It is somewhat unfair to demand of innovations that they make significant differences in institutional surveys. After all, the political process of reducing threat to vested interests and complying with existing values means that only small deviations from the *status quo* are very likely. As Bachelor of General Studies data as well as evaluations of Contemporary University, Opportunity Scholars and, later, University 101 revealed, these experiments were meeting their objectives in ways satisfactory to faculty and administrative judges. They were providing meaningful alternatives for a few hundred South Carolina students. Teaching seminars, University 101 training and other Venture activities were providing new skills and knowledge to perhaps a tenth of the university faculty. But the felt need was not that only a handful of students needed a more stimulating and involving education. It is one thing to provide exciting options on the periphery and quite another to make major improvement in the mainline experience of students. The latter, however, was the problem suggested by 1971 questionnaires and workshops. The "big picture," therefore, is a legitimate barometer of institutional effectiveness in improving educational health over the three years 1971-74.

There were survey signs that things were improving at the University of South Carolina. The percentage of professors perceived by students mainly as dispensing knowledge or assigning sources which the student should master decreased from 45% to 39%, and students reporting no influence at all over course structure and content decreased from 40% to 35%. These shifts in response were not statistically significant and should be conservatively viewed, but they did approach significance in shifts toward more active mental activity out of class, including a statistically significant increase in the number of students spending over half their study time focused on the application of knowledge.

There was a significant increase from 58% to 71% in students who reported frequently feeling "confident and competent" in their courses, and a significant increase from 48% to 57% in the number who frequently felt "challenged to do your best thinking" in those courses. Faculty-student contact had not increased, nor had most of the possible areas of faculty impact on student development. Exceptions however, were important. Significantly fewer respondents (from 43% to 30%) reported only minor faculty influence on "sense of purpose"; and significantly more respondents (from 33% to 41%) reported major faculty influence on "intellectual competence." Finally, the CUES "Scholarship" scale made a significant shift upward, moving South Carolina from the fourteenth to the twenty-fifth percentile nationally. Twenty-five percent of the respondents in 1974 reported being "very well" satisfied with their educational experience at USC contrasted with 17% in 1972. That represented a

It is one thing to provide exciting options on the periphery and quite another to make major improvement in the mainline experience of students.

80

significant increase in students highly satisfied, while the proportion "fairly well" satisfied remained around 58%. In general, therefore, all the energy put into undergraduate improvements did appear to be paying off, although changes in responses of independent samples three years apart are subject to various other interpretations. The institution still had a considerable distance to go, however, before it could say it was providing a highly challenging and exciting education for the majority of its undergraduates.

On the organizational side, *Institutional Functioning Inventory* (IFI) responses from faculty revealed decreases in perceived university emphasis on campus cultural events and on democratic procedures, the latter remaining below the tenth percentile nationally. The IFI was administered prior to the new president's attempts to involve faculty in decisions, while administrative shifts were occurring without widespread faculty involvement, before AFPC had visibly asserted itself, and during a year of senate quietude. Nevertheless, the recent efforts to democratize governance apparently were not yet of sufficient magnitude to impress faculty. Faculty were no more unhappy with faculty-administrative relationships than in 1972. "Institutional Esprit" remained at about the twenty-second percentile nationally, not strong but not indicating grievous conflict. Most notably, both "Concern for Undergraduate Learning" and "Concern for Advancing Knowledge" had risen since 1972. Table 3 compares the undergraduate learning profiles for the two years. It indicates that faculty perceive considerably greater interest on the part of their colleagues in getting to know the nature and needs of their students. Once again, however, the picture is one of improvement but not full scale problem resolution. Nearly ninety percent of the college and university members using IFI rated their institutions stronger than did USC faculty in "Concern for Undergraduate Learning." Finally, faculty reported no change in a weak university emphases on "Self-Study and Planning" despite the Strategies and IGI studies and the new Academic Forward Planning Committee. Apparently the impact of these activities and structures had not been seriously felt by faculty in general.

MAINTAINING MOMENTUM
Would, or could, the new administration pick up the momentum toward improvement of undergraduate education? Whether the administration pressed for change or not, was there sufficient momentum and influence in the faculty to keep things going? In February of 1975, we interviewed about twenty faculty members and administrators close to university-wide action. We asked them about the status of innovations implemented earlier as well as new or continuing efforts to make undergraduate education more invigorating for students and decision making more effective in solving institutional problems.

One consistent response was that faculty involvement in university decision making was increasing under the new president. Selection of some executive administrators had involved faculty, and the president had asked AFPC to study selection of department chairpersons. The new Facilities and Grounds Committee was active in decisions on a new

All the energy put into undergraduate improvements did appear to be paying off.

81

Whether the administration pressed for change or not, was there sufficient momentum and influence in the faculty to keep things going?

TABLE 3
University of South Carolina
Item Analysis of Scales that Changed[1]
"Concern for Undergraduate Learning"

ITEM NUMBER	ITEM DESCRIPTION	1972 PERCENT	1974 PERCENT
006	There are established procedures by which students may propose new courses	30	28
017	Faculty promotions/tenure based primarily on estimate of teaching effectiveness	8	9
032	There is not much contact between faculty and students outside classroom	26	36
033	Senior professors seldom teach freshman or sophomore courses	40	51
037	Extensive independent work on tutorials are an important part of the curriculum	49	53
045	How best to communicate knowledge to student does not concern many faculty here	47	61*
049	Professors get to know students in their undergraduate classes quite well	15	28*
051	Most professors do not wish to spend much time talking about students' personal concerns	42	49
058	Pressures of other commitments keep many professors from adequate course preparation	57	65
059	Most faculty quite sensitive to needs, interests, and aspirations of undergraduates	42	56*
063	In recruiting new faculty, teaching ability is as important as scholarly contribution	31	41
068	Capable undergraduates are encouraged to collaborate with faculty on research projects	72	72

*Change significant at .05 level, symmetric test.
[1]Proportion of responses contributing to the scale score. Some items had four-point response scales and the proportion reported here combines the two responses (e.g., "strongly agree" and "agree") which contribute to the scale. For complete description of the scoring process, see the IFI Technical Manual.

history building and had worked with the president in securing a building for a faculty club. The senate itself had passed a new policy changing the grading system back from the A, B, C, No Credit scheme passed in Student Movement days to the use of D's and F's. Students concerned about getting jobs and graduate school entrance had joined faculty concerned about meritocratic standards in returning to the use of negative sanctions. The new president and new provost had abruptly announced that the College of General Studies would be merged into other colleges, a move viewed by some as a sign of a shift away from mass education and non-traditional teaching, for which General Studies was noted. But after flack from the General Studies dean, students and some political forces in the state, the president took the more democratic route of asking AFPC to study the situation and recommend an action. In yet another move to increase faculty involvement, AFPC had been involved in developing a new tenure and promotion committee of senior faculty which would replace some of the administrative control over the crucial reward function. Finally, the former president and the 1973-74 heads of the faculty and student senates had launched a special committee to develop a University Senate which would combine administrative, student and faculty representation.

Some interviewees, especially young, innovative faculty, were not so sure that all this activity was making decision making more openly democratic or increasing concern for the improvement of undergraduate education. Certain oldline faculty were suddenly at the forefront of special committees. The tenure and promotion committee would be made up of senior, probably conservative, faculty. AFPC may be so consumed with responding to presidential requests that it would not be an active force in its own right. The senate appeared to be dominated by conservatives again, as witnessed by quick passage of the University Senate proposal. The residential college proposal was still alive, but the president did not support its placement in the central "Horseshoe" area. Contemporary University had been reduced to a smaller independent study program in an administrative effort to balance costs with income. All these signs, plus a perception that the new president himself was an old-line educational conservative, at least in comparison with the past president, led several innovative interviewees to be less than sanguine about the institution's current openness to non-traditional ideas. The place may be more democratic, but because the majority were not nearly as concerned about undergraduate learning as they were the research-oriented model of the university as shown on the IFI scales, the change may not bode well for undergraduate improvement.

On the other hand, it was the new president who staunchly advocated BGS, the new provost who pushed IGI, the new associate provost who used the Venture funds to stimulate teaching innovation and the new vice president for instruction and the AFPC chairperson who as senior faculty members had become active in Strategies, the discussion group and IGI. Although the president was unavailable for an interview, each of the other key administrative leaders expressed strong commitment to a continuation of efforts to improve undergraduate education. Some inter-

Certain oldline faculty were suddenly at the forefront of special committees.

83

viewees still saw plenty of support for change at the top and felt the new participation would help develop broader faculty commitment for new ideas than was possible in earler presidential initiatives. Clearly, it was too early in the new order of things to tell which perspective would turn out to be right.

One action intended to keep the momentum was the Strategies task force's action plan, developed at the Saratoga workshop in the summer of 1974. It called for a retreat of about fifty faculty members, potential opinion leaders who were interested in undergraduate education, plus an equal number of students. Administrative re-alignments caused a delay from October, 1974, to March, 1975, but an expanded task force got busy in the fall to design the workshop and recruit participants. In looking at the 1972-74 surveys, and after discussion among themselves, the task force members decided that student-faculty relationships remained the central problem. They decided to focus the workshop on three action agendas: "(1) Creating a more stimulating academic environment and mutual rapport among faculty and students; (2) Learning and communication experiences within and outside the classroom; and (3) Faculty accessibility and advisement."

The session opened in the late afternoon with a brief role-playing skit in which three students displayed the case against serious faculty commitment to helping students, followed by three faculty members returning the compliment concerning student willingness to engage in serious learning.

The affair itself followed the format so enthusiastically received in the IGI workshops. The session opened in the late afternoon with a brief role-playing skit in which three students displayed the case against serious faculty commitment to helping students, followed by three faculty members returning the compliment concerning student willingness to engage in serious learning. Familiar and hard-hitting stereotypes thus got out in the open, softened by humor. The associate dean of student activities and I followed with brief comments on the Strategies data, after which small task groups worked through a student-prepared dinner (delicious) to generate specific recommendations for university action to improve faculty-student relationships. Course and teacher evaluation; faculty development; advisement time, training and rewards; individualization of instruction; and encouragement of wide diversity in teaching approaches and learning experiences were some of the group emphases reported that evening. The task force had not considered itself a body to coordinate and encourage follow-up on these recommendations, but I urged that a well-organized and politically well-linked advocacy group would be needed if this were not to be another groovy workshop without consequence. The group did decide to follow through. As of this writing, it is planning strategies for significant improvement in faculty-student relationships.

COMMENTARY

The University of South Carolina in the early 1970's was rapidly emerging as a modern university, but several problems in undergraduate education and in organizational ability to solve those problems were identified repeatedly by both a special faculty-administration-student retreat on academic life and by the interviews and surveys of the Strategies for Change and Knowledge Utilization Project. Widely diverse students were not being challenged and excited by undergraduate educational experiences. There was little faculty-student interaction. Open collaboration to solve these problems was desired but not present.

In the course of four years, a variety of innovations were introduced, some by presidential fiat, which got prompt action but generated little support, and some by painfully slow committee deliberation, a process more satisfactory to faculty but one leading only to small pilot projects made as compatable as possible with traditional academic values. Aggressive entrepreneurship by the president, steadfast "issue sponsorship" by the provost, connection of several administrative and faculty leaders to innovative models outside the university, intentional efforts by an *ad hoc* group of young turks and senior opinion leaders to make faculty governance more supportive of undergraduate reform, feedback of data about university goals and practices, special action-planning work shops, continuing relationship with a few consultants, creation of planning and staff development structures and considerable variety of innovative thrusts seem at first glance to be planned change tactics which made a difference. At the end of the four-year record, post-tests indicated some signs of improvement in more active learning and teaching, stronger faculty-student relationships and more collaborative decision making. Certainly a number of specific innovations had been launched and most of them had survived: Contemporary University, University Without Walls, Bachelor of General Studies, University 101, Opportunity Scholars, a new freshman advising system, a committee on teaching, outdoor places for faculty-student interaction, the Academic Forward Planning Committee, an Educational Development Officer and a Vice President for Instruction, a new media center, increased faculty involvement in facilities and personnel decisions. Still, the evidence suggested that it would take much more than these changes to alter significantly undergraduate educational experiences in the directions desired by most faculty and administrative respondents.

It is too early to draw conclusions regarding critical planned change factors and strategies, except to say that no one of the models described in Chapter One appears to do justice to the complexity of this case. We could call most of these innovations R&D demonstration projects or adaptations of external models, but I would not call the University of South Carolina faculty passive consumers. Hardly. We could say the most important aspect of the change process was the way existing innovations were introduced through a social network which connected external models to executive administrators (for the most part) and, through them, to a sufficient number of open "early adopters" to permit trial of fairly compatable, simple, divisible innovations with at least some apparent relative advantages. But that explanation does not do justice to obvious political dynamics. The president used his authority when possible to innovate by fiat, but faculty members and administrators who felt such actions violated democratic or collegial rules of the game or threatened their interests retaliated with their own political weapons: faculty governance and departmental or individual ability to refuse to participate in these innovations. Eventually, conservative external political forces caught up with the president. Lest we conclude that political hassles are the essence of planned change process, we should recall that faculty, students and ad-

85

No one of the models described in Chapter One appears to do justice to the complexity of this case.

ministrators could identify common goals and needs and could collaborate together on the few occasions when, with the aid of process consultants, the Problem-Solving approach to planned change was tried at South Carolina. And such open collaboration was a strong desire among diverse groups.

It begins to appear that each planned change model tells a part of the story, but only a part. The whole is something else. But I am leaping to conclusions on too little evidence, just as I warned not to do. Let us turn to another case history, this one a liberal arts college, before speculating further.

5 Developing Institutional Supports for Academic Renewal: Hartwick College

"Self-renewal," like a child in spring, has managed to get pretty soiled since John Gardner sent it out to play over a decade ago.[1] But, scrubbed clean, the term still offers us important instruction regarding how to improve ourselves as persons, as professionals, as departments and as organizations. As Gardner used self-renewal, there are two sides to the coined phrase. One side is keeping up with social change. The self-renewing professor or college must be up on the latest changes in the profession and in post-secondary education, on changing economic and social conditions and on new learning needs and advancements in knowledge about teaching and learning. And, more important, the self-renewing individual or institution must be willing and able to adjust current practices so as not to fall behind the future.

Some of the tarnish on "self-renewal" may be that often only this responsiveness-to-social-change side of the coin is visible. The college or professor whose only motivation is to keep up to date falls victim to faddism, change for change's sake, trying to be something we are not, bandwagonism and other shallow characters. Gardner emphasizes that self-renewing individuals or institutions must respond to social change within the context of their own basic character, talents and purposes. That does not mean myopia, preoccupation with self or re-invention of the wheel. Nobody thinks much of those characters either. It means that the self-renewing individual or institution knows itself as well as its environment and changes not just to meet the future but to fulfill better its unique potentials and aspirations. It is one coin with the usual two sides.

What does a complex organization need in order to be self-renewing? Certainly a heavy emphasis on structures, roles, values and norms which perpetuate current practices does not leave much attention to renewal. Somebody, sometime, needs to be able to step back from daily pressures and see whether this is what we should be doing as well as we could be doing it. Opportunities for administrators and faculty members, not to mention students, to reflect and plan are vital. So are expert services to aid that reflection and change. Social psychologists of complex organizations call the structures and roles for self-renewal "adaptive subsystems."[2] The Academic Forward Planning Committee and the Educational Development Officer at the University of South Carolina are such renewal units. A fair hypothesis is that to the degree an organization develops and maintains structures, functions and expertise for renewal, to that degree is renewal likely. Of course, few colleges and universities have the required units, officers and activities to diagnose needs, the professional development centers and linking agents to bring innovations into the institution,

The college or professor whose only motivation is to keep up to date falls victim to faddism, change for change's sake, trying to be something we are not, bandwagonism and other shallow characters.

or even much time free from business as usual. Accordingly, few colleges have much luck at academic renewal.

This chapter describes a four year effort to build strong academic renewal capacity in a moderate-sized liberal arts college of fifteen hundred students. The institution is called Hartwick. It is situated on a beautiful outlook in the south central region of New York State. It attracts many students from the greater New York City area. The college boasts an excellent science division, field and foreign opportunities, increasing attention to the arts, and top-ranked soccer and basketball teams. Students tend to be middle class whites, moderate in politics and educational aspirations, and "collegiate" in orientation. During the 1960's, an aggressive president rapidly built buildings and academic departments. At the end of the decade, that person resigned. The new president had been dean of New College, Hofstra University, one of the earliest cluster colleges, and was closely tied to innovative trends in post-secondary education. One of his early acts was to ask Arthur Chickering to speak to faculty about the student development theories expounded in *Education and Identity*.[3] That external contact led in turn to Chickering's invitation that Hartwick join the Strategies for Change and Knowledge Utilization Project; as a result, systematic efforts to build structures and commitments for academic renewal began in earnest.

The president did not immediately exert his formal authority to establish educational alternatives at Hartwick. He did, however, use public addresses and other means to suggest that a traditional liberal education taught and evaluated the traditional way was not going to make Hartwick sufficiently unique in character or effectiveness to compete as private education grew more expensive, public education expanded and the college age population dwindled. He told Strategies interviewers that he felt he must play the gadfly, the catalyst, the provocateur of academic renewal, not the bureaucratic authority. He said, "Unless the faculty and the students, who are by and large more conservative than the faculty when you come right down to it, unless they pick up the ball, forget it." He could start the ball toward innovation and renewal, but renewal itself must come from the personal commitment of campus members. In four years, his few deviations from that rule occurred mainly when the ball was about to be kicked out of bounds, when innovators were about to be denied tenure or financial stringencies were about to choke off innovative programs. He exerted administrative authority to keep the innovation and renewal agendas on the field of play.

88

1971-1972: BEGINNINGS

Did that strategy, essentially a Problem-Solving approach without a process consultant, work? Let's see. An early catalytic action was the president's personal interaction with the art department chairperson in an effort to persuade that department away from building an art major and toward integrating art and creative expression into general liberal education. The department did decide on the latter course. Another presidential attempt to stimulate reflection on Hartwick's effectiveness and future was to invite Royce (Tim) Pitkin, founder of the Deweyian Goddard College, to observe the college from time to time (beginning during the president's inaugural week) and ask the kinds of penetrating questions about educational goals and means which Pitkin is masterful at asking. Also, the president brought in Pitkin's former assistant at Goddard as associate dean to head up fledgling efforts in off-campus and independent study.

Then came a third Goddardite, Art Chickering. When he first invited Hartwick through the president to join the Strategies project, the president recalled, "We never took any formal action on it, but we talked about it all over the place, and I took at face value the enthusiasm that I had seen for Chick on the campus. It seems to me that at that time there was a very clear feeling that if the grant came through, we ought to get into it." The grant, however, did not come through. Not then, in 1970. A year later, Chickering called in the middle of a trustees meeting. The president and dean held a quick caucus and decided to go ahead. A project called "Strategies for Change" had been initiated by the executive administration, and Chickering, its leader, was the third person from experimentalist Goddard to descend on the traditional Hartwick since the new president himself had come from an experimental college. The president said in the fall of 1971 that he "sensed no particular objection" to the decision: "I assumed that there would be some who didn't want to have anything to do with it. As time went on, we worked out a procedure which made this a voluntary thing for any faculty member or group of faculty to be a part of it. So I think that any stigma of being forced into something has been removed."

Our own interviews in the fall of 1971 gave a different perspective. Some of the twenty-five faculty members and administrators picked for interviews because of their recent involvement in college issues were enthusiastic. Others, perhaps persons who would not share their feelings with an innovative president, were irritated and suspicious. One said,

> There is definitely a small number of faculty who feel that administration should not be attempting to influence faculty. And therefore, when one became aware that evaluation [of students] tended to be the one consistent factor that [the president] would discuss, I think they saw this as, "There! He's really going to push us into it now!" by having that as the topic. I think there are people who are fearful that this whole Strategies for Change is not that which it is set up to be, but it is an underhanded means of making change. You know, you've got to make this change now because here you are in this experiment and you can't not do this.

The past president had been, by everyone's account, authoritarian, but his agenda were clear and traditional. "You knew where you stood," and that was on familiar ground. The new president did not tell people what was about to change. Instead, he made speeches about the need to re-examine educational assumptions and brought in these unorthodox Goddardites and talked about unorthodox Sarah Lawrence College. The change in styles led some faculty to feel he must have an agenda. But it was, as yet, hidden. We heard one faculty member swear she had seen the cover of a "master plan" that the president, Pitkin and Chickering had drawn up for the college. We found no evidence of such a document.

We heard one faculty member swear she had seen the cover of a "master plan" that the president, Pitkin and Chickering had drawn up for the college, though we could find no evidence of such a document.

> *What is it they want us to do that they're going to convince us to do by doing research? . . . I had said [in a Campus Council meeting] that it seemed like it was part of the "master plan" that everyone was talking about because you're entering into change for what purpose. You can't have research of that nature and not have some change effected. . . . Otherwise, why bother? So, then, what is the nature of the change that you want? There is some thought that Sarah Lawrence is the proto-type of student-faculty evaluation.*

A student interviewee saw threat to security as the faculty's main reason for uneasiness: "A group of people [were] deathly afraid that this group [Strategies for Change] was coming in here to push and pull a few strings and see what happens. They're leery of having strings pulled on them and being watched. Many of them are happy with the *status quo*. That's where they want to be left."

Part of the discontent stemmed from the fact that the president not only initiated the Strategies participation but also appointed the dean of students as "vice president for institutional research" and, with the new vice president, personally selected the twenty members of a new "committee on planning and research." The president also set the new group's agenda:

> *Ever since the Strategies for Change idea came up, I've been convinced that some approach to evaluation should be our problem. . . . I suppose it's something that's been bugging me for seven or eight years now. And I saw it happen at Hofstra, too, that this [traditional evaluation of students] was the limiting factor in the learning process. Everything had to be squeezed to fit that shape, and what I guess I'm looking for in a broad sense is trying to find some ways to make ourselves more honest with respect to what we say we know is happening to a student.*

"What I guess I'm looking for in a broad sense is trying to find some ways to make ourselves more honest with respect to what we say we know is happening to a student."

Each Strategies "intensive" institution was expected by the grant to designate at least a half-time on-campus leader, was supposed to create a renewal group and was supposed to pick some curricular, teaching or evaluation issue as the focus of action and research. The president had fulfilled these obligations himself.

In order to compensate for this top-down action, the president and vice president carefully selected the committee on planning and research to represent, as the vice president wrote, "the several philosophies of education within the faculty and a balance of professors by age and disciplines. This was done so as to build support for the project and to spread information about the project widely among the faculty." Suspicions did not abate, and the well-balanced group spent its few 1971-72 meetings debating whether to act or not. The agenda itself remained at issue. The vice president's first press announcement about the project claimed that "Hartwick College . . . has indicated the desire to investigate those methods that should be used to evaluate student learning and personal development." Well, the president and vice president liked that topic, but much of the rest of Hartwick College was yet to be convinced. The president and the vice president, therefore, soon took a less aggressive approach to agenda setting. The vice president wrote a position paper called "Why Should We Choose Evaluation of Students As Our Project?" His second press notice said "while the College has not selected a final topic of study, it will probably deal with new modes of student evaluation."

The first meeting among any part of the new committee was also the first inter-institutional workshop of the Strategies for Change and Knowledge Utilization Project, October 25-28, 1971, in Philadelphia. The vice president for institutional research attended and brought along his assistant, a recent Hartwick student leader; a long-time Hartwick associate professor of psychology interested in research on student development and, according to the vice president, "academically conservative"; a junior student interested in making the college a more educationally vigorous place; and the chairperson of biology, a senior opinion leader widely respected among faculty and students for his student orientation and up-to-date department. The workshop stressed the importance of two change strategies: first, systematic information on internal goals and practices as well as on new developments outside the institution should be gathered and used to catalyze and inform the renewal process. Second, Goodwin Watson's speech emphasized the need for those who must implement changes to "own" their own diagnosis of needs and development of solutions while receiving strong institutional supports during the implementation process.

These sessions, plus ambiguity about their own agenda in the absence of the president, contributed to broad-ranging discussions within the Hartwick group. The vice president wanted to pursue the evaluation of student development. The psychologist was interested in studying student development and reporting such research to the faculty. The biologist felt that much better communication among campus groups was needed and that the first step toward renewal must be clarification of the college's educational goals. The one common point of agreement Chickering heard when sitting with the team was, "they clearly don't want any more input from Goddard types." Long after this workshop, the debate would continue over whether they should develop new evaluation systems, study student development or build a better system of interaction leading toward the clarification of goals. And so would the low credibility of consultants with experimentalist backgrounds. The action plan which the vice president wrote at the workshop's end was a general proposal to seek "Evidences of Change in the Individual Student" through campus discussions, use of internal research, examination of goals, encouragement to faculty members "to experiment freely with methods of assessing student change within their courses and in other education situations" and improvement of communication. Consultation monies available from the Strategies coordinating center would be used, wrote the vice president, to visit colleges and universities with unusual evaluation methods, to visit student development and evaluation experts, and to bring to Hartwick such resource persons as Esther Raushenbush, (the former president of Sarah Lawrence), Goodwin Watson and Harold Hodgkinson (the former dean of experimentalist Bard College and a noted expert on innovations in higher education). Also, money was requested to support the psychologist's preparation of the *College Student Questionnaire* (CSQ) data the next

Goodwin Watson's speech emphasized the need for those who must implement changes to "own" their own diagnosis of needs and development of solutions while receiving strong institutional supports during the implementation process.

91

summer. The first task, however, was to "write [a] chronology of events about how Hartwick College became involved in 'Strategies for Change'." Explain ourselves to the suspicious.

After that first workshop, the vice president and his assistant got busy establishing contact with expertise and innovative models concerning student evaluation. The planning and research committee, meanwhile, debated whether it had the proper mandate and responsibility to do any of the actions proposed in the vice president's plan. In order to gain some faculty participation in his knowledge linkage activities, the vice president set up a small "Campus Staff" of new assistant professors and student leaders known by him to be interested in changing the evaluation system. He wrote another position paper describing this team's functions in terms of Havelock's "Linkage" model, although the group emphasized the "extension agent" role of connecting campus members to innovations far more than "process consultation" on campus problems or "research and development" of new evaluation models. Literature in higher education on innovative evaluation systems, pass/fail grading, accountability and college goal-setting was distributed to the full Committee on Planning and Research. The vice president visited the University of Michigan (which happened to be his *alma mater*) and talked with Wilbert McKeachie, Richard Mann, Stanford Erickson and Gerald Gurin to glean their ideas about evaluation of student development. Gurin recommended that he talk with Chickering, but the vice president was looking for people who came from such traditionally presitigious places as his university. He did visit Brown University and Sarah Lawrence, however. Esther Raushenbush did come to Hartwick to discuss her book, *The Student and His Studies*,[4] and evaluation at Sarah Lawrence. At least the vice president was becoming personally connected to many external sources of knowledge. Other campus members received entensive written material, and some heard Raushenbush speak. These activities may have raised the general awareness of alternatives to Hartwick's evaluation system, but they did not lead to agreement in the Planning and Research Committee.

In March of 1972, part of the "Campus Staff" and the president attended the second Strategies workshop, held at the same time and place as the national conference of the American Association for Higher Education. Our idea was to help teams plan and learn about change in the context of all the expertise and practical experience which gathers together each year in Chicago. The team made direct contact with Harold Hodgkinson during the AAHE meeting to propose that he visit Hartwick. At the workshop, Ronald Havelock and David Bushnell led sessions focused on the problem-solving process and factors. The Hartwick team's plan, again written by the vice president, reconfirmed the objectives of their Philadelphia action plan but described a shift in thinking leading to an emphasis "less on grading, more on philosophy and process." A new objective also was added: "to create a climate sympathetic and supportive of planned change and situations conducive to it." No specific actions to achieve any of these general objectives were spelled out by the team. No specific follow-up, except for the vice president's reports to the committee on his latest contacts with external sources of information, occurred.

The planning and research committee, meanwhile, debated whether it had the proper mandate and responsibility to do any of the actions proposed in the vice president's plan.

92

Planning and Research Committee members registered considerable frustration as the academic year neared a close. As one later observed, "The problem early in the project was that evaluation as such was going in so many different directions, with so many different thoughts, that it was hard to focus it in any direction." Others observed that some committee members did not want to take any action, some wanted a new evaluation system, some wanted to do social science research on student development and some wanted to improve communication and clarify goals. No one faction could build a coalition strong enough to move the group, nor was the vice president able to lead the group in a way which identified common concerns or interests. The short evening meetings once a month provided time enough only for the opposing views to be expressed; the next month, the same arguments would be repeated. The voluntary nature of the group meant each meeting would have persons ignorant of the last meeting and therefore not ready to go beyond redundant debate. The vice president was praised for his diligence in searching out external information, but he was criticized for not being open to alteration of his own agenda and for being ineffective as a group facilitator or coordinator of participative follow-through. The president himself did not attempt to lead. When he did attend committee meetings, he tended to say the same phrases heard frequently before by faculty about the college's need to meet future competition with evidence of unique effectiveness in adding value to student lives. Interviewees found him persistent and some found him inspiring; they also felt he was redundant.

The frustration did lead the vice president to call together what he saw to be the more interested members of the committee, plus innovative young faculty members he previously had not included because he thought they were possibly too well-known as innovators, for a two-day retreat in May of 1972. More resistive committee members were not included. He then drafted a "working paper" which called for a pilot project with student-faculty collaboration in setting learning objectives and evaluating their achievement, and with use of journals, portfolios and written evaluations to supplement letter grades. Instead of generating action out of external stimulus and general discussion in a representative group, he now would try to launch a small pilot project among interested faculty. William Hannah and I were invited to attend in order to consult in the retreat process and to provide connection with the Strategies project.

The retreat focused first on a recent faculty meeting in which the faculty had split nearly in half over three innovation proposals. I had written in an earlier report to the college that there seemed to be in the faculty a strong traditionalist camp, concerned with tough grading and a focus on disciplinary or classical liberal arts requirements, and a group of "experimentalists" interested in giving students greater control over their programs and a variety of on- and off-campus learning experiences focusing on personal as well as intellectual development. Two retreat members well-known for teaching experiments latched onto this report. They said the faculty meeting revealed a traditionalist coalition which would pull the college back from openness, tolerance and innovation. One of the con-

"The problem early in the project was that evaluation as such was going in so many different directions, with so many different thoughts, that it was hard to focus it in any direction."

93

They said the faculty meeting revealed a traditionalist coalition which would pull the college back from openness, tolerance and innovation.

cerned retreat members, an assistant professor of English who was interested in personal development, said this group should attempt to bring the two faculty factions closer together in understanding and appreciating what the other is attempting. After the retreat itself, several participants made statements similar to the person who commented, "I went into the retreat not knowing or trusting many of the participants very well, and I left the retreat feeling the same way." I gave the group some direct observations on what I thought was their somewhat meandering and avoiding behavior as well as on the president's tendency to distract the group from specific tasks. That was the first appearance of what would become an increasing attention to group process among these persons, but at the time my comments only briefly raised the issues of openness, confrontation and structured follow-through on tasks.

Further discussion at the retreat continued to demonstrate disagreement between the social scientists, who felt the group should stick to researching student development, and the vice president, who wanted to get his pilot evaluation study off the ground. Also, student participants were largely silent. When I asked them why, they said that faculty members and administrators in the group ignored them. The faculty would tell each other what students want and think right in front of the students themselves. Also, they said it was very hard to summon the courage and skill to interrupt professors. One student who had designed an impressive student evaluation form in an independent study was sufficiently irritated that she did not return for the second day of the retreat.

Still, out of this worry about tolerance and openness and the continuing debate over committee purposes came a major re-organization of the Strategies project at Hartwick. The group agreed that the politically representative but bulky "Committee on Planning and Research" should be disbanded, as should the "Campus Staff." In their place would be a "Committee on Institutional Research" (CIR), a voluntary group of persons interested in studying and improving student development. It would have several catalytic and facilitative functions:

a. to ask questions
b. to observe change
c. to encourage educational inquiry
d. to facilitate consideration of long range planning
e. to facilitate consideration of change
f. to aid and advise standing committees
g. to suggest courses of study and action
h. to involve itself in all matters relevant to the responsibilities of the Office of Institutional Research

Several specific projects would begin CIR's life: (1) a survey of current faculty approaches to evaluation; (2) pilot evaluation projects by the Sociology, Nursing and Psychology departments, each of which had interested members on CIR; (3) a new freshman advising program to be developed by a CIR subcommittee in 1972-73 and installed in the fall of 1973; (4) on-campus workshops to study data being gathered by the Strategies staff; (5) campus visits by Wilbert McKeachie and Harold

Student participants were largely silent. When I asked them why, they said that faculty members and administrators in the group ignored them.

94

Hodgkinson; and (6) luncheon or late afternoon faculty seminars to share novel teaching approaches or new research. The group decided that the two-day retreat accomplished more than a whole year of two-hour meetings; consequently, CIR meetings would be held all day Saturday once a month at an off-campus location, despite the personal sacrifice of a significant part of those weekends.

Summer vacation curbed follow-up for everyone but the vice president for institutional research. He began to lay the groundwork for the CIR projects and also recruited delegates to Strategies' first annual "review and planning" workshop in Saratoga Springs. In an effort to involve senior, academically conservative opinion leaders, he invited a history professor who was regularly elected to lead the faculty procession at commencements and convocations. The faculty had no elected president or chairperson. In addition to himself and his assistant, he added the president of the student senate, a trustee, and the president to the group. None of the young, interested faculty members at the May retreat were included. The vice president had gone back to a representational strategy for inclusion; it was still his project. At the three-day workshop, the Hartwick group reviewed the year's progress, examined Strategies survey and interview data on the college arranged in loose-leaf "Self-Study Packets" and discussed with Harold Hodgkinson several broad questions concerning the future of private liberal arts colleges. The president focused attention on this latter topic. The vice president wrote up another general action plan with the same heading as before, "evidences of change in the individual student." It proposed to accomplish the May retreat projects and to have a CIR subcommittee consider on-campus uses of the Self-Study Packet. We on the Strategies staff were left with the impression that the only persons who were prepared personally to follow-up on the plan were the vice president and his assistant.

1972-1973: MORE TALK, A LITTLE ACTION

The vice president's first act in the fall of 1973 was to bring Goodwin Watson to campus to discuss ways to help students clarify individual learning objectives. Watson was a major implementor of the University Without Walls system and shared with faculty ideas about individualized education. Later interviews revealed a pattern similar to those of the past. Faculty members and students interested in educational innovation met with Watson and found him stimulating. Others could not remember much about his visit or felt he was another of the president's outside agitators for experimentation. During the fall, the vice president also surveyed all faculty members regarding their evaluation practices and developed profiles of innovative evaluation efforts in fourteen other liberal arts colleges.

In general, interviewees on CIR felt their meetings in the fall of 1973 were quite an improvement over the year before. The biology chairperson said,

> It's in a healthier state than it has been since its inception from the standpoint of being able to grab the imagination of those whom I would consider to be key people on campus. What I mean by key

The group decided that the two-day retreat accomplished more than a whole year of two-hour meetings.

95

"It's in a healthier state than it has been since its inception from the standpoint of being able to grab the imagination of those whom I would consider to be key people on campus."

people are people that do develop a sense of commitment and will
work with each other. I think we finally have that nucleus now.

Several persons found the all-day Saturday meetings with specific agendas far better than the brief, sporadic and rambling sessions of the previous year. The chairperson of education, a recent graduate of an innovative program at the University of Massachusetts and member of the earlier "Campus Staff," felt that the key to recent progress was "to pick one or two items and pursue them so we had some definite results that would be of use to us and to the campus, then to redirect from that point rather than continually gather more information." A psychologist in the student counseling center had become active in the fall and said that CIR committee members themselves had begun to take charge, to urge action. The new organization meant nay-sayers were no longer around to block movement, and members were no longer leaving everything to the vice president. The professor of history who had attended the Saratoga workshop said he now had an interest in seeing more evidence about what is happening to Hartwick students. As for visiting consultants Raushenbush and Watson, the very clear message was that a combination of their experimentalist backgrounds and rather poor on-campus planning for their visits led to minimal impact among persons not already interested in change. In summary, interviewees said, commitment was increasing, specific topics were being consistently pursued, a sustained meeting time had been found, leadership was emerging among committee members and the focus was shifting from utilization of external knowledge concerning evaluation of college learning toward internal self-study. In general, ownership of the issues and activities of the group had moved from president to vice president to certain faculty members. The vice president's Social Interaction strategy was becoming a Problem-Solving strategy. Still, interviewees on and off the committee observed that the group had not yet carried out a project. There remained a restlessness to get things done.

In early November, CIR met for one of its all-day sessions. I was there to observe the group's process. A detailed report of this meeting may give you a better understanding of the dynamics which were helping and hindering progress. About eighteen people, including the president, were seated in a circle in the president's living room. The first agenda item introduced by the vice president was consideration of the committee's responses to the fourteen innovative evaluation models he had summarized and mailed to committee members. Most preferred were approaches using journals, portfolios and individual learning contracts. The vice president therefore urged a pilot similar to his earlier proposal, but an associate professor of English blocked the way by saying, "I'm a conservative on change, and I don't think we've committed ourselves to making a proposal to the faculty."

For the next hour, three Committee members dominated a debate about the uses of evaluation (judgment of performance or assistance in learning), the control of evaluation (student, teacher, external test), and the appropriate content of evaluation. Finally, one member said, "It's still a problem of how to get hold of the problem, isn't it?" The vice president several times tried to summarize or draw conclusions, but each time one of

96

There remained a restlessness to get things done.

"It's still a problem of how to get hold of the problem, isn't it?"

the primary debaters raised a different question or contributed an opinion not directly related to the vice president's statement. Another twenty minutes into this debate, the director of physical education, whose doctorate was in student development, said, "I'm direction-conscious. We all seem back in a hodge-podge. Three schools [in the vice president's compilation] the majority picked have a definite trend toward close advising relationship and written evaluation. Are we backing off? I'd like to look at some of these systems." More discussion ensued. The associate dean for off-campus programs suggested that most members seemed to feel various evaluation approaches worth trying, while the psychologist who studied the *College Student Questionnaire* data urged that the group rely on the survey of its own faculty rather than on outside models. These two views each had supporting statements from other participants. Then, a half-hour later, the vice president asked his assistant to read the minutes so far. He read, "We've agreed that obtaining much evaluation information is valuable, that the information is primarily for student uses, that encouraging evaluation alternatives is desirable, and that there are elements in the majority-supported evaluation schemes of other colleges that we support." A brief silence followed. Then the associate professor of English commented, "These aren't official minutes, are they? I don't feel they've covered all that we've talked about this morning." On this note, the group broke for coffee. I, as an observer, felt I had just seen a good example of the reasons CIR had debated without action for over a year. The innovators were checked by the cautious, and the group leaders were missing their chances to find and build on common ground. After coffee, the chairperson of nursing took over discussion to present nursing's competency-based evaluation as a potential solution, but others quarreled with the relevance of professional training evaluation to liberal education evaluation. Finally, the group decided to have the vice president and any interested others draw up evaluation proposals for the December meeting.

The meeting shifted to uses of the Strategies data on "educational and organization health" at Hartwick. A subcommittee, composed of the counseling center psychologist, an assistant professor of psychology interested in college student identity formation and a social science student concluded that "the data have nothing in particular to tell us." The evidence may answer the questions of the Strategies staff, but those are not our questions. The physical education director, the vice president and the nursing head, however, responded that they had all learned useful things from the data and felt others should see it. The vice president volunteered to disseminate the data, and the nursing head recommended a workshop or series of them to study this information and the CSQ. The biology chairperson urged such meetings at the academic division level. Because the subcommittee remained uninterested in disseminating this information, the group decided once again to let the vice president work with the subgroup to design a way to get the Strategies' data used.

The next agenda item was the questionnaire on faculty evaluation methods at Hartwick. The vice president had a thirty-seven percent response so far. He noted that in their evaluations most faculty members emphasize knowledge accumulation and development of cognitive skills

The evidence may answer the questions of the Strategies staff, but those are not our questions.

related to understanding the subject. Affective growth, general problem-solving skills and application skills were not emphasized, though they were deemed important by some committee members. The group urged the vice president to try to increase the response rate and to relate evaluation techniques to teaching objectives. Then, at 3:20 p.m., the associate professor of psychology reported on his analyses of responses to the *College Student Questionnaire*. He had put the data into composite profiles of "John or Johanna C. Hartwick." The average Hartwick student was from a middle class, conservative background, had not been involved in many high school activities and did not expect to be politically active or to get involved in social service programs such as VISTA or Peace Corps; most did expect to do graduate work. Sophomores showed increases in cultural sophistication, were about as academically industrious as the average in other colleges and did not feel any great academic pressure. He used a Chickering article to explain his interpretation that the peer environment was particularly influential in increasing cultural sophistication. Group response to the presentation was positive. The assistant professor of psychology in fact made a formal motion (the first one that day) that they request funds to extend the administration and analysis of CSQ II to seniors. The associate professor of psychology said there were other data available, such as the subject area tests of the *Undergraduate Record Examination*, which rarely got used. At 4 p.m. the nursing head moved to table the motion to extend CSQ to seniors because the issue needed more study. It was tabled.

That November, 1972, meeting may or may not have been typical, but its dynamics support interviewee claims and my earlier observations. Several points stand out. First, in comparison with earlier meetings, the agenda was much more specific, developed by the group instead of the vice president and backed by extensive preparation. Second, those who wanted innovation were still effectively countered by those who did not or those who wanted more research instead. Third, the vice president and his assistant did not have the leadership skills and group support necessary to break such stalemates. Fourth, a few action-oriented persons such as the associate dean, the biology chairperson, the physical education chairperson and the nursing chairperson were no longer sitting back. They were trying to get the group to end debate and act. Fifth, the group was split between those who felt they should create changes solely out of their own internal research and development and those who found the Strategies diagnoses and the fourteen innovative evaluation systems helpful. Sixth, when it came down to action between meetings, all that was still up to the vice president for institutional research. CIR members owned the meeting discussions and were gaining control of the agenda, but the legwork was left to the administrators.

Between the November and December, 1972, meetings, the vice president wrote and mailed to faculty two "Office of Institutional Research Memos" dating from his visit to the University of Michigan. One presented Richard Mann's thinking about evaluation, and the other described Michigan's Center for Research on Learning and Teaching. He also announced that Wilbert McKeachie, from Michigan, would visit the

98

CIR members owned the meeting discussions and were gaining control of the agenda, but the legwork was left to the administrators.

campus in January. Also distributed to CIR members was a proposal by the counseling center psychologist and an assistant professor of psychology. It called for a study to test the hypothesis that students with clear, intrinsic, course-appropriate goals to which they are committed will perform better academically than others.

In the December CIR meeting, the chairperson of nursing focused the group on learning objectives. The psychologist in charge of CSQ analyses presented the goals of male students as CSQ reported them for the past three years. The education chairperson presented a proposal for spelling out course objectives. The vice president presented a long proposal for a new system of evaluation, one part of which was clarification of student objectives. In short, the biology chairperson's original support of objectives was gaining stronger footing. No action was taken in December on any of these proposals. In January, McKeachie spent a half day with CIR, as Watson had earlier. Later interviews made it clear that most remembered little of his visit except that, despite his pleasant personality and obvious grasp of the research on teaching effectiveness, he was low-key and nonassertive. Other participants dominated the meeting. In the same meeting, the assistant professor of psychology presented still another list of learning objectives, these from his studies of freshmen. Like earlier lists, this one emphasized personal and intellectual development much more than subject mastery.

The vice president was not to be dissuaded by this talk of objectives from his constant purpose: to get approval for an experiment in student evaluation. He organized a small team of CIR members to work on his lengthy proposal at the next Strategies workshop, scheduled for late January of 1973, at Quaker Academic College (a pseudonym). One student, the chairperson of nursing, the CSQ analyst and the vice president attended. Because of his high position and strong rapport with academic conservatives, the academic dean was recruited but, at the last moment, pulled out. Just prior to the workshop, I mailed to all fall interviewees at Hartwick an "Interim Report" summarizing their responses to general questions concerning educational problems at Hartwick and the institution's ability to solve them. Interviewees had focused on inadequacies in evaluation of students *and faculty* and on narrow, undemanding, incoherent and "ivory towerish" curricula as major academic problems. As for their ability to solve those problems, strengths mentioned included a general openness to new ideas in several departments, the faculty colloquium and the vice president's information. Major problems included the inability of faculty members and administrators to confront each other openly, the president's constant emphasis on innovation, a fragmented and cumbersome governance system, "reactive rather than proactive change" and weak student involvement in educational problem-solving. Self-study and redesigning governance were principle recommendations for action. I did receive feedback from the dean and a few others that the report was accurate and useful in airing problems. The vice president on January 17 distributed to chairpersons an outline of available data, which summarized earlier survey and interview information, and the "Interim Report." The summary contained descriptions of the kinds of data avail-

The vice president was not to be dissuaded by this talk of objectives from his constant purpose: to get approval for an experiment in student evaluation.

99

able, plus a few unexplained graphs at the end. Anyone desiring to study the evidence was encouraged to stop by the vice president's office.

At the January workshop, I sat with the task force and noted its early discussions. A major concern was that a history professor did not get tenure. The chairperson of nursing and the associate professor of psychology intimated, I thought, that the president somehow manipulated the decision because the person was conservative. The vice president argued back. After an hour of this, I suggested to the group that everyone was talking at, not with, others, and that the problem seemed to everyone to be the other guy's. I suggested they might do better to share their goals for the workshop, then follow through on a common objective. The vice president said he felt they should work on his proposal, for up to then the broader committee had talked a lot but had done little. The students agreed. So did the nursing chairperson but added that they should try to develop a proposal and a strategy for presenting it which would result in faculty approval. I suggested that someone be designated to keep the group on track. Everyone turned to the nursing chairperson, and she agreed to attempt to fill that function.

For the next two days, assisted by Royce Pitkin, the task force labored long hours. The outcome was a plan to develop fuller evaluation in manageable and hopefully acceptable stages rather than trying to gain passage for the vice president's long proposal all at once. A key part of any fuller evaluation, the group decided, would be the advising system. Strengthening the advising process would be step one. Step two would focus on development of a more complete student record, perhaps including a journal or portfolio. Step three would be "Development of a more sophisticated evaluation process" focusing on extended written evaluations, examination of graduation requirements and study and use of taxonomies of educational objectives.

The next CIR meeting, February 10, 1973, saw two additions to that group's procedures: (1) formal motions and votes and (2) minutes taken by the chairperson of biology instead of the vice president's assistant. First off, the committee unanimously approved the priorities developed by the task force at the Quaker Academic work-shop. They then decided to start with freshman advising. It was moved and passed that the task force meet with those administrators in charge of freshman advising to discuss the plan, then have the whole contingent meet with the committee March 3, its next meeting. The nursing chairperson had indicated at the Quaker Academic workshop that the rest of the faculty must be involved in the committee's thinking. After discussion of means, "It was moved and agreed that the Committee members should move ahead with getting input on the developing advisory proposal from departments, divisions, and residence halls as soon as possible before March 3, 1973." Finally, the group discussed a questionnaire developed by Strategies staff to identify faculty attitudes and behaviors related to academic change. Once again, concern was registered that this questionnaire was less a benefit than a nuisance. It was not their questionnaire and was not, they felt, focused on issues of concern to them; several persons said they doubted that it could help the committee in its own study.

At the next month's meeting, the committee discussed what advising, and advisors, should accomplish. Then a subcommittee composed of the counseling center psychologist, the biology chairperson and an associate dean in charge of advising was formed to develop for the afternoon an advising proposal based on the morning's discussion. A final plan for a voluntary freshman advising program was passed that afternoon. The Committee on Institutional Research had finally made a proposal for innovation.

Harold Hodgkinson did visit Hartwick March 23 and 24, and he met with the Committee on Institutional Research one of those mornings. Later interviews indicated that those campus members who tended toward innovation were most stimulated by his array of information concerning new developments in higher education, while "traditionalists" wrote him off as one more campaigner for the president's experimentalist point of view. Hodgkinson himself provided some written comments on his visit. Two of his observations concerned teaching practices and communication gaps:

> Passing back along classrooms I certainly got the impression reinforced that most of the teaching done at Hartwick is traditional and in the lecture mode. I have not seen so many rows of chairs uninterrupted for quite a while.
>
> Probably the greatest single problem I encountered at the college was the problem of ineffective communications. It is always difficult to pinpoint the origin of such problems, but it is clear that there is a large amount of rumor and misstatement of fact going around the campus. One reason for the communication difficulty is that the faculty seems to spend most of its time in small enclaves and very seldom gets together as an entire faculty. In addition, the faculty and administration as a group do not get together on a regular informal and casual basis. There seems to me to be a need for somebody within the administration to begin functioning as the communication linkage, with the faculty and with student groups.

This perceived gap, present at the Project's start, mentioned in subsequent Strategies reports, and lurking in the background of the committee's work, would shortly come to a head in a faculty move toward unionization. But first, let's turn back to the committee's own agenda.

On March 21, 1973, the advising pilot program came under the review of the Faculty Council. A few members of that body, and particularly the AAUP president, argued against its approval because it was presented as an "evolving proposal," an experiment, rather than a settled design with high probability of success. Interviewees later said an underlying but unspoken concern was that this was another presidential scheme to slip innovation past the faculty. After supportive arguments by CIR members and administration from the Office of Advisement, however, the council gave its approval on a voluntary, pilot basis. On April 7, CIR met with a group of faculty who were interested in volunteering for the program as well as with four freshman students. After discussing advising needs and problems, the committee decided to set up "in-service" meetings for volunteers and to establish a committee to work with the Office of

Later interviews indicated that those campus members who tended toward innovation were most stimulated by his array of information concerning new developments in higher education, while "traditionalists" wrote him off as one more campaigner for the president's experimentalist point of view.

101

The committee's first formal action was moving into implementation along the familiar lines of a small, voluntary, pilot program.

"I think ideas arise in committee that sound exciting, but there is no follow-through."

102

"I have had frequently the feeling this year that we get started on something and begin to narrow it down to the point where maybe we could do something and now all of a sudden, another huge whopping issue gets introduced and we're off on that somehow."

Advisement to further develop the proposal. So, the committee's first formal action was moving into implementation along the familiar lines of a small, voluntary, pilot program.

During April, a member of the Strategies staff conducted interviews and observations on campus. He asked committee members how their group was now getting along. Although there was a new optimism over the success in working through the advisement proposal, some members still were not sure how well the group would work. The biology chairperson observed:

> For the most part I think the committee has been ineffective and still remains so in large measure because those individuals who serve on it have so many other responsibilities. . . . I think ideas arise in committee that sound exciting, but there is no follow-through. Now, the lack of follow-through probably involves two factors. First, the individuals who bring up ideas are simply so overwhelmed with other types of responsibilities that they cannot follow through on their own. . . . They bring the ideas up, hoping they will be expedited through the structure of Institutional Research somehow. The other [factor] is that there's no coordinated effort to follow through firmly enough established on the part of that office which is structured, in my estimation, to follow through.

A third problem one interviewee noted was that "The Committee on Institutional Research has been ineffective, in my judgment, in establishing an appropriate kind of interplay with the general community." Still, the difficulty of the vice president in meshing his agenda with the committee's was mentioned:

> He seems to lose sight of the main directions that the committee is going in. He may have an idea, for example, that he would like to follow through on, but he's ineffective perhaps in getting the committee to buy that idea and then in the process still clings to the idea while the committee is going elsewhere.

Several members, particularly the biology and nursing chairpersons, the counseling center psychologist and the associate dean for off-campus programs, had asserted themselves in recent months to be sure there was follow-through on ideas. They sought consensus point by point in committee, and they took charge of meeting minutes to be sure the minutes reflected the group's decisions. Three or four of these people met before meetings over lunch to plan strategies for keeping the committee on track. By summarizing group progress in meetings, doing meeting minutes and making inputs to the vice president's requests for agenda items, these few emerging leaders helped keep the advisement proposal rolling. An advocacy group had appeared on the scene.

A fourth concern expressed by interviewees was that CIR, until advisement became the focus, was still handling too many large issues at once. As the counseling center psychologist noted, "I have had frequently the feeling this year that we get started on something and begin to narrow it down to the point where maybe we could do something and now all of a sudden, another huge whopping issue gets introduced and we're off on that somehow." An introduction of the "Self-Study Packet" seemed such a diversion to this interviewee. And the subject of evaluation itself seemed to her also to be too global and complex to keep motivation high: "It takes a lot of persistence to stick with it. It is a difficult area, very foggy." Fifth, there was little informal interaction among members between meetings. That kind of linkage was not available for moving work along. A recent exception was the close interaction among the counseling center psychologist, the assistant professor of psychology and the two associate deans. Their frustration with inaction and their social ties led to between-meetings strategizing about how to get the committee moving. A final, persistent problem was the lack of clear goals for the college and in the committee. The latter group became more committed to taking action, but for what purpose remained unstated.

Hodgkinson, during his visit, continually asked, "What are you trying to accomplish?" He stated over a dozen times, as recorded by a Strategies observer, that the answer to a question asked him would depend on the goals of the college or the committee. He repeatedly commented that he could not get a response to his question on goals. "I've had great trouble in understanding the directions you want to move kids." In the March 27 committee meeting, the same confusion emerged concerning the advisement proposal. Hodgkinson asked what educational function it was to accomplish, but no one answered. The Strategies observer asked the same thing. Finally, Hodgkinson said, "As I've heard it, [the purpose of the advisement program is] to inspire greater student contact with faculty." The associate dean for off-campus programs, the counseling center psychologist and the nursing chairperson agreed. But the associate professor of psychology asked, "Do we know this is needed?" That question was not answered. Finally, interviewees were unsure what the committee would do next. There were "Step 2" and "Step 3" of the January action plan, but interviewees were not sure if they would take up those steps.

During March and April, the institutional climate affecting the committee darkened. Because of data indicating reduced enrollments and the prospect of little offsetting revenue from other sources, the president proposed to the trustees an austerity budget which included no faculty raises. A group of faculty met in protest over what seemed another aribtrary presidential act against their interests. Unionization was proposed. A small group of senior faculty, less at odds with the president and more confident that shared rather than adversary governance was possible, made a counter-proposal to establish a "planning council" which would be chaired by the president, have a faculty plurality and report straight to the trustees. In a heavily attended and, a Strategies observer reported, highly emotional meeting, most faculty decided to back the shared governance approach. Shortly thereafter, a trustee-sponsored committee containing several of the senior faculty who favored the council motion was established. The language of the "moderate" counter proposal suggests the severity of the problem as it was perceived by faculty:

A RESOLUTION OF CONCERN

It is the strong sense of the undersigned that the college currently suffers from a lack of direction *that seriously interferes with the educational climate of the college. Representative of our concerns are the following:*

1. *A climate of rumor, discord, and distrust exists that seriously hampers cohesive action and discussion between the faculty and administration concerning both the short-term operation and long-term goals of the college.*

2. *The Bylaws of the College charge the Faculty with establishing sound educational programs but the Faculty is not provided fiscal information required to make informed judgments, e.g.*

   a) *We have been unable to establish meaningful communication concerning the fiscal implications of short- and long-term educational decisions.*

   b) *There is a strong reluctance on the part of the President to freely disclose the current and projected budgetary profiles of the College relative to administrative, faculty and other personnel salaries.*

   c) *No clearly-defined means of establishing the costs and educational benefits of on-campus and off-campus programs have been disclosed.*

3. *Unilateral administrative decisions are not fully enough discussed with the faculty and, further, are too frequently not communicated directly to the faculty but rather by way of rumor, innuendo and interviews in the campus newspaper. Frequently decisions affecting the individual faculty member are made without any opportunity for faculty input, e.g., faculty salary freeze, health insurance plans, personnel cutbacks, etc.*

4. *The very fact that a sizable number of the faculty consider it necessary to investigate systems of arbitration and collective bargaining in an attempt to establish effective faculty influence indicates to us a serious breakdown in the sense of community that should comprise the fabric of a liberal arts college. We must draw ourselves together and re-establish those qualities of trust and good will that will enable us to get on with the main business of providing a high quality educational experience for our students.*

"A climate of rumor, discord, and distrust exists."

104

On March 5, the president addressed the faculty in defense of his austerity budget and appealed that Hartwick cannot maintain enrollment in the face of higher costs unless it increases its students to faculty ratio, without increasing class size.

The traditional answer to such a dilemma is to increase class size. Unfortunately, if it ever was a good answer, it certainly is not now, because it would jeopardize those aspects of our community which I believe attract students to us. Within the next few weeks I will submit to you a proposal that may provide some other possible answers. At least it will be a basis for discussion. I'm willing to put my head on the block first. . . . This proposal may be construed by some as the ultimate revelation of the secret plan for Hartwick College which I alledgedly have been harbouring in my bosom these many moons, and which purports to transform Hartwick into a copy of some wicked experimental college or other. Don't you believe it. You see, the fatal flaw in most experimental colleges of the past has been that they depended on a very low student-teacher ratio, a condition I recognized at least a dozen years ago as a limitation to their general acceptability.

On April 9, 1973, the president proceeded to propose "Some Suggestions for Change" to the faculty. He charged everyone to help design a more educationally effective and financially efficient college, and said,

Though we agree on this objective, we will surely disagree on its ultimate pracitcal form. Nevertheless, if we are to succeed, we must reach consensus, or that ultimate form will never be creatively implemented. I trust, therefore, that to that end you will help me establish continuing patterns and procedures for discussion; and that all of you will assume the obvious responsibility of being part of those planning sessions. If you do not, you cannot honorably wave the flag of protest against alleged unilateral decisions made by the administration.

He proceeded to suggest that faculty must get to know students and their progress much better if they are to determine how well the student measured up to the college's goals as stated in the catalog. He proposed that it might be more important to measure the size of the student-teacher group than the faculty-student ratio. Five faculty in a subcollege of one hundred students may be better than a one to fifteen ratio. He suggested that faculty may have to spend more time in advising, counseling and guiding; peer learning might be emphasized. He said the freshman may need more attention than the senior in order to develop independent learners. Freshmen might be started into major or problem-centered interdisciplinary programs to build on their interests right away. Grades and credits are ill-suited, he said, to measure adequately "creative and scholarly effort, independent study, individual programs, and off-campus programs."

And we should be happy for this, since it is in these non-standardizable areas of intellectual growth that we as an institution are least vulnerable and can most easily express our uniqueness—and that uniqueness will have a lot to do with our durability and health institutionally.

I will let these comments suffice for the present. There is, I hope, enough specific to stimulate argument and discussion, but not enough to stifle imagination. If there are those among you who feel these suggestions are worthy of further exploration—let's explore. Those of you who judge these matters are of no concern to you probably don't belong here anyway.

"This proposal may be construed by some as the ultimate revelation of the secret plan for Hartwick College which I allegedly have been harbouring in my bosom these many moons."

105

The speech fit the president's self-identified leadership style: to catalyze with ideas and needs, to gadfly and challenge; but to leave action to those who must carry it out. Most interviewees found such speeches stimulating, although some said they could not judge the accuracy of his financial and enrollment predictions because the administration kept the information and because such predictions hung on easily debatable evidence anyway. I felt in that last paragraph what interviewees called "little zingers." One consultant wrote to Strategies staff the same observation: "I get the feeling, occasionally, that he treats faculty as if they were 'hired hands.'" Harold Hodgkinson, who was on campus around blow-up time and who had received from the president copies of his speeches, wrote to the president,

> *I like the proposals contained in your April 9 letter to the faculty very much. But it does seem to me that the style of the presentation is something like a very large rock dropped into a very small, calm pond. Rather than having some of these ideas dropped from on high, as it were, it might be better to work through a number of possible ideas with representative small advisory committees of faculty and students first, so that any public pronouncement of the options (and I gather that your statement was simply a listing of some of the options) could be made with some feeling of comfort that others had been involved in the selection of viable options.*

In CIR, the biology chairperson finally took the initiative. He proposed administration of the *Institutional Goals Inventory*, which he had discovered through involvements in the Strategies project. The Committee agreed. A couple of members had just returned from a conference on "Faculty Effectiveness as Evaluated by Students," and they urged development of a course and teacher evaluation, just as the independent study student had urged the year before. The minutes, now being written by the counseling center psychologist instead of the vice president's assistant, concluded, "It was agreed that the priorities of the committee are: (1) Student evaluation and (2) Considering the differences between goals for the college as they are perceived by different members of the community. In other words—ULTIMATELY, ON WHAT BASIS DO WE GRANT A DEGREE." In one follow-up action, the Faculty Council, on which several CIR members sat, authorized CIR to look into student evaluation of teachers.

Two important actions for institutional renewal at Hartwick took place in the summer of 1973. One was the work of the special committee to design a campus planning council. Three action-oriented members of CIR were on that group: the biology, nursing and physical education chairpersons. Also selected were the dean of student services, a philosophy professor of long tenure and long service in drafting major faculty policies and the psychology chairperson, the latter reputed by all interviewees to be in dead opposition to the president and to deviations from traditional ways of teaching, learning and evaluating. He had been observed as an effective gate closer in high committees and was just elected president of the local AAUP chapter.

The second significant development was Hartwick's first involvement

"The style of the presentation is something like a very large rock dropped into a very small, calm pond."

106

in a faculty development project initiated by the College Center of the Finger Lakes (CCFL), a consortium to which Hartwick belonged. The vice president for institutional research, who was liaison to CCFL, begged and cajoled seven faculty members, nearly all members of CIR, to attend the first, week-long workshop of that new project. Later interviews with five of the seven supplied unanimous rave reviews. Each said he or she had been reluctant to attend, for it sounded like more of a "touchy-feely" experience which had bombed for Hartwick participants a year before. Yet all five were extremely enthusiastic about their workshop experience. Initial individual interviews before the workshop with each faculty participant by one of the three consultants got them "thinking seriously about their role as teachers." It also established a colleague relationship between trainers and participants, interviewees said. Low-key morning groups were offered in which faculty members from the four participating colleges and across several disciplines shared their teaching aspirations and problems. Afternoon "mini-universities," in which a wide variety of teaching techniques were attempted, allowed them to further explore their own interests in the non-threatening atmosphere of the off-campus retreat. Especially important, each member said, was the increasing sense of ownership by participants as the consultants turned over planning sessions to the faculty. Each college group of participants was to become a faculty development team which, both by the individual example of its members and by group efforts, would stimulate broader involvement. The Hartwick team decided to assume a low profile on campus "because of all the fears around" about plots to change people. It called itself "The Seven Dwarfs."

The Hartwick team decided to assume a low profile on campus "because of all the fears around" about plots to change people. It called itself "The Seven Dwarfs."

1973-1974: THE COLLEGIUM

When I heard the Strategies staff member's report in which he agreed with the faculty's report of a "climate of rumor, discord and distrust" on the Hartwick campus, I wrote to several faculty and administrative leaders to urge that they openly confront and resolve the conflict instead of letting it simmer over the summer. I suggested that key persons on the faculty and administrative side might use the annual Strategies workshop in Saratoga, with process consultant Goodwin Watson as facilitator, to work on the problem. Instead, several members of the planning council drafting committee showed up and spent the workshop intensively designing a new body politic to be called a "Collegium." It would be composed of students, faculty and administrators with a faculty plurality and would report to the president instead of straight to the trustees. Current governance was reconstructed into three parts—academic, student life, finance and development—under the Collegium. These also would be collaboration between students, faculty and administration with faculty dominating the academic side, students their own affairs and administrators outnumbering others regarding finance, facilities and capital development. The faculty as an independent governance system, the *status quo*, was ignored in the design.

After some modification in the full special committee, the Collegium proposal was presented in a special September meeting of faculty. It drew attack from senior faculty members known to be active leaders in the current faculty governance system. They said the proposal radically changed governance without demonstrating where the faculty as a separate entity, the academic departments and the president fit into the scheme. In response to these criticisms, the faculty members of the special committee caucused and altered the proposal to drop all the new structures under the Collegium and substitute current governance. The new body, they reported, "will not usurp the authorities and responsibilities conferred upon the President and Faculty by the by-laws of the College, and upon the Student Senate by the students of the College; nor will it endeavor to perform the functions of these constituencies." Also, "During the second year of this experiment its effectiveness will be evaluated by the Collegium and by the other segments of the College community, and at the end of the two years the Collegium may be terminated by action of any one of its three constituencies." That is, the faculty, the administration or the students could scuttle the new ship. All faculty members on the planning council committee except the AAUP president supported the revision. He had been silent in most special committee sessions, and other members were irritated that he would vote against their proposal without bothering to state his reservations.

In the next faculty meeting, the same senior professors who had spoken before now won a series of amendments to further reduce the new body's powers by changing such words as "establish" to "develop" and "propose" to "suggest." The physical education chairperson rose in irritation to say "As amended, we've taken a step backward. The faculty doesn't want done the job it wanted done last spring." Interviewees later indicated that it was the senior, traditionalist faculty which had "emasculated" the proposal because they felt that by adding students and administrators in strong numbers to the council, faculty control would be diminished. Between faculty meetings, the dean summarized the process to date in a position paper. He observed that the faculty the last spring "said through its resolution that it wanted more power without giving up any of its present authority." Since that time the proposal had been succeedingly stripped of power. "Please notice how far the proposal has moved from May to November: from an all encompassing, broadly-based Planning Council reporting directly to the Board to an organization which would threaten no one and would merely make suggestions and proposals. . . ." He then proposed a simple procedure to accomplish what now seems the faculty's desire: create a standing faculty committee on long-range planning. "From the point of view of the Faculty, there would be an attractive feature since the Committee would be *created* by the Faculty, it would be held accountable directly to the Faculty." He then moved a Committee on Long-Range Planning which would be predominantly faculty, would not have the president as chairperson and would not include a mechanism for selecting a "Chairman of the Faculty," as the Collegium proposal did. The latter charge had raised questions in discussion concerning the function of the dean, who was *Dean of the Faculty*. In this motion, I felt the dean was proposing what the faculty by November was willing to pass. He also was giving support to those reputedly conservative

He had been silent in most special committee sessions, and other members were irritated that he would vote against their proposal without bothering to state his reservations.

108

"As amended, we've taken a step backward. The faculty doesn't want done the job it wanted done last spring."

faculty who feared loss of faculty power, not gain, in the Collegium. Finally, he was siding against the president, who had expressed support for the Collegium. (It might be useful to note here that Hartwick had attempted a faculty-student-administrative "Campus Council" two previous years, but the dean had moved that it be dissolved because, he said, it was poorly attended and accomplished no useful purpose. However, some of its members, particularly students, had found it a very helpful forum for discussion across faculty, administrative and student lines.)

On December 10, 1973, the faculty easily passed a new Planning Council along the lines proposed by the dean, although the chairperson of the faculty position was retained. The eventual innovation, therefore, was only a mild departure from the *status quo*, and one which would increase faculty influence over college development if it resulted in change at all.

The Committee on Institutional Research underwent leadership changes in the fall of 1973. The president had asked the vice president for institutional research, who had not been able to get self-study and planned change going, to resign. In his place, the president appointed the counseling center psychologist as "Coordinator" rather than "Vice President" for institutional research. He also formalized a half-time position as "Faculty Associate for Institutional Research" and placed the CSQ analyst in that job. The freshman advising program was off the ground and included several CIR members as volunteers. The committee itself spent its fall meetings considering new agenda, orienting new members and discussing its role in the college; participants in the CCFL faculty development project were among the most active members. The October minutes describe the new coordinator's summary of discussion on CIR's role: "our function is to look at the college and its needs and to act as a provocateur: to raise issues, ask questions, make proposals to appropriate groups, ask for cooperation in studies." "To look at the college" instead of to look at external research and innovation marked a major strategy difference between the new institutional research coordinator and the past vice president. Another new strategy was to formalize CIR's linkage to campus governance by having the new coordinator meet "with some regularity" with the major college committees. A second kind of linkage was a series of bag lunch seminars sponsored by faculty members involved in CIR and focused on college issues or new faculty teaching or research. These followed a series of late afternoon discussions maintained the year before by a small group of faculty.

Mostly, however, CIR continued to debate its goals and roles. When asked in late fall interviews if CIR now had a clear direction, one member answered, "Oh, Lord no!" Another said, "I don't think it accomplished anything last year, and it is accomplishing less this year." Interviewees said CIR members were too diverse in interests or willingness to act, too fluctuating in attendance and too overburdened with other work to set specific objectives or to follow through. The one action of the previous year, the freshman advising program, was reported by those faculty in it to be only marginally effective because they had no time to give these students special attention. The faculty members already heavily involved with students and committees tried to add yet another burden. The

The eventual innovation, therefore, was only a mild departure from the status quo, and one which would increase faculty influence over college development if it resulted in change at all.

109

A second kind of linkage was a series of bag lunch seminars sponsored by faculty members.

motivation was strong but the time available was not.

I had been asked by CIR leaders to visit and help the group more often than other project institutions had sought Strategies staff assistance. Proximity to the campus may have been one reason they asked. Hartwick is only ninety miles from Saratoga, while Mountain College is fifteen hundred miles. Hartwick members knew I could get there quickly and cheaply. Also, I had written the "Self-Study Packet" analyses and the "Interim Report," which some people found helpful. Third, I was not a Goddardite but was from the same traditionally prestigious university as was the vice president for institutional research, who made initial contacts with me. I liked and respected the faculty members and administrators who were struggling to make the college distinctively effective for students, and I was intellectually interested in the faculty ownership strategy slowly evolving there. Several CIR members became interested in task group process, and I was the staff resource in that area. Finally, I was the one visiting fireman who kept coming back. Over the years Hartwick and I got to know and feel comfortable with each other. This long term relationship with a single external consultant seemed to have greater benefit for the college than a series of short visits by a variety of experts. Soon, Bonnie Buenger Larson of the College Center of the Finger Lakes would establish a similar on-going relationship with the college.

I was invited again to join CIR in their December, 1973, meeting. I led off the session by summarizing recent interviews. Lower enrollment and tight finances had raised faculty concern that the college develop and present a distinctive image. Communication, trust and tolerance between traditionalists and experimentalists, between faculty and executive administrators, was a bit improved but still weak. CIR members had told me the group talked too much about too many agendas. They wanted to set action priorities and get on with it. In response to the last point, I suggested that they rapidly list on newsprint all the topics they had in mind, then put them in rank order and make an action plan for at least the top item. This they did. The top concern was to help the college decide its educational objectives. The group decided to conduct an *Institutional Goals Inventory* survey and to collect and give college members other data describing the current internal and external environment of the college. Subgroups volunteered to begin work on these tasks. Their strategy was not to have some researcher do the study, for "people need to become involved in the process."

During December, the faculty associate administered the IGI to the members of the Committee on Institutional Research. He reported the results in January. CIR turned out to be especially concerned to improve "Community," to build a climate of openness, candor, trust, respect and commitment to the college. It also had high concern to improve the intellectual and aesthetic climate of the college and to strengthen intellectual and personal development of students. Committee members commented that they appeared to be more student-oriented than the faculty as a whole was likely to be, but they had enjoyed the IGI exercise and wanted other groups to do it. They decided to administer it to standing committees, a student sample and the trustees. They all volunteered to

The group talked too much about too many agendas. They wanted to set action priorities and get on with it.

help tabulate results. Subgroups also began considering what internal research about the college and external data about prospective student interests, population and occupational trends and state priorities should be shared with college members.

Following this January meeting, the faculty associate, who had high interest in the IGI, continued to lead that activity, and CIR members did pitch in tabulation time and persuaded committees to take the instrument. Energy, clear understanding and interest in the external/internal environment assessments, however, waned. Analysis and feedback did not occur. Instead, CIR began considering other agenda items, such as evaluation of the freshman advising experiment, a topic encouraged by the appearance at a CIR meeting of Student Senators complaining about the inadequacy of advisement; evaluation of the college's "India Term"; college attrition; and, once again, CIR's functions. On the latter item, several CIR members were concerned that the committee merge the faculty development interests of some of its members and the research interests of others. Late in the spring of 1974, a subcommittee composed of the chairperson of biology, the director of institutional research and the associate dean for off-campus programs (all of whom by then had been involved in CCFL faculty development workshops) presented a new statement of functions:

> *The Committee on Institutional Research includes volunteers (from faculty, students and administration) who are actively committed to helping themselves and others to better accomplish their educational aims in a way that supports personal, professional and institutional renewal. Among their responsibilities are:*
> a. *Serving in an advisory capacity to the Office of Institutional Research—particularly in helping to establish priorities and in insuring maximum utilization of the resources of the office.*
> b. *Assisting in collecting, interpreting and disseminating research findings.*
> c. *Consulting with those who want support in their own efforts toward personal, professional and institutional renewal.*
> d. *Initiating and implementing plans and proposals leading to the realization of personal, professional, and institutional renewal.*

The functions were approved in ten minutes, though debate over what to call the committee went on for two hours. No agreement could be reached that any alternative—such as committee for "renewal" or "development" or "action-research"—did not raise red flags, so the old name was kept. I observed to the group that the old split between those who wanted CIR to do social science research and those who wanted it to catalyze college improvement through action proposals or professional development seemed to remain; there was, however, less opposition to action and greater control by action-oriented faculty than there had been the year before. Also, the former vice president for institutional research's third agenda, a new evaluation system for individual student development, had

CIR members were concerned that the committee merge the faculty development interests of some of its members and the research interests of others.

111

had sunk below other priorities since he left. During 1973-74, the chairperson of biology, with his steadfast interest in clarifying objectives, had been unanimously elected CIR chairperson in a move initiated by the coordinator of institutional research to free her for other duties and to increase faculty ownership of the committee. In May, the English professor who consistently had been generating innovations to attend to the personal development of students was elected 1974-75 CIR chairperson. Both of these leaders were members of the original faculty development "Seven Dwarfs." In a final act to strengthen CIR, the committee asked for and got from the president approval to move the coordinator of institutional research from half to full time, to add a half time secretary and to rearrange office space so as to make room for the faculty associate for institutional research. In short, 1973-74 saw more aggressive faculty leadership and ownership of CIR: clarification of functions covering research, innovation proposal and professional development; strengthening of administrative capacity; steady membership by an interested core of about ten to twelve people; and agreement that encouraging the setting of college objectives was the first business of CIR.

Meanwhile, the new planning council was getting underway. It met first on March 25, 1974. The biology chairperson was elected chairperson. He immediately advocated that the group should focus on the future mission of the college. As a first step, the council asked the faculty associate for institutional research to administer the IGI to this new group. In April, the dean of the faculty announced his resignation. He had been asked by the president the year before to resign at this time. He and the president had not worked well together because of clashing educational philosophies and greatly differing leadership styles. A group of senior faculty members, irritated that the president had taken this action without faculty consultation, had asked him to rescind his decision, and he had. But then the dean found an attractive position elsewhere. The new council seized on this resignation to propose a faculty-trustee-administrator-student search committee for an acting and permanent dean, as well as to examine the structure and functions of the dean's office. The president approved this proposal, as did the trustees. Also in the spring of 1974, the new council initiated establishment of an Affirmative Action Committee. Finally, to insure close linkage with other major governance units, it developed regular contacts with the trustees' executive committee, invited standing committee members to its meetings, had each council member make connections with one standing committee, and invited the master at writing minutes (the coordinator of institutional research), to serve the same function for this body. By these actions, the planning council quickly established itself as the committee concerned with the identification of future goals and the search for executive personnel and thus integrated itself rapidly into the current structure of college authority. In its final meeting of academic year 1973-74, the planning council decided that the task of fitting a statement of educational objectives to graduation requirements "is fundamental to all others and needs attention first."

The full council statement reveals that all the prior linkage to innova-

1973-74 saw more aggressive faculty leadership and ownership of CIR.

112

The planning council decided that the task of fitting a statement of educational objectives to graduation requirements "is fundamental to all others and needs attention first."

tive ideas by the president and CIR was not in vain. The council felt the college might evaluate student development in college, the value added by Hartwick, instead of normal test performance; might use learning contracts worked out between the student and a faculty team; might use competency-based evaluation instead of a series of "hurdles over which to jump"; might diversify student pathways to graduation; might use portfolios and external evaluations of student work; might stress the freshman year. The group had become quite knowledgeable about solutions. Now the problem was to clarify goals and fit the appropriate solutions to them. The council decided to continue work through the summer in order to develop a proposal for faculty consideration. Two summers before, a committee had developed a proposal for a year-round calendar which the faculty, suspicious of economic rather than educational motives and uninvolved in the committee's learning, shot down. The year just past, a committee had formulated a fancy "Collegium" only to face more faculty suspicion and lack of persuasion in the fall. Would the same strategy meet the same reception a third time?

CHANGES IN EDUCATIONAL AND
ORGANIZATIONAL HEALTH, 1972-1974

Faculty members had begun to take charge of Hartwick's self-examination and renewal between 1972 and 1974. A good deal of innovation-oriented consultation and knowledge linkage had occurred. Three new participative renewal functions were being built: institutional research on education, faculty development and planning. All of these efforts had been slow in coming and still involved only a few of Hartwick's members. Only a small living learning project, a small off-campus and independent study program, a small freshman advising project and individual changes by a few faculty members had occurred. Most energy had been directed at clarifying who we are and where we want to go rather than at implementing change. How, then, did Hartwick's educational and organizational health, as roughly measured by Strategies evidence, look in 1974 as compared with 1972?

Educational process, for the most part, appeared stable. Over 40% of the professors both years, according to students, primarily "dispense knowledge or assign sources which the student should master." More flexible, collaborative or resource roles were equally frequent both times. About 68% of the students both years said they had minor or no influence over course content and structure. About a quarter of the students coasted through their work in both years. About a quarter in both years studied primarily to fulfill graduation requirements or to get good grades rather than for more intrinsic reasons. Class time heavily emphasized listening and note-taking in 1972 and 1974, as opposed to more active thinking or participating; and study time focused mainly on memorizing and interpreting, with lesser emphasis on analyzing, applying, synthesizing and evaluating. About 65% of the students each year had fewer than six conversations lasting over five minutes with faculty members or administrators during the last semester. There were significantly fewer students in 1974 who reported *no* conversations with advisors about future plans or

113

About 65% of the students each year had fewer than six conversations lasting over five minutes with faculty members or administrators during the last semester.

with faculty members about general topics. But students reported no differences in impact of faculty contacts except for a significant increase in the number who reported only minor impact on "increasing my range of feelings, sensitivities and awareness (aesthetic, social, spiritual)." More students in 1974 reported studying over 30 hours a week (14% to 24%), but more reported spending no time during the last week in informal discussions of general issues (13% to 24%). More in 1974 did report major peer influence on "increasing my intellectual competence and curiosity" (10% to 20%). And, finally, more 1974 students found themselves "interested, attracted" to the randomly selected course on which they reported (64% to 74%). The CUES "Scholarship" scale, however, had not changed significantly. Hartwick remained below two-thirds of the national group on this scale. In general, it would appear that few differences had occurred in the educational process at Hartwick, but the student body had shifted in a somewhat more diligent, interested direction. The college's CSQ data support this interpretation.

On the organizational side, six *Institutional Functioning Inventory* scales had significantly *decreased*, while one ("Meeting Local Needs") had increased. "Institutional Esprit," which we were increasingly convinced was a scale highly sensitive to college issues during questionnaire administration, had taken a nose dive. The IFI had been administered in 1974 during the period when rumors were just surfacing regarding the president's earlier request that the dean look for a job elsewhere. Later interviewees said that when the dean left campus and the selection committee got rolling, the ill-feeling dissipated considerably. "Concern for Innovation" had dropped as well. Item analysis suggests that greater awareness of external innovations which were not being used, plus the financial pinch, instead of less emphasis on innovation, accounted for the change. In 1974, 82% of the respondents agreed that there is a "general willingness here to try innovations that show promise elsewhere," compared to 62% in 1972, but "this college would be among the first to experiment with a novel educational program" dropped from 88% agreement to 68%. Eighty nine percent agreed in 1974 "in the past few years there have been major departures from old ways of doing things," compared to 39% in 1972. We are innovating, but we now know enough about other places to know we're not the first to do what is new to us, the data seem to say.

As for finances, only 66% in 1974 (80% in 1972) *disagreed* that "curricular changes are decided more on financial bases than on educational merit." The college was suffering an enrollment slump. There was much more talk about what we need to do to attract student dollars. Notably, "Self-Study and Planning" significantly *decreased* in faculty perceptions despite CIR, the new planning council, the Strategies data and the IGI. Part of the explanation may be that during the 1972 administration of the IFI, the college was completing a five year Master Plan required by the state. Part may be that CIR had spent its first two years mostly in internal discussion rather than self-study. Part may be that the planning council and the IGI were just getting underway when the 1974 IFI was administered. Part may be a residual skepticism from the president's handling of the dean. One major drop, from 52% to 26% disagree-

114

We are innovating, but we now know enough about other places to know we're not the first to do what is new to us, the data seem to say.

ment with the statement "recent changes here are a result of internal/external influences, not of institutional purposes," hints at the president's actions but also suggests that the financial pinch and the parade of nontraditional consultants were leading faculty to conclude that the institution was responding to only one side of the self-renewal coin. Table 4 reports the "Self-Study and Planning" scale results.

Change in the "Concern for Undergraduate Learning" scale also suggests a greater skepticism in 1974 than in 1972. The three items which changed significantly, plus the other items which changed at least ten percentage points, reflect a more critical view of learning and the degree to which professors are student-oriented. Table 5 reports those items. These results in particular—but also the responses on esprit and self-study and planning—suggest that the relative complacency of 1972 had been upset. The 1972 data revealed little felt need to change. By 1974, however, respondents appeared to be quite unhappy about faculty-administrative relationships and decreasingly content with self-study, planning and the level of faculty concern for students. Yet student respondents to the ECQ did not see much difference in educational experiences in 1974. Could it be that although education at Hartwick had not altered much in those years, faculty had become increasingly unwilling to praise the *status quo?* The thrust of the self-study data, the long debates of the Committee on Institutional Planning, the president's speeches about the need to change in order to meet the future, the biology chairperson's insistence on clarifying mission, the administration of the IGI, the intervention of consultants and written information critical of traditional practices, the faculty development project and the actions leading to formation of the planning council all were aimed at raising and clarifying a need to change the *status quo*. The drop in enrollment got the same message across in the graphic terms of dollars for salaries. If these efforts had been successful, faculty might well feel less positive about the college in 1974 than in 1972 and might be more ready to do actively something to solve the problems they now saw. That appears to be confirmed by the IFI scores as well as the growing core of action-oriented faculty members. Rather than failing, all of these efforts appear to have succeeded in building a substantial need for renewal. The question is, would this increasing discontent result in educational and organizational improvement?

115

Rather than failing, all of these efforts appear to have succeeded in building a substantial need for renewal.

1974-1975: FROM NEED TO ACTION
The third annual Strategies review and planning workshop in Saratoga Springs took place July 21-24, 1974. Hartwick sent a large group with overlapping membership in CIR (six of the eight), faculty development (five of the eight) and the planning council (five of the eight). Among them were the president and his wife, the coordinator of institutional research, the biology chairperson, the associate dean for off-campus programs, the innovative professor of English who was now CIR chairperson, the philosophy professor so active in major committees, a history professor who had become interested in change through experiences in the CCFL faculty development project and another associate dean who had been active in promoting and supporting flexible, student-oriented programs

TABLE 4
HARTWICK COLLEGE "SELF-STUDY AND PLANNING"

Item #	Item Description	Key Agree	1972 Percent	1974 Percent
076	There is a long range plan for the institution. It is published for college-wide distribution	Y	21	45*
078	Reports of institutional studies are announced generally and available to faculty/staff	Y	75	84
081	One or more persons are now engaged in long-range planning for the college	Y	85	89
084	College has a long range plan based on a reasonably clear statement of goals	Y	41	50
088	Greater emphasis on departmental planning than on institution-wide planning	N	60	46*
092	Analyses of philosophy, purposes, and objectives of college frequently conducted	Y	71	49*
093	Planning here is continuous rather than one-shot or completely non-existent	Y	82	70
103	Recent changes here a result of internal/external influences, not of institutional purposes	Disagree D-SD	52	26*
108	There is wide discussion about what the college should do five to ten years in the future	Agree SA-A	81	72
110	Most administrators and faculty see little real value in data-based institutional studies	D-SD	78	56*
125	Institutional research agency here does more than just gather facts for the administration	SA-A	60	59
132	Planning for the future of the college is high priority activity for senior administrators	SA-A	91	77*

*Change is significant at .05 level, symmetric test.

TABLE 5
HARTWICK COLLEGE
"CONCERN FOR UNDERGRADUATE LEARNING"
1972-1974

Item Description	Response Key	1972 Percent	1974 Percent
There are established procedures by which students may propose new courses	Agree	67	53*
There is not much contact between faculty and students outside the classroom	Disagree	70	57
How best to communicate knowledge to students does not concern many faculty	Disagree	80	66*
Professors get to know students in their undergraduate classes quite well	Agree	77	67
Most professors do not wish to spend much time talking about students' personal concerns	Disagree	78	66
Most faculty are quite sensitive to the needs, interests, and aspirations of undergraduates	Agree	89	74*

*Difference significant at .05 level, symmetric test.

117

and was just appointed acting dean for 1974-75. Most of the active educational renewal leaders were there.

During the workshop, the group struggled over whether to spend the summer drafting a detailed statement of objectives and requirements or to design a process by which wider faculty groups could become participants instead of critics. The philosophy professor pointed out that the year-round calendar and collegium proposals had met defeat because an isolated committee had made them so specific that "when the opposition succeeded in dislodging one brick in the edifice, the whole thing collapsed." But he admitted that he still believed a specific proposal should be written, as did the biology chairperson. These senior leaders were countered this time by younger faculty members and administrators who valued an openly participative problem-solving process from the start. A compromise was effected. "Sample" statements of objectives and requirements would be drafted by the committee, but then a series of interactions with departments, divisions, standing committees and the faculty as a whole would continue throughout the fall. At the end of this

"When the opposition succeeded in dislodging one brick in the edifice, the whole thing collapsed."

process, the planning council would submit to the faculty a formal proposal.

The Saratoga group also designed a one-day faculty-administrative retreat, with families, to kick off the fall in a way which might begin to bring the campus community together. In addition, a sub-group designed with me a day and a half "intensive" meeting of CIR to get its fall activities off to a good start. I was struck in each of these action planning meetings by how aware of group process and increasingly skillful were those persons who had been involved in the CCFL workshops. What used to take meeting after meeting to resolve now was handled fairly expeditiously. Also, the notion of early involvement of "potential adopters" in the diagnosis of need and the development of change proposals, a Strategies theme, was now a strong commitment of emerging leaders at Hartwick.

During 1974, CCFL training workshops were accelerating, thanks to a grant from the Lilly Endowment. Administrators such as the director of institutional research and the associate dean for off-campus programs had joined new faculty initiates in enthusiastic reports about the personal insights, innovative techniques and motivation to improvement they had gained in their workshops. By the end of 1974-75, nearly half the faculty had experienced some workshop or on-campus consultation regarding professional development. A group of ten faculty members and a student advised the project. The English professor who chaired CIR was selected to be half-time "Faculty Associate" for the on-campus "Educational Consulting Service," a position funded for three years through Lilly. Besides "Basic Faculty Development" workshops like those the Seven Dwarfs had experienced,[5] "Basic Administration" workshops off-campus and "thematic" workshops on-campus, not to mention workshops for students and clerical-secretarial staff and the nursing department all took place in 1974-75. The action-oriented nursing chairperson took over the CIR chairperson function from the English professor. The trustees approved the position of "Chairman of the Faculty," and the chairperson of biology was unanimously elected to it. The president brought in a "Vice President for Planning and Development" to strengthen renewal supports in both those areas. The acting dean continued to make that office a more congenial and renewal-oriented function. The campus newspaper put educational developments and issues on the front and editorial pages. The coordinator of institutional research wrote in a letter to me, "there's a general note of optimism around."

The Committee on Institutional Research did hold its "intensive" fall kick-off according to plan, with me as process consultant. After some discussion of the usual, wide-ranging agendas, the group broke into small interest groups each of which would focus its interest—research, professional development, planning—on assisting the college in clarifying educational objectives and graduation requirements by Christmas. Once again, the biology chairperson was the advocate of this focus. A major theme developed during the meeting was that the time for "just talk" had passed.

One CIR action plan called for the coordinator of institutional research to send to the faculty a summary of the IGI results. She did. Her

118

A major theme developed during the meeting was that the time for "just talk" had passed.

conclusion was that the same objectives emphasized in the earlier *College Student Questionnaire*, Strategies evidence, the nursing department's objectives, and CIR itself held for faculty in general: intellectual and personal development as well as community were the major areas needing attention. The mastery of academic subjects was highly valued but more effectively accomplished than the other objectives, according to faculty. "So," she wrote, "apparently we'll need to work hardest in the areas where we care most": helping students learn how to learn; motivating them to keep on learning; helping them to become effective problem-solvers; helping them understand themselves and others, to clarify purposes, to become open; and helping all of us work together in open collaboration. She did observe that students and administrators desired personal development of students more than faculty; that students were more interested in career development than were faculty and administrators (except, perhaps, their own); that students felt more need to increase democracy in governance and extra-curricular opportunities than did others; that faculty were more concerned about developing reading, writing and math skills, as well as the college's academic reputation, than were others; and that both faculty and administration were worried that a plan for the college's future needed to be quickly set. The common concerns support the notion that college members were becoming increasingly aware of needs to build a closer community and to help students grow intellectually and personally. The subgroup differences, however, suggested tensions which might lead to disagreements; students, administrators and student-oriented faculty might, for example, line up against traditional faculty members regarding personal growth goals. And as responses from committees and departments trickled in to the planning council, these differences became apparent. The academic standards committee, chaired by a traditionalist, had little interest in changing current objectives and requirements. The student affairs office used Carl Rogers to make an eloquent case against the current system and for development of whole persons in their whole environment.

I had pledged in CIR's intensive meeting to report Strategies data related to objectives and requirements. Robert Guerrin, Susan Koffman Plante of the Strategies staff and I wrote a paper called "When Goals Meet Practices . . ." and mailed it to the college in December just before a major faculty development workshop. We attempted to relate our student reports on educational practices to the *Institutional Goals Inventory* responses and teaching-learning research. The message was that one highly valued Hartwick objective, subject mastery, was represented fairly well in teaching practices and requirements (as, indeed the IGI responses indicated), but much more active, interactive and experience-based learning and teaching would be needed to improve in the objectives areas so much a concern to faculty, students and administrators: intellectual and personal development. It was a theme redundant to CIR members but now presented in a new package of research and theory. The report became the focus of the workshop's first evening meeting. The meeting summary concurred "that we are more satisfied about the way in which we achieve *Subject Mastery* than the way in which we accomplish *Intellectual* and

119

Much more active, interactive and experience-based learning and teaching would be needed to improve in the objectives areas so much a concern to faculty, students and administrators: intellectual and personal development.

Personal Development goals," and that "this is the stuff of Faculty Development." During the second day of the workshop, nearly a third of the Hartwick faculty, including such "traditionals" as the psychology chairperson, attended seminars and experiential sessions on teaching improvement led by their own colleagues. The new Faculty Associate for faculty development led the overall workshop and, said later interviewees, established himself as not just a far-out, somewhat suspect teacher to traditionals, but as a skillful consultant for various faculty concerns. His credibility broadened. Regarding the Strategies' report, the coordinator of research wrote, "Your timing is exquisite and the report the Strategies staff produced is excellent." Jack Noonan, the workshop keynoter, said it was one occasion in which he saw the powerful potential of educational-effectiveness research for stimulating a common concern to improve teaching. A targeted purpose relating to internal concerns and the connection to a special internal event, as well as brevity, differentiated this feedback from the "Self-Study Packet."

At mid-year, the institutional research, planning and faculty development programs entered new phases. The planning council decided it now was time to draft a formal proposal for educational objectives and graduation requirements. A subcommittee, consisting of the history professor, the philosophy professor and a young assistant professor of foreign languages (who had replaced the biology chairperson as council head), put together a draft and presented it in February to a full faculty meeting, the Faculty Council, the Academic Standards Committee and the Individual Program Committee "because of their particular responsibilities." The Committee on Institutional Research had completed the IGI feedback. Out of thirty-seven possible agenda items compiled from past minutes by the director of research, the group selected four for winter and spring work: (1) the freshman year; (2) course and teacher evaluation; (3) faculty workload; and (4) student satisfaction. In order to establish openness and to encourage participation, CIR led small group discussions on this agenda in a faculty meeting. The four topics were supported with one amendment: the evaluation group should design an evaluation of administrators as well as professors. Members preferred the task group arrangement developed in the fall over the former large group discussions followed by the director of institutional research or faculty associate actions.

Each action topic was followed up by task groups. The freshman year group, which met over lunch, drew as many as twenty faculty and student participants. It came up with about ten freshman seminars, taught by faculty volunteers (primarily biology) for the fall of 1975. The course and teacher evaluation group, with the aid of the Faculty Associate for Institutional Research, created a form to be used in the fall of 1975. CIR also endorsed a longitudinal study of student personality development by an enthusiastic new assistant professor of psychology, while the Faculty Associate for Institutional Research put together a general rationale and model for systematic study of student development at Hartwick.

The faculty development project remained a top concern within CIR. In winter and spring, a core group, led by the Faculty Associate and a new assistant professor of history, followed up on a faculty inventory of skills and knowledge that campus members wanted to develop or were willing to share. Practicums on classroom techniques and advising met during April and May. The nursing faculty held a one-day workshop on the use of simulations with Bill Bergquist as consultant. A two-session workshop for secretaries also was held, as was a May workshop on learning skills for students. Faculty were recruited for three major off-campus development workshops.

The IGI responses had indicated students felt that governance was not sufficiently democratic. A January incident confirmed that feeling. Early in the fall, the student government had communicated to administrators a student complaint that one of the college parking lots was too narrow and therefore unsafe for emergency vehicle passage. City officials confirmed that the area was in violation of safety laws, claimed the campus newspaper. But, the newspaper reported, "the underlying issue which eventually led the Student Senate to call a strike was that of repeated frustration of student efforts to communicate with or get a response from the administration" over a six month period. It was a brief demonstration by several hundred students, but it did succeed in establishing a special Task Force, headed by students, which could examine important issues and report its concerns directly to the Trustees. Students later said that administrative indifference came from the top, that the president was not very open or responsive to student concerns. The president, in turn, noted that "Not once did any student directly report this grievance to me." The blame, according to both parties, lay with the other. The president did, however, support establishment of the special Task Force.

I visited Hartwick in late February to meet with CIR, to observe the faculty meeting on objectives and requirements and to learn from persons active in renewal activities their perceptions of the current educational and organizational health of the college.

First, most interviewees said they could see little change in educational effectiveness or process. Most classes were being conducted much as they had been in the past. Students said many of their professors still read out of the text and provided little challenge or relevance to student lives. Many faculty members were hard to find outside of class. Students themselves appeared to most interviewees to be rather passive, of average ability, a fairly unmotivated bunch on the whole. There were, however, repeated mentions of three increased demands, increased needs to change this situation. First, some students were insisting that they get better teaching, more career preparation and more personal and intellectual excitement for their rising tuition. A faculty member noted, "Students are putting the pressure on faculty, and faculty feel it." Second, faculty members who had become involved in CIR, the IGI study or faculty development said they were much more concerned about students and about effective teaching than they had been, and they wanted to help the school improve in these regards. As one said, "Teachers, including me, were talking to the walls. We thought we were hired to teach a subject, not a student." Third, pressure was beginning to come from faculty members

The IGI responses had indicated students felt that governance was not sufficiently democratic. A January incident confirmed that feeling.

121

"Teachers, including me, were talking to the walls. We thought we were hired to teach a subject, not a student."

not involved in CIR or faculty development but known to be concerned about academic standards and traditional education. They wanted to tighten up on what they saw to be an "anything goes" approach to education. In general, these interviews confirm the 1974 survey data. Not much had changed educationally in recent years, but such new activities as faculty development and self-study, along with the economic pinch, had raised a need to improve. There still appeared to be considerable disagreement about how to do this, with one influential group of long-term professors wanting to tighten standards and trim such non-traditional learning experiences as off-campus study (which was indeed being trimmed) faced by an increasing group of faculty and students wanting more flexible learning built on student needs and interests. The growing size and willingness of the second group to act was the most recent change.

Interviewees consistently found 1974-75 more relaxed and open in regards to college administration and governance. The acting dean and the new chairperson of the faculty both exuded a relaxed, humorful informality and a respect for a wide range of students and faculty. Budget information seemed more accessible, and some faculty felt the president was displaying stronger leadership. Faculty meetings were less tense, more open and more interactive as persons involved in faculty development three times used small group structures to generate open discussion in full faculty meetings. But several needs were emphasized by most interviewees. One was a need to restructure governance in order to reduce confusion, overlapping responsibilities and waste of time. Several faculty members of top faculty committees also saw the need to put administrators on such committees as Budget and Salary and Faculty Council, and to merge those two groups, because decisions required both faculty and administrative input and both financial and educational information. Some faculty members and administrators saw this concern, and recent faculty approval for putting an administrator (the new vice president for planning and development) on the planning council, as a sign that the all-college governance system sought by "collegium" sponsors was occurring "through the back door." Most interviewees were well aware, after the student demonstration, that students felt excluded from decision-making, and most agreed that part of the problem was that, in their perception, the president and a few influential senior faculty regarded students as transients who were not sufficiently responsible, accountable or knowledgeable to take a strong role in college decisions. Others felt part of the problem was an extremely complex and confusing reporting relationship of student government to faculty and administration. They were seeking to develop a streamlined student affairs governance model that also would be college wide in membership and would not report to faculty standing committees. Finally, there was much speculation about who the new vice president for academic affairs (the dean) would be. The only woman in the running had very favorably impressed interviewees as bright, personable, of strong academic standards but open to innovation. She seemed to me the odds on favorite, and she did turn out to be selected as the new dean.

There were several consistent interview responses regarding the

Faculty meetings were less tense, more open and more interactive as persons involved in faculty development three times used small group structures to generate open discussion in full faculty meetings.

122

planning council's proposal to alter educational objectives and graduation requirements. First, those directly involved felt that the process of involving subgroups and slowly building a proposal out of their reactions was far superior to the old process by which a few "wise men" would go off and write a polished proposal which would quickly be rejected. Second, most interviewees felt that the proposal itself was a "lame revolution" on paper. If it were to result in significant educational improvement, it would be because of extensive follow-through in operationalizing objectives, training faculty as educational advisors and competency teachers, and changing the reward system to favor those who successfully implement the objectives. Most interviewees were skeptical that such implementation would occur. Departmentally-oriented teachers, and others, divided on what they saw to be the proposal's problems. Because it allowed for the demonstration of competency outside the course-class structure, some senior faculty members said it was too loose and would allow students to avoid what is difficult. Because departments would be the main evaluation units, several persons interested in interdisciplinary or experiential learning felt the proposal was too restrictive and would result in departmental competition for heavy major concentrations.

Members of the committee on institutional research reported that the organization and leadership of the coordinator of institutional research and the strong leadership of the nursing chairperson, plus the frustration of three years' talk without much action, had made CIR a much more efficient and active force in 1974-75 than in the past. The sub-groups on freshman year, the faculty workload, faculty-administrative evaluation and student satisfaction were hard at work. The freshman year group would succeed in launching about ten seminars with faculty volunteers, and the evaluation group was developing an instrument for fall use. Most interviewees said they had found the IGI helpful in raising their own concern for intellectual and personal development of students and the need for a stronger sense of community in the college. Most were uncertain, however, if either the task groups or the IGI would pay off in college improvement. Interviewees did say CIR had gone through a major shift in strategy from relying heavily on external experts and studying innovations elsewhere to a focus on internal ownership of a collaborative problem-solving process using a continuing relationship with a couple of consultants, such as Bill Bergquist and myself, instead of one-shot "big name" experts. Most interviewees did not feel, however, that internal research was yet being gathered or disseminated in an effective way. The Faculty Associate was helping, but reliance on systematic information was not yet a regular way of proceeding at Hartwick.

The student newspaper continued to show increased attention to college issues. The February 27 edition filled most of its front page with an interview of the student representative to the planning council. He discussed the objectives/requirements proposal as something that "will not involve any great change in course offerings or requirements, but will mainly create increased student-faculty relationships" because of the greater possibility for working out one's own degree program with faculty advice and ongoing counsel. The February 27 issue also had a report on

If it were to result in significant educational improvement, it would be because of extensive follow-through in operationalizing objectives, training faculty as educational advisors and competency teachers, and changing the reward system to favor those who successfully implement the objectives.

123

the student satisfaction task force, the vice presidential search committee, the off-campus program and the special Task Force's recommendations on the parking lot problem. Also, a letter to the editor expressed student discontent about being heard in decisions, this time in relation to the president's comment that a proposed new business administration major favored by students (as demonstrated in student IGI responses) might not be unique enough "to draw students to us instead of these other colleges." The letter-writer concluded, "This seems to be the way things have been going, doesn't it. Students, whom the college has done so much to attract, quickly become aware that, because they will only be at Hartwick for four years, their opinions on all but trivial or ephemeral matters, count as not much more than a minor nuisance." The student advocated a business major distinctively designed "as part of a liberal arts education" but ended with some skepticism. "So let's say this is not a complaint, but a warning: Hartwick seems to me to have a future full of eager applicants, disillusioned students and unenthusiastic alumni."

If, however, the many activities of CIR, the planning council and faculty development continued, this student's sad prophecy may prove wrong. As the 1974-75 academic year drew to a close, there lay ahead the promise of formal objectives and requirements encouraging flexible and student-oriented education, an elaborate and highly effective professional development program to help implement those objectives, new freshman seminars and course/teaching evaluations, increased capacity for and use of internal research, a closely linked set of academic renewal structures, a solid core of committed and increasingly skilled leaders and an apparently dynamic new dean entering with faculty blessing. The president's strategy of catalyzing renewal but leaving it up to the faculty was slow in jelling, and five years after he began the outcome still was in doubt. But at least this observer felt there was plenty of evidence to support optimism if the momentum could be maintained.[6]

124

There was plenty of evidence to support optimism if the momentum could be maintained.

COMMENTARY

Hartwick College, over a hundred faculty members and fifteen hundred students perched on a hill in central New York, entered the 1970's on the impetus of recent expansion of buildings and academic departments. Little in the way of non-traditional education was practiced or much respected. Enter a new president, deeply involved in innovative education himself and convinced by available evidence of educational, economic and political trends that the usual college fare practiced with no more than the usual skill would not permit the college a long and distinctive place in higher education. Like the South Carolina president with his connections to external information related to undergraduate education, the Hartwick president took quite a different tack. Instead of using entrepreneurial skills and bureaucratic authority to launch a variety of experiments, he catalyzed action by speeches and the establishment of a Research and Development committee and office, then waited for faculty to assume ownership themselves of institutional renewal. It was basically a Problem-Solving approach, although the president was not trained in facilitating such a process and had no one on the staff or in consulting roles who was an experienced problem-solving consultant or group facilitator.

Without such guidance, a large and politically representative group floundered for nearly two years. Its head was a vice president whose main role was to link the group to external resources and to draft action proposals. Unfortunately, his linking did not follow Social Interaction guidelines. Instead of continuing personal contact between opinion leaders and highly credible resources in their eyes, he relied on the written word about non-traditional institutions and practices and on brief, one-shot visits by non-traditional spokespersons. These activities stimulated the small group already interested in academic reform, but it at best missed and at worst irritated more traditional faculty leaders. In addition, his proposals and action plans tended to be complex packages incompatible with existing structures or practices and developed in insolation from the larger group.

When the president began his tenure, few campus members shared his strong concern that serious academic renewal may be necessary. Data suggested a fair degree of satisfaction with things as they were. He perhaps could have used his authority to dictate reforms, but faculty commitment would not have been present. So he waited, encouraging innnovations and protecting innovators but not taking major initiatives himself. Slowly, concerned leaders among the faculty began to emerge. Their involvement in the Strategies project and the College Center of the Finger Lakes faculty development project gave them information and skills which they employed to make the college's problem-solving process more effective. The new Committee on Institutional Research changed from a politically representative stalemate to a voluntary group of persons committed to study and improve education in the college. It shifted to longer meetings and small task forces in order to move past general speech-making to collaborative action. It left broad, unfocused discussions and took up structured agenda which attempted specific, manageable projects one at a time. Some of its leaders and others took the occasion of a serious faculty-administration rift to initiate a planning council which, once reduced, simplified and made compatible with faculty governance (as Social Interaction theory emphasizes), was approved. Instead of the one-shot non-traditional stars, continuing relationships with a few consultants expert in the problem-solving process were established. Faculty members were given release time to lead institutional research and professional development instead of assigning an executive administrator those tasks. Certain faculty leaders who strongly favored more traditional models used high standing governance positions and back-room politicking to block renewal efforts, but they were increasingly countered by highly respected leaders like the biology chairperson who used such new renewal structures as the Committee on Institutional Research, the Planning Council and the Chairman of the Faculty to push a clarification of college mission and a vigorous pursuit of more effective teaching and learning practices.

After four years effort to improve both educational and organizational health, educational practices themselves had not changed on the whole. A few pilot projects had been launched and several faculty

125

members were trying new techniques in teaching, but the overall educational experience of most students did not appear much different in 1974 than it did in 1972. Still, complacency had been replaced by wide concern. Faculty leaders had emerged. Renewal structures had been established. Goals had been clarified. Task groups were beginning. A new and supported academic dean had entered the scene. In short, organizational ability and desire to renew significantly the institution had changed considerably.

As was the case at South Carolina, no one planned change model does justice to the Hartwick process.

As was the case at South Carolina, no one planned change model does justice to the Hartwick process. The Problem-Solving strategy was central: catalytic leadership, participant collaboration and ownership in clarifying need and building solutions, use of external consultants to help the problem-solving process rather than to give answers, shift of that facilitating skill and activity on to campus leaders themselves, use of in-depth meetings or workshops and task groups. And that approach did appear to be paying off. But Social Interaction also explains much of what happened. The president got his ideas from external contacts. Consultants and articles and conference attendance did stimulate other interested campus members to desire change. It was the re-constitution of the Research and Planning group into a combination of innovators and open opinion leaders that got this body off dead center. It was a shift to less complex, more easily divisible and more compatible action plans which seemed to increase support for such innovations as freshman advising and the planning council.

126

At the same time, politics and power was much of the ball game. The president used his bureaucratic authority to initiate and protect innovative activities, if not to impose solutions on the college. Resistant faculty members used the standing committees of faculty governance and coalition formation among sub-groups of the faculty assembly to block change proposals, while renewal leaders built their own renewal structures. Finally, Research and Development was apparent in several ways. The Committee on Institutional Research eventually moved toward using task forces to research and develop change proposals. The Planning Council sought to organize college development along rational planning lines. The council, institutional research, freshman advising, competency evaluation, faculty development, individualized degree programs and the living-learning program, are just a few local developments that in part were adaptations of external models—"demonstrations" if you will. Hartwick members had a strong need to do their own research and build their own solutions. They resisted attempts to get them simply to adopt Sarah Lawrence or Goddard or University Without Walls or even University of Michigan answers to their concerns. Still, their solutions were more adaptations than inventions.

Still, their solutions were more adaptations than inventions.

We rarely get a chance to follow closely planned change process in both a large state university and a liberal arts college. Two cases, however, do not build a theory. Despite common educational and organizational problems (low student motivation, low faculty-student interaction, low intellectual and personal development, low sense of collaborative community), even these two settings may be too dissimilar from each other and from your or my institution to permit generalization. I turn, therefore, to another liberal arts college, smaller than Hartwick but very similar in its starting point: administrative concern that the college had to develop a distinctive mission and effectiveness in order to serve successfully its students and meet the increasing competition.

127

6 Seeking a Unique Identity: Quaker Academic College

There are hundreds of small liberal arts colleges tucked away in rural America. Like suburban houses, most of them are expensive and hard to tell apart. As inflation, looming recession and the decline of eighteen to twenty-two year olds became factors in public postsecondary education, some of these colleges folded. Others, called (not very kindly) "invisible colleges" by Alexander Astin,[1] strove to develop a visibly unique identity which would attract students. This is the story of how one such college sought in the early 1970's not only visibility but also distinction through academic self-renewal.

Quaker Academic College (a pseudonym) is located in a small midwestern town. In 1970 its core curriculum was traditional liberal arts fare taught for the most part in traditional ways. It was distinctive, however, for sizable programs in agriculture, industrial arts and education, all of which reflected its Quaker work tradition. Its catalog and some of its faculty and students also were distinctive for their attention to Quaker concerns: social issues and service, non-violence, internationalism, "community in diversity" and governance attempts to use Quaker consensus (or sense of the meeting) for important issues. Strategies staff especially enjoyed visiting Quaker Academic, for faculty there seemed particularly capable and interesting. We frequently commented that the place seemed to us much more intellectually lively than its invisibility suggested.

In 1971, the major academic innovation at Quaker Academic was "Man in Focus," an interdisciplinary freshman program centered on contemporary social problems. Its initiation lay in a former president's suggestion in the early 1960's that the college take the reports of the Eisenhower commission on "Goals for American Studies" as themes for student-faculty discussions and papers worth one academic credit. Interviewees noted that this idea found sympathy among faculty oriented toward the Quaker tradition of social concern. External stimulus, support and initiative at the top and congruence with institutional and individual values: that is a familiar formula for change to us by now.

But, recalls the director of institutional research, this program began to "lose steam" in the late 1960's. At the same time, a new breed of student was enrolling in the college. Instead of local, rural, fairly conservative students, they were, according to the director,

> *more upper class [and] better prepared, . . . who came to Quaker Academic with more social concern and social consciousness, students who had quite good high school backgrounds. They were finding the freshman year tedious and repetitive. They wanted*

129

External stimulus, support and initiative at the top and congruence with institutional and individual values: that is a familiar formula for change to us by now.

*something more exciting and interesting than having to sit through
courses similar to the ones they had in high school.*

The president again took the initiative to meet this need by setting up in
1967 an "Instructional Improvement Committee" with the director of
research as chairperson. That group developed and implemented "Current Issues Seminars" on the "American College," the "Inner City" and
"America's Role in Vietnam." In 1969, a greater influx of socially concerned students followed publicity about a Peace Corps program focused
on agricultural development. Unfortunately, the influx came from upper
middle class students with suburban or urban backgrounds instead of the
farm kids sought by the Peace Corps. The program was cancelled in
August, too late for many enrollees to go elsewhere. The college would
have to find another way to meet these students' interests. One response
was to introduce an independent study option for B average students.

In 1968, a new provost came to the college. For several years he had
been involved at Rensselaer Polytechnic Institute in providing "a broad
context for people who are going into a professional field," and he saw a
similar problem in relating liberal arts to the industrial arts, education
and agriculture programs at Quaker Academic. He recalls that, "I guess I
came in thinking that innovation would be a good idea." Rather than
capitalizing on his "honeymoon" period to install a flurry of changes,
however, he invited all faculty members to join him periodically in his
home to discuss innovation. "Certain people who had innovative ideas
promptly showed up," he remembers. But as Social Interaction research
indicates, less innovative folk would need more reason than the provost's
invitation. The provost's second initiative was to begin a program of
institutional research on student characteristics.

130

> *I was aware of a tremendously varied student body and I knew
> practically nothing about them. I don't have any expertise in it, but
> I said one of the things we ought to do is to get a better picture of
> our own students and to find out as well as we can what is
> happening to them. At RPI we had used the* College Student
> Questionnaire, *and I know Marty Trow who had worked on
> that, so I got a little money to try the CSQ out with a bunch of
> students in the spring of '69 and was astonished when the profiles
> came in to realize that we were different from national norms, or
> small college norms, or anything else in three ways. We had a much
> more liberal student body, a much more socially concerned and a
> much less grade-motivated. . . . That kind of led me to think that,
> besides the problem I had seen all along, of getting the vocational
> student to be more aware of the context in which he was going to
> operate, I sort of was beginning to see the other half of the coin
> which was to get the liberal, socially-concerned student to the point
> where he was willing to work hard at particular bodies of knowl-
> edge in order to be able to do something.*

This diagnosis of needs, both by survey and by discussion in his home, led
the provost, along with the director of research, a Quaker history professor
long active in the peace movement, and a young assistant professor of
sociology, to propose to the faculty in the spring of 1969 a pilot program

for freshmen. It would include a "Survey of Contemporary Problems" taught by the historian, the sociologist and the director of research (an English professor) in the fall, something similar to the "Current Issues Seminars" in the winter, a special section of freshman English called "The Human Condition" taught by the provost and, in the spring, an independent research project on a contemporary problem. The faculty approved this package as a small pilot program for fifty students. Interviewees recall very little argument over the program. It was small and only a pilot, it would be taught by volunteers who were respected intellectually and professionally, it was apparently responsive to a student need, most of its components already existed and its social problem focus was rooted in the school's Quaker tradition. All the Social Interaction criteria were met. Also, by adapting freshman English and "Introduction to Government" requirements and by using sabbaticals or other temporary teaching assignments, it could be implemented without special cost or burden on faculty load.

Implementation was not so easy. The next four years would be marked at Quaker Academic by attempts to learn how to teach this interdisciplinary, problem-centered program and how to broaden its impact within the college. The first implementation problem was a lecture survey of world problems fed rapid-fire to fifty highly independent students. That was not sensational pedagogy. Students complained that the course was confusing, superficial and impersonal. Worse, all those world problems all at once was downright depressing. The winter seminars and spring independent projects went well enough, however, that the director of research summarized, "Overall, we thought it was a pretty good start."

Two strategies were employed to bolster the program. The director of research sought and won an American Council on Education administrative internship which he used to study interdisciplinary freshman programs at Hiram and Beloit Colleges. Thus, at least one implementor gained first hand acquaintance with other models of the kind of program he was attempting. The second strategy was the provost's decision to seek external funding for an expanded program. He approached the National Endowment for the Humanities (NEH) with the argument that Man in Focus, as he called the new program, was just the ticket for "critical and dissatisfied young people":

> Aware of the urgency of contemporary problems, critical of hypocrisy and impatient with the patience of the academic world, they have little interest in shaping themselves to fit into prepared slots in the "system," little concern about their own economic futures, or about the academic mechanism—grades, credits, and degrees—which are traditionally used both to motivate and to measure.
>
> Many of them, however, are among the ablest and most sensitive of their generation. Yet they stand a fair chance of becoming among the least effective also, unless they can focus their concerns, acquire the hard disciplines of problem-solving, logical analysis, organization, and communication, and learn to combine flexibility with concern, imagination with information.

As one student put it, the goal was to develop "pragmatic idealists." This

The next four years would be marked at Quaker Academic by attempts to learn how to teach this interdisciplinary, problem-centered program and how to broaden its impact within the college.

131

As one student put it, the goal was to develop "pragmatic idealists."

outcome would be accomplished by expanding Man in Focus to include half the freshman class by fall, 1973; by extending it into the upperclass years not only through the existing Field Term and Current Issues Seminars but by establishing special projects or "institutes" focused on specific social problems; and by integrating other faculty members and other disciplines into interdisciplinary functioning. Program evaluation would test how effectively problem-solving skills and knowledge were integrated with social concern.

While awaiting word from NEH, the few innovative volunteers went ahead with the second year of their small program, this time with seventy-five students. Admissions data revealed that these students were somewhat higher achievers than the first group. But they still complained about the shotgun survey of world problems. They added that when they weren't being lectured at by faculty, they were being harangued by "bullshit artists" among their fellow students. The criticism did not overwhelm the program, however, and in March of 1971, NEH came through with a $300,000, three year grant. Money was to be used to subsidize participant salaries, conduct summer training institutes for faculty and provide funds for field work, audio visual equipment, consultants and guest faculty.

The provost was not done scaring up external resources. He managed to get a Man in Focus faculty team accepted into the summer, 1971, Danforth workshop on liberal education. There, the group of initial innovators and a few new volunteers planned curriculum and faculty development activities for the 1971-72 program. It would appear that Man in Focus was well-endowed and well-prepared for effective implementation. There were, however, problems.

One implementation problem was that the program was particularly owned by the provost and the director of research. The former was the person seeking "pragmatic idealists," and he would have a hard time throughout the program trying to get faculty to develop problem-solving skills in the "turned off girl from Scarsdale" attracted by the contemporary problem focus. The director of research, in turn, did not involve participating faculty in ways very satisfactory to some of them. As one observed,

> I think he very much took the leadership role there, somewhat to the dismay of those of us involved who would have liked more to say about what it became. As I recall, the first year, it was pretty much determined what the content of it was, what the books were. He took suggestions, but it was pretty clear he was deciding. The evaluation of it was pretty much up to him. I think a lot of good has come out of it too, but I think a source of frustration has been that it has been difficult to get ideas to him. He would be dismayed to hear me say that because I think he looks at himself as being very open. But he has a very definite idea of what he wants to do, and sometimes your ideas get translated into what he wants to do.

The director of research saw the same issue from a different perspective:

> Well, I think committees are okay, but it seems to me that, particularly in something innovative, there's a problem in how you

"I think he looks at himself as being very open. But he has a very definite idea of what he wants to do, and sometimes your ideas get translated into what he wants to do."

do it. I think there's a gestation period, sometimes it's informal—I prefer that—a spontaneous way of developing things rather than meetings where an idea gets compromised away until it's something no one is strongly against and really doesn't mean anything anymore. Then I just forget it.

He did not see his avoidance of committee process as a limitation on the faculty's ability to have a say in the program: "We [the provost and he] sort of set up a structure within which you could operate. But then faculty have gone ahead and made their own plans and operated within that in their own ways with quite a bit of freedom and flexibility."

One problem with his approach, according to interviewees, was that Man in Focus faculty did not hold the regular working sessions called for by the Danforth workshop group in order to develop team teaching, to learn how to create practical idealists, to learn from consultants, to help each other and to strengthen program evaluation and feedback. They did hold three-week summer workshops supported by the NEH grant, but these sessions focused primarily on redesigning the program so as to have more student involvement in the fall, not on training faculty to help idealists become problem-solvers. It was decided that five separate groups—on population, pollution, urban problems, war and peace, and educational reform—would replace the team-taught survey. That move split up the team even more but did reduce student criticism the following fall. A new student complaint, however, was that as lecturing decreased and discussion increased, the bullshit index also rose. If such foreign and difficult tasks as developing hard-nosed problem-solving skills in turned-off idealists were to happen, it would appear that the provost and director of research would have to find more effective ways to involve faculty.

The provost continued to find yet more external resources. Through contacts with the dean of a nearby college, he heard about the Strategies for Change and Knowledge Utilization Project. That sounded to him like an excellent opportunity to gain expert consultation and to strengthen the data-gathering on students to which he had been committed for some time. He and the director of research attended the first Strategies workshop in October, 1971. Other participants accepted them in place of Antioch College, which had withdrawn at the last minute. The NEH funds would be used to finance the workshop and consultant expenses for Quaker Academic's "intensive" participation. The first Strategies intervention was a visit to the college by the central staff in January, 1972. Arthur Chickering was asked by the provost to address the faculty at that time regarding ways to develop problem-solving skills in students. Chickering introduced the notion of contract learning, which he was busy implementing in the first year of Empire State College. That seed, we will see, fell on fertile ground.

During 1971-72 the major academic committee at Quaker Academic, called the Educational Policies Council, was busy discussing what knowledge and skills the college should emphasize in its curriculum, teaching and evaluation. The immediate impetus for these discussions was the English department's proposal that the freshman English requirement be dropped. As Cohen and March observe, into that decision event ("gar-

133

Chickering introduced the notion of contract learning, which he was busy implementing in the first year of Empire State College. That seed, we will see, fell on fertile ground.

bage can") was being dropped everyone's agenda for the college.[2] The provost himself was encouraging the idea of open curriculum and flexible calendar. He presented to the EPC Whitman College's open program, which stressed not requirements but ten guidelines concerning "the sorts of knowledge and skill which a college graduate should have" (competencies if you will). Shortly after Chickering's visit, a young philosophy professor new to the college but already known to be very student-oriented presented to the EPC (of which he was a member) a proposal for a completely individualized system based on learning contracts written by each student under supervision of a faculty advisor (essentially the Empire State model). At the same time, the biology professor who taught the Man in Focus course on pollution (and who also was a member of EPC) proposed that the college have only one requirement: successful completion of 124 credit hours. Individual programs would be worked out by the student and his department or advisor. The major difference in the proposals was that the philosophy professor envisioned a complex advising role and a variety of learning experiences besides faculty-designed courses. The biology professor was talking about regular courses. The minutes of the meeting suggest the committee's reaction: "Questions raised were the practicality of the [philosophy professor's] proposal and the problems involved with the transition period from our present system to the new system. [The biology professor's] proposal was suggested as a possible intermediate step. Other questions involved getting student opinion and when to present the proposal to the faculty."

On April 7, 1972, the EPC introduced into a full faculty meeting three proposals for changing requirements. The chairperson of the committee, the same assistant professor of sociology who helped launch Man in Focus, reported that discussions of educational philosophy and objectives had been triggered in the EPC by the English department's proposal to drop freshman English. That had led to a full-blown discussion of what should be learned and, perhaps therefore, required to accomplish the Quaker objective of "bringing a person to the teacher within." The three proposals the committee was presenting (one to shift departmental to divisional requirements, one for the 124 credit hour requirement only, one for contract learning) "are to be regarded as attempts to functionalize a philosophy rather than as concrete proposals."

Faculty response was: "let's talk about the philosophy before considering the proposals." Debate then waged between those who felt the college and the faculty must set requirements for students, largely because faculty know more about it and do not have time to advise extensively each student, and those who felt that students needed to be helped to design and take charge of their own education so that it fits their individual needs and helps them become independent learners. In short, they debated means, not desired outcomes. The provost, as clerk of the meeting, observed after considerable discussion "that the faculty was deeply divided and discussion would have to continue further." He adjourned the meeting "with promises of further discussion in the near future." A faculty observer reported to the Strategies staff that the faculty's reception of the contract and no specified requirements proposal was "stormy," "but

134

Faculty response was: "let's talk about the philosophy before considering the proposals."

apparently the [EPC] intends to persist in proposing a type of contract system without any specific requirement." It would appear that the committee, having several innovators in its midst and having taken ideas from external sources and discussed them together for several months, had left the rest of the faculty somewhat behind instead of seeking ways to share its learning and thinking as it went along. In order to find out just what the faculty did want, an associate professor of English who sat on the EPC proposed that "each teaching faculty member be sent a questionnaire to determine whether the faculty in general are satisfied with the present core requirements."

Meanwhile, the provost was up to his old tricks. He had met and enjoyed Royce (Tim) Pitkin at a Strategies workshop; Pitkin was founder and long-term president of Goddard College. The provost brought him to Quaker Academic with NEH money in order to speak to persons developing an upperclass "Peace Institute" for Man in Focus; but he also asked Tim to describe Goddard College education to the EPC. Several interviewees on that committee remarked later that Pitkin had great impact on the group because he had a rich understanding of educational philosophy, spoke of student learning experiences in vivid detail and was "hard-boiled and practical" about it all.

Two days after Pitkin's visit, on April 26, 1972, the faculty met again to discuss requirements. The committee's survey showed that only one respondent liked the requirements as they were. Eighteen wanted some change, while twenty-three felt there should be "major discussion." The provost "expressed a need for the faculty to come to grips with the question of the core requirements and questioned how to proceed." The EPC chairperson said she felt the major issue dividing the faculty was "who should be responsible for the student's program—the student or the faculty?" The committee was criticized for not bringing other faculty into the discussion of core requirements earlier. Some said formal requirements would provide needed structure, ensure adequate distribution of study and maintain high standards. The assistant professor of philosophy and the chairperson of education (another new and innovative member of the college), said these features could be as well or better fulfilled on an individualized basis. The provost, again after some debate, said further discussion was warranted. He suggested that EPC hold open meetings on the topic. One faculty member felt that would mean one more meeting a week "for every responsible faculty member." Another suggested that EPC, which now seemed to favor this contract and open curriculum model, "perhaps needed to more accurately reflect the faculty cross-section of opinion." The EPC chairperson responded that the group originally represented "many differing views, but through discussion and working together had grown together." Another faculty member asked whether the underlying philosophy should be discussed but the committee member from English reiterated an earlier point that it was more feasible to react to a proposal than to resolve philosophic differences in the abstract. Finally, the financial officer pointed out that the 1973-74 catalogue would be published next summer, so some decision would have to be made soon if it were to be incorporated in that volume. The provost

Pitkin had great impact on the group because he had a rich understanding of educational philosophy, spoke of student learning experiences in vivid detail and was "hard-boiled and practical" about it all.

135

then said the next step should be to consider one proposal. Again, this meeting revealed the gap between the committee, which had been working on these issues for months, and the rest of the faculty, which had not been persuaded of the need or its solution.

Two common problems in faculty governance appeared in the faculty's critique. First, although EPC was criticized for not involving faculty earlier, some faculty now did not want to consume any more time in meetings. "Involve us but don't take our time" is one enigma of faculty governance. Second, when a group, through study and discussion, ended up with views at odds with people who had not gone through that educational experience, it was criticized as unrepresentative. Such a view seems a rather anti-educational perspective on the duties of a committee.

On May 1, 1972, the EPC did as the faculty asked and came up with one proposal, 124 hours and a major concentration, with distribution requirements worked out between each student and an advisor or group of advisors. The associate professor of English proposed that "serious consideration" should be given to a program similar to Goddard's as outlined by Tim Pitkin, perhaps as a small experiment for the next year. He was assigned with the assistant professor of philosophy and a professor of chemistry to draft an honors program along those lines. On May 10, the faculty met again to consider EPC's proposal. The "honors" or student-designed option also entered the discussion. After much debate, the provost again said he saw no resolution in sight. Because June 1 was the catalog deadline, and vacations were near at hand, he recommended that discussion of requirements should be postponed until the next fall.

At the May 15 EPC meeting, a former student, now an admissions counselor at Western College, described that institution's new modular program, which functioned without requirements, departments, faculty ranks or letter grades but with formal courses as the primary educational experience. The representative said students had so far registered high interest in the approach and were taking quite traditional courses of study. She emphasized the relationship between faculty tutor and student as the key to program success. The provost then

> suggested that the following points be the topic of discussion at the faculty meeting Wednesday: (1) the required aspect of the core be eliminated as of September 1, 1972, (2) the distribution requirement be retained, (3) an ad hoc committee be established to assist students and advisors with distribution guidelines, and (4) the graduation requirements of 124 hours, 40 upper division hours and 30-40 hours in a major field be retained, and the minor or second major be eliminated.

The committee approved this suggestion.

But the May 17 faculty meeting had a full agenda concerning grading, academic appeals and pay for students to teach courses. Subsequent EPC and faculty meetings were preoccupied with a proposal from Sociology to allow one-third of the courses in that major to be taken pass/fail. Core requirements were not formally considered again until fall, 1972.

"Involve us but don't take our time" is one enigma of faculty governance.

EXTERNAL DIAGNOSIS OF QUAKER ACADEMIC'S NEEDS

During 1971-72, while Man in Focus was being implemented and core requirements were being examined, the Strategies staff was gathering data on the educational and organizational health of the college. In late July of 1972, the provost, director of research and two English professors studied the data at the Saratoga Springs workshop. They saw on the IFI that Quaker Academic was over the seventy-fifth percentile nationally in academic "Freedom," in "Human Diversity," in "Concern for Undergraduate Education," in "Democratic Governance," in "Concern for Innovation" and in "Institutional Esprit." Attention to "Self-Study and Planning" was also high, at the sixty-fifth percentile. That is a different profile for innovation than Hartwick's. In 1972 both enjoyed high concern for undergraduates and for innovation, some attention to planning and strong faculty-administrative esprit. But Quaker Academic was much higher than Hartwick in diversity and very strong in academic freedom, as one would expect of a Quaker college. That could make change more difficult, for diverse campus members would have diverse views on any proposal, and political norms would grant them much involvement in decisions and great autonomy to implement changes as they wished. Strategies for change, therefore, would have to focus particularly on generating personal concern for needs, interest in solutions and commitment to implementation among individual faculty members.

Educational data showed somewhat traditional teaching roles and student influence, with a bit more attention to listening and memorizing than other educational activities, but there was more variety in teaching approaches at Quaker Academic than was evident at most other Strategies institutions. Faculty-student contacts were infrequent and faculty impacts on student growth were at best moderate, according to students, but the picture was no worse than elsewhere. The director of research found the profile of student experiences fairly attractive. The English professors, however, commented particularly on the interview data, a more familiar kind of evidence to them than survey statistics. And that information did suggest several problems. Faculty members reported that Quaker consensus was a desirable governance model in the abstract, but in practice it could drag out proceedings and could pressure people to go along with an expressed sense of the meeting in order to avoid being a "poor sport" or extending debate even longer. "It stifles some real dissent" and "there is a wearing down process" were representative comments. Another problem was the school's $500,000 deficit and increasing difficulty in recruiting students. The college was losing many of the Eastern liberal students who had come in recent years. There were differing opinions regarding how to stabilize enrollment and attract other income, but everyone agreed that here was a problem needing rapid solution. Because the college had rapidly grown a few years before, there was a feeling that factionalism was increasing and the old traditions or old constituencies were being forgotten. Senior faculty were perceived to be taking a "back seat" concerning recent change efforts. But "they are still a very powerful faction." The influx of the Eastern students and a sizable group of Blacks raised concern that too much diversity may be detrimen-

That could make change more difficult, for diverse campus members would have diverse views on any proposal, and political norms would grant them much involvement in decisions and great autonomy to implement changes as they wished.

137

"Common agreement on values hold us together, but I'm not sure what that whole something is."

138

The president declared his educational agenda for the college.

tal: "I'm not sure at all you can have in a small community a great variety of cultures coming in conflict with each other and still survive. Common agreement on values hold us together, but I'm not sure what that whole something is."

Strategies staff had interviewed faculty in January of 1972 to learn their views about Man in Focus, and those perspectives also were available in July. Most said it was a valuable program, but several criticisms were consistently expressed. One worry was that it was creating a "two track college," one for bright Eastern seaboard kids and the prominent faculty who taught in the program, the other for the "more average ones." Another concern was that instead of effective interdisciplinary team teaching, Man in Focus sounded "as if it was going to be a general mishmash discussing in a kind of bullsession fashion the issues to be attacked." Rigorous discipline appeared lacking. Third, faculty members, including some Man in Focus faculty, did not feel that problems were tackled in a truly interdisciplinary fashion. As one noted, "I still feel uncomfortable to talk about areas outside my domain," and no concentrated training for interdisciplinary teaching occurred. The provost himself was disappointed that there was not much attention to development of practical knowledge and problem-solving skills. Courses for the most part consisted of readings, discussions and papers. Field work or simulation involving the solution of real problems was not integral to most Man in Focus courses, with the partial exception of a biology course which examined the pollution of a local creek (but did not actively try to reduce it). The director of research observed that the faculty's considerable freedom had permitted them to avoid seriously tackling the problem of developing practical problem-solving skills in impractical and equally independent students.

The Saratoga team made plans to present the "Self-Study" data to the faculty in a two-day fall retreat. This affair would be joined to a longer series of activities aimed at clarifying institutional mission, with the *Institutional Goals Inventory* as one tool. The director of research would continue developing Man in Focus. As an aid to that activity, another two-week workshop for about fifteen faculty members was conducted in early August. I visited to consult on ways to build problem-solving experiences into Man in Focus courses, but I heard little expression of interest in helping students move beyond the traditional academic emphasis on diagnosing the problems. The workshop focused primarily on curricular planning rather than training for new teaching objectives.

For the past year, impetus for educational change had come from the Educational Policies Council, the legitimate faculty governance group for such activity. The president, new to Quaker Academic in the last year, had been busy working with the College Planning Committee which had been meeting on capital building and renovation in the room right across the hall from EPC. It apparently did not seem odd to these groups to plan programs and facilities separately. The president also had been preoccupied with issues of rules for student conduct, which were liberalized in that year. In his annual report for 1971-72, however, the president declared his educational agenda for the college:

Quaker Academic must find ways of combining flexibility with challenge, of substituting intrinsic motivations for extrinsic ones, of demanding high-level performance in individual courses, while permitting the student greater leeway in designing his overall program. Moving in this direction, Quaker Academic will need to increase the strength of its allied programs in agricultural education and industrial arts, while providing new opportunities for students who are interested in fine arts, communication, administration, community development and political and social action. And it will need to maintain strong work in the disciplines while developing problem-oriented interdisciplinary work and increasing involvement in the world outside the campus.

The provost's concern to train "pragmatic idealists" through contemporary problem-solving and EPC's desire to give students more responsibility for designing their own programs were now joined to a new emphasis on the college's occupational training programs.

The first opportunity in the fall of 1972 for faculty to discuss the college's needs was the October 6 and 7 retreat near Earlham College, another Quaker institution. The provost and president had asked Warren Bryan Martin, a Strategies advisor they had met at the inter-institutional workshops, to keynote the affair. Later interviews with faculty members indicated that this speech made a strong impression: "He talked about the values of the Quaker tradition, and he got the faculty to the point where they wanted to talk about those Quaker values. The faculty really wanted to examine and assimilate these values into the program." Consensus, a caring community, simplicity and such social action as the peace movement were raised as basic commitments the college should foster. But several interviewees felt Martin gave mixed, and confusing, messages. In the morning session, they reported, he stressed the need for innovative approaches to take advantage of the Quaker tradition, to take an experimental approach toward liberal arts and to develop the vocational programs of the college. Then, after talking with faculty, he said in the afternoon (recalled interviewees) that because most faculty seem pretty traditional in their notions about curriculum and teaching, perhaps the bulk of Quaker Academic's program in the next few years should be traditional. Nearly every interviewee felt the end result of Martin's statements was confusion: "He left us confused and distorted"; "very confusing"; "that really confused a lot of people." But it got them talking about what Quaker Academic's future should be. As one "confused" interviewee concluded, "The whole thing ended up being very healthy. It forced us to begin talking. It helped in bringing out the president's paper." Strategies survey data also were presented by the director of research, but interview data surfacing problems were not passed out to faculty.

The "president's paper" was a memorandum distributed to faculty October 31, 1972. The president stated that the paper was not meant to dictate change but instead to stimulate discussion about how the college can become visibly distinctive instead of another of Astin's "invisible colleges." He observed that Quaker Academic currently does best

in the area of what traditionally is characterized as liberal arts instruction (with an interdisciplinary twist), but this is not and is

139

"The whole thing ended up being very healthy. It forced us to begin talking."

not likely to become sufficiently distinguished to insure the clientele. The youth seeking such an education are not growing in numbers as rapidly as are the institutions seeking to meet these needs, and institutions not already possessing reputations of excellence in this highly competitive area are not likely to compete successfully for existing clientele.

He wrote that the college's attention to vocational as well as liberal arts preparation was distinctive. "I maintain that our distinctiveness is rooted in the maintenance and now refocusing of technical skill training. . . . In a nut shell, we are characterized by a desire to equip youth for democratically managing change within this institution as well as in society at large." The president went on to say he supported cultural diversity in clientele, particularly if that diversity becomes educationally productive rather than fractious, and he agreed with Warren Bryan Martin that the college needs to meet students "where they are in terms of needs, life styles and college expectations." He wrote, "A primary program need is exploration of new career possibilities which benefit from the service orientation and training in change management we stress." That "probably" would mean emphasizing the social sciences and applied studies, along with communication. "We cannot operate without considerable breadth in the other divisions, but we do not need comparable depth." He said departments and departmental majors should be re-examined. "Perhaps the interdisciplinary thrust should lead to divisional rather than departmental majors." Also,

The more student-focused, rather than discipline-focused, our programs of study become (e.g. cluster major, field-study and independent study, and our commitment to accepting students where they are in terms of needs and abilities), the more pressure we will come under to tailor faculty-student interaction to the expressed needs of students. . . . What we very much need here at Quaker Academic is more mutual instruction in teaching at the college level.

He ended on student recruitment. He suggested recruiting more selectively to get students who were committed to the college's goals and therefore less likely to drop out. He concluded by saying that better strategies to market the college must be devised.

Accompanying the president's memo was a short description by the provost of three distinctive college student and faculty orientations: "Acad," the traditional focus on intellectual development and success in the academic world; "Vocat," the concern to develop technical competence, to get and handle professional jobs; and "Altern," concerned about social change and personal growth, finding a way out of the *status quo*. He described the differences between colleges whose primary emphasis was one of these orientations, with allusion to Chickering's similar college typology in *Education and Identity*:

The tendencies represented here are, of course, all present in Quaker Academic. We are not Acad, or Vocat, or Altern: but in some sense we are all three—hence the frequent charge that we try to be "all things to all men." A large number of our students, for example, come here looking for Altern. Many of the faculty, on the

"What we very much need here at Quaker Academic is more mutual instruction in teaching at the college level."

other hand, would probably be happiest with Acad. Vocat is taking on new life at the college, but is, to some extent, being modified by Altern.

My own view is that Quaker Academic cannot afford to become pure Acad, Vocat, or Altern. We must continue to be a mixture and to endure the tension which results; but we need a more consciously planned mixture. I also see Altern as a necessary ingredient at the college which shapes and turns the rest. But Altern can, of course, be anything—from St. Johns to Evergreen to Goddard. I have purposely slanted the description toward what appears to be Quaker Academic's version, and I suggest that its particular character is, and probably should be, related to the college's Quaker (especially Service Committee) background.

A new strategy had been launched. Instead of the EPC as the proposer of new formulations for college mission and program, the executive administration was taking the lead. And instead of catalyzing faculty action to identify problems and to build solutions, the president was presenting a fairly specific prescription on college needs and remedies. The summer apparently had made EPC's initiatives old history.

The president and provost discussed their written statements at the November 1, 1972, faculty meeting. They reiterated the emphasis on preparing students for "societal change and improvement," the consistency of this plan and the college's traditions and faculty abilities, the need to develop a new clientele committed to a reasonably coherent educational purpose and the need for more integration across disciplines and continuity across the four undergraduate years. They reminded faculty that proposed changes would not be "a call for de-emphasizing anything, but rather a projection for where additional emphasis (money, etc.) should be placed." The president announced that the memo would be discussed by each academic division. After brief discussion, the faculty agreed to meet again in three weeks to discuss the memo further as a total group. The president stressed in this meeting and in subsequent division meetings that all he asked was that any resulting college direction (1) be responsive to the student market; (2) prepare students for future social roles; (3) build on the institution's traditional values and skills; and (4) be reasonably clear and coherent. He set up a January faculty workshop as the deadline for creating a "Clarification of Distinctiveness."

Many faculty were not cordial to this new approach. A Strategies staff member directly observed the social science division's reception of the president and his memo. Faculty members said they already had various applied programs, but does Admissions know we're for real academically and intellectually? Does the administration know these applied programs exist, for they're not in the catalog! One faculty member said he thought students wanted hard academic work even if they intended to go into applied areas. They want challenge. The president agreed. Faculty went on to say we must get rid of snap courses. The president said one problem now is that current courses just prepare students to fit in, not to effect, social change. The division chairperson said the president was putting the rap on students for the college's problems. There is an awful

A new strategy had been launched.

141

142

lot going on here if you give us adequate money, faculty and students to do it. The president asked why the college doesn't have enough students. The chairman blamed public relations, and another faculty member agreed. Those people should get together with faculty to understand the program. The president said some changes were being made in Admissions, but it would be important to involve faculty in the recruitment process. The provost said when programs had changed, enrollment went up. A faculty member said there were biases in institutional data. The president emphasized that whatever the program, the faculty should stress career opportunities. One faculty member said Man in Focus students had no idea nor much concern about careers, and a business professor said his problem was to bring the liberal arts to students preoccupied with career preparation. One faculty member questioned the assumption in the memo that managing change was a proper focus. The president reiterated that the college's focus on its Quaker Service Committee values, plus the combination of applied and academic preparation, would bring a distinctiveness which would attract and keep students. The observer summarized the meeting: "The main thing which struck me was that there was a good deal of animosity toward this plan, faculty wanting *standards*, and *excellence*, and to *be academic* or rigorous. If you go vocational, it has to be theoretical also, it has to be hard, *demanding*." It also seemed that, although everyone agreed there was an enrollment problem, everyone believed the problem was someone else's fault. The president seemed to faculty to be blaming their curricular organization and teaching. They in turn blamed the administration for ineffectively selling the program. After other divisional meetings like this one, no further movement had been made toward institutional renewal.

The Strategies project made another intervention about this time (January, 1973). It sent back to twenty-six interviewees an "Interim Report" summarizing their views on educational problems and organizational abilities to resolve these problems. One problem still mentioned frequently was that neither Man in Focus nor the college in general had found a way to introduce intellectual challenge and practical skills into the education of "Altern" students. Some faculty members said part of the problem was that Admissions sold an experimental college image, emphasizing Man in Focus and thus attracted intellectually turned-off students. Others, however, felt faculty should learn how to challenge such students more effectively. Student interviewees said the challenge problem was compounded by an anti-intellectual dorm life. Strategies staff stayed in the dorms and found them extremely noisy, not exactly conducive to quiet thought and study but certainly a practical social problem begging solution.

A second problem repeatedly mentioned was labeled in the report "Fragmentation of Campus and Curriculum." Interviewees said that Quaker values, the "Q Factor," were in the catalog but not in campus life. One student said, "You want to hear students laugh? Ask them about the Q Factor. It's a joke!" Interviewees felt there was little consensus about what values and experiences were essential to education at the college. Students said wide gulfs separated three subcultures: "the greeks, the freaks, and the straights." These groups rarely interrelated and had very low tolerance for each other's life styles and values. Blacks seemed to compose a fourth, isolated, subculture. Departmentalism, high faculty turnover and curricular separation of the liberal arts, vocational and Man in Focus programs were said to add to fragmentation. The report summarized:

> No consensus on goals or values, serious gaps between student subgroups, and piecemeal curriculum: these are the main components of interview concern for fragmentation of campus and curriculum.

Additional problems cited by some interviewees were (1) the need for financial economies; (2) the failure of Man in Focus to teach problem-solving; (3) the burden of piling independent study coordination on top of already heavy faculty loads; (4) the need to give students more say in designing their learning experiences; (5) the need to give students fundamental training before taking some Man in Focus courses; and (6) the need to expand Quaker Academic's student market.

As for institutional strengths for solving these problems, the most apparent one was that both faculty and administration are strongly committed to the college and to making its education as effective as possible. A fairly democratic system, honest and capable administrative leaders and high competence within the faculty were also pointed out. Yet, as weaknesses, people felt that institutional problem-solving was not done systematically, that intergroup communication was inadequate and that there just was not enough time available to spend in tedious committee meetings. Also there was a perceived lack of openness to contrary points of view among students, faculty and administrators. In order to solve the college's problems, most interviewees agreed that educational objectives must be clarified. Interviewees reported that the October retreat and the president's memo did provoke debate. The problem now was to work through to consensus. A second general solution raised by several interviewees was to conduct in-service training in ways to motivate diverse kinds of students, in ways to handle the consensus form of governance, in more effective ways to diagnose and solve problems and to conduct and evaluate field experience.

This report was sent directly to interviewees by Strategies staff, both to fulfill an obligation to persons who took time to be interviewed and to be sure the feedback would not be kept from the college community. The executive administration alerted faculty that copies were available from the director of research, but a decision at the top was made not to distribute the report more broadly as other Strategies institutions had done with their own. The director of research explained,

> We thought it was a more divisive document than a helpful one. [The provost] and I advised the president not to distribute the report. It came at a time when faculty morale was low. There was much complaining going on. It was best not to cause more. It occurred to me at the time that quantitative data would have been more helpful.

Two approaches obviously were in conflict. The Strategies staff felt that

"No consensus on goals or values, serious gaps between student subgroups, and piecemeal curriculum: these are the main components of interview concern for fragmentation of campus and curriculum."

143

"We thought it was a more divisive document than a helpful one."

the best approach would be to get faculty concerns out on the table—a Problem-Solving assumption. The local administration felt it wiser to avoid confrontation with disturbing information. The director of research had made a similar decision in not disseminating disturbing interview data during the fall retreat.

Another Strategies intervention was the holding of its semi-annual action planning workshop for campus teams at Quaker Academic upon the president's invitation; he hoped more faculty would become involved if the workshop were held on campus. The workshop once again put emphasis on two areas: team action-planning with consultant help and information exchange sessions on such topics as freshman programs, use of self-study data, evaluating innovations, learning contracts, faculty development and, of course, strategies for change. The college's formal team had eight members, including students, faculty, the provost and the president. Others dropped in on various sessions. One problem was that because the workshop was held on campus, team members attempted to catch the action between their scheduled classes. It was difficult, therefore, to develop coherence and momentum in the team.

By workshop's end, however, the team did have an action plan. Through consultation with Strategies Advisor David Bushnell of the Human Resources Research Organization, the group decided to administer the *Institutional Goals Inventory* to help involve the campus community in clarifying the institution's educational objectives. That instrument was administered in February, 1973, and discussed in a faculty workshop with Bushnell in April 24, 1974. The second plan of action was to provide information and ideas obtained at a workshop on faculty development, calendar and curriculum for consideration by the Educational Policy Committee. These issues and information were discussed in EPC throughout the spring. Third, faculty visits to other colleges to observe their innovative programs would be attempted, using funds from the Man in Focus grant. One visit, at least, did occur: the ombudsman went to Ottawa University in Kansas. That visit would be crucial in designing the process by which campus consensus on the direction of the college would be sought. Fourth, Man in Focus efforts would continue in the upperclass Peace Institute and would move into a Community Studies and independent study segment in the spring. Also, the 1973 Man in Focus faculty workshop would be designed and preliminary planning for the fall Man in Focus and other interdisciplinary programs would be tentatively planned that spring. These intentions were carried out by the director of research.

Throughout the fall of 1972, the Educational Policies Committee had not carried through its spring efforts to clarify core requirements and to consider such innovations as contract learning or calendar change. Instead, the group reacted to several proposals from departments for new courses or programs, in particular international studies. The provost reminded both EPC and the faculty of the need to clarify core requirements, calendar and grading, but, except for the October retreat and the divisional meetings regarding the president's memo, the governance system had not dealt extensively with these issues since the previous spring.

In February of 1973, however, attention on campus shifted. First, the

144

That visit would be crucial in designing the process by which campus consensus on the direction of the college would be sought.

ombudsman journeyed to Ottawa University in Kansas to learn how that small college had managed extensive planned change and just what the nature of that change was. Ottawa had been suggested to Quaker Academic members several times by me as a college whose academic program and change process were well worth examining. At Quaker Academic was a faculty member (the assistant professor of philosophy) who had attended Ottawa, while both the president and the ombudsman had worked at the University of Kansas. Upon the ombudsman's return, he told the president and provost that they might consider altering their approach to planned change. He had learned that President Armacost of Ottawa had set the stage for change by getting the trustees to create a larger deficit in order to retain the faculty, raise all salaries and pay faculty to embark in the summer of 1967 on an intensive effort to set basic educational objectives. Outside consultants as well as threatening talk about declining enrollment, cuts in faculty, merit pay, student evaluation and presidential decrees all were avoided. It was to be an inside renewal effort owned by the faculty and heavily backed by administration and trustees. On hearing this positive reinforcement and internal Problem-Solving strategy, Quaker Academic's president and provost decided to give it a try.

Both the people at Ottawa and Strategies had emphasized the value of small group discussions across departmental and other subgroup lines as more likely to stimulate openness to change than general faculty meetings or departmental meetings. The Strategies workshop and the Ottawa experience further suggested the value of a group's getting off by itself for sustained, uninterrupted interaction. The president and provost therefore decided to hold small, interdepartmental group sessions at one of the college's farms as the next step toward obtaining consensus on college objectives and requirements. The meetings would be late afternoon-evening affairs, with supper, for about a dozen faculty plus the president and provost. The provost told me in mid-March that each mini-retreat had resulted in commitment to academic reform among those present. I asked in particular about the reactions of certain opinion leaders who might be expected to be less than enthusiastic. The provost said all those named, with the exception of one on sabbatical, were extremely enthusiastic and committed.

Besides this "faculty-owned" process of change, the ombudsman brought back from Ottawa several suggestions concerning academic content, costs and faculty development. He reported to EPC on Ottawa's contract learning system, which placed heavy emphasis on faculty advising. Both economy and faculty development were aided, he said, by increasing course loads twenty-percent but then giving faculty members a half year off every three years for their own study and professional renewal. The ombudsman summarized to the committee that Ottawa had managed to integrate into one program all the things Quaker Academic had been trying to do.

Out of these mini-retreats, an *ad hoc* committee put together a proposal for a new program of "Individualized Educational Planning" (IEP). The central component would be the learning contract, "which begins with the student's personal, intellectual and career goals, and which

It was to be an inside renewal effort owned by the faculty and heavily backed by administration and trustees.

145

The central component would be the learning contract, "which begins with the student's personal, intellectual and career goals, and which enables him to maximize options in planning and commencing a life-long learning process."

enables him to maximize options in planning and commencing a life-long learning process." Programs would be put together by the student and a committee of three faculty members. Majors and distribution requirements would be dropped; faculty roles would shift from a heavy emphasis on course instruction to an emphasis on advising, counseling and coordinating independent study or informal courses. Special faculty development workshops, training leaves and growth contracts would be introduced. Off-campus learning opportunities would be expanded. Career orientation would be enhanced by engaging local professionals in advising and teaching.

At the March 30, 1973, faculty meeting, the *ad hoc* committee presented a proposal that starting the next fall, all freshmen and interested sophomores would develop an individual learning program with the advice and consent of a faculty team. Most faculty were in attendance, as were some student leaders and thirteen trustees. Discussion first focused on the committee's request for a vote on this issue. A "weighty Friend" (a Quaker term for highly esteemed mebers of the faith) preferred consensus. A committee member explained that "the *ad hoc* committee's procedural recommendation was based on the need for a clear cut reading of the strength of support for the philosophy of individual program planning." It was agreed that a secret vote would be taken, then discussed to see if there was enough agreement to implement the proposal. The discussion turned to which students should be involved the next fall. Student leaders felt upperclassmen should have a chance. They maintained, "Exclusion of upperclassmen will only further reduce morale and will tear the college apart." The president felt upperclassmen were too close to graduation to develop a strong advising relationship with a faculty member. The issue was not clearly resolved. Another major topic concerned the nature of the advising process. The president emphasized the need to retrain faculty for this role, and he said he assumed the major brunt of advising help would be for sophomores and juniors wrestling with career choices. The provost stressed the value of asking a student "what do you want to do," and others concurred that it was good to put planning responsibility on the student. There was some concern that students could avoid tough subjects this way and that IEP might saddle those professors interested in advising with overwork.

After an hour's discussion, the secret ballot was taken on

> an advising program which would be based on each student working out his own program with a team of advisors. These advisors will help the student develop a program which is oriented to the student's own career goals within a broad objective guideline which is yet to be worked out by the faculty. This system is to apply to all freshmen entering in the fall of 1973 and to some present students. How many present students and which present students has not yet been agreed upon.

Sixty persons with faculty status approved the principle of individual program planning. Ten were opposed. The president asked those with reservations to state their concerns. The Man in Focus history professor said there were too many blanks yet to be filled out, too many unknowns.

146

Sixty persons with faculty status approved the principle of individual program planning.

The associate professor of English who had been critical of Man in Focus said it was not clear what results would materialize, and she was concerned that upperclass students might be neglected. So was another faculty member. Another associate professor of English felt the issue of redefining faculty role "causes problems for some," and another felt "advisors may not be as good as they want to be." Yet another faculty member felt increased personal advising might not be worth the loss of personal contact in classes which would result from the larger class sizes needed to accommodate more advising. The provost asked if there were any persons still desiring discussion or wishing to stand in opposition to the proposal. After several moments of silence, the provost "expressed his own realization of the risks undertaken through commitment to the development of a program enabling students to make good use of intellectual and academic resources in the development of their own goals." He then adjourned the meeting.

On April 11, 1973, the faculty took up the issue again, this time to decide just which students should be allowed to submit individual program proposals for fall, 1973. Discussion centered on several issues: (1) should the option be open to upperclassmen, despite some concern that they might use it to circumvent requirements and might be too close to graduation to build a sound plan; (2) should students develop proposals with an advisor and committee or draft them alone and then submit them to the proposed IEP Coordinating Committee; (3) are faculty able to help develop or judge proposals prior to the proposed summer training institute and can students submit later proposals if the first one is not accepted; and (4) how can both depth and breadth be insured in each program. The faculty finally agreed, "after much disjointed discussion," say the minutes, "to send a letter to all students presently enrolled explaining the individual program planning system and the option of submitting a proposal this spring." One final request, by a student, was that students be included on the IEP Coordinating Committee. The meeting was adjourned.

The strategy of generating proposed changes out of cross-departmental, small group retreats and an *ad hoc* faculty committee apparently was much more effective at developing faculty interest and approval for major changes in requirements and educational practices than was a presidential memorandum. Ownership of the problem-solving process by decision-makers and implementors (meaning faculty, in particular, for academic policy) was again successful. Of course, the past year's external resources such as Chickering, Pitkin, Martin and the Strategies workshops joined the ombudsman's visit to Ottawa University as key links to sources of new ideas. The earlier study and proposals to faculty by the EPC warmed the water and built a group of advocates. The Strategies interim report, said some who were interviewed, added to convictions that something needed to be done. Even the president's memorandum, despite the ire it raised, did provoke concern over the college's future. This synergy of prior change effort perhaps prepared the way for the culminating series of retreats, committee sessions and faculty meetings.

The strategy of generating proposed changes out of cross-departmental, small group retreats and an **ad hoc** *faculty committee apparently was much more effective at developing faculty interest and approval for major changes in requirements and educational practices than was a presidential memorandum.*

147

THE INSTITUTIONAL GOALS INVENTORY

Campus change does not necessarily happen in neat sequence. After the decision to go ahead with Individualized Educational Planning on April 25, 1973, the faculty met with David Bushnell of the Strategies advisory board to consider results of the *Institutional Goals Inventory*. Clarifying goals, at least as far as the IGI was concerned, was not the first step to change. Bushnell opened his remarks on the IGI by observing three significant changes in factors affecting college. Student values, especially those of the affluent, are changing toward greater interest both in personal growth and vocational preparation. The job market for college graduates is declining and shifting toward human services and middle management. And the population is leveling off. These factors, he said, put increased pressure on colleges to clarify goals which respond to student needs and to improve effectiveness in an increasingly competitive market. The IGI scores in general showed a high desire at Quaker Academic for an emphasis on "Intellectual Orientation," "Individual Personal Development" and "Freedom," but only moderate interest in "Vocational Preparation" and "Meeting Local Needs," the areas stressed by the president in his memo. He had been trying to push the faculty into goal areas it did not highly value. Faculty did desire, however, to increase substantially both the liberal and professional emphases from current practices. Some goals, such as "Research" and "Traditional Religiousness," were given little emphasis as current or desired goals *in general*, but wide standard deviations (1.13 and 1.08 respectively) indicated that there was considerable disagreement about how much emphasis each should be given. Emphasis on "Individual Personal Development" (standard deviation .90), "Graduate Professional Training" (1.07), "Public Service" (1.04), "Social Egaliterianism" (1.03), "Off-Campus Learning" (1.02), "Meeting Local Needs" (.99) and concern for "Accountability/Efficiency" (.93) all showed considerable faculty disagreement.

Discussion among faculty after Bushnell's presentation raised several points. First, top-ranked goals showed fairly high consensus between students, faculty, administrators and trustees. Second, discussants felt the data revealed more concern "To educate students in a particular religious heritage" than there should be. Third, faculty felt too much emphasis was being put on the goal "To encourage students to spend time away from campus, gaining academic credit for such activities as a year of study abroad, in work-study programs, in VISTA, etc." Fourth, students wanted more emphasis on credit or degree by examination. Especially pertinent to the new individualized program, there was agreement on the value of "Individual Personal Development" but substantial disagreement about current emphases. Faculty and trustees felt there was substantially more current emphasis on this goal than did students and administrators. Bushnell noted that administrators generally felt current emphases on desirable goals was less than did faculty, students or trustees. This accounts, perhaps, for the largely administrative push toward change and the faculty complaint that administrators were not recognizing what was already being done. Again pertinent to IEP, all groups desired substantially more effort "to increase the desire and ability of students to

Faculty did desire, however, to increase substantially both the liberal and professional emphases from current practices.

148

undertake self-directed learning."

Pertinent to the governance issue and the concern for administrative heavy-handedness in pushing change, all groups agreed that more attention must be paid to maintaining "a climate in which communication throughout the organizational structure is open and candid" and "a climate of mutual trust and respect among students, faculty and administrators." Bushnell commented later to Strategies staff on what he heard about the usefulness of an outsider such as himself in helping the college work through this kind of information:

> One other important point commented on by a number of the people involved in arranging for the feedback exercise: they seemed universally in agreement that it is important to have an outsider come in and present the initial findings both to establish the objectivity of the results and to win over any potential opponents who were ready to pick at the methodology because they were threatened by the substantive findings. One or two people told me that [the director of research] had tried to communicate the findings at the Institutional Research Committee meeting but had not made very good headway. It will be interesting to see whether or not the various committees and planning groups that currently exist on campus will in fact meet at later times to discuss the implications of the findings further.

Interviews in December of 1973 did reveal that EPC, Long Range Planning and the Educational Policies Committee of the trustees all took up further discussion of the IGI results. A "developing rift" between a member of EPC and a member of the long range planning committee "lessened considerably so that we are looking to more inter-committee cooperation." The trustee group decided in May of 1973 that "the Board of Trustees be provided with a list of decisions to be considered in relation to the top priority goal areas: intellectual orientation, community, individual personal development, and vocational preparation." One administrator summarized the perceived usefulness of this intervention:

> The timing of the IGI study was excellent. It served as a reassurance to the faculty; disgruntled faculty were exposed to this and shown the potential purposes of the college. This study can be attributed to Strategies for Change involvement. The data was well-received by the faculty and a good part of its success was due to when it was administered and when it was received by them. Dave Bushnell was a low-key presenter and he was greatly appreciated by all who heard his presentation.

It is interesting that this effort to clarify goals *followed*, not preceded, a major decision on a new approach to education at Quaker Academic. Because goals stressing individual development, both intellectual and personal, were highly emphasized, the exercise may have served to solidify support for the individualized program planning. Then again, the moderate faculty interest and considerable difference of opinion about locally oriented, vocational and off-campus programs suggests that what faculty desired was individualizing the *on-campus* program, not the kind of outreach described in the president's earlier memo and in descriptions of the

All groups agreed that more attention must be paid to maintaining "a climate in which communication throughout the organizational structure is open and candid" and "a climate of mutual trust and respect among students, faculty and administrators."

149

It is interesting that this effort to clarify goals followed, not preceded, a major decision on a new approach to education.

likely content of future individual programs. One might predict from this information a campus-bound implementation of Individualized Educational Planning.

EXTENT OF INNOVATION: A COMPARISON

Man in Focus was completing its second full academic year under NEH support and its fourth year as a coordinated effort. At a July workshop of the Strategies project, the president, the director of research and an assistant professor of education who taught in Man in Focus made plans to carry forward upperclass institutes and program evaluation. Strategies information on faculty also was examined, and part of that evidence indicated the degree of faculty support for Man in Focus. Table 6 compares faculty involvement in that innovation with Messiah faculty's perspective on their 4-1-3 calendar (see Chapter Eight) and South Carolina's Bachelor of General Studies degree. A fair summary of the first percentages seems to indicate that Quaker Academic faculty were better informed than South Carolina's but less than Messiah's during the development of each innovation. The Messiah Task Force, we will see later, put great emphasis on informing faculty, while South Carolina, with a far larger faculty to inform, had made little effort to do that. During implementation, Messiah faculty, all of whom were expected to participate in the intensive term, were much more involved than Quaker Academic faculty, while comparatively few South Carolina faculty members were touched by BGS. Involvement in formulation and implementation appears to correlate with attitudes toward the innovation. Messiah faculty were most enthusiastic, followed by fairly solid support at Quaker Academic and less than majority interest at South Carolina. There are many other factors involved in generating support for these three innovations but Table 6 does strongly suggest that it helps greatly if faculty are informed and involved in formulating the change, then equally involved in planning, training, participating and evaluating its implementation.

The provost's report claimed that Man in Focus now would move "from a somewhat peripheral position in the curriculum toward the center," for "it is already clear that this new approach will heighten the demand for problem-focused, interdisciplinary courses":

> Students will henceforth not be set apart as Man in Focus freshman. They will be offered a variety of Contemporary Problems seminars with a contemporary emphasis each term and a variety of Human Condition seminars, with a more historical and humanities-fine arts emphasis, and will be invited to put these together in various combinations, as one approach to breadth and as a means of exploring fields and disciplines. These courses will be open to freshmen and sophomores. We hope in this way to attract into the program more vocationally oriented students as well as those socially concerned ones who have previously enrolled.

IMPLEMENTATION OF INDIVIDUALIZED EDUCATIONAL PLANNING

As the fall of 1973 approached, therefore, the provost of Quaker Academic

Involvement in formulation and implementation appears to correlate with attitudes toward the innovation.

150

TABLE 6
FACULTY SUPPORT FOR INNOVATION

1. EXTENT OF INVOLVEMENT DURING FORMULATION	Quaker Academic "Man in Focus"	Messiah 4-1-2	South Carolina BGS
Worked on the committee that developed the program	17%	13%	9%
Sought additional information about it from colleagues and campus media	44	60	32
Read about similar programs elsewhere	21	42	21
Went to other campuses or conferences to learn about such programs	8	13	3
Studied teaching and learning research and theory pertinent to the proposed change	16	23	7
Studied evidence on our students and/or institutional objectives to determine its suitability	36	33	12
Actively supported it as a valuable addition to our school	40	39	15
No participation in formulation stage	21	24	60
2. INVOLVEMENT IN IMPLEMENTATION			
Participated in planning the implementation	23	48	7
Participated in training for the new roles, knowledge, and skills needed to implement the program	29	18	8
Participated as a faculty member in the program	39	69	14
Participated on the team which evaluated the program	12	20	2
No involvement in implementation	21	24	61
3. ATTITUDES TOWARD PROGRAM			
I don't know enough about it to say	23	24	40
It is not up to the standards of the regular program	15	16	28
It was not carefully thought through	8	9	6
There should have been more research conducted into the nature of our students, practices elsewhere, and teaching-learning in general before it was passed	14	29	16
It did not receive adequate faculty review	15	18	19
It appears to meet student learning needs which were not met before	48	56	44
It appears to meet student learning interests which were not met before	62	73	39
It seems to hold promise despite apparent problems	60	76	38
I would like to see similar programs developed or expanded at my institution	60	62	38

still planned to make interdisciplinary, problem-focused courses central to the college. He also established an Individualized Educational Planning Coordinating Committee. An assistant professor of music, an associate professor of mathematics and physics, a professor of history (the Man in Focus professor), an assistant professor of literature and language, an associate professor of agriculture, an associate professor of sociology, a professor of psychology and an associate professor of education made up the committee. It was, clearly, an interdisciplinary group which ranged across the age, rank and tenure spectrum at Quaker Academic. The provost sought external funding to implement IEP just as he had for Man in Focus. He submitted a proposal to the Fund for the Improvement of Postsecondary Education, but it was rejected. He turned then to the Lilly Foundation, for the president of another Quaker institution had become an officer there. This time he secured a $200,000 implementation grant. With part of the money, he and the president appointed the ombudsman to be IEP director. They also hired a career counselor, for that person would be an important part of the effort.

In early July of 1973, the IEP Coordinating Committee and director met for a week to set policies. The resulting document stated that the core of the new arrangement would be planning teams composed of the student, three faculty members representing at least two academic divisions and, "wherever feasible and useful, one person from outside the campus community." These teams would be established in the sophomore year; consensus would be their decision making mode. An "initial advisor" for freshmen would "focus the student's attention on goals beyond graduation, . . . encourage exploration, the pursuit of stated interests, remediation if necessary, experimentation with new fields and disciplines." But as soon as the team was put together, it would develop a plan for the rest of the student's undergraduate education. Such plans would have to emphasize both depth and breadth of learning. Depth could be covered by a traditional major or a "cluster major," an interdisciplinary concentration devised by the student (an innovation which had been introduced into the college several years before). Resources for individualized program fulfillment included the college's own curriculum, independent and field study, courses in neighboring institutions and tutoring by skilled individuals in the community or on the campus.

The last section of the document shifted from describing policies to outlining faculty needs required for the successful implementation of the program. "It must be recognized by everyone involved that this period of transition will be very stressful and possibly threatening." A four year period was recommended as the time to shift from the current to the individualized program. Emphasis would be on "re-tooling our own people rather than bringing in new members." Everyone should be sensitive and responsive to feelings of uneasiness and threat. Professional development, especially in the areas of advising and career counseling, would be needed. Because of heavy advising-teaching loads, "frequent, standardized sabbatical leaves" would be needed to keep up in one's discipline. Developmental contracts for faculty should be introduced to help clarify and guide development of the skills needed to implement IEP.

152

"It must be recognized by everyone involved that this period of transition will be very stressful and possibly threatening."

Faculty differences in strengths, whether teaching or advising, should be recognized: "there should continue to be a place at Quaker Academic for the faculty member who is primarily concerned with formal teaching in his or her own discipline." Three kinds of "organized assistance" were proposed: (1) help to develop new courses, especially interdisciplinary courses, "which can help equalize loads"; (2) help to "improve their success in various kinds of teaching situations"; and (3) aid to "improve their success as advisors."

When fall arrived at Quaker Academic, it brought fewer students than in years past. Particularly absent were the liberal Easterners who had been a major impetus for Man in Focus. The provost presented the new student profile to faculty in late October. The data revealed more local students (up from 17% in 1971 to 29% in 1973) and more in-state students (up from 33% to 51%). Average Math and Verbal SAT scores had dropped from 500 in 1971 to 473 in 1973. In 1972, 40% of the new enrollees were first generation students. Now it was 51%. In 1972, 50% of Wilmington's new students were "very or somewhat dissatisfied with their secondary education"; in 1973, the percentage was 36%. Faculty commented in later interviews that this new bunch was more conservative, compliant and vocationally concerned than freshman classes of the recent past. Enrollment in general was down. When a Strategies staff member visited Wilmington in early December, "If we survive" prefaced many comments.

In this climate of decline, the president decided he could not wait around for Man in Focus and IEP to give Quaker Academic a visibly distinctive and attractive image to students. He had been alert to the planning for a public community college to be built nearly adjacent to the college. He saw here two opportunities, one to provide liberal arts teaching for the new college and the other to articulate a four-year program for community college graduates. He spent much of the 1973-74 academic year working with college trustees and local leaders to insure a strong role for Quaker Academic in the new institution. He did seek advice from the Planning Committee, but otherwise he considered the development of support in the external community too delicate a matter for broad faculty and student involvement.

Meanwhile, Man in Focus and Individualized Educational Planning continued toward implementation. Neither, however, was spreading much beyond a few interested faculty, in some cases the same innovators for both programs. When a Strategies staff member interviewed in December, he again heard that Man in Focus still fell short of being truly interdisciplinary or effective at developing problem-solving skills. Its courses were focused on contemporary issues. It did stimulate use of outside speakers, films, field trips and independent projects. These, apparently, would be its legacies to curriculum and teaching at Quaker Academic. Students were enjoying the program, partly because the planning team had done away with the large survey the year before, but also, faculty said, because this group was somewhat more conservative and willing to listen. It apparently was not so much a case of Man in Focus's meeting the needs of the bright, turned off idealist as it was a better fit

Faculty commented in later interviews that this new bunch was more conservative, compliant and vocationally concerned than freshman classes of the recent past.

between the same program and more traditional students. As for IEP, only a handful of faculty members, most of them on the IEP Coordinating Committee, were enthusiastic about or involved in the program. The IEP director was dismayed at the lack of faculty support. He himself tended to be argumentative and closely identified with the president—both problems, he felt, in his being persuasive to faculty. The IEP Coordinating Committee was not providing leadership in implementation; it was instead preoccupied in the review of student degree plans.

Upon hearing the Strategies staff member's report, I decided to see if the project might lend IEP a hand in broadening faculty involvement. The director and I met in January of 1973 and worked out a plan to develop a faculty team which would take charge of implementing the Lilly grant. The group would begin its new role in a team workshop sponsored by the American Association for Higher Education and held during its annual national conference. The Strategies project and NTL's "Training Teams for Campus Change" project[3] would lead that workshop.

Shortly before the AAHE conference, the IEP director submitted to the provost a report on the committee's activities. He noted that 259 students, 202 of them new to Quaker Academic, were enrolled in IEP. That was about a third of the 1973-74 student body. Fifty-five faculty members were involved in program advising, with about five advising committees per faculty member the average load. He said program advising was getting done, and students were quite appreciative of the new career counseling service. Among problems, he found that very active participation came from only a few faculty in a few departments. He also found that advising quality appeared to vary greatly and that many advisors "have expressed uneasiness about going beyond purely academic advising." He had the following to report about general faculty support:

> *While faculty enthusiasm for the program is . . . difficult to measure, it is possible to say that positive responses and helpful criticisms or suggestions have been outnumbered by statements and actions reflecting an unwillingness to co-operate or understand the reasoning behind various aspects of the program. However, responses of either nature have been relatively few.*

He reflected that the Coordinating Committee was consumed by rulings on individual cases. Neither it nor the July workshop participants had managed to develop a statement of philosophy and objectives which could guide program implementation. Other problems involved lack of articulation between the program and such offices as Records, Admissions, Career Development Services, foreign study and field study.

The director projected that as IEP expanded into the upperclass years, advising loads would amount to over an hour a day for all faculty, considerably more than the current rate and a continuing distraction, he thought, from other professorial work but not enough to motivate faculty to become highly skilled in doing it. He urged training in non-directive counseling rather than the directive advising he felt was currently the mode. He recommended orientation of both faculty and students to the non-traditional teaching-learning processes a full implementation of IEP would mean. He urged rapid development of cooperative arrangements with nearby educational institutions. His major recommendation was that, in order to develop a program that starts with the student's purposes and builds an open, flexible program to fulfill those purposes, an "academic counseling center" needed to be established and staffed by a rotating team of faculty "mentors." They would handle all freshman planning and all planning team chairpersonships—about 40 freshmen and 40 chairpersonships per mentor. This service would provide intensive training and mentoring experience for most faculty, eventually.

The team which attended the AAHE workshop was selected by the IEP director and the provost. In addition, it included four members of the IEP Coordinating Committee and the director of research. The group met long hours with the director's report as their focus. They developed strong commitment to IEP as "the right way to go." The program was acknowledged as not being radical; what "will make us unique is the way we put our program together and support it as a total college community." An impasse, however, developed in a problem that emerged between the faculty members and the administrators in the group, who invited me as one of the workshop consultants to help them work through the issue. I joined the team and simply asked questions to try to understand the concern. I gradually concluded (perhaps influenced by earlier impressions as much as current discussion) that the provost and director of IEP were regarding the group as advisory, not as equal partners in a collaborative team; yet the faculty members seemed to me as committed to IEP, as knowledgeable about its situation and better-linked to other faculty than the administrators. They did not seem at ease with the way the administrators were discussing faculty non-cooperation, nor was I. I also knew from previous Quaker Academic change activities and information that faculty did not care to be told what to do—they were high on the IFI "Freedom" scale and I assumed that changes in the individual teaching habits of faculty would need their commitment.

I attempted to put myself in the place of a faculty member on that team, then share with the administrators present that I was feeling like a second-class citizen in that role as I heard the way the administrators described the problem (uncooperative faculty) and the solution (administrative decision after advice from the four faculty members). The usefulness of my input would depend, of course, not only on its accuracy as perceived by team members and on an outsider's freedom to say what insiders are reluctant to express to campus authorities, but also especially on the administrators' openness to the message that they might have to play a less visible leadership role and take a chance on faculty leadership. Both the provost and the director of research expressed agreement with the diagnosis of the situation as I and other team members hypothesized it.

Everyone agreed that the four faculty members of the Coordinating Committee should take the visible leadership, with the administrators offering solid, behind-the-scenes support. One person suggested that the four faculty members write up a report on this team's recommendations, distribute it to faculty, and then lead a faculty meeting to discuss the recommendations. I suggested that first they personally seek out faculty

I gradually concluded (perhaps influenced by earlier impressions as much as current discussion) that the provost and director of IEP were regarding the group as advisory, not as equal partners in a collaborative team.

155

opinion leaders and persons especially suspicious of manipulation so that these individuals might be persuaded in a low-key, one-to-one conversation rather than in the formal debate atmosphere of a large forum. By meeting's end, team members appeared to me genuinely excited by what had happened. They said they felt they had broken through the impasse and were on their way. Would, however, the faculty members take charge, or would the pattern back home return to administrative thrust and faculty parry?

Following the conference, the four faculty members did write a brief report and circulate it to all faculty. It was, however, a reaction to the IEP director's report, not their own proposal. They agreed with the director that "what is needed is a different *kind* of advising, not just more time spent by faculty." That would require more faculty involvement in advising by some faculty members than was now the case. But, without endorsing the "academic counseling center" proposal, they raised some questions about it.

> *(a) What is the effect of cutting specific courses normally taught by the mentors? (b) What are the implications for faculty load? (c) How can a mentor maintain professional competence in his own field? (d) How will a mentor's faculty status be defined? (e) How do we build in some kind of accountability between the mentor group (however it is defined) and the faculty? (f) Given differing individual and departmental attitudes toward advising, shouldn't we emphasize* voluntary *participation in advising rather than relying on administrative appointments? (g) If we decide in favor of the mentor structure, shouldn't each division be involved in selecting the specific individuals and the number of mentors that best fits the needs of each division. (h) Are summer workshops the best way to prepare faculty in advising? (i) Whatever advising structure we choose, how will we deal with the breadth objective? (j) If we go to a mentor structure, what will be the role of the IEP Committee? Of student advisors?*

Attached was a memo to the IEP director by the director of research:

> *I'm concerned however with your suggestion that a small group of mentors advise nearly all freshmen and serve as chairpersons for all committees. This change seems to me unwise logistically and psychologically. It would alienate other enthusiastic faculty from the program, make more rigid the attractive openness students now have in "selecting their own teams" and it would create pressures and fatigue for the mentors during the orientation week and at registration times.*
>
> *I'd recommend instead that the mentors assume a substantial share of the advising, that uninterested faculty be excused from IEP advising to devote themselves instead to full-time teaching, and that other faculty (the majority I think) be given moderate advising loads, allowing the mentors to provide liaison with them. Advising relationships that are now established and that are working well ought not to be disturbed, and students and faculty who wish to work together should be encouraged to do so.*

With this critique of an administrator's recommendation in hand, the team called a meeting for interested faculty. The four faculty members did not meet informally with opinion leaders beforehand. They did not share with the larger group their own experience in Chicago and the excitement that created for them. They did not take strong leadership roles, for they felt that their having been selected as a team by the administration did not give them legitimacy. "We just opened it up, and all the conflict came out," one recalled. There were suspicions that the four were "administrative lackeys" and "they thought we already had decided things and were just working them up to it as soon as they saw we had something in mind." "Mentoring" as a special role was not appreciated. One member of the team summarized the group's feeling: "We blew it!"

Later in March, a full faculty retreat was held to consider IEP. Small group discussions preceded general meetings. Most discussion focused on the director's report and recommendations. It was the "president's memo" again. The provost was asked by the team to show strong support for the group and to define the problem. He did not play an active role, according to team members. Mentoring came up in the last session, and interviewees said the faculty argument was that if you are for mentoring, which would take a great deal of time, you are against teaching. Also, such an approach would defeat the traditional liberal arts, it was argued. One faculty member asked for a show of hands among those who desired to be mentors. One member of the team of four raised his hand. Some interviewees later said the strong role of the director during the meeting in pushing his proposal and the fact that centralized mentoring would swell his central office led faculty to believe he was "building a nest for himself." He took heavy criticism. The vote clearly demonstrated no support for the mentoring notion.

After the retreat, the team met to consider what to do now. One faculty member suggested summer workshops to help faculty members learn about career counseling. The director said no, he preferred letting individual faculty members use the Lilly money however they wished to prepare themselves for IEP participation. The Coordinating Committee was activated to lead implementation, however, and an enthusiastic member of the AAHE team was appointed chairperson by the IEP director. Then the director left for a visit to Israel. The committee met weekly and enjoyed close rapport and commitment because, one commented, most members had been to the AAHE workshop together. The committee held several meetings with chairpersons of the IEP faculty teams to get the problems out. Few problems had answers, but at least discussions among faculty had begun. Also, the Coordinating Committee chairperson put together an IEP handbook to guide teams and made a report on the program to the Academic Council, which consisted of the division chairpersons plus the provost and president. Besides this involvement of faculty, the provost appointed two members of the four-person faculty team to work with the IEP director part-time, although they were carefully not called "mentors." Some faculty who became involved in Individualized Educational Planning teams in 1974-75 commented during interviews that the process of listening, questioning and exploring with a student was

"We just opened it up, and all the conflict came out."

157

The committee held several meetings with chairpersons of the IEP faculty teams to get the problems out.

IEP, like Man in Focus, was still only partially adopted midway into its second year.

I feel some confidence in saying that renewal objectives were being realized.

highly rewarding for the faculty member. And many students had designed programs to which they were highly committed. Other faculty members, however, still saw little student interest in all that planning and little educational accomplishment for the faculty time required. IEP, like Man in Focus, was still only partially adopted midway into its second year.

UP WITH EDUCATION, DOWN WITH MORALE

The administration had been pushing change for two years. A few faculty members had responded enthusiastically to Man in Focus and IEP, but many were skeptical of these thrusts. What had been the consequence for education and organization? Strategies data suggested that Quaker Academic in 1974 was more flexible in teaching than in 1972. In the earlier year, 42% of the student respondents to ECQ described one of their professors (randomly selected to represent courses in general) as "dispenses knowledge or assigns sources which the student should master." In 1974, only 29% of the teaching roles were characterized that way. Greatly increased, from 21% to 31%, were professors who "direct efforts flexibly to help students learn." Accompanying that shift was an increase in "fairly important" or "major" student influence over course content and structure from 37% in 1972 to 48% in 1974. Man in Focus attempts at more flexible, student-oriented teaching, as well as IEP increases in student influence, probably helped stimulate these changes. They had not, however, significantly changed the mental activities students reported in class and during study, though students were studying more for intrinsic reasons: to master material (7% to 12%), to broaden understanding (24% to 28%), to learn something vocationally useful (23% to 28%) and because the course is "enjoyable and interesting" (8% to 14%). Fewer studied just to meet requirements (27% to 13%) or "to get good grades" (6% to 3%). They tended to feel more confident (65% to 72%), less bored (28% to 18%), more interested (67% to 78%) and more challenged (57% to 64%) by their courses in 1974 than in 1972. These statistics certainly fit what one would hope to accomplish by letting students choose their own degree program and by gearing course work to contemporary concerns instead of following set requirements. Finally, students reported spending significantly more time in 1974 than in 1972 talking with their academic advisors about academic arrangements and future plans, another IEP feature. Some part of these shifts may be explained by a better fit between the less independent, turned-off students of 1974 and the college; but the data are so logically tied to the new program thrusts, and so little otherwise changed in student responses, that I feel some confidence in saying that renewal objectives were being realized.

Yet morale had plummeted. The *Institutional Functioning Inventory* responses showed significant drops in faculty perceptions of "Democratic Governance" and "Institutional Esprit." The latter had tumbled below 97% of the institutions using the IFI. Table 7 shows how low faculty-administrative esprit had gone. Most interviewees pointed to four causes of this change. First, enrollment drops had depressed everyone and made

TABLE 7
QUAKER ACADEMIC "INSTITUTIONAL ESPRIT"
1971-1974

Item #	Item Description	1971 Percent Agree	1974 Percent Agree
097	Most faculty consider the senior administrators to be able and well qualified	80	36*
104	Generally, top level administrators here provide effective educational leadership	89	39*
106	Generally, communication between faculty and administration is poor	91	41*
111	Staff infighting, backbiting, etc. seem to be more the rule than the exception	94	49*
112	The college is currently doing a successful job in achieving its various goals	74	33*
116	Close personal friendships between administrators and faculty members are common	87	71*
117	Compared with most other colleges, faculty turnover here appears somewhat high	87	46*
121	Although they may criticize some things, most faculty seem loyal to the college	93	83*
122	There is a strong sense of community here, a feeling of shared interests/ purposes	80	43*
123	In general, faculty morale is high	85	21*
126	Faculty in general is strongly committed to acknowledged purposes of the college	83	64*
131	Most faculty would not defend the college against criticisms from outsiders	91	74*

*Change significant at .05 level, symmetric test.

159

faculty tense, even defensive. Second, the president and the IEP director had made aggressive change attempts which, because they were comparative outsiders and were not skillful at openly involving faculty in diagnosing the problem and formulating solutions, increased rather than decreased resistance. The Man in Focus director was a long-term insider and did involve faculty in summer planning sessions, but he too did not help develop strong faculty ownership for the program. The provost, although admired, was criticized for equivocating rather than playing a strong, visible leadership role. Third, no faculty leader or group had taken on the task of consistent advocacy. The closest attempts were the EPC in 1973 and the AAHE workshop team in 1974, but both soon fizzled. Fourth, many felt that too much had changed too soon. IEP was launched before Man in Focus was fully implemented, and rumors about relationships with the new community college shifted much attention from IEP implementation. Although both Man in Focus and IEP benefited from external funding, that money was used primarily to staff and support the programs, not to tackle the problem of broadening faculty involvement, and commitment and skill.

The next academic year, 1974-75, was more a year of waiting than action. The provost was absent on a sabbatical leave in the fall. The president resigned early in the fall and was a lame duck. The IEP director was regarding 1974-75 as his final one at Quaker Academic. The IEP Coordinating Committee was absorbed into the functions of the Educational Policies Council. Negotiations with the new community college and cuts in staff necessitated by further enrollment decreases preoccupied the executive administration and Academic Council. Faculty interviewees said there was a leadership vacuum and much waiting for the community college arrangement to be finalized; the president was criticized by the student newspaper for not involving the college community in this move. Man in Focus was no longer a formal program. Instead, its ingredients were to be merged into the regular curriculum, and some faculty members were enthusiastically teaching interdisciplinary, problem-centered courses. Faculty were unsure whether either it or IEP would survive if the main mission of the college were to become community college teaching. Late in the year, a new president was selected. He was a Quaker Academic alumnus, current trustee and generally a popular choice.

I have not had opportunity to interview or observe in this college since the appointment of the new president, but what little I hear suggests that the new educational gains are being joined by improvement in faculty-administrative rapport. Applications for admission are up for fall, 1976. All that work appears to be paying off not only in educational practices but in organizational health as well.

COMMENTARY

Over the course of nearly a decade, this small, Quaker-affiliated college in the rural midwest struggled to find educational practices and an institutional image of distinction. Once again, executive administrators took the initiative. First the president, stimulated by a national commission, and then a new provost, motivated by his prior experiences and research on the nature of Quaker Academic students, took steps to introduce contemporary problem-centered interdisciplinary work. Rather than designing and proposing a program himself, however, the provost invited faculty members to join him in informal discussions of academic needs and solutions. From these sessions emerged a small cadre of interested faculty members who launched Man in Focus. Probably because the program was initiated by respected colleagues, was a small pilot program with volunteer faculty, was compatable with institutional values, appeared appropriate to a new breed of liberal students and was able to attract outside funding, it drew little faculty opposition. Probably because little concerted effort was made to broaden the program goal, and because the "Scarsdale radical" stopped coming to Quaker Academic in large numbers, the program's legacy was not a major change in educational practices but, instead, a minor increase in interdisciplinary and contemporary efforts, as well as the use of audio-visual material, guest lecturers and field work in college courses.

A small group of faculty members, some the same ones involved in Man in Focus, continued meeting with the provost, this time in the Educational Policies Council. Discussions of innovative practices in other institutions, often stimulated by the first-hand exposure to colleagues from those institutions, led this group to propose individualized degree programs rather than traditional requirements. In this case, the interested were asking others to alter their own practices and were seeking not a temporary experiment but a major policy change. These others had not discovered a need to change for themselves, nor had they searched through potential solutions with EPC. They were not about to agree, and strong Quaker norms concerning freedom and consensus did not allow for a bureaucratic decision or even majority rule. After a summer's hiatus, new tactics were tried. The president and provost drafted position papers on the college's future which they discussed in academic division meetings and the faculty went into retreat to discuss together and with an outside consultant the need to change. These actions stirred widespread discussion but did not lead to agreement. Then the executives, stimulated by an outside model of institutional renewal process, shifted back to collaborative discussion with small, cross-disciplinary groups in "mini-retreat" sessions, instead of following a more threatening and bureaucratic approach. It was, essentially, the tactic which led one faculty group to initiate Man in Focus and another to propose individualized degrees, only this time all faculty members were involved. Near consensus was reached and Individualized Educational Planning was begun. Again, the provost exercised entrepreneurial skills to secure an outside grant to support early implementation. But, again, the one person in charge of implementation did not broaden faculty ownership nor conduct extensive training so that complex "mentoring" skills could be employed. Few professors, therefore, helped students plan their degrees in very innovative ways.

These academic changes were by no means failures. Teaching was significantly more flexible and students more interested and challenged in 1974 than in 1972, and students spent significantly more time talking with their advisors about academic plans. Several faculty members recited

Discussions of innovative practices in other institutions, often stimulated by the first-hand exposure to colleagues from those institutions, led this group to propose individualized degree programs rather than traditional requirements.

161

what were for them exciting outcomes of these changes both for their own teaching and for their students. Still, faculty-administrative esprit sagged and both programs had a hard time moving beyond the committed few faculty and administrative participants. I felt two problems stood out.

First, this institution expecially has strong collegial norms around freedom and consensus. Change must arise from problems felt by faculty and solutions developed by faculty. When that happened, in the proposal to start Man in Focus and the mini-retreats on college mission and Individualized Educational Planning, agreement was reached. But administrators had few skills in such collaborative problem-solving and dropped back into bureaucratic or laissez-faire approaches to implementing both programs and bureaucratic tactics in developing other major changes in the college (career orientation and the merger with the new community college). These actions failed to increase faculty commitment to change; for some, they increased resistance.

Second, despite the difficulty of developing "pragmatic idealists" or independent educational planners and learners, faculty development was little practiced. During a period when half the Hartwick faculty experienced some contact with faculty development without any new program challenge as impetus and focal point, hardly any Quaker Academic faculty got help in exploring highly complex new teaching roles. Although considerable education innovation was managed without these ingredients, training and consultation in collaborative institutional and student problem-solving seem critical but missing ingredients in Quaker Academic's renewal process. But in truth, few administrators saw much need to improve their collaborative skills, and few faculty members sought help to develop pragmatic idealists or student abilities to propose and plan education.

162

What does this case add to our understanding of planned change process and factors? We see the importance of administrative initiative. We see the value of establishing contacts with existing external innovative models, for Man in Focus and Individualized Educational Planning, not to mention the renewal process itself, were adaptations of approaches used elsewhere in higher education. We see the likelihood that only a small number of faculty members (mostly young but with some veterans and covering a range of disciplines) will join innovative efforts early on. We see that information on students goals and practices can stimulate concern for change and that outside consultants can play the same role. We again see the importance of following prevalent political norms, of making changes that are compatible with existing values, of starting small, and of initial grant support. We see that groups which identify needs and develop solutions in isolation will have great difficulty persuading other members of the organization that the need is real and the solution right. We see that major policy changes are not major changes until this commitment spreads beyond initial advocates. We see the importance of leader skills in collaborative problem-solving and of training for complex new roles. We see that in the absence of sophisticated and coordinated planning for change, fits and starts are more likely than impressive movement.

We see, in short, all the planned change models of Chapter One. Research and Development, Social Interaction, internal Problem-Solving, together with bureaucratic, collegial and democratic dynamics, are all present. As I lived with these cases, this general point kept suggesting itself to me, as it may have by this time in your reading. I am not easy, however, to convince. Three cases are not as solid a basis for conclusions as are seven. Also, I am not sure yet just what I would include, with what emphasis, in a planned change strategy which might join prior research to the experiences of South Carolina, Hartwick and Quaker Academic. Let us turn, therefore, to somewhat condensed accounts of planned change attempts in three other organizations: an Eastern, private university, a black college near the Mason Dixon line and a former Catholic women's college in the West.

7 Other Institutions, Similar Dynamics: Commuter Private University, Black Cooperative University, Mountain College

Joining South Carolina, Hartwick and Quaker Academic in the Strategies project were three institutions whose leaders asked that their institution be kept anonymous. I shall call one, a private Eastern university of about six thousand students, Commuter Private, for most of its students lived at home in its metropolitan New York City area. A second, Black Cooperative, alternated work and study for twelve hundred blacks from Northern urban centers and Southern rural high schools so poor that virtually every student received some form of financial aid. The third, Mountain College, had been a traditional Catholic women's college but, under a new president, entered the 1970's in search of a new identity as a coeducational, secular institution. These organizations appeared on the surface to have little in common with each other or our three earlier cases. In early workshops of the Strategies project, teams from these colleges said they could see little to gain from interacting with the strange bedfellows Arthur Chickering had somehow gathered together. Yet their educational and organizational problems had much in common. At the level of educational practice, each had three and a half month courses organized by academic discipline and mostly learned by reading books, sitting in classrooms and taking tests under the guidance of professional scholars who had no training for teaching and who were seldom seen by students outside class. For organizational change, each relied on administrative initiative, committee proposal, political debate and pilot projects, all of this activity conducted by individuals without training in planned change. Could these educational and organizational practices be improved? In 1971, some members of Commuter Private, Black Cooperative and Mountain College thought there was room for improvement. This is the story of their efforts to introduce change into these complex organizations.

DIVERSITY AT COMMUTER PRIVATE

Commuter Private University straddles a highway on mid-Long Island. In the 1950's, it was a liberal arts college whose members took pride in their scholarly ways and their ability to get students into Harvard and Yale. During the 1960's, however, the college joined many others in rapidly expanding to serve a wide variety of student capabilities and interests. Professional schools at Commuter Private grew and an innovative provost initiated an experimental sub-college whose job would be the development and testing of new models for curriculum, teaching and evaluation. Public higher education was rapidly developing on the Island, however, and when the student population boom slowed, Commuter Private's enrollment suffered. Its administrative leaders began to search after new ways to compete with their far less expensive neighbors.

One such leader was an associate provost who had been on the university faculty for decades and was the director of a small "Center for the Study of Higher Education." The provost, a person who long had pursued under-graduate innovation, involved Commuter Private in the Strategies project and turned over internal leadership to his associate, who was at least as well linked as himself to trends in higher education. Both persons were interested in the Strategies for Change and Knowledge Utilization Project primarily because it offered a way of gathering data about university functioning. Once in, they also agreed to identify an innovation issue which Strategies staff could watch. The associate provost decided that the univeristy "will try to move forward incipient plans for establishing small college units serving different student purposes." He called the idea "diversity." Various college units would diversify teaching and learning approaches, educational objectives, schedules and degree formats; each program unit would itself clarify and emphasize its unique differences from other units. He later admitted, "the whole thing was purely my idea. I was asked to produce some proposal at the Chicago workshop in July, 1971 [a Strategies event], and I came up with that idea. In a way, it's a collection of many separate ideas I've toyed with now and again." He based his proposal particularly on a recent publication of the Carnegie Commission, *Less Time, More Options*, and cited trends in higher education toward a greater diversity of college students and life-long learning options.

He sent his proposal to the Provost's Advisory Council with the recommendation that a committee be established to examine the options and propose ways to diversify education at Commuter Private. The council did okay a committee, which the associate provost was to establish. He said he "chose people who were interested in change, both positively and negatively. I tended toward the positives, of course, but mostly I wanted *attitudes*, of whatever inclination: activist faculty. And I chose people who were already active and well-known . . . opinion leaders. My third criterion was diversity in constituency." The committee was given the diversity proposal but told it could "set up its own specific goals and procedures; its primary function is to study ways of implementing changes in the university."

The first gathering of committee members was the first Strategies workshop for campus teams in late October of 1971. A new associate dean of education and another associate dean of arts and sciences, the second an influential faculty leader, joined the associate provost in that Philadelphia meeting. They debated whether to do anything at all in the project. The arts and sciences dean was unimpressed by the survey instruments to be used in Strategies studies and argued with Strategies National Advisor Warren Bryan Martin over whether or not the university merely offered a traditional education under shifting innovative names and would do well, as Martin suggested, to stick to its traditional character. He did, however, find the Strategies staff competent and liked a discussion of governance literature I did for the workshop. He began to see some advantage in having Strategies staff interview various individuals at the university and

The associate provost decided that the university "will try to move forward incipient plans for establishing small college units serving different student purposes."

observe the process of planned change. The full committee agreed in its first on-campus meeting to study five changes already underway. A young assistant professor of economics fresh from innovative activities at the City College of New York (CCNY) joined the group and urged that it take an active stance. I also wrote the committee to say I thought Commuter Private and Strategies could benefit from their study of current change attempts. When no meetings or action occurred between November and February, primarily because all the committee members were over-committed leaders within the university, the assistant professor of economics and the associate dean of arts and sciences had this oral exchange:

> *Associate Dean: "Could we clear up something as to what we had last done? My understanding is that the associate provost had informed the staff that we would not be sponsoring any projects on campus, that the off-campus group would be invited on to monitor and distribute questionnaires, and that we would cooperate in that."*
>
> *Assistant Professor: "No. I think if you read the associate provost's recent memo on it, that he sort of made the decision, based on some input, that we would go back and do the projects we had talked about. The January 18th memo. So that really, if everything goes well, we would really have a fairly full level of participation in the Project. . . . [You] really were the one who started the debate about us not participating."*
>
> *Associate Dean: "I liked [Lindquist's] proposal that we not try to start . . . I mean, I suggested that we get out of it, but I like Jack's suggestion that we have the off-campus group come on and monitor ongoing innovative proposals with our cooperation, but that we not sponsor any particular one. That's where I thought we were."*
>
> *Assistant Professor: "You mean without sponsoring any? But really, how can you monitor change if we don't do those projects we talked about?"*

Because the associate dean was upset over an attempt by a trustee to merge several departments into a "School of the Arts" and the assistant professor wanted to bring about the adoption of a plan he brought from CCNY to change three credit, three contact hour courses to four credit, three contact hours, the two eventually agreed to study these two change attempts as examples of "top down" and "bottom up" strategies. The second Strategies workshop in March of 1972 provided the occasion and pressure for them to nail down an action plan to complete these studies by mid-June, which they did. That would be the only activity of the committee in 1971-72. But as one committee member told our staff, this project was not exactly of burning interest. The associate provost and assistant professor of economics were able to get the group to do the studies simply because "We said we'd do it, so we'll do it, but without any great glee or joy or any expectations that it was going to change anything."

The associate provost's diversity proposal had disappeared. The committee never took it up, and the associate provost sought no other avenue of acceptance that year. When later asked why, he explained: "I'm

167

willing to push on administrative things but not on things like this. If people don't want it, I'm not going to push it. And without a strong advocate, it disappeared. The others were too busy with other things to really push it." The associate provost was not willing to become an issue sponsor for the idea, although he remained interested and would come back to diversity during the next two years.

The next mention of diversity occurred in the Strategies projects' first annual review and planning workshop in Saratoga Springs. Information gathered the first year of the project was given to the provost, the associate provost, the assistant professor of economics and the president of the student senate. This information revealed to these people considerable diversity in teaching styles and learning experiences, a wide range of student and faculty characteristics and a very low score on the closeness of "Community." Also, earlier interviews and this survey data suggested that the participative governance system was so cumbersome, with so little executive initiative, that "death by terminal committee" had become a rampant disease. Strategies staff member Judy McCormack made this report on team discussions:

> On examination of the data on the first morning of the Workshop, two problems were highlighted: (1) it was difficult to ever reach consensus at Commuter Private because of its diverse population (the diversity supported by the questionnaire data), and (2) the decision-making machinery was so cumbersome that many new ideas were squelched (this supported primarily by interview data and inputs from the university people). Tim Pitkin [Strategies National Advisor] asked if it was feasible to exploit Commuter Private's diversity rather than try to buck it and attempt to reach consensus. His line of questioning initiated animated discussion concerning possible ways of capitalizing on diversity. Tim suggested the formulation of separate schools with differing educational philosophies as a possible model for the university. All four participants picked up on this idea and much time was spent during the remainder of the workshop examining and embellishing upon it. At one point, the institutional representative was questioned about the fact that his initial Strategies proposal dealt with the diversity issue. He concurred, but seemed to want to minimize any connection there.

> Strategies were discussed for presenting the data to the appropriate people in appropriate ways so as to raise interest and awareness on campus of some of the institutional problems suggested by the data. The hope was to spark interest in exploiting Commuter Private's diversity as a possible solution to these problems.

> At the time the group departed, there was a shift in focus of the project, and it remained unclear whether or not there would be any follow-through with respect to studying the School of the Arts or the four credit plan.

The team's action plan called for further examination of the data and formulation of action questions related to it. According to the plan, "A

"Death by terminal committee" had become a rampant disease.

major finding of the data is *diversity* with regard to academic programs, environment, teaching techniques and goals—consequently a major question will be how this diversity can be best accommodated." It was the young economics professor, however, rather than the associate provost, who had time to follow up on the Saratoga plan for disseminating this information; according to the professor, the data told a different story than that identified in the action plan:

> *As the tone of my report makes clear, the major finding of the data, in my opinion, is not diversity but rather weakness in our educational product. In particular, our results on the CUES "Scholarship" scale, "Campus Morale" scale, "Community" scale, and on the IFI "Concern for Undergraduate Education" scale give me great cause for concern.*

These scales showed that students did not experience much intellectual or scholarly vigor nor much closeness with other students or faculty, while faculty reported little concern for undergraduate students. He concluded that, "Based on our discussion at Saratoga, as well as my interpretation of the data, I feel our committee should become more action-oriented. That is, we should become more agents of change and less observers of the process of change." He then called a meeting of the "Saratoga Four." The associate provost could not attend but a long-tenured professor, now special assistant to the president, was added. The group decided not to disseminate the data further because of low response rates but to build from their own understanding of it several workshops to "Make a Better Commuter Private." Advising, a concern of the special assistant, would be one focus. An *ad hoc* committee would spend a semester studying, advising and drafting a proposal which was not to be officially acted upon by the administration.

Tim Pitkin had suggested in Saratoga that action on diversity would have to come from the top, from the provost, in order to succeed. When interviewed in the late fall, the provost said he still was committed but had been preoccupied with staff cuts necessitated by enrollment drops. The associate provost in turn was busy chairing the search for a new president and taking over the computer center. He said he saw diversity as the only viable long-term answer for the university, but he just couldn't get to it. The only person active in leading Strategies-related activities, the economics professor, was busy with the large *ad hoc* committee formed to study advisement.

But the idea would not die. In February of 1973, Tim Pitkin and I visited Commuter Private in preparation for a scheduled faculty-administration-student workshop. While chatting with the associate provost, Pitkin asked whatever happened to that diversity idea. The next morning, the associate provost opened another conversation with us by saying, "You always get me thinking, Tim." He proceeded to say he had been up since five that morning roughing out a program and course catalog along the lines of the *Whole Earth Catalog*, with each ad designed to illustrate one diverse aspect of the university. He thought such a catalog, with ads contributed by departments, could sell the institution's rich diversity at the same time it alerted some faculty and administration to

"A major finding of the data is **diversity** *with regard to academic programs, environment, teaching techniques and goals — consequently a major question will be how this diversity can be best accommodated."*

169

"You always get me thinking, Tim."

diversity itself. He already had typed out twenty lively and humorous pages. With follow-through by the young economics professor and his student government friends an *Alternative Bulletin* came out that summer. Its impact was not determined, however, and its student editor killed it the next year because "the quantity of material submitted [by departments] was minimal, the quality outrageously poor but for the material submitted by the Sociology department." It was an innovation dependent on people who were neither interested nor skilled in it.

In March of 1973, the associate provost, provost and economics professor hosted a workshop for faculty and administrative opinion leaders and some student leaders. One session, attended by a half dozen of the thirty-odd participants, concerned the associate provost's diversity proposal. Immediately an arts and sciences dean for freshman programs claimed that diversity could become a chaotic disaster. Instead, Community Private should cut back on some of its current diversity and become well-known for doing a few things at high quality. The university's new dean of arts and sciences tried to effect some line of agreement between this view and those supporting diversity. The associate provost's report to the full workshop stated that the group had supported three kinds of diversity: student diversity (but perhaps not in intellectual ability, it said), degree or course credit options and different kinds of educational experiences. No specific follow-up on this workshop was planned, although the provost had wanted to use this beginning as a way to become more active in academic leadership. Distribution of reports from sessions such as the associate provost's were delayed by the assistant professor of economics until fall.

I interviewed a dozen participants in that workshop one year later, in February of 1974. I asked whatever became of the diversity report. One answer, by the assistant professor of economics, was that the cluster college idea had become a major interest of a four member "Wild Card Committee" appointed by the dean of arts and sciences to brainstorm about the future of that school. The economics professor was on that committee, which had held sessions with most of the departments of the School of Liberal Arts and Sciences (LAS) to discover their views of the future. The group learned that many faculty felt disciplinary training as currently offered was essential. Yet in their sessions with students they learned that many students felt "uninvolved, undedicated, put upon by the establishment [and] lacking in educational commitment." The students "feel that their education is meaningless, don't know anyone, and have nothing to do." They learned that despite a friendly faculty atmosphere and loyalty to the university, departments were "distant islands" from one another. "Nobody knew on this campus what the hopes, aspirations are. But what was worse, I found this was true within a department. Individuals within a department didn't know what the other guy was teaching, what he hoped to do for students, what he saw his contribution to that particular field to be." The Wild Card Committee, by this time consisting of only three members (the fourth had withdrawn), drew the following conclusions from their year of study, discussions and interviews:

The cluster college idea had become a major interest of a four member "Wild Card Committee" appointed by the dean of arts and sciences to brainstorm about the future of that school.

They learned that many students felt "uninvolved, undedicated, put upon by the establishment [and] lacking in educational commitment."

WHAT'S WRONG WITH THE PRESENT EDUCATIONAL SYSTEM?

1. *The over-standardized curriculum has too little room for the special needs of individual students.*
2. *The present curriculum is too closed to have room for a growing tip of new courses and curricula.*
3. *It has been too much (and too ineffectual) a dedication to the "liberal arts" as the only set of materials worth pursuing.**
4. *It relies on an unfounded conviction that specialization in a field is the mark of an educated man.*
5. *There is too little concern for new possibilities for a more general and comprehensive type of education.*
6. *There is too little responsiveness to a changing student population in a changing world.*
7. *Departments have become too nationalistic and insular—not to mention arrogant in their splendid isolation from the crunch of contemporary problems. This leads to each department vying to dominate the curriculum with the accompanying alliances, power struggles and antipathies so hostile to an educational community.*
8. *Students are apathetic, unawakened and lacking in enthusiasm.*
9. *There is haphazard advisement by persons without sympathy for students and themselves lacking the kind of educational breadth which would permit imaginative and creative advisement.*
10. *There is too much conviction that a lacklustre curriculum can be remedied by the mere proliferation of new courses.*
11. *There is failure to realize that without interested and inspired teachers the best curriculum can go aground.*
12. *There is failure to bring faculty and students together in groups with similar intellectual interests and goals, with the concomitant failure to develop commitment to learning and a sense of community in a common enterprise.*
13. *There is failure to provide mechanisms whereby students and faculty would together be responsible for the development, evaluation and repair of the curriculum.*
14. *There is failure on the part of the institution to provide the funds for personnel and equipment necessary for an effective learning experience.*

*One member of the three disagrees with #3.

171

Based on this inventory of problems and their own educational views, the committee set forth seven educational principles:

1. *The goal of education should be not only to provide the student with the ability to understand his world but to give the student some competence in being able to cope with it.*
2. *The educational process should be flexible enough to provide a variety of ways of doing this.*

3. *Classroom experience needs to be revitalized and made relevant to the student's life and times via whatever new types of learning experiences particular fields of inquiry permit.*

4. *The notion that a field must be studied in depth is indeed the typical standard for traditional curriculum and we give our allegiance to this conception of education. Yet we wish, as well, to make room for studies in breadth which permit students to gain a rudimentary competence across many fields. This type of "general education," we feel, is more useful than the traditional one in many of the newer interests and pursuits for which students are now coming to college.*

5. *The need for coherence (not standardization) within a curriculum is of utmost importance in providing the basis for intellectual commitment.*

6. *The essence of education lies in motivated teachers and students. A good educational institution focuses on their involvement with each other and with inquiry.*

7. *The heart of the educational experience does not lie so much in particular subject matters which are sometimes thought to make it up but in the process of learning itself and the type of vision.*

The Wild Card Committee's proposal for resolving Commuter Private's educational problems in accordance with these principles (and an awareness of departmental entrenchment) was that two kinds of majors be offered: "the traditional subject matter major which should be left intact" and "thematic cluster majorships yet to be developed." The latter would be a group of courses bound by a common theme or problem. They also proposed that all departments be grouped into "area units" that might stimulate cross-disciplinary interaction about "substantive intellectual matters" and curricular review. They then proceeded to outline several kinds of thematic majorships they recommended, among them urban problems and ecology.

No formal action was taken on these proposals. The Wild Card Committee continued to meet among themselves and with the remaining nine departments in LAS. From these meetings they relayed departmental gripes to the dean. Their own sessions now focused on information outside the university. Members read the Newman Report, several Carnegie Commission reports, Jerry Gaff's *The Cluster College*, and the Riesman, Gamson, Gusfield study of Oakland and Monteith.[1] The latter was particularly interesting to the members who were interviewed, for it related directly to their concern for integrating the disciplines and the student's concerns. They also became increasingly interested in cluster colleges as they heard students complain primarily that there is at Commuter Private "no sense of community and no sense of relationship; they feel lost." In addition, they searched out other literature and attended AAHE's national conference in Chicago.

But many faculty were not eager to consider thematic majors or cluster colleges. As one Wild Card member said,

The faculty, I found out, are very resistant to change, very resis-

172

tant, largely because they don't know what it's going to mean to them, to the way in which they have taught. They're afraid that someone is going to tell them, "Look, you have to teach this new course you never taught before, and you have to do it in a new way."

The associate dean of LAS put the same concern another way: "Interdisciplinary work is a pain in the neck. We are organizationally and intellectually structured by disciplines. Don't create another rut which would be very expensive in time and energy." It should be mentioned that the associate dean himself was coordinating development of area studies programs for underclassmen.

The committee found resistance particularly acute in the natural sciences. It was, in fact, a natural scientist who had dissented and dropped out of the committee. They learned, one member said, that many scientists felt "this interest in matters educational belongs to those idiots in the social sciences" and "there is a real, hard-core discipline that's got to be taught and to hell with it, it's got to be taught." Again, defensiveness seemed the order of the day. One Wild Card Committee member noted:

> Despite the fact that I came into every one of those interviews literally on my hands and knees backward, apologizing for being there, said many many times that we were the learners, that we wanted their best opinion, insisted that we would be guided by what they had to say, everyone felt evaluated. And negatively too. This was the most pervasive experience that I had with this. I, of course, began to be concerned about educational innovation under these conditions. This was a defensive reaction, as if they were being graded on their insufficiencies in knowing what other people were doing in their field, their insufficiencies in knowing about innovation.

The dean himself was encouraging development of problem or special topic-centered freshman programs, but he did not take the cluster idea further. He essentially closed that gate on the Wild Card Committee. This year the provost was not acting as provost but head of a special commission on university goals, and he felt a cluster college structure might be one kind of model to propose. The idea would stay around awhile. The associate provost, however, now was acting provost and had no time for his own proposal, he said.

During 1972-73, a trustee had assumed the role of acting president and had taken bold strokes to balance the budget in the face of rising costs and declining enrollments. He was most supportive of the Strategies project, especially an "Interim Report" I wrote to summarize interviews about the institution's educational health. That report cited interview and questionnaire data. One common theme was "Misconnections Between Faculty and Student," a consistent interviewee complaint that many faculty and most students just were not getting together in meaningful ways. Student life was not intellectually stimulating, despite agreement among students and faculty that the latter were highly qualified scholars and loyal to the university. Interviewees saw the need for stronger administrative leadership for determining the institution's future course instead

"The faculty, I found out, are very resistant to change, very resistant, largely because they don't know what it's going to mean to them, to the way in which they have taught."

173

The associate provost, however, now was acting provost and had no time for his own proposal.

of merely responding to external or internal pressures.

The acting president avoided educational leadership as being out of his businessman's league. In 1973-74, a permanent president was in office, and his theme, repeatedly emphasized in speeches, was excellence and distinction. He decided to use a second on-campus "Strategies for Change" workshop of university leaders, set for April, 1974, to begin focusing on the few things the university could do extremely well rather than attempting to do something for everybody. He keynoted that workshop by quoting a recent speech by Lewis Mayhew, which urged narrowing down to a few distinctive functions. The associate provost (now acting provost) again led a session on diversity, on "human-sized communities" which might be cluster colleges or thematically organized groups of faculty and students, each with high academic standards. Each sub-group turned the workshop topic of "distinction" into "excellence" or "quality." There was a pervasive concern that Commuter Private re-establish a reputation for very high educational standards. The president confirmed this tendency by opening the last session with a letter he intended to place in the New York Times. It stressed the university's commitment to raising admissions standards:

> The first principle that will guide our admission practice is this: we will accept only those students whom we are prepared to serve, which means students who are ready and able to profit from what our university has to offer. This will exclude marginally qualified students, simply because such students require far more help than we are able to give.

Quality, in short, would be accomplished first by raising student performance at entrance. The second strategy proposed by the president was to raise internal standards for student performance. One of the workshop consultants, Tim Pitkin, wanted to know what Commuter Private was going to do to deserve these so-called students with high standards. He was doubtful that the university could change its quality and reputation just by declaring it and by setting new admissions and performance standards. Another workshop speaker, however, Joseph Campbell of Sarah Lawrence College, said "I'm very sympathetic" to raising standards, that "high quality" students left Sarah Lawrence when entrance standards were lowered, and, as for faculty, "People who are willing to teach uninteresting students are often uninteresting people." Some students in the workshop were irritated by this talk and felt the president's position was elitist and snobbish. But most faculty members and administrators in attendance spoke in favor of toughening standards.

The acting provost attempted to summarize the day. He said he still saw diverse programs, "possibly even diverse cluster colleges," as the way to go within a general theme of excellence. "What we can try to do is to provide alternative routes to a quality education." The next step, he felt, was to define "quality," the heart of Commuter Private's educational philosophy. Several other people then proposed what should be done next, though no specific plans were made.

The day after this workshop, the president uncovered for Strategies interviewers his tentative design for the university. It would have three

174

He was doubtful that the university could change its quality and reputation just by declaring it and by setting new admissions and performance standards.

tiers. A "Low College" of two year liberal arts programs in academic disciplines would involve particularly student-oriented faculty. A "Middle College" of three years would have scholars present their specialties to students, with a masters degree at the end. The third tier, "Upper College," would include traditional doctoral programs but also life-long learning through an "Alumni College." These tiers would be wed by a commitment to high academic standards and the traditional disciplines. He said, "I am not enamoured of the cluster college concept because traditional disciplines have stood the test of time." In an interview with the former provost the same day, Strategies staff members learned that he viewed the three-tiered plan and the cluster college approach as of equal merit. His major concern was that the previous day's workshop might represent a simplistic approach to the intellectual development needs cited in my earlier report.

> After reading your stuff [Strategies reports], my hunch is that a key factor in Commuter Private's future might well be how your understanding of intellectual development permeates the president's and others' definitions of excellence. You're writing about substantive changes in most of our professors' approach to teaching, the data suggests, while I suspect a good number of those who would have to change are interpreting excellence as license to do what we've been doing, but with more academically eager and successful students. Better admissions standards will shape up this place. I hope that hunch is wrong.

The former provost was not in a strong position to influence definitions of excellence, for his goals commission was off to the side of governance and he himself was near retirement. The acting provost was about to be replaced by the arts and sciences dean. Within a year, he would lose his associate provost position, the computer center directorship and the Center for the Study of Higher Education directorship. The assistant professor of economics, whose activities had been sponsored by the associate provost, retreated back into economics instead of putting together a "whole series" of workshops on Commuter Private education, at one time his plan for the next year. Leadership of the Strategies project passed to the new provost. He sent a team of an associate dean of arts and sciences, two faculty members and the dean of the experimental sub-college to Strategies' third annual review and planning workshop in Saratoga in late July of 1974. The group was new to Strategies and expressed suspicion that the project was part of past agendas. It did produce a general report which was submitted to the provost. No evidence of its impact was made available to us. There have been no indications that follow-up on the diversity proposal has occurred.

During the years from 1972 to 1974, teaching and learning at Commuter Private changed somewhat toward the tougher emphasis on professorial standards favored by many faculty and administrative participants in the 1974 workshop. The CUES item "Lectures follow the textbook" went up from 40% in 1972 to 53% in 1974. "If he wanted to, a student probably could pass this course mainly on 'bluff'" went down from 31% to 22%. Students indicating substantial influence over course content and

"I am not enamoured of the cluster college concept because traditional disciplines have stood the test of time."

175

Visible changes suggested a faculty adhering more to traditional tests and grading standards and a student body responding in kind without becoming either more or less involved or satisfied.

An idea without high level leaders dedicated to seeing it through was not going very far.

structure went down significantly from 28% in 1972 to 17% in 1974. Studying "to broaden general knowledge, understanding, or background" went down from 24% to 16%, while studying "to get good grades" went up from 4% to 11%. Interest and challenge did not significantly change, according to students. Student satisfaction remained moderately high. Visible changes suggested a faculty adhering more to traditional tests and grading standards and a student body responding in kind without becoming either more or less involved or satisfied. The data did not reveal any more or better diversity of teaching and learning.

The diversity idea had found several routes into Commuter Private. The experimental sub-college and diverse new programs for new students spoke to this agenda in the 1960's. But neither the associate provost's nor the Wild Card Committee's proposals had progressed very far. Why? One answer seems to be that although the idea found gatekeepers high enough in the system to get a hearing (the Provost's Advisory Council and the arts and sciences dean), no persistent, skillful, high status issue sponsors appeared. The associate provost kept his idea afloat but had neither the time nor the inclination to push it. The provost was interested but could not muster decisive leadership at the end of his tenure within the university. The arts and sciences dean supported a diverse cluster program for freshmen but chose not to pick up the ball on the Wild Card Committee's more ambitious proposal, and the committee members felt they must not agitate beyond their charge to deliver recommendations to this administrator. The energetic assistant professor of economics at first saw other concerns as more burning than diversity. The president in 1971-72 was on the way out; the 1972-73 president was an interim businessman; the president since fall of 1973 was interested in high standards and discipline-based liberal education rather than diverse clusters. As the associate provost observed, an idea without high level leaders dedicated to seeing it through was not going very far.

A second reason for failure appeared to be a clash in values. Persons interested in meritocracy thought the best route to the future was by traditional means: high admissions standards and the presentation or pursuit of disciplinary expertise with tough evaluations. To them, diversity sounded like trying to do everything for everybody and thus doing nothing well. Others were most concerned about finding ways to make education exciting and meaningful for the diverse students Commuter Private had and, they thought, would have to have, to meet salary and mortgage payments. Student complaints about uninvigorating education seemed to them reason to change education; the first group seemed to be more interested in changing the level of entering students than the ability of the university to meet diverse student needs. The first group, supported by the new president and several senior faculty leaders remaining from a more elitist past, held the trump cards.

Third, both the associate provost and the Wild Card Committee identified a need and developed a proposed solution in relative isolation from those who had to be convinced. Because most leaders saw things differently, they were not persuaded by the written word. They had not been to those department sessions with the Wild Card members. They were not up on the evidence which lay behind *Less Time, More Options*. The experimental sub-college in their midst seemed to attract students quite unlike the serious young scholars which many faculty leaders preferred. These leaders did not go into the dorms or the student center to ask students what was the matter, and when students did complain at the Strategies workshop, they were called unrepresentative, picked by the "radical" economics professor or part of the left wing of student government. Strategies data was equally identified with the change-oriented associate provost and economics professor. A couple of one-day workshops over two years was not enough to open people to evidence contrary to their beliefs.

Perhaps a slow, open involvement by leaders of high status and credibility to traditionalists would have helped get a substantial hearing for diversity. But as incompatible as the idea was with prevalent desires, despite its fit with current reality, it is perhaps unlikely that it could overcome senior faculty preferences without strong support from executive administrators. Warren Bryan Martin appeared correct in 1971 when he said, based on earlier observations, "Faculty at Commuter Private looked to status institutions for benchmarks, and to traditionalists. These men want the university to gain stability and excellence in the traditional sense." Most agreed with the associate provost and the Wild Card Committee that there was a need to improve the vigor of undergraduate education, but they saw the solution quite differently. Don't change basic curriculum or teaching. Change incoming students and toughen traditional academic standards.

NON-TRADITIONAL TEACHING FOR NON-TRADITIONAL STUDENTS

Black Cooperative is an institution serving about twelve hundred students, mostly black, from the urban North and rural South. Its long-term president had led the adoption of the cooperative work and study curriculum but by 1971 found himself pre-occupied with building new campus facilities and finding funds to cover both tuition and other costs of educating poor students. Internal administrative leadership fell to a dual academic deanship. One dean was a white man, who helped obtain grants and otherwise facilitate institutional development but who was looked on as a guest, not the legitimate leader of the black school; the other was a black woman, the daughter of a previous president. She was somewhat unhappy with the dual arrangement.

The white dean knew Chickering from their days as colleagues at Goddard, and he enlisted Black Cooperative in the Strategies project. Chickering described initial campus reactions as follows: "Moderate level—not much bounce from rest of staff to material circulated, so no clear commitment of faculty. The president reacted immediately positively to study of what happens to students in college and using that information. Commitment at administrative level without much grassroots reaction." When funding was delayed a year, even this amount of support was questionable. The white dean saw the president's active involvement as crucial, for others looked to him as to a father for signs of

A couple of one-day workshops over two years was not enough to open people to evidence contrary to their beliefs.

177

Chickering described initial campus reactions as follows: "Moderate level—not much bounce from rest of staff to material circulated, so no clear commitment of faculty."

what is worth doing, but neither the dean nor our staff could ever get anything more than verbal support of the project from him. The first participant instead was a young assistant professor of psychology in charge of institutional research who attended a Strategies "institutional representative's" meeting in Chicago in July, 1971. He wrote a plan to study student experiences, but by fall, the dean reported that the psychologist "has been buried in classes and overdue work, and I have not seen him for two minutes on end." This was the first of many instances in which other demands on Strategies participants, all of whom carried heavy loads and were attempting other innovations, would prevent follow-through.

In late October of 1971, however, the dean did get a young instructor of English, the director of alumni and an older student involved in student personnel at the university to attend the first team workshop of the Strategies project in Philadelphia. The psychologist could not attend, and the others were not researchers. They worked on the idea of studying students but were not sure what good such a project would do. Then they ran into Tim Pitkin and Warren Bryan Martin, Strategies National Advisors. The English professor vividly reports that interaction.

It seemed that when all the data were gathered and analyzed, there would just be a lot of analyzed data and no clear direction for action.

178

> *The project staff seemed reasonably content with the program as I had outlined it and revised it, with our project as we had developed it, until Saturday afternoon. Prior to this I had some reservations about this project's being wide enough in scope to serve the needs of the university. It seemed that when all the data were gathered and analyzed, there would just be a lot of analyzed data and no clear direction for action. Also, the task force felt a sense of inadequacy in terms of pre-workshop meetings such as had been held by the Mountain College team consisting of an administrator, faculty, and two students which were already welded into an efficient unit before arriving at the workshop.*
>
> *So things went along pretty evenly with fascinating and educational small-group and large-group meetings, the latter run by Chick, until Saturday afternoon at 1:30. We had our plan for research pretty well figured out, and thought we could take about 15 minutes to write it up and then spend the afternoon watching the game on TV or possibly visiting the Liberty Bell (which I had never seen), but that wasn't quite the way it happened.*
>
> *When there are approximately six staff members and six visiting consultants available for conferring with about eight schools, and when two staff members and three consultants descend en masse on the Black Cooperative contingent, it gives one a strong feeling that someone somewhere was not happy with our program content. We met in one of the suites . . . reserved for the project, and the first thing said was Tim Pitkin's "What made you pick this particular project?"*
>
> *I hastily disavowed any responsibility, tactfully, and said it was an outgrowth of the prior workshop where [the institutional representative] had worked out with the Project Staff.*
>
> *"And who's [the institutional representative]?" said Tim.*

"Well . . . he's our Director of Institutional Research. . . ."

"And where's [the institutional representative]?"

"Well . . . he's back home with the flu and if he were at all able he would be here and would be much better able to answer questions?"

"Why are you here?"

"I'm only a participant observer [to help gather Project Data] and serve in that capacity but [the institutional representative] thought it would be good for the project and for me to be here. . . ."

"Does your faculty know anything about this?"

Now, about this time, our defenses were rather shot. It was as close to an encounter session as I have ever been, and Tim gave one the feeling that he could see straight through you—physically as well as psychologically, which maybe he could—and that there was no sense in being anything less than totally honest. So I said, "No."

"Who got you into this?" he asked. I replied that it was probably the Dean. Tim proceeded to ask us to describe what our school was really like, which we tried to do.

The consultant who took over after Tim demolished us was Warren Bryan (Dick) Martin from Berkeley. He had the most fantastic array of information stored in some kind of computer he uses for a brain, and we had a 15 minute dialogue which went like this.

"Have you heard of the _____ experiment?"

"No."

"Well, if you write Dr. _____ at _____, no, he just moved to _____ and his street address is _____, then you could get information on that if you are interested. On the other hand, it might be helpful to use _____. Have you heard of that?"

"No." Etc.

He sifted through half a dozen different ideas and plans before he decided that what would best suit our expressed needs, i.e., a lack of a sense of community within the student body (except when they boycott), within the faculty, within the administration (?), maybe, and certainly between [these groups] would be the Institutional Goals Survey . . . used with the Delphi Technique. And we agreed thoroughly. We also agreed that our encounter with Dick was undoubtedly one of the most exciting experiences any of the three of us have ever undergone.

179

The team's action plan, submitted at workshop conclusion, was to administer the IGI along with a process to increase goal consensus, but just when this process would take place was not specified: "The project staff was interested in a strict time schedule being constructed for our progress, but it did not seem feasible to create one, considering the large number of variables still to be dealt with. As soon as the inventory is acquired, then a schedule can be developed."

We also agreed that our encounter with Dick was undoubtedly one of the most exciting experiences any of the three of us have ever undergone.

The team met again on campus and still intended to administer the IGI, but by January nothing had happened. The psychologist explained that

> people are not too excited about looking at objectives. We are reminded by [the black dean] that the school has been through this to a limited extent. We helped the president work out a list of goals that he had to have in written form. As I remember it, we had some Saturday workshops. Faculty couldn't get turned on to that sort of thing. . . . One of the reactions to this project was, "The first attempt wasn't very exciting anyway, so why do you want to do it again?" We just wanted to say that, actually, we don't know what the heck we're doing.

A need had been stimulated by Pitkin's penetrating questions and Martin's charismatic suggestions, and an essay by Richard Peterson of ETS about IGI had "gotten me excited," said the psychologist, but there was no such generation of need among other faculty members and administrators. It seemed to be a rerun of a previously unproductive exercise. The English professor added,

> Maybe this is true at all institutions, but faculty at Black Cooperative tend to work to capacity and everything has priorities. I don't think that this has reached a position of peak priority. . . . The important thing right now is that we are just going into the North Central Association review for accreditation, which means that all minds are really tuned to this, especially the administration.

They wanted a project with more immediate payoff and executive support before they would in reality add this work to already overburdened schedules.

The four Strategies task force members were too low in rank to get the goals study incorporated into the North Central preparation, nor did they think to try that. Mostly they were trying to keep their heads above water in their own duties. They wanted a project with more immediate payoff and executive support before they would in reality add this work to already overburdened schedules.

Arthur Chickering met with the task force in the winter of 1972. He proposed a return to the original idea favored by the president: study student experiences with Strategies data, put the evidence against already existing goals and identify improvement targets out of the discrepancies between goals and evidence of practices. Again, it was a consultant's idea rather than the team's. The members said it sounded good, but they were unsure how to do it and whether it would eventually lead to improvement. The earlier strategy, on the other hand, at least would meet one immediate need they felt, that of stimulating dialogue between faculty and administration. When the team attended the second Strategies workshop of March, 1972, in Chicago, it therefore spelled out in step-by-step detail a plan to build interaction around clarification of goals. Some of the social events and discussion meetings in that plan were carried out, but the psychologist and English professor, both white, decided to cease active leadership after a confrontation between the white dean and several black staff members late that spring. Two new members of the task force, both black, also ceased involvement at this time, one out of concern that he would lose rapport with black colleagues and the other because she saw no active support from the president.

In July of 1972, data gathered during the past academic year were given to the male dean, the psychologist and a new, young English instructor persuaded to attend when neither the president nor a biologist opinion leader could be persuaded to do so. The evidence indicated that students found the curriculum, teaching and administration unduly regimented and unresponsive to student needs. Moreover, 82% of the faculty respondents agreed that "Generally speaking, communication between the faculty and administration is poor." An interviewee commented, "They don't communicate with students. Sometimes they do, but treat them paternalistically, which is wrong." A student commented that "There is a barrier between administrators and students a mile wide." Others, especially students, said faculty lecture and disappear. Many said there was no time free of heavy teaching or administrative burdens and little faculty or administrative leadership. As for governance, 74% of IFI respondents agreed that "In reality, a small group of individuals tend to pretty much run this institution." Faculty morale was very low. Only a third of the faculty respondents agreed that "there is a strong sense of community, a feeling of shared interests and purposes, on this campus." Only 18% agreed that "Generally speaking, top level administrators are providing effective educational leadership."

The small group decided that these data were, according to their perceptions, accurate but too devastating merely to be sent out to campus members. They asked me to rewrite the report and personally deliver the information to the president. This I did, and he showed much concern. He concluded the meeting by telling his secretary to send out the report under his signature. He said he was particularly concerned about the apparent emphasis on rote learning and the apparent faculty-student-administrative communication gaps. He hoped his fund-raising responsibilities would lighten enough in the next year to permit his involvement in following up this data feedback.

The president did not have opportunity to follow up. Instead, the woman dean gave a brief ("lukewarm," said observers) critique of the data in a faculty meeting. She explained later,

> We here at Black Cooperative are tired of answering questions for researchers. We have analyzed our own problems and know what they are. Outsiders have visited the university ad infinitum, and all these studies are not received here with glee. It is our opinion that people from outside see things in other lights. We have had these consultants up to here. We do not enjoy feeling put upon.

The dean may not have given public credence to the complaints about weak faculty-administrative relations, but she did take aggressive action to improve the situation. After a long discussion of the data with William Hannah, a Strategies staff member she greatly respected, she held several faculty meetings in her home, focusing on college concerns. She supported use of a governance structure of faculty committees. Interviewees said her relations with them became much more warm, open and supportive. The white co-dean had resigned the past summer, so her actions had the effect of changing the nature of academic leadership at the university in general:

"They don't communicate with students. Sometimes they do, but treat them paternalistically, which is wrong."

181

"Outsiders have visited the university ad infinitum, and all these studies are not received here with glee."

TABLE 8

BLACK COOPERATIVE UNIVERSITY
ITEM ANALYSIS OF SCALES THAT CHANGED
"INSTITUTIONAL ESPRIT"

Item #		Key	1972 %	1974 %
097	Most faculty consider the senior administrators to be able and well qualified	Agree	33	48
104	Generally, top level administrators here provide effective educational leadership	Agree	18	58*
106	Generally, communication between faculty and administration is poor	Disagree	18	49*
111	Staff infighting, backbiting, etc. seem to be more the rule than the exception	Disagree	48	77*
112	The college is currently doing a successful job in achieving its various goals	Agree	33	71*
116	Close personal friendships between administrators and faculty members are common	Agree	51	38
117	Compared with most other colleges, faculty turnover here appears somewhat high	Disagree	33	80*
121	Although they may criticize some things, most faculty seem loyal to the college	Agree	66	84
122	There is a strong sense of community here, a feeling of shared interests and purposes	Agree	30	61*
123	In general, faculty morale is high	Agree	24	49*
126	Faculty in general is strongly committed to acknowledged purposes of the college	Agree	48	84*
131	Most faculty would not defend the college against criticism from outsiders	Disagree	45	81*

*Change significant at .05 level, symmetric test.

182

In November of 1972, Strategies staff checked the progress of the local task force. We learned it had "fallen into disarray" because none of the task force members had much time, none believed that they had a project with a clear payoff and none felt a burning need to get people to look at the data. Also, the psychologist was setting up a basic skills lab, the English professor had a reading lab off the ground, the biology professor had a federally funded project underway and another erstwhile task force member was putting an audio-visual support system together. The psychologist in addition had organized weekly bag lunch discussions around articles in *Improving College and University Teaching*. Each was pursuing innovation which responded to the student needs in the data. They just could not get the less immediate and more team-oriented project going. Survey data later confirmed the positive impact of these efforts, especially the dean's, to improve institutional vitality. Faculty responses to a second administration of the *Institutional Functioning Inventory* reported a significant improvement from 1972 to 1974 in "Institutional Esprit," as Table 8 illustrates. "Concern for Innovation," "Democratic Governance" and "Self-Study and Planning" also rose. "Concern for Undergraduate Learning" made significant gains, as did academic and personal "Freedom."

The January, 1973, Strategies workshop for campus teams was held at Quaker Academic, within easy driving distance from Black Cooperative, partially to enable a sizable Cooperative team to attend. Just prior to that workshop I reported to the university interviewees an "Interim Report" summarizing their fall concerns. A major item was titled "Traditional Teaching and Non-Traditional Students." Respondents found the textbook and lecture form of education unsuited to students who had not succeeded under such pedagogy before. As one faculty member put it, "We are trying to fit students into a learning box which does not meet their needs or interests instead of fitting the learning arrangements to the student." The large Black Cooperative task force at the workshop decided to tackle this problem by first finding out just what went on in the classroom. The dean led this planning. The action plan emerging from the workshop prefaced the survey of teaching practices design by noting that "We have a particular project that is well-defined and workable as well as important. We have been frustrated up to now with the enormity of concerns of the university that has resulted in a lack of cohesion and singleness of purpose for the task force." Once faculty were queried about current practices, the task force would locate and disseminate alternative teaching and evaluation models. Then it would encourage experimentation with these alternatives through workshops and seminars. To provide leadership for this third phase, division chairpersons would receive from the dean some release time.

Back on campus, this last provision hit a snag. The chairpersons were reluctant to take release time from other duties until they saw the information on current and alternative practices. The psychologist was in charge and did design a questionnaire for faculty, but there the project bogged down. Some interviewees blamed the psychologist who, others said, "has a real problem following through. He starts with a burst of enthusiasm, does damn good work, then fizzles." The psychologist himself gave ac-

"We are trying to fit students into a learning box which does not meet their needs or interests instead of fitting the learning arrangements to the student."

"So far, failure here. No one can get these meetings set up."

184

Once again, lack of active administrative initiative and support plus the heavy workloads of task force members were the explanations given by interviewees.

counts of frequent occasions in which he launched new efforts with administrative backing, then found that backing gone when he needed it to get implementation. The associate dean admitted, "I fault myself for not doing more than I did, which was practically nothing, to encourage it. We all let it be [the psychologist's] project." The Strategies task force did meet a couple of times and decided to set up divisional meetings to administer the psychologist's questionnaire, but in March the psychologist reported, "So far, failure here. No one can get these meetings set up." The only action to assess teaching styles was a series of classroom visitations by administrators "purely to observe various techniques," the dean's memo to faculty said. No formal follow-up to identify alternative styles and to train faculty members in their use occurred in the academic year 1972-73.

In July of 1973, the associate dean and the institution's planning officer attended Strategies' second annual review and planning workshop. Again, Strategies staff made an attempt to get the president to the workshop, but he was out of the country. The twosome came up with a plan to have the university's participative Planning Committee study Strategies research from interviews, the *Institutional Functioning Inventory*, the *Experience of College Questionnaire*, and the *College and University Environment Scales*. Also, the teaching styles plan would be implemented in the fall, course and teacher evaluations would be reviewed and improved and, finally, the Planning Committee would "consider utilization of the *Institutional Goals Inventory* as an input to the continuing five year plan updating procedures" required by a large Ford Foundation grant. A final decision was the planning officer's intention to try to shift some of that Ford money from new personnel salaries to the development of current personnel, a change I and William Hannah urged when asked to review the Ford proposal. The notion was that when the Ford money ran out Black Cooperative would not have a stronger continuing staff than it had in the beginning if all the money went into new positions which the university would not be able to sustain on its own. I also urged that a black consultant, such as some I earlier had recommended, be used on campus to help implement these plans instead of (or together with) me or Hannah.

Data use did not happen. In December of 1973, the associate dean said the administration squelched it because "We feel right now that it is too soon to face them with that data." No follow-up on the teaching styles plan occurred, although the psychologist did study some appropriate literature. Once again, lack of active administrative initiative and support plus the heavy workloads of task force members were the explanations given by interviewees. The planning officer went on half-time and could not build an effective influence base with administrators or faculty. Still, innovations continued. A National Endowment for the Humanities grant supported a director and committee which changed general education from very large prescribed courses to smaller area requirement courses with some student choice. Freshman English was revised considerably by the English department toward a competency model supported by reading labs, while mathematics also shifted toward a competency-based, basic skills program. A series of small freshman seminars was initiated by the associate dean. A small Lilly Endowment award permitted a committee to hold luncheon workshops on effective instruction led by faculty members honored for their teaching. The dean and a few faculty members began attending regional meetings on new teaching techniques ("which work, not theory," said the dean). The governance system was made more democratic in adherence with another grant expectation, and the dean generally supported this system of working committees reporting to the faculty. Students were about the same in 1974 as 1971 in background, though interviewees found them less hostile toward authority in 1974. Nearly all these changes occurred as a result of strong administrative initiative in the fulfillment of the conditions of external grants. In contrast, the Strategies project offered very little financial incentive and was initially an effort by junior faculty members and administrators without sustained executive backing. The new ideas—competency-based basic skills programs, reading and learning laboratories, uses of audio-visual equipment, freshman seminars—were introduced by a very few individuals who were mostly administrators and well-connected to external information channels. Most were specific structural changes that could be quickly implemented, whereas the self-study proposals of the Strategies task force were more vague and long-range in terms of possible payoff. It would appear that "Support at the Top," "Capacity" (time, money, skill), and "Linkage to Innovation Channels" are some general factors which help explain why some and not other innovations were implemented at Black Cooperative University. The school was losing enrollment, down from about 1200 in 1971 to under 900 in 1975. Interviewees suggested that lack of good co-op jobs, terrible food and living conditions, a woefully inadequate library and lack of quiet study space, the isolation of the campus and a perceived indifference to students among business personnel were some of the reasons students either did not attend or quickly dropped out. But the academic program and academic administration were far less the subjects of student criticism in 1974, interviewees thought.

Nearly all these changes occurred as a result of strong administrative initiative in the fulfillment of the conditions of external grants.

185

NEW DIRECTIONS VS. OLD TRADITIONS

Mountain College was a small, Catholic, women's, liberal arts institution until the mid-1960's. Then its board brought in a new president who had interned under Jim Dixon, former president of Antioch, and decided to seek a distinctive position as a co-educational college. By 1971, when the Strategies project came on the scene, the new president had recruited new trustees with interest in innovation and had hired several executive administrators supportive of her ideas. What were those ideas?

> I guess I would have to admit that the only vision that I had was that, in fact, Mountain College was on a dead-end path prior to 1965. What I knew of what students were saying and the kind of questions I was raising personally, about the validity of doing things the way they had been done in terms of credits and courses and majors and departmentalizing knowledge, just indicated to me that there had to be, not one way, but multiple ways to reach what I think the end of education should be, i.e. the ability of persons to be self-directive and thereby capable of learning exclusive of other

186

people or institutions. So I suppose that if I were going to sit down and plan a college, it wouldn't be Mountain College as it is. The option I had was to revitalize, or revamp, or renovate, or open up, or whatever term you want to use, an institution that was already steeped in tradition and a way of being and had a lot of its tentacles plowed deep in the past which it didn't seem to me realistic to completely uproot.

Her goal was to help students become independent learners through diverse and personalized learning experiences. But she faced a fairly lock-step curriculum and departmentalized structure to which students were dependent for learning and credit. The question was, how could the president shift the focus from formal curriculum to individual student?

Her first strategy had been to recruit trustees and administrators sympathetic to this goal. Next she received from the new board a mandate to come up in one year with a long-range plan for the college. She appointed a fifteen-member long-range planning committee to direct a participative effort. Volunteers also were welcome, and meetings were open. The committee met a couple of hours a week throughout the year. But, with little direct guidance from the president nor much access to external expertise or systematic research on internal practices, "nothing would jell." A general statement of philosophy was written, and numerous proposals were made. After the president replaced the traditionalist vice president for academic affairs with an innovative one, even more ideas percolated. At the end of the year, however, a unified plan was not forthcoming. Perhaps more significently, the open and voluntary process had not involved several senior, influential faculty members. While a third of the faculty talked and studied and brainstormed, others went about their business relatively untouched. Some of these later became vocal opponents of the eventual plan.

The president decided to take the situation into her own hands. In late December of 1970, she took the new vice president and her friend the dean of students up into the Rockies, and there they pulled together the long-range planning materials into a document called "New Directions." She felt it was a "compromise of a whole number of compromises . . . not nearly as daring as we would have wanted it to be." It was a general statement with eleven points aiming to personalize and make more flexible learning at the college. Before submitting the plan to the faculty, the president phoned the trustees and held a trustee meeting to get their approval. She later explained, "On occasion, I decide the only hope of doing something is to use some power." The upshot was that faculty members gathered together in an early January faculty institute found New Directions a *fait accompli*. Several were angered that a supposedly collaborative planning process had suddenly become bureaucratic fiat. Because much of the plan called for individual faculty members to alter their teaching and advising so as to take a more personalized, individualized approach, and because there was no ready means to enforce individual changes in teaching or advising, several faculty members simply avoided implementation of New Directions. One structural change, a shift from academic departments to three interdisciplinary divisions, however, was administratively implemented. Division chairpersons nevertheless found considerable resistance to the new structure and, within a year, it was revised into several smaller program units. Core requirements, however, were subsequently abolished in line with New Directions, and stayed abolished.

Two academic innovations quite in keeping with New Directions also emerged in 1970-71. One was the University Without Walls. The president's contacts with Antioch included the Union for Experimenting Colleges and Universities. When that consortium launched University Without Walls, the president enlisted Mountain College as one of the charter locations. The Office of Education and the Ford Foundation picked up the first year's costs. A director and small staff were hired, and college faculty served as advisors or instructors. The program started small, with only eighteen students the first semester, and it was carefully evaluated. The director kept the faculty assessed of enrollment and expenses. Because most University Without Walls students were older than other Mountain College students, the program quickly established itself not as a competitor with existing programs but as a strong source of new tuition for a college experiencing declining enrollment. Also, although some faculty found the University Without Walls too much a departure from traditional courses and curriculum for their comfort, survey data showed that the college's faculty as a whole was more interested in undergraduate learning and had greater frequency of student-faculty contact than other Strategies institutions. There was faculty support for the personalized approach which marked the new program. In the next few years, as evaluation and accreditation legitimized the University Without Walls and increasing percentages of new college enrollees came to take degrees through that program, this essentially external innovation, formally disseminated through the president, became a mainstay of education at Mountain College and probably the best example of "New Directions" in operation.

The second sizable innovation launched in 1970-71 took quite a different route. Instead of an externally and administratively disseminated model, this was the brainstorm of two long-tenured faculty members. They became interested over the years in improving the learning experiences of freshmen. As one recalled:

> It really developed when we had some discussions of short stories with some students the year before (i.e. 1970) in my home. We watched the thing evolve and it went very well. We saw a lot of enthusiasm on the part of the students. We talked to them about what kind of learning experiences college should bring to you. That's where the idea originated.

In another part of the college, a few faculty members and student personnel staff were attempting a living-learning experiment. Though this program was highly unstructured and collapsed after one semester, the idea of uniting living with learning in a continuing relationship with a few faculty members appealed to the two faculty friends. One of the two found herself on the curriculum sub-committee of long-range planning, and, as that group explored ways to create independent learners, she worked up a

There was faculty support for the personalized approach which marked the new program.

187

188

proposal which she said "got buried" in the committee's reports. The only reference to it in New Directions was a call for "an intensive orientation which involves many members of the college community."

During the faculty institute in January of 1972, however, consultant Arthur Chickering spotted that line and extolled the virtues of an intensive freshman orientation to various modes of higher learning. One interviewee reflected the responses of others when she said, "I think Art Chickering had a great deal to do with administrative consideration. . . . He thought a freshman program had a great deal of validity, and it seemed to spark, I think, people to look into it." One of the proposal's originators agreed but commented, "I might add parenthetically that there was some resentment on the part of the people who knew about the idea to begin with that it took an outsider with a big name to suggest it before it was ever considered—it got buried before." On the basis of faculty and consultant interest, the president established a task force to design an orientation for all freshmen plus an experimental, semester-long orientation for a few. The dean of students was put in charge of the group, which quickly divided into two sub-groups in order to accomplish the two agendas.

On the semester-long orientation sub-committee was the English professor who made the proposal to long-range planning. When group discussion "bogged down in typical committee ways of dealing with things," she, another faculty member and two students got together to formulate a proposal. It was essentially her earlier proposal, and the committee bought it after little discussion. One member felt "it isn't structured enough" and another worried that "it sounded too much like sensitivity training." The dean heard some members say they thought it had been "ramrodded through" the sub-committee. But it was passed. Because orientation was regarded as an administrative matter, the vice president for academic affairs approved it without faculty review. He was unsure that such review would be favorable, he later said, so he decided to go ahead even though the program carried thirteen credit hours, nearly a full semester's load.

By this time, however, summer was approaching and the new program had myriad details yet to be worked out. Also, the Strategies project had entered the institution through the president's contacts with the Union and Art Chickering. The president wanted the college to be an "intensive" participant, which called for identification of an innovation to study, establishment of an action-research task force and appointment of a half-time institutional representative. She decided to focus the Strategies resources on the freshman "core" program, and she gave institutional representative duties, including directing the freshman core, to one of her new, innovative administrators, the humanities division chairperson. In order to plan the program properly, its implementation was delayed a semester (in contrast to the immediate launching of the small University Without Walls pilot).

The new freshman program director faced a couple of obstacles not faced by the University Without Walls director. First, his divisional and teaching duties were already full-time, so the freshman program became the third "half" of his work. Second, the program already had "owners," the faculty and students who had proposed it. He was foisted upon them, and the two originators were not pleased. A third problem was that he really did not know much about the program except what he read in the rather general proposal. For these reasons, he quickly decided not to *direct* but to act as a resource for a team made up largely of persons who had helped design the project. One of the originators was elected to lead the committee.

During the fall of 1971, the freshman core task force defined the program, tried to establish a good working relationship within itself and recruited students. When the "new" and "old" members reached a major impasse, one of the originators proposed a weekend retreat with a group facilitator. All the "team" members later said that experience made quite a difference in identifying common agreements, building closeness within the group and increasing commitment. For the next few months, there was no lack of volunteers for tasks, no problem in meeting attendance and no leadership conflicts of much magnitude.

The task force relied primarily on the knowledge and experiences of its own members. During the first inter-institutional team workshop of the Strategies project, however, five members of the group became aware of relevant literature and other living-learning programs. A trip by some to an experimental college conference at the University of Nebraska enabled direct contact with people already implementing similar programs. Some task force members began reading such books at Heist's *The Creative College Student*[2] and Jerome's *Culture Out of Anarchy*,[3] a report on experimental colleges. Not all task force members, however, valued external sources of knowledge. The two originators of the core felt it must emerge from local experiences. One said,

> From my standpoint, I'm tired of all the explorations of what others have done. It seems to me that what we were doing would grow out of the experience of the type of students we have, out of what we are as a faculty, as an administration, as a college. I think I've been bothered before by an innovation or change that works somewhere else which we try on our campus. I think it's possible to look at those programs, but I really think the other way of doing it, of evolving it from our own institution has much more value.

On the other hand, a student observed,

> Since the Philadelphia workshop, I think I'm very aware of how little we use outside information and resources. The goals and procedures sort of arise from the creative ideas of the group rather than from what someone else has done somewhere else. To me that's not sufficient, because I think that if we had more knowledge about the living-learning situation, then maybe we could foresee some of the kinds of problems we are going to encounter.

It is ironic (but not unusual in the Strategies project) that professors who emphasize external authority and not experiential learning in their classes were the ones who insisted that change should be built out of their own personal experiences and opinions rather than from systematic external knowledge resources, while students such as the one above were more

All the "team" members later said that experience made quite a difference in identifying common agreements, building closeness within the group and increasing commitment.

189

academic in their approach to college development. But there it was. The core never did rely much on other programs or research or theory. Nor was there any systematic training of team members to prepare for their complex new roles. They learned and designed as they went. Nevertheless, the external contacts at least provided some reinforcement. As one member said, "One of the biggest things I got out of it [the Nebraska conference] was, we are not alone."

The team at Philadelphia had worked out a design to introduce the freshman program in a faculty meeting by having task force members lead small groups instead of by the usual stand-up presentation and oratorical rebuttal. The group also met with academic divisions and the curriculum committee. These meetings did raise some interest and quell some rumors, interviewees in and outside the task force said, and they also were a surprising aid to task force thinking. One member noted,

> You get so wrapped up in what you're doing, and you're so convinced that it is the right thing to do and has no problems. Then you have these people asking you questions you haven't thought of before, and you are answering defensively. People are saying, "Why are you doing that?" It helps. It keeps you in contact with people outside the program.

Recruiting students for a second-semester "orientation" proved most difficult. Freshmen were settled in dorms, had established relationships, were figuring out how to make it in the traditional academic system. A new dorm, a new group and a highly non-traditional learning mode were attractive mainly to students turned off by the traditional system and contemplating dropping out. Only twenty-five instead of the hoped for sixty students enrolled in the core, and many of them were vague about their objectives and unmotivated academically. The team could not agree on how to handle such students. An initial "Lifebound" experience in the Grand Canyon and the Denver ghetto rapidly built a sense of community and self-scrutiny—"a kind of high"—but the unstructured and less dramatic nature of follow-up activities quickly depressed that spirit. Each student was to work out with the team an individual learning contract in six areas besides Lifebound: Small-Group Encounter, Interdisciplinary Seminars, Body Awareness, Community Involvement, Creative Experience and Independent Study. But whereas Lifebound was organized and led by trained professionals hired by the team, the other areas of study were disorganized and led by team members almost as new to them as their students. A group of faculty evaluators and the team itself agreed at semester's end that more structure and more academic emphasis were needed.

190

The program had all the bugs and conflicts one might expect in a new program run the first time by inexperienced people without much reliance on external sources of knowledge. It was costly because of low enrollment, and nearly 50% of its students dropped out of the college at semester's end. It hardly enjoyed University Without Walls reputation as a moneymaker. Yet the academic vice president was convinced that much had been learned and the program, with revisions and a full-time director, should be continued. Faculty leaders objected to this expenditure in the face of serious deficits and enrollment decline, but the vice president saw in the core program a way the college, in the long run, could become distinctive as a creator of independent learners.

The core was to last two more years, never attracting many students but increasingly well-run as its leaders gained experience. Its legacy, claimed a later dean, was mainly to help awaken faculty to the needs of students and to alternate teaching-learning modes. University Without Walls also picked up its community service and interdisciplinary seminar ideas.

The president of Mountain College resigned in the spring of 1972. She felt she had done what she could to introduce New Directions. Continuing opposition from traditionalist faculty leaders got her down, but she did not wish to take the advice of some other administrators and "hang the saboteurs" of her plan. Within a year, the new president, who had been the development officer and was hired to stabilize finances, had removed the academic vice president and the new division chairpersons. His stance was to seek a way for "traditionalists" and "experimentalists" to survive together. In a workshop response to the feedback of Strategies data indicating a faculty concerned about students but a lack of intellectual vigor, a decision was made that every faculty member specify for each course an "expectation outline" which would be discussed with their students and with the program chairperson.

The dean in 1973 called that intervention and action "overall, the most significant result of Strategies for Change and Knowledge Utilization." It was a low score on the CUES "Scholarship" scale, and stress on that in a data summary I included in a "Self-Study Packet" given the new dean and president in a Strategies off-campus workshop, on which the on-campus workshop focused its attention. As Table 9 reveals, that scale did change markedly from 1972 to 1974, surely in part because of the "expectation outline" and other emphases on intellectual and academic effort triggered with the aid of data feedback. That emphasis plus the removal of core requirements and the existence of University Without Walls opportunities reduced student complaints about lack of vigor and flexibility. The college still is scrambling for students and probably has not fully fulfilled the New Directions vision of the former president, but it does seem much closer to her dream of developing independent learners than it was when she began her quest in 1967.

Several change factors stand out in this case. First, the president's initiatives confirm the necessity of strong and active support for change at the top. Second, the continuous opposition of senior faculty leaders who were traditional in their academic views confirms not only the presence and strength of senior faculty oligarchies but also identifies an essential weakness in the president's approach. She opened the development process to these people, but she did not go out to expand their knowledge of local need and external knowledge nor seek their support. Nor did she go out of her way to make New Directions compatible with their values. Instead, she brought in young, non-traditional followers and placed them in administrative positions more traditional faculty members once had. It was not an action likely to increase openness. Another problem with the

TABLE 9
LORETTO HEIGHTS
COMPARISON OF SCORED ITEMS
IN CUES SCHOLARSHIP SCALE

POSITIVE ITEMS

Scholarship Scale Item	Key	1971-72 %	1973-74 %
Most of the professors are dedicated scholars in their fields	T	89*	93*
Most of the professors are very thorough teachers and really probe into the fundamentals of their subjects	T	73*	87*
Courses, examinations, and readings are frequently revised	T	82*	84*
Careful reasoning and clear logic are valued most highly in grading student papers, reports, or discussions	T	75*	74*
A lecture by an outstanding scientist would be poorly attended	F	40	73*

*Items scored (+) if more than ⅔ responded in keyed direction

192

She swung too far from participatory democracy to autocracy.

president's strategy seemed to be that she swung too far from participatory democracy to autocracy. She let the planning group go, then turned around and acted unilaterally in establishing New Directions. A leadership style which combined administrative initiative and faculty-student-trustee involvement, a collaborative give and take, would appear preferable.

In the case of University Without Walls, we see a familiar change formula: an external model is introduced by administrators as a small, voluntary experiment subject to faculty review not in competition for funds or students in existing programs. Strong leadership, contact with faculty, legitimation by external accreditors and success in attracting new students to the college all were helpful. Also, the personalized emphasis of the program did fit the interests of many faculty at this highly student-oriented college.

The freshman core had the advantage of persistent advocates within the tenured faculty. The two originators kept the idea alive through the first semester of implementation. It also benefited by being on the long-range planning and then the orientation task force agendas through the involvement in governance of its originators. It received important legitimation by an external and credible consultant on student development. Administrative backing was solid, as long as the New Directions group remained, and the Strategies project helped develop plans to increase faculty awareness and support as well as to utilize external knowledge resources. The program was plagued, however, by ownership conflicts

NEGATIVE ITEMS

Scholarship Scale Item	Key	1971-72 %	1973-74 %
The professors really push the students' capacities to the limit	T	18*	31*
There is very little studying here over the weekends	F	7*	49
Students set high standards of achievement for themselves	T	15*	49
The school is outstanding for the emphasis and support it gives to pure scholarship and basic research	T	16*	63
Students are very serious and purposeful about their work	T	18*	65
Standards set by the professors are not particularly hard to achieve	F	18*	38
Students put a lot of energy into everything they do in class and out	T	22*	63
There is a lot of interest in the philosophy and methods of science	T	24*	55
Most courses are real intellectual challenges	T	25*	60
Most courses require intensive study and preparation out of class	T	31*	54
Class discussions are typically vigorous and intense	T	31*	54
People around here seem to thrive on difficulty—the tougher things get the harder they work	T	31*	37
It is fairly easy to pass most courses without working very hard	F	33*	60

*Items scored (−) if less than ⅓ responded in keyed direction

between more academic and more experiential task force members. It suffered from weak organization and an unskilled, inexperienced staff. It did not use external resources in any consistent way to help the leaders learn how to do the program. Its experiential components were less compatible with traditional academic values than most University Without Walls contracts. It was expensive and did not attract students. It became part of the irritation many senior faculty felt toward the president and academic vice president, and its own leaders were too new or low-ranked to carry much clout in the faculty. The freshman core was a fascinating design for introducing students to themselves and to alternative modes of higher learning, I thought, but it was an extremely complex undertaking with low financial and human capacity to pull it off.

Together, however, the president's new trustees and administrators, the participation in long-range planning, New Directions, the freshman core program, the data feedback and "expectation outlines" and especially University Without Walls generated a "synergy" of thrusts which moved this small college closer to one of the most important goals of higher education: producing independent learners.

COMMENTARY

These last several change attempts certainly support the value of research and development. The University Without Walls was an already designed innovation for which Mountain College was a "demonstration site"; the foundation and government money sunk into this development phase paid off. Only at South Carolina in our project did a University Without Walls unit meet rejection, there because of mismanagement and direct conflict with existing values and interests. Besides University Without Walls, the cluster college, competency-based education, basic reading or math skill labs, living-learning programs, schools of the arts and four-credit plans all were innovations developed elsewhere, then proposed to Commuter Private, Black Cooperative or Mountain College. Except for University Without Walls which did have a dissemination network in the Union for Experimenting Colleges and Universities, none of these developments were "packaged" and "sold" except through articles, books, conference proceedings and informal contacts. It was an internal advocate in most cases who tried to convince institutional authorities that these innovations were worth trying. The University Without Walls example does suggest that innovations in higher education can be formally disseminated by their developers through administrative channels. It may be important that such "products" be as malleable and as capable of adapting to the local situation as the University Without Walls is. Still, federal or foundation money put into not just the development of a particular program on a particular campus but the dissemination of that innovation throughout the institution and throughout postsecondary education would seem well spent.

Several of these innovations did not get "sold," however, and other planned change models suggest the reasons why. Social Interaction theory is especially helpful. We see in these cases once again the crucial role of the "Cosmopolitan Local," that person well-linked to external news about innovation but also well-linked to internal authority. The trustee, the associate provost and the provost at Commuter Private, the young economics professor there, the administrators and a few faculty members at Black Cooperative, the president of Mountain College: these were the people who brought new ideas into their institutions and obtained a hearing for them. Also quite visible in these cases is the vital role, for or against change, played by internal opinion leaders. Two associate deans of arts and sciences and their dean were effective in blocking development of the diversity idea at Commuter Private. In contrast, the strong support of senior faculty for the new president's "excellence" theme gave that proposed change quick support. At Black Cooperative, the Strategies task force could not get anywhere as long as the two key authorities, the president and dean, showed no signs of commitment. At Mountain College, the president could not offset the influence of senior faculty leaders

194

We see in these cases once again the crucial role of the "Cosmopolitan Local," that person well-linked to external news about innovation but also well-linked to internal authority.

despite her recruitment of trustees and executive administrators who backed her cause. In each place, a senior group of faculty and administration, which in rank and tenure and high position constituted a clear oligarchy, appeared to have great influence, usually resistive, over change proposals.

Social Interaction research stresses the importance of demonstrable relative advantages to the adoption of innovation. University Without Walls showed clear income-producing advantages at Mountain College. The basic skills and competency programs, as well as the increased faculty-administrative interaction at Black Cooperative, also had the advantage of bringing in needed grant money, fairly visible differences in behavior or substantial research evidence to support them. Diversity, cluster colleges, the core freshman program, self-study, the four-credit plan and the school of the arts did not have such clear advantages. Diversity and cluster colleges were clearly advantageous to persons who studied them and wanted to meet the needs of diverse and isolated students, but these innovations did not make much sense to persons who wanted to focus on limited kinds of programs for limited kinds of students. The freshman core at Mountain College could not demonstrate that it would help achieve college objectives or attract students at reasonable cost. At Black Cooperative, the goals and practices self-study seemed to have such delayed and vague payoffs that the team just could not get energized to do it.

Divisibility and trialability are other Social Interaction factors which help explain what happened. University Without Walls could be instituted on a small, test basis. So could basic skills labs, competency programs and a few meetings in the dean's home. So could the freshman core program, although the non-divisible requirement that each student take all seven learning modes created internal resistance. New Directions, however, was sweeping in its rhetoric.

Value compatibility provides yet another Social Interaction insight into these innovations. Practical improvements in student competency and closer faculty-administrative relations were highly valued at Black Cooperative, while scrutiny by outsiders was not. University Without Walls found an environment which stressed considerable support for personalized instruction at Mountain College though several senior faculty were not sure the program would measure up to their academic standards. "Excellence" was most compatible with the somewhat elitist standards of many Commuter Private faculty. Diversity, in contrast, appeared to contradict meritocratic values, while New Directions and the freshman core seemed to go too far toward sensitivity-oriented and permissive education.

The Problem-Solving perspective reminds us that all of these innovations were proposed because of a felt need within each institution. At Commuter Private, the associate provost saw a need to capitalize and improve upon existing diversity in students, programs and teaching approaches. The new president and senior faculty saw a need to establish a reputation for high academic standards. The president of Mountain College felt education must be altered so that it creates independent learners.

*Sometimes
awareness of an
innovation such as
University
Without Walls or
cluster colleges
may have helped
increase felt need,
but innovations
which did not
address some local
person's or group's
needs did not get
raised or adopted.*

196

*"Potential users"
of educational
innovations do
want to make them
over into their own
image and do not
like being "sold"
someone else's
answer.*

And so on. Sometimes awareness of an innovation such as University Without Walls or cluster colleges may have helped increase felt need, but innovations which did not address some local person's or group's needs did not get raised or adopted.

Action-research such as that conducted by the Strategies project is itself a Problem-Solving strategy. At Commuter Private, data feedback and external consultation helped clarify for some people the presence of great diversity, misconnections between faculty and students and lack of scholarly and intellectual vigor. At Black Cooperative, feedback and consultation concerning low esprit between faculty and administration helped motivate the task force and dean to bring these groups closer together. At Mountain College, feedback of the low CUES "Scholarship" rating by students served as the catalyst for the development of course "expectation outlines." In each case, feedback with consultation in off-campus workshops to a few key people was followed by on-campus scrutiny. The gathering and feeding back of systematic research on educational and organizational health, with the aid of consultants and workshops, does seem an effective strategy for clarifying or raising the need to change.

The Problem-Solving model assumes that changes developed internally and relying heavily on internal resources are more likely to stick than solutions borrowed from elsewhere. Certainly that was an assumption held by the originators of the freshman core at Mountain College. Still, University Without Walls, the competency programs and basic skills labs were not local inventions but were instead adaptations of existing models. And they stuck better than the core freshman program. It would appear that Problem-Solving assumptions hold to the degree that "potential users" of educational innovations do want to make them over into their own image and do not like being "sold" someone else's answer.

Process consultation, another Problem-Solving strategy, was not much in evidence among these cases, except for the intervention with the Mountain College task force. That proved highly beneficial to the team in the short run, though the brief weekend retreat was not sufficient to resolve lasting differences between the more academically and the more experientially inclined. I did not do much process consultation in these institutions, partly because of distance and limited time, but also because there was little call for such intervention. Some problems, such as Black Cooperative's gap between faculty and administration, moved toward resolution without a process consultant. These cases do not "prove" that such intervention is not a helpful contributor to planned change. I often felt one or another of these institutions could benefit from such aid. But they do confirm that process consultation is not a very usual part of college and university change.

The Problem-Solving model regards collaboration as the most effective decision-making process. People who must decide and people who will be affected by decisions should be involved together in diagnosing need, finding solutions and making choices. Certainly at Black Cooperative, an increase in "worker" involvement with the dean in academic governance had a salutary effect on morale, just as the retreat helped the Mountain College task force feel better about working together. At Commuter Private, interviewees frequently complained of too much collaboration and too little decisiveness by academic leaders; several of that institution's change proposals got bogged down in the elaborate committee system. That system, however, did not foster open, collaborative, skillful problem-solving. It seemed to resemble more a series of debates between conflicting interests. A remedy could well include both stronger leadership and more skillful collaboration in the Problem-Solving sense. At Mountain College, collaboration also was not collaboration. The president authoritatively turned the participative planning process loose, then grabbed it back. She was authoritarian, then permissive, then authoritarian, and that combination got her a large University Without Walls unit but not the cooperation of senior faculty leaders. In each case, a problem-solving process which included active leadership together with collaborative involvement could well have improved a rocky planned change process.

Finally, these cases give us several images of the campus political process at work. At Commuter Private, the diversity issue managed to get on a couple of special committee and workshop agendas. Administrative gates opened enough for that. But subsequent gatekeepers swung the gate closed again. The associate provost and Wild Card Committee were not sufficiently powerful issue sponsors to get past these high formal authorities. Also, both the Strategies and Wild Card activities were outside formal governance bodies and were not regarded as quite legitimate change formulators because of that. At Black Cooperative, little change could occur unless top authorities were not only open gatekeepers, as the president was in welcoming the Strategies project, but active issue sponsors. People below were not willing to support change actively unless the person in power in this quite hierarchical organization was visibly supportive. At Mountain College, formal administrative authority helped establish University Without Walls and the freshman core, but the informal power of senior faculty blocked the president. Their interests and hers clashed. They stayed and she went, albeit with a substantial legacy left behind.

As before, it appears that each major model of the planned change process, each grand strategy, does tell part of the story, but only part. Somehow, these parts must be blended into a whole. The final case, Messiah College, comes as close as any Strategies institution did to such a wholistic strategy for innovation and renewal.

Finally, these cases give us several images of the campus political process at work.

197

8 Enhancing Teaching-Learning Flexibility: Messiah College

There was not another institution in the Strategies project quite like Messiah, nor one quite so distant from my undergraduate days at the University of Michigan. The unchallenged authority of the doctrine of the Brethren in Christ, the "straight" garb and manner of its friendly staff and students, the quiet, rural setting, the acceptance of limited freedom and strong administrative direction all seemed leagues removed from the hurly burly of Ann Arbor, UCLA and other institutions more familiar to me. Indeed, its clear focus on Evangelical education and its administrative authority perhaps makes it closest to business and industry as an organizational type. And Messiah is not alone. Hundreds of small, liberal arts colleges with close ties to Christian churches and somewhat authoritarian norms dot the landscape of American higher education. Since chancing upon Messiah five years ago, I have worked with several such colleges and have come to hold great respect for the members of these institutions. Perhaps, as I was told on my first visit to Messiah by a local humorist, "that, Jack, is the first step to grace."

What has such a college in common with the University of South Carolina or even Quaker Academic? What can we learn or confirm about planned change that other institutions have not taught us already? We slowly learned that the answer to these questions is, simply put, plenty! For one thing, we found that the teaching-learning problems identified by Messiah faculty members and administrators were very similar to those registered elsewhere. The college had participated in Chickering's earlier *Project on Student Development in Small Colleges*, and several members saw in the evidence of that project what by now is a familiar problem. Teaching appeared to be too much lecture and learning too much note-taking and memorizing. Greater flexibility in teaching approaches and learning experiences seemed to these persons necessary if students were to become less passive and dependent, more capable of learning on their own beyond college. A second thing we found in common with other institutions was that neither administrative dictate nor the usual committee process was very effective in implementing academic innovation and reform. Even in a college with relatively bureaucratic norms, simply telling faculty what to do would not do.

An early response at Messiah to the teaching-learning problem was development in 1969 of a satellite campus adjacent to Temple University in Philadelphia. This idea originated in discussions between the president and a consultant to Mennonite Colleges, then was fleshed out with Ernest Boyer, a Messiah trustee and, at that time, chancellor of the State University of New York. The wide options of Temple University, an urban

199

Even in a college with relatively bureaucratic norms, simply telling faculty what to do would not do.

experience for Messiah's mainly rural students and a living-learning center would supplement the limited fare possible on the Messiah campus. The idea was discussed with department chairpersons and generally approved by the faculty as a small, inexpensive pilot project run by volunteers. The advantages were apparent and presidential initiative did not upset faculty in this school. So this innovation, spurred by evidence of an internal problem, connected to a solution through administrative linkage to external consultation, and proposed by the top authority, gained general faculty sanction. It did not, however, gain very widespread faculty or student involvement. Few students or faculty members had discovered the need and were excited about the solution themselves. It is all right to let others do it, but spare me. This limited participation hardly made it the answer to the college's teaching-learning concerns.

Another focus of the need for change was the "integrated studies" program of required general education. Interviewees in 1971 complained that despite thematic foci and team-teaching, much of what happened in that program was disciplinary lecturing and listening. Faculty participants were not very happy with this state of affairs, but they said that they had little time to develop or carry out truly interdisciplinary courses and that there was no training available in how to do that anyway. Support for implementation was lacking. Also, the process of developing this proposal did not gain much more faculty commitment than the satellite program. A faculty-student-administrative committee did develop the program over a summer, but the rest of the faculty were involved only after a final proposal was completed. It became a shooting target for almost a year of faculty meetings before, with the dampened enthusiasm such a process can produce, it passed.

A third program related to the development of a need to create new ways to diversify teaching and learning was a one-week "intersession" first conducted in January of 1971. This attempt to stimulate diversity through a calendar re-arrangement was criticized by faculty members and administrators as too hastily conceived and too jammed with reading assignments and lectures. Thought had been put into a new structure but not into the most appropriate way to behave in that structure.

One person who had exerted leadership in these changes and who was especially concerned that learning be broadened to include much more than lecturing and memorizing was the academic dean. He was widely respected on campus for his knowledge of higher education and for his creative ideas. At the same time, faculty who felt academic change must be faculty business slowly considered found the dean a bit too aggressive in his leadership. In the spring of 1971, the dean got another idea:

> *Through all this I had felt that variety was much needed in the curriculum, that we either had to reduce requirements or increase the electives available to students. We needed a better distribution, but when mentioned, this always seemed to meet with a negative response. During the spring [of 1971], I started to review the literature on college impact on students. The literature made the point that the first part of a student's experience in college was*

200

The literature made the point that the first part of a student's experience in college was crucial to changes in the student's academic orientation. So I came up with the idea of a calendar change.

crucial to changes in the student's academic orientation. So I came
up with the idea of a calendar change, and I discussed this in May,
with the President. My proposal to him was a 1-3-1-3-1 calendar,
and he thought it would be worthwhile.

As with the Project on Student Development and the development of a satellite campus, an external catalyst, this time the literature on student development, stirred an interest in internal change. And a specific change was proposed—a 1-3-1-3-1 calendar. But one-owner academic innovations, Messiah's recent history suggested, were not likely to run as well as one-owner used cars. The dean had to find a way to get a calendar change adopted by the faculty. Here entered the Strategies for Change and Knowledge Utilization Project.

CREATION OF A SUPPORTIVE CARRYING STRUCTURE

Almost simultaneously with the dean's ruminations in the spring of 1971, the Strategies Project got underway; the president and dean signed on Messiah at the "Associate" level. The college would cooperate with the research on educational and organizational practices but would not be committed to a heavy investment in change activity. One part of each institution's involvement, however, would be designation of an academic innovation just beginning to receive campus scrutiny. Project researchers would follow that innovation as it occurred, and a campus task force of faculty, students and administrators would be established (if one was not already in existence) to assist the research and support the innovative action. The dean recommended to the president that a calendar study be Messiah's innovation focus. The president agreed. The dean thereby found a structure—a Strategies task force—for his idea, although he provided flexibility by making the charge a study of various calendar options rather than just the 1-3-1-3-1. He "owned" the latter preference, and he no doubt hoped the task force eventually would agree. But he apparently knew they needed to develop their own eventual proposal.

201

The dean then went about selecting the task force. As chairperson of the task force and institutional representative to the Strategies project he selected a young but widely respected mathematics professor. The two of them then picked two senior faculty opinion leaders who represented academic divisions other than their own, plus the two top student officers.

There remained, however, the structural problem of what governance body would review the task force's eventual recommendations. In order to establish linkage to faculty governance, the dean at first planned to ask the Academic Affairs Committee, which he chaired, to establish the task force as a subcommittee. He shortly became reluctant to do that, however, for he and other interviewees regarded that body, which included senior division chairpersons who were irritated about the dean's aggressive change initiatives, as a "bottleneck" which "often beats things to death." It was Messiah's version of the oligarchical stronghold found on many college and university campuses. But, during the summer, an alternative presented itself, once more by linkage to external sources of knowledge. The dean and president, in August of 1971, attended the annual conference of the Council for the Advancement of Small Colleges (CASC). The

He and other
interviewees
regarded that
body, which
included senior
division
chairpersons who
were irritated
about the dean's
aggressive change
initiatives, as a
"bottleneck"
which "often beats
things to death."

topic that year was long-range planning, and the president immediately decided to establish a Long-range Planning Committee at Messiah. The dean then recommended that the calendar study, which very much concerned the college's plan for the future, be placed under that group. He also proposed that the Long Range Planning Committee include himself and, as secretary, the mathematics professor. The president concurred. Faculty later selected their own representatives, one of whom was also a member of the calendar task force. Thus overlapping membership and avoidance of a more conservative channel promised a sympathetic review of the task force's work.

So far, however, it was the administration's ball game. Data from the *Institutional Functioning Inventory* and interviews confirmed that Messiah faculty held their administrators in high respect and accepted their authority (as, some interviewees explained, they accepted Biblical and pastor authority). Still, earlier change efforts by administrators had been slow to gain acceptance and effective implementation, and Messiah faculty, like others, did regard academic issues as their professional concerns. After the Strategies project and the "tentatively identified" calendar study were formally introduced to faculty by administrative memorandum, the issue of faculty ownership became a live one. As one professor said in a fall, 1971, interview:

> *I resent a bit making some type of calendar change. The fact that it was presented to the faculty in the way it was caused me to feel that this kind of change is more effectively presented if the faculty kind of spurs the idea; that is, rather than the administration's saying, "We are going to do this."*

In fact, of course, the faculty was not spurring innovation. It took administrative initiative catalyzed by external information and individuals to get action going.

In fact, of course, the faculty was not spurring innovation. It took administrative initiative catalyzed by external information and individuals to get action going. Yet this initiative increased the difficulty involved in moving the general objective of more varied learning experiences and the specific means, a calendar change, from the lone advocate—the dean—to awareness, interest, trial and adoption by the faculty at large. That task became the central business of the Strategies task force.

AROUSING AWARENESS AND INTEREST AMONG THE FACULTY

The task force's first activity was to send delegates (the dean, the institutional representative, and one of the faculty members) to the Strategies action-planning workshop in Philadelphia. Goodwin Watson's emphasis on reducing the psychological resistances to change through collaborative problem-solving and the attention of Strategies staff and advisors to knowledge utilization were not lost on the Messiah team. Their action plan was a sequential strategy to involve faculty in the calendar study and to use a variety of knowledge resources. The committee would first survey the literature related to calendar alternatives. Then two person teams of task force members would visit three nearby colleges which were organized under a 4-1-4, a 4-4-1, and a modular calendar. These visits would then be discussed with faculty and students in open forums. Also, JB Lon Hefferlin, a nationally known consultant on academic reform, would be invited to the campus to expose the faculty to the full range of calendar options. Following all this effort to raise awareness and interest, a questionnaire would be sent to all faculty to solicit their calendar preferences. Results again would be discussed in open forum. Finally, the task force would draft a proposal and submit it to the Long-Range Planning Committee. March, four months hence, was set as the deadline to obtain a faculty decision so that any change could be implemented the following year. No other team's plan reflected this extent of faculty involvement and linkage to information. Staff concluded in workshop wrap-ups that because of this ownership and knowledge utilization, because of the well-detailed plan and because of the organization, openness, and warmth exhibited by the institutional representative, Messiah's plan was most promising.

What actually happened? The whole plan. The literature was reviewed and, reported task force members, found helpful in broadening their awareness of calendar options. The other colleges were visited and spurred task force interest in the teaching-learning potentialities of short, concentrated learning units. As for general faculty awareness and interest, Hefferlin's visit was reported by all interviewees to be immensely informative and stimulating. As one psychology professor summarized, "Dr. Hefferlin had a great deal of information for the faculty and made a tremendous impression. The possibilities were clear. It showed us the value of an outside resource person." Another simply said, "There's nothing like an expert." The institutional representative later reported that lively discussion of alternatives occurred well after Hefferlin's visit. Had other task forces managed to carry out the extensive knowledge linkage considered in that same meeting in Philadelphia, similar faculty interest might well have been a consequence.

Before other parts of the action-plan were carried out, the Strategies staff visited the campus to interview task force members and general campus opinion leaders and to interact with the task force regarding next steps. A familiar and potent organizational development approach—feedback of survey or interview data regarding the process of institutional problem-solving—was first used by Strategies staff in a brief report to the task force regarding repeatedly heard concerns. These concerns were reported as follows:

> 1. Several respondents indicated that the impetus for change frequently came from the administration. One person said, "We were told at a faculty meeting that we were going into a calendar revision study. The man had already been picked to lead it." This suggests that some faculty do not feel the sense of "ownership" of ideas that Watson noted as being so crucial to successful change.
>
> Is it possible to create ways to increase faculty participation in initial deliberations about potential changes?
>
> 2. Another concern of several interviewees had to do with perceived rapid pace of change at Messiah. These people stated that time was not taken to properly evaluate implemented changes. As a result, according to one person, changes suffered from uncorrected weaknesses.

"Dr. Hefferlin had a great deal of information for the faculty and made a tremendous impression. The possibilities were clear. It showed us the value of an outside resource person."

203

Are plans being made by the Calendar Committee to ensure any calendar change is evaluated by a committee which is broadly representative of all shades and varieties of campus opinion?

3. One of the more conservative people said that faculty-administration communication was not always sufficient to keep faculty informed about proposed changes.

With regard to the calendar study, is the committee working to keep faculty fully informed about its calendar investigations and discussions? Have attempts been made beyond the faculty forum to follow up on Lon Hefferlin's presentation or group visits? Have there been attempts to solicit opinion from all faculty groups?

4. Interviewees found JB Lon Hefferlin's visit and presentation most helpful and stimulating. One person responded that Hefferlin's presentation was a "real eye-opener." People also reported that the visits to colleges were very fruitful.

Has the committee given further thought to using outside resource people? Might other interested faculty be encouraged to visit colleges with differing calendar programs?

5. Some respondents indicated that they did not see much difficulty in changing calendar because it would only alter the timing of traditional teaching activities.

Has the committee tried to increase faculty awareness of the creative potential of various calendar options? Has the committee considered implementing structures to assist faculty and students in fully realizing potentialities of calendars— workshops, retreats, on-going implementing committees, incentives for creative approaches to new calendar?

Ownership and knowledge utilization thus were reiterated but this time expressed by faculty leaders rather than out of research and theory. New themes—careful evaluation and implementation assistance—would become major components of later task force plans.

On January 24, the Faculty Forum was held. A report on the earlier workshop with Hefferlin was redistributed to refresh memories and interests. Calendar committee members who had visited the three other colleges made brief reports. Ensuing discussion showed no clear consensus on any calendar model but rather a wide range of opinions. Two days later, the Student Forum was held. Seventy of the school's 800 students turned out. The institutional representative reported that most students asked informational questions, but, "the students who gave opinions generally liked the modular type calendar because of its flexibility."

After these forums and the Strategies feedback, the committee decided that more discussion should take place among faculty and students concerning the different calendar options before the committee should attempt to develop a proposal. To facilitate discussion, committee members developed in detail four calendar models: a modified 4-1-4, a 4-4-1, the dean's 1-3-1-3-1 and a modular calendar. These were presented to faculty on February 14 and discussed in the February 21 faculty meeting. At that meeting, the notion of a questionnaire to survey preferences was introduced and passed, thereby becoming "owned" by the faculty. It was administered the next week. Twenty-four of the respondents (out of a faculty of 51) favored 4-1-4. The next highest was 1-3-1-3-1, with twelve in favor. Only four rated the present calendar as their first choice. Interest in change apparently had been well-seeded.

The second Strategies workshop for campus task forces was held March 2-5, 1972, in Chicago, just prior to the annual conference of the American Association for Higher Education. The dean, the institutional representative and one senior faculty member of the Calendar Committee attended. This group spent most of the three days drafting a calendar proposal to submit, after full committee approval, to the Long Range Planning Committee. The committee's proposal was to adopt a modified 4-1-4 calendar (actually 4-1-3 plus a faculty institute in May and a summer session) for 1972-73, a 4-1-3-1 for 1973-74, and the dean's 1-3-1-3-1 in 1974-75. Review procedure included in the proposal indicated that it would go directly from Long Range Planning to the faculty, thus bypassing the senior faculty stronghold, the Academic Affairs Committee. If approved, an implementation committee would be formed and a workshop would be held to bring outside resources and faculty together to begin to work out intensive term courses. Finally, in May of 1973, a one-week faculty institute would be held to evaluate the first intensive term.

The proposal sailed through Long-Range Planning with only minor alterations. On March 20, 1972, the faculty met to consider it. The first year's calendar (4-1-3) was passed "with little opposition or discussion" reported the math professor. Then came the 1973-74 proposal (4-1-3-1). As the professor reported,

> The recommendation regarding the 1973-74 calendar seemed to arouse in faculty all the latent opposition that is there for change. There was a great deal of opposition because some faculty members felt as though the academic consequences of such a calendar were not fully explored. Faculty also felt that this would incur too many changes in too short a period of time, not allowing a sufficient time for evaluation. This sudden surge of strong opposition was very difficult for me to understand since the only difference in this calendar seems to be to add a May term which appears very much like adding an additional summer term and faculty had already acted favorably on the general format of the calendar and the summer sessions. When the recommendation seemed sure to suffer defeat, the dean very astutely offered a substitute motion "to adopt a calendar for the 1973-74 school year similar to the one proposed for the 1972-73 school year instead of the one suggested by the Long Range Planning Committee." This substitute motion then passed.

The next day, in a continuation of this meeting, the 1-3-1-3-1 proposal for 1974-75 was quickly tabled. One thing at a time, then evaluate and decide. That appeared to be the faculty's message. The intensive term committee, implementation workshop and 1973 evaluation institute were approved.

Only four rated the present calendar as their first choice. Interest in change apparently had been well-seeded.

One thing at a time, then evaluate and decide.

FROM DEMAND TO DECISION: A BRIEF REVIEW

Why did the modified 4-1-4 pass the faculty? Certainly one reason was that it was advocated all the way by the highest ranking academic officer and was supported by the presdent; these two officers enjoyed wide respect and tolerance for strong leadership among the faculty. The dean served as both gatekeeper and issue sponsor. It is what Goodwin Watson calls "Support at the Top." Those change attempts not blessed by initial executive support would do well to make the obtaining of that backing a major action agenda. A second reason appears to be that extensive linkage to knowledge resources and heavy faculty involvement served to raise awareness and interest among enough faculty to approve the new calendar. "Ownership" and "Knowledge Linkage" were broadened.

Third, a need to provide greater teaching and learning flexibility had been registered earlier, and, more specifically, criticism of a brief "intersession" raised a campus concern to improve or modify that version of an intensive term. There was a "Clear Need." Fourth, the Strategies Project provided a carrying structure, consultation and planning time of which the Messiah team took full advantage, while the CASC conference catalyzed establishment of an overlapping review body which allowed circumvention of a governance "bottleneck." Fifth, the task force leader was a respected faculty member only recently tarnished by a half-time administrative appointment, and his own leadership skill was aided by well-articulated action plans. Sixth, efforts to use outside resources and involve campus members were frequent and varied. A "synergy" of effort, Havelock notes, is often a key ingredient in successful change. Seventh, the dean did not insist on his own pet solution but was open to whatever the task force and faculty approved (while being sure to get in his licks on the way).

In brief, a general concern to improve teaching and an existing calendar, strong advocacy, support and openness at (and for) the top, responsive action and review structures, competent leadership and intervention of several external resources, widespread, detailed planning, plus various and repeated faculty and student involvement (and who knows what else) all combined to obtain favorable passage of the modified 4-1-4 calendar. It was not a simple formula. The three new ingredients for Messiah, however, seemed to task force members and staff to be the action-planning, the heavy emphasis on faculty involvement and the establishment of links to sources of information. The institutional representative summarized his own annual report by stressing these last two factors:

> The major strategy that our committee used was to attempt a "community-arrived-at proposal and decision." This was in contrast to, for example, the General Education study in 1967 in which a committee worked for several weeks in the summer and brought a finished proposal to the faculty in the fall. For the calendar study we attempted to disseminate as much knowledge as possible and to have a rather wide discussion before the committee even worked on a proposal. . . . I have reaffirmed my commitment to the importance of dialogues in making corporate decisions even

though at times this dialogue was very difficult to achieve. I have also learned how important it is for a group to feel ownership of an idea before it is accepted by them. This feeling of ownership is very seldom achieved; however, the degree of acceptance of an idea seems to be directly related to the degree of ownership felt by the group.

IMPLEMENTATION

A decision to change is not change, although many studies of change stop there. If the decision is understood and owned by a very few of those who must carry it out, it may be a long way from change. At Messiah, earlier decisions, such as the satellite campus and integrated studies, had experienced implementation problems. Did the increased information and involvement of the calendar development build greater readiness? Did faculty and students increase teaching-learning flexibility, as the 4-1-3 objectives stated, or did they merely force old behaviors into uncomfortable new structures?

The first steps toward implementation were a faculty workshop in May of 1972 to expose faculty to alternative ways of teaching the January term. An intensive Term Committee was established to provide participative leadership and coordination. The workshop brought in administrators from the three colleges previously visited. Later interviews suggested that, as in the Hefferlin workshop, both information and enthusiasm were transmitted by the visitors. Coupled with that promising start, the nominating committee named the dean, the institutional representative and another member of the calendar committee to the new Intensive Term Committee along with faculty and student representatives from each academic division. The institutional representative was elected chairperson and the dean secretary (not an inconsequential office, as readers of creative minutes know). Formal leadership thus carried over from development to implementation. The Intensive Term Committee itself was included in the calendar proposal as another structural device to avoid the Academic Affairs bottleneck, for barriers to college approval can also be barriers to implementation. As the dean observed,

> *The Academic Affairs Committee always takes a great deal of time to move through agendas. We thought a sub-committee would expedite the intensive term courses thing more quickly. There was a press for time. We had to get the schedule out quickly, so giving the power to the committee to approve courses without going to Academic Affairs seemed reasonable.*

Meanwhile, the Strategies task force—the calendar committee—appeared out of a job. Its proposal had been passed and several members were busy leading implmentation. But, in its meeting of April 19, 1972, the group decided that several agenda items called for continuation of a special task force: "(1) to evaluate the success or failure of the intensive term; (2) to organize the faculty workshop for May, 1973 [a participative review of the first intensive term], (3) to identify and pursue any spinoffs from the calendar change, and (4) to carry out our continuing involvement with the Strategies for Change Project." There would be a participative body not only to implement the change but also a participative

This feeling of ownership is very seldom achieved; however, the degree of acceptance of an idea seems to be directly related to the degree of ownership felt by the group.

207

208

body to evaluate it and follow-up on further change considerations.

Before that task force reconvened in the fall, the president and the institutional representative attended Strategies' first annual review and planning workshop, July 17-19, in Saratoga Springs, New York. The central agenda for that meeting was feedback and study of diagnostic data collected over the year by project staff. The Messiah pair carefully worked through this evidence with the help of Roger Voskuyl, then Executive Director of the Council for the Advancement of Small Colleges. Voskuyl was familiar with Messiah and had been president of a similar small college. The president and the institutional representative found him most helpful, and the staff was reminded of a discovery they had made with other institutions, that consultant-college matches in which each had knowledge of the other and respected each other's status and values and in which a continuing rather than one-shot relationship existed were most likely to bear fruit. Other sessions of the workshop emphasized that data feedback which allows campus members to determine their own questions and find their own answers—with consultant assistance in locating, interpreting and validating the data—may well be superior to a polished research report that makes an easy shooting target. The principles, once again, were knowledge of internal data, external consultation and ownership by those involved.

The data concerned institution-wide educational experiences and decision-making practices. Up to that point, most Strategies-related activities had focused on specific innovations. Staff therefore introduced the notion that academic "self-renewal" might best operate at both the program and institutional levels in a systemic, mutually reinforcing fashion. Messiah's president and institutional representative immediately picked up on this two-level focus.* Both said they reconfirmed the need to increase teaching-learning flexibility in general, for Chickering's *Experience of College Questionnaire*, administered in both 1967 and 1972, revealed little decrease in the authoritarian, information-dispensing teaching role and the dependent, memorizing student role. Their action plan therefore called for the task force "to shift the focus of our action project from that of calendar to a major spinoff which concerns Teaching and Learning." And both agreed that faculty should have the chance to draw these conclusions for themselves:

> We felt as though these data should be shared rather fully with the entire faculty in afternoon and evening workshops during the academic year. Upon sharing these data it was hoped that faculty would identify the problem areas suggested in the data. It was felt that we should not try to interpret it for the faculty, but rather let them interpret it for themselves. This conviction seemed to grow out of the fact that we enjoyed discovering what the data said and in drawing our own conclusions from these data. It was felt, therefore, that all faculty members should have this privilege.

Because the dean, the institutional representative and another task force member were heavily engaged in the Intensive Term Committee, a new task force was selected, this time composed of five full-time faculty, one from each division, and two student officers.

As a follow-up to the July workshop, I mailed out some suggestions about ways to "broaden ownership of the evidence." These included administrative and student involvement but focused primarily on faculty. Specifically, I suggested (1) small-group discussions with the information in hand (as opposed to general presentations and orations) using task force members as group leaders; (2) assistance to standing committees as they study parts of the data relevant to their concerns in sustained, uninterrupted sessions; (3) the use of outside facilitators to provide technical assistance and a detached perspective; and (4) a follow-up structure and plan. Messiah employed the suggestions regarding small groups and sustained sessions, and the task force provided follow-up.

The first workshop, a four-hour affair held from 4 p.m. to 8 p.m. (including dinner) was held on the day regularly scheduled for the faculty forum. Its focus was the *Institutional Functioning Inventory*. Although participants found the initial presentation too long and the group discussions too brief and too broadly focused to get very far, one concern that was clearly identified was the very low score on "Meeting Local Needs." Continuing education for the surrounding community was an interest of the dean's and had been stated as an action concern by Long Term Planning the year before. The Strategies task force later proposed establishment of a Continuing-Cooperative Education Committee, and that body was established by the faculty in the fall of 1973.

The second four-hour workshop focused on the *Experience of College Questionnaire*. More time was given to small group discussions, and each group focused on only part of the data (such as course experiences, faculty-student interaction, peer relationships or extra-curricular activities). Strategies staff were in attendance to lend assistance and outside perspective. Students were present, for it was their experience being discussed. The institutional representative summarized:

> *Judging from the reporting of the groups' discussions, the general problems of teaching and learning seemed to surface. The students served to remind us that teaching and learning are really very closely entwined. This workshop seemed to lay a good foundation for the May Faculty Workshop in which these questions of teaching and learning were explored much more deeply.*

Faculty now were raising the same concerns felt by the president and the institutional representative the summer before. One senior member of Academic Affairs said he wanted to see less memorizing and more conceptualizing and synthesizing. He said how a student is taught and tested relates to the kind of thinking she develops: "We must teach and test more for concepts than facts. We talk about that every meeting I attend, but the data indicate we aren't doing much about it." Student involvement in course planning, creative projects, field work and independent study were recommended by various faculty. At one point, a faculty member challenged the data's indication that many faculty just lecture from the text. Several students assured him that faculty do and that it is deadly.

*An appropriate third level of improvement, individual self-renewal as in faculty or administrative development, later became a concern on several Strategies campuses, including Messiah.

209

"The students served to remind us that teaching and learning are really very closely entwined."

"We must teach and test more for concepts than facts. We talk about that every meeting I attend, but the data indicate we aren't doing much about it."

Two reporters said their groups were struck by the strong vocational orientations among students. Others were unhappy that students were both highly dependent and highly satisfied. These concerns led one faculty member to propose that (1) liberal education oriented toward specific careers should be developed and (2) students should be gradually encouraged toward more independent learning. Interviews with faculty following the workshop confirmed that a concern to develop less authoritarian teaching and dependent learning had been raised by the data and workshop discussions. The desire to increase educational flexibility had been part of the dean's concern at the beginning of the project, and Long Range Planning had stated in October, 1971, that "Teaching methods must be kept flexible" and that "new techniques must be found for information dissemination so that classroom time can be used more creatively." Now, however, the concern was raised by faculty out of information contributed by students.

The next project event was an inter-institutional workshop in January of 1973. The Messiah task force developed a detailed plan for evaluation of the first intensive term and for its May Faculty Workshop. Substantial portions of the *Experience of College Questionnaire* were applied to the first task. The May workshop was to involve prominent external resource persons, data analysis and eight days of discussion and decision-making concerning the Intensive term, the general education sequence (a center of the rigidity-flexibility debate) and teaching-learning alternatives.

Did the calendar change, the initial strategy for increasing teaching and learning alternatives, achieve that objective? Both the task force evaluation and interviews of all faculty by Strategies staff suggest answers. First, students were asked on the ECQ how they felt about their intensive term course experiences while taking them. These data were then compared with responses regarding regular terms, as Table 10 illustrates:

TABLE 10
PERCENT OF RESPONDENTS REPORTING THE FOLLOWING
FEELINGS FREQUENTLY OR MOST OF THE TIME ABOUT
THEIR COURSES IN 1967, 1972, AND J-1973.

	1967	1972	January 1973	Percent Difference 1972-J-1973
Worried, tense	18%	28%	20%	− 8%
Confident, competent	49	55	65	+10
Bored, uninterested	25	36	17	−19
Interested, attracted	56	59	78	+19
Challenged to do best thinking	58	54	67	+13

The intensive term fostered greater confidence, interest and challenge than the regular terms. Students also reported being more up-to-date on assignments in the January term. Students reporting that "the teacher encourages class discussion" increased 11% for the intensive term. As Table 11 indicates, several professors did adopt a more flexible teaching role in the short term.

The intensive term fostered greater confidence, interest and challenge than the regular terms.

TABLE 11
PERCENT REPORTING THAT EACH STATEMENT DESCRIBES
THE ROLE OF TEACHER IN 1967, 1972, JANUARY 1973

	1967	1972	January 1973	Percent Difference 1972-J-1973
Teacher dispenses knowledge, or assigns sources, which it is the student's job to master	33%	45%	31%	−14%
Teacher directs his efforts flexibly in order to help students learn	36	30	31	+ 1
Teacher and students work together as both he and they increase their understanding of the subject	18	11	24	+13
Teacher serves mainly as a resource for students, while students have principal responsibility for making and carrying out their own plans	13	15	13	− 2

Student mental activities fit these shifts. In the 1972 regular term, 14% of the student respondents said they spent more than half their time in class "doing your own thinking about ideas presented (as opposed to taking notes)," while 29% spent more than half their class time in the January term doing this kind of thinking. Although 51% of the respondents said they spent more than half their out-of-class study time memorizing in the regular term, only 31% reported this in the 1973 intensive term. In contrast, time spent synthesizing and applying concepts and information increased.

The task force's questionnaire to faculty revealed that 78% found adequate class preparation time, 61% felt "concentrating on one course at a time made it possible for the student to do better work" (52% of the student respondents agreed) and 68% agreed that "flexible periods of instruction enhanced the process of learning" (64% of the students agreed). But only 23% said "I would like to teach in more than one intensive term during the 9 month academic year." As their vote the year

212

before suggested, one intensive term a year was enough of that good thing for most faculty.

The Strategies staff evaluation suggested that adoption of the calendar change had occurred among about half the faculty at best. Interviews with almost all faculty revealed that 45% reported changing their course structure and 50% said they had changed their teaching techniques. Unfortunately, students did not see it that way. Among a small sample, only 15% said their course structure deviated from regular term fare, and 33% said the teaching technique changed. But 78% of the student interviewees and 88% of the faculty questionnaire sample were well-satisfied with the first intensive term. It seems safe to conclude that *the idea* of an intensive term and more flexible teaching had been adopted in the majority while *actual alteration of practices* included something less than half the faculty. Institution-wide change was still ahead, but a solid foundation had been laid.

Yet another Strategies intervention was a brief "Interim Report" summarizing one-hour interviews conducted in the fall of 1972 with twenty-four task force members and campus leaders. Once again, the passive-dependent nature of student educational experiences, the relationship of liberal education to career and adult learning and the inflexibility of general education were most cited by faculty as major academic problems. Regarding institutional problem-solving, interviewees said there existed a well-organized system of collaboration, a general openness and concern to improve and excellent leadership in the college. But on the negative side, several faculty still felt that the administration was too dominant, that there was tension between senior faculty and administrators and that this tension was politely avoided rather than openly confronted. Some of this feeling was precipitated by a recent administrative objection to the establishment of an informal faculty discussion group initiated by discontented senior faculty.

The report was mailed to all interviewees. An immediate impact was administrative irritation (for criticism as well as praise had been directed there) and support for the report among the senior faculty who sat on the Academic Affairs Committee. One wrote to me:

> *I have just read your report on Messiah College, and I want to say it is a great piece of work. I don't see everything the way you see it, but that is where I can learn from you. One of the great blessings of the report is to hear what the other sides are saying (including about me), something we don't know about, as your report implies.*

Another senior professor wrote:

> *You have perceptively focused upon our strengths and weaknesses as these relate to capacity for constructive institutional change. . . . Since a particular stress point seems to be campus inter-personal relations, you have helped me to reassess my own attitudes and role in campus life.*

Later interviews indicated that subsequent discussions, individually and in groups, centered on that interpersonal difficulty. A governance study, already initiated on the recommendation of a Middle States accreditation review, included consideration of ways to improve interchange between faculty and administration. The Interim Report themes were reiterated in the Governance Study Committee meetings. Faculty interviewees said a key to improving interaction was the willingness of criticized administrators to join in seeking solutions to the problem. Despite initial irritation, they had openly confronted the issues instead of denying them. From our point of view, the resolution of this interpersonal problem was not tangential but directly related to the ability of the college to improve its teaching-learning flexibility. Energy spent in conflict was energy—and cooperation—unavailable for academic improvement.

The May Faculty Workshop came off essentially as planned, with the addition of a faculty meeting to consider the recommendation of the Governance Study Committee. Outside resource persons, especially George Akers, President of Columbia Union College and Kenneth Eble, Professor of English at the University of Utah, evoked considerable discussion concerning post-secondary trends and improvement of teaching as they apply to the Christian college. Continuing education, individualization of learning and the integration of subject matter were central themes under both topics. A group evaluation of the January term, using a single implementation objective as the organizing focus for each group, came up with the following recommendations:

> *OBJECTIVE: to provide for creative innovation by both students and faculty in the development and offering of new courses.*
> *SUGGESTIONS:*
> 1. *We must make clear that January is a time for truly innovative non-catalogued courses which nevertheless may substitute for other courses and requirements. This latter factor is a divisional decision which does not require faculty approval. We should remember that experimental new courses should remain un-catalogued for the most part.*
> 2. *Another intensive term regularly scheduled in May or August or some other time would enhance the kind of intensive term developments which are intended for January.*
> 3. *Yet to be investigated are opportunities for:*
>   *a. adult education*
>   *b. cross-cultural opportunities*
>   *c. required courses offered in a different way*
> 4. *In a wide range of courses the opportunity should be explored for taking students to the [satellite] campus for up to two weeks.*
>
> *OBJECTIVE: to provide for a greater variety of experiences for both students and faculty.*
> *SUGGESTIONS:*
> 1. *Professors need to be encouraged to try more new techniques in January.*
> 2. *One week between January and Spring Term is necessary. A break is very necessary after the faculty's intensive effort as well as the students.*
> 3. *Make the 3 of the 4-1-3 an honest 3 months, that is, allow more*

Energy spent in conflict was energy—and cooperation—unavailable for academic improvement.

213

time for the Spring Term.

4. Restructure General Education for more flexibility..

5. Handel wrote "The Messiah" in a 28-day intensive term.

6. The tight major requirements for graduation make innovative courses in the January Term very difficult.

OBJECTIVE: to encourage a greater variety of teaching techniques.
SUGGESTIONS:

1. In order to have flexibility and innovation we would encourage students to have only one course so that time and pressures do not conflict.

2. To have science or music or other curricula so tight that students must take or faculty must offer required courses seems not to allow the atmosphere of interaction that intensive term strives for.

3. We need a day or so break between terms.

4. We think there should be fewer or no required courses.

OBJECTIVE: to enable students and faculty to take advantage of experiences on other campuses.
SUGGESTIONS:

1. An effort should be made through the Consortium and other channels to bring more students and faculty to this campus for January and to exchange with other colleges.

2. Earlier planning facilitates exchange.

OBJECTIVE: to provide the opportunity for full-time field experience.
SUGGESTION:

1. An intensive term is very good. However, due to primarily logistical problems an intensive term in May would also be very helpful, thus 4-1-3-1.

Synergy was again apparent. The intensive term objectives and discussion re-emphasized the concern for greater curricular and teaching flexibility. Although some people in the Natural Sciences division and the Music department persisted in the belief that their course needs could not be adapted to the one-month term, most comments focused on improving rather than halting the modified 4-1-4.

BUILDING MOMENTUM

In 1973-74, the "Project Change Task Force," as the writer of its minutes now identified it, met regularly to move toward the objective of improving teaching flexibility and effectiveness. The chairperson of the committee was now the dean. Otherwise, the membership remained the same as the 1972-73 group—the professor of mathematics (who was still the institutional representative), a professor of education, an associate professor of chemistry, an assistant professor of English, an assistant professor of history and a professor of religion. Most members had joined the college after 1967. Only the institutional representative, who arrived in 1962, and

In 1973-74, the "Project Change Task Force," as the writer of its minutes now identified it, met regularly to move toward the objective of improving teaching flexibility and effectiveness.

the professor of religion, who joined the college in 1951, could be called "old guard" in 1974.

The first task force action was to consider action-plans developed by the dean and the institutional representative at the Strategies summer workshop in Saratoga Springs. The plans called for submission of a proposal on further calendar changes, consideration of a recommendation to propose establishment of a Continuing-Cooperative Education Council, dissemination and use of Strategies questionnaire results on faculty attitudes and behaviors and study of the academic organization structure. In particular, the task force was to "consider methods to institute in-service education for faculty in the areas of: (a) effective teaching and course planning techniques for intensive term courses, [and] (b) motivation for learning."

In its first meeting, on August 31, 1973, the Task Force adopted the plan. It also elaborated the faculty in-service education areas to include:

1. *Funds for retraining faculty.*
2. *Training in speech instruction for Integrated Humanities faculty.*
3. *Motivating faculty for publishing.*
4. *Incentive to faculty to work out an integration of faith and their respective disciplines.*
5. *Exchange professorships.*
6. *Sharing sessions between faculty from other Christian colleges and Messiah faculty in areas of common academic concern.*

At its next meeting, the task force put the final touches to a proposal to establish the Continuing-Cooperative Education Council; the faculty shortly thereafter approved that new body. The group then turned to consideration of proposals to revise the academic division structure. To gain legitimacy from the faculty as the proper body to suggest a new structure, the task force asked for and received in late September approval from the faculty to do that, provided the president chaired those deliberations. The major debate that developed in those discussions was between a divisional structure proposed by the associate professor of chemistry and a departmental arrangement proposed by the institutional representative. The dean spoke in favor of the departmental model, as did four of the six faculty members. The argument in its favor was that it eliminated one level of control, thereby linking the dean and departments more closely together. Concerns about inter-disciplinary education could be handled other ways, perhaps through in-service faculty programs. To an external observer, the move appeared to be another attempt to avoid the conservative bottleneck of the division chairpersons. In subsequent meetings, the departmental proposal was refined, then was aired in an open faculty hearing and revised on the basis of criticisms expressed during that meeting. Faculty proceeded to ratify the new departmental structure in December meetings. Once again, open involvement of faculty during proposal development rather than afterward appeared to pay off.

In January, the faculty passed an Academic Affairs recommendation to maintain the modified 4-1-4 calendar. It also instructed the Strategies task force to continue seeking ways to create flexibility in curriculum and

215

Once again, open involvement of faculty during proposal development rather than afterward appeared to pay off.

teaching. The task force decided to attend a team workshop at the American Association for Higher Education conference in March "in order to study the matter of making the curriculum more flexible." Also, the dean proposed that the May Faculty Institute be focused on faculty development. His notion was that faculty members would submit proposals to use that time in various personal or academic improvement efforts. "Mini-grants" of up to $200 apiece could be allotted to development projects. The task force agreed with those suggestions; according to the calendar revision, all faculty were obligated by contract to participate in two weeks of professional development. Now those two weeks could be individually designed. The group then decided to begin to stimulate faculty input on their charge of examining the curriculum in general as well as to begin to garner evidence about the curricular requirements "at three or four representative colleges." A faculty questionnaire would follow open hearings. In short, the group continued to seek both linkage to external information and faculty involvement.

The faculty hearing on the curriculum, held February 11, 1974, focused in part on a multi-college comparison of curricular flexibility developed by the task force. Most noteworthy in terms of the group's objective—increasing flexibility—was that Messiah equaled the least flexible of six other small Christian colleges in its general education and major requirements and in its electives. Only 11% of the students' courses, on the average, did not fall either in general education or major blocks, although the percentage varied by major. The follow-up questionnaire revealed that over 75% of the faculty who responded felt that more flexibility was desirable. Interaction with evidence had its impact. The team attending AAHE therefore decided to focus on ways to increase curricular flexibility. At the convention the team discussed the contract method of individualized education with Arthur Chickering and the provost of Quaker Academic College and heard from Strategies staff about a faculty development project just getting underway in the Council for the Advancement of Small Colleges (CASC). Their plan of action was as follows:

Final Action Plans

The final action plans as developed at our last session include:

A. *Faculty Development*

 1. *Facilitate new departmental structure;*

 2. *Utilize experiences of individualized projects of May faculty workshop;*

 3. *Tie in with faculty development project of CASC.*

B. *Making Curriculum More Flexible*

 1. *Task Force to identify three theoretical models*

 2. *Hold Faculty Workshop (or workshops) in which models will be discussed in small groups*

 3. *Gather departmental reactions to the models*

 4. *Task Force formulate proposals*

 5. *Faculty Action*

A THREE YEAR PERSPECTIVE

Up to this point, the Strategies task force had introduced a major curricular change, conducted several workshops and institutes, utilized external consultation and self-study data, established a Continuing-Cooperative Education Committee and held a faculty hearing on curricular flexibility. Considerable effort had been made to expose faculty to external knowledge, internal data and proposals in early stages of development, and to involve representative faculty in the task force so that knowledgeable decisions and a sense of ownership could be fostered. So what? Was Messiah any closer in 1974 than in 1972 (or in 1967, for that matter) to teaching-learning flexibility? A partial answer is the information concerning the intensive term. In the first year, that innovation did engage nearly half the faculty in new approaches to teaching. But was there any carryover? One study of intensive terms suggests that they do not have decided impact on the behavior the rest of the academic year.

Information collected by Strategies at the end of the project again offers some clues regarding the progress of these strategies. For example, the one IFI scale which significantly increased in 1974 was "Meeting Local Needs," a change reflective of the dean's and the task force's efforts to attend to continuing and cooperative education needs. "Institutional Esprit" remained close to the 90th percentile nationally, suggesting that faculty loyalty to the institution, sense of common mission and respect for administrators remained strong despite evident conflicts between some faculty and the administration. In teaching practices, the emphasis on dispensing knowledge as the primary instructional approach decreased slightly, although student influence over course structure and content did not change. The class time spent in "doing your own thinking" increased significantly, however; in 1972 only 13% of the students reported doing this kind of thinking in class, while the figure had risen to 21% in 1974. Class discussions, however, were slightly less participative.

On the other hand, significantly *less* study time was spent memorizing and more spent interpreting and applying. These shifts were accompanied by student reports that significantly more students were "frequently or most of the time" interested in the course (59% to 69%) and challenged by it (54% to 65%). In faculty-student relationships, significantly fewer students (15% to 8%) reported no conversations over five minutes with faculty members or administrators, and significantly more students (28% to 37%) reported "major" faculty/administrative impact on increasing their "intellectual competence." On the CUES "Scholarship" scale, Messiah students rated their institution at the 69th percentile nationally in 1974, compared to the 33rd percentile in 1972. In general, significantly more students (16% to 34%) reported being "very well" satisfied with their educational experiences at Messiah.

This information, in short, tells a very promising story concerning change at Messiah College. Students were doing more active thinking and more interacting to greater effect with faculty. They found course experiences and the academic atmosphere much more invigorating. Concern to meet local and continuing educational needs was increasing. Apparently the strategy of involving faculty in diagnosing needs, linking to knowledge

So what? Was Messiah any closer in 1974 than in 1972 (or in 1967, for that matter) to teaching-learning flexibility?

217

Neither the dean nor the task force members felt that the task of increasing teaching-learning flexibility was fully accomplished.

resources and developing solutions, if spear-headed by a well-organized and respected planned change team and supported at the top, pays off.

NEXT STEPS

Neither the dean nor the task force members felt that the task of increasing teaching-learning flexibility was fully accomplished. In fact, activities were increased in 1974-75. First off, a team of three faculty members, the dean and the institutional representative attended the one-week CASC workshop on faculty development in August, 1974, at Oklahoma Christian College. They returned to campus with a detailed plan of action. Its objectives were to strengthen sense of community among faculty and administration as well as to foster individual faculty member initiatives for their own professional development. Several projects were undertaken toward those ends. The initial project was to increase team membership to nine faculty members, nearly a fifth of the faculty. Another effort was to use CASC and Strategies funds to send faculty members to conferences on college teaching and to bring to campus consultants Harold Hodgkinson (on governance and adult development) and Jack Noonan (on faculty development); both had interacted with the team of Oklahoma Christian.

Another project involved ten faculty members for part of the year in systematic classroom diagnosis using videotape. In an attempt to increase friendly interaction and openness in faculty meetings, a social coffee period was held prior to each week's meeting. Several interviewees said this affair tended to make the atmosphere of the meeting itself much more cordial and open. The idea of professional growth contracts, picked up by the team at the CASC conference, was introduced to department chairpersons and tried out by the team itself. A questionnaire soliciting faculty development needs was distributed to faculty so that the team could reflect broader interests. Faculty responses emphasized the need to improve administrative relations with faculty, a concern to reach consensus on college mission and a desire for broader faculty discussion about teaching.

Stimulated by discussion of "ad hocracy" and "trial balloons" in a CASC regional workshop and in conversation with Hodgkinson, the team decided to present to faculty a proposal to reduce standing committees to four, rely on *ad hoc* committees, and allow standing groups to finalize faculty decisions if publication of such trial balloons did not result in petition by five faculty members that the whole faculty review the decision. The objective was to reduce faculty time spent in governance without reducing faculty opportunities for influence. The proposal, however, called for the president to chair two of the standing groups, for the dean to chair the third and the dean of students the fourth. Neither faculty members nor administrative found that arrangement attractive. They did approve the trial balloon policy, however. Finally, the team set up a professional development browsing shelf in the college library, and this was well-used. Looking back, team members and others felt that much progress had been made in encouraging faculty members to learn about new ways to teach, and some progress had been made on the issue of faculty-administrative relations. Interviewees said there was still work to do to break through the personal barriers to change on both fronts.

The Strategies task force, meanwhile, went ahead with its own efforts to make learning more flexible. One of its tasks was to query faculty about the first set of professional growth projects and approve requests for the 1975 version. It expended about $3,000 in grants of up to $200 for 1974 projects. Faculty evaluation of this effort was extremely positive. The institutional support and the flexibility of individual projects were appreciated. A second agenda, spurred by the dean, was a meeting with the general education committee to explore ways to make the freshman year more flexible. Not much room for student choice was found that way, but a faculty member who had attended the AAHE team workshop the spring before proposed consideration of individual learning contracts, and the institutional representative suggested credit by examination as a way exceptional students could quickly meet initial requirements. These ideas were developed and presented to faculty in the manner first tried with the calendar change: draft a rough proposal, present it in a full faculty hearing, revise it and present it again. Both quickly passed, with amendment of the contract learning proposal (calling for each student and a three-faculty member team to develop a program) to be sure early review would be conducted by the academic affairs committee. Neither change was viewed as a threat to departmental majors. And by this time, faculty members themselves had seen and raised the need to provide diverse learning opportunities well-fitted to student concerns. A final and major act of the Strategies task force was to screen and approve requests from each faculty member for the two-week professional growth project required by the calendar change. Although some faculty members still were not attempting improvements in weak areas, there was a wide range of projects deemed highly promising by task force members. It appeared that a great deal of innovation was occurring. Now would come the hard part: change in depth and change among the laggards. But that was a project for 1975-76.

PLANNED CHANGE THEORY AND MESSIAH COLLEGE

How did change happen at Messiah? What theory applies? It is certainly apparent that the involvement of the dean and increasing numbers of faculty members and administrators established an important social interaction network linking knowledge resources to users. The satellite campus and 4-1-3 calendar were adaptations of innovations existent outside the college and introduced through cosmopolitan contacts. JB Hefferlin, Harold Hodgkinson, Kenneth Eble, Jack Noonan and Strategies staff members were only a few of the outside consultants who helped introduce new ideas into the institution. Trips to other campuses or teaching-learning conferences, and visits by colleagues from other institutions added to the richness of this contact. Linkage to knowledge resources for innovation was a major strategy of the task force, and it paid off. In at least this general sense, therefore, the Social Interaction model fits Messiah's change process.

Intervention of evidence about need, however, was another major strategy. The ECQ data on teaching and learning provoked faculty and

Interviewees said there was still work to do to break through the personal barriers to change on both fronts.

219

Linkage to knowledge resources for innovation was a major strategy of the Task Force, and it paid off.

administrative concern on several occasions. The IFI results helped clarify the need for continuing and cooperative education. The Interim Report helped stir attention to administrative relations with faculty. Campus members reported that this data did aid in building commitment to change. And progress was made toward resolving problems identified in the data. This Problem Solving emphasis on systematic diagnosis of need was a second effective part of the process.

Third, ownership of the problem-solving process by those who must decide and implement academic changes—the faculty—was frequently cited as an important factor in building greater commitment to the 4-1-3 calendar and faculty development than had been true for earlier planned changes. Collaboration is another Problem-Solving assumption. At the same time, it was the executive administration which provided much of the initiative, knowledge linkage, institutional support and planning structure for change. Their credibility as respected and accepted leaders, their persistent advocacy and their gatekeeping and issue sponsorship appeared necessary if anything were to happen beyond academic business as usual. This role of key authorities fits Political assumptions about change.

Strategies staff were consistently impressed by how well-organized and effectively followed up were Messiah's action plans. The task force, the Long Range Planning Committee, the Assistant Deanship and the Growth and Development Committee each gave the institution formal structures for change planning and follow-through. They helped link one action, such as gaining approval of 4-1-3, to later actions to meet the same objective. Both RD&D and the Problem-Solving models stress systematic organization of change attempts.

Variety and redundancy of effort was certainly apparent and useful. The satellite campus, integrated studies and the one week intersession made some dent in curricular and teaching inflexibility. The calendar change made quite an opening. Data feedback stimulated interest. Professional growth projects and faculty development widened that interest. Any one change project would not substantially increase teaching-learning flexibility, but taken together they amounted to a major change. Havelock's "synergy" factor demonstrated its importance.

Any one change project would not substantially increase teaching-learning flexibility, but taken together they amounted to a major change.

Linkage to knowledge resources, systematic need diagnosis, support at the top, persistent advocacy by skilled and respected leaders, faculty ownership, well-organized action-planning and political process and synergy: these were the change factors which appeared to be especially important at Messiah College. As at other Strategies institutions, this melange suggests that change requires a combination of theories and strategies. If such a combination is mounted, the evidence of Messiah College does suggest that substantial change in behavior will occur.

Section III

Innovation as Adaptive Development

The case histories of Section II depict efforts by local organization members to solve local problems in response to external pressures with the stimulation and guidance of innovations elsewhere. Section III synthesizes these cases and prior research into a general model describing what it takes to accomplish planned change in professionally staffed organizations such as colleges and universities. Chapter Nine outlines the "adaptive development" model. Chapter Ten discusses the change agent roles and skills, plus the organizational service units, which are needed to make adaptive development happen.

This section can be of particular use in re-examining one's own roles and skills, whether one is an organizational leader, member or consultant. It also is useful in considering whether your organization has sufficient investment in the various "adaptive subsystems" which keep attention and energy focused on adaptation to new needs and conditions.

9 Strategies for Adaptive Development

We cannot afford to be dilettantish or partial about planned change in organizational behavior. If we do not take charge of the development and implementation of our futures, either the inertia of the past or the vagaries of the forces around us will dictate our actions. The literature in Section I and the cases in Section II tell us that taking charge is far from easy. Even the best Research and Development is not enough, though important, for less rational factors enter change decisions and, as is the case in education, powerful evidence of R&D outcomes is hard to obtain. Even the most sophisticated linkage between innovations and their potential adopters is inadequate if the innovations are not impressive or the local need is not clear and strong. Even skillful human intervention to clarify goals and needs and to collaborate in development of locally owned changes is weak if it takes place in isolation from the stimulation and guidance of external knowledge resources. Even a combination of Rational Planning, Social Interaction and Human Problem-Solving is less than promising if it is not well-integrated into local formal and informal systems of influence and decision-making. And none of this has much payoff unless followed up by training for new roles; by renewal and innovation structures; by skillful leadership; by adequate time, money, and materials; by appropriate rewards; and by formative as well as summative evaluation.

I hypothesize from the literature and cases that all these models and strategies must be combined in order to have a serious chance of bringing about innovation and renewal. But how should we go about it? In this chapter, I will describe the planned change process in such complex organizations as colleges and universities as the literature and cases define it. That description constitutes a synthesis of planned change models, not a competitor to but a combination of prior strategies. I call this synthesis "adaptive development" because planned change is a local development, but one which is stimulated and guided by the adaption of external innovations rather than the invention of new ones. In many ways, it is the organizational analog of Piaget's theory of human development.

223

I hypothesize from the literature and cases that all these models and strategies must be combined in order to have a serious chance of bringing about innovation and renewal.

DEVELOPING INNOVATIVE MODELS

The Bachelor of General studies degree at South Carolina was adapted from models already in use at the University of Iowa and the University of Michigan. The Contemporary University, Opportunity Scholars and University Without Walls were essentially demonstration projects at South Carolina, the testing of models which might spread within the university and elsewhere. University 101 at South Carolina and Man in Focus at Quaker Academic were adaptations of the freshman seminar innovation sweeping the country in the early 1970's. The Academic Forward Planning Committee was modeled after the University of Virginia's example, and the Educational Development Officer was the National Laboratory for Higher Education's idea first. Messiah adapted 4-1-4 calendars and satellite campuses, both familiar innovations in the early 1970's, to its own situation. Hartwick, Mountain College and Commuter Private had their versions of living-learning programs, and Mountain College tested out University Without Walls as well. Black Cooperative adapted co-op education and basic skills laboratories. Quaker Academic and Messiah tried out their versions of contract learning. Faculty development was not born at Hartwick and Messiah, nor was it simply bought wholesale by them.

All these innovations were assembled locally by the Strategies institutions, and I will look at that adaptation process later. The point here is that nearly every local innovation had a model as a stimulus and guide. These were not pure inventions; no one built their programs from scratch. It appears critical to organizational change, therefore, that innovative models be developed and tested. Research and Development *is* important. A general strategy for change which omits the development of model innovations for adaptation elsewhere would ignore the evidence of these cases.

The cases indicate, however, that human interaction innovations such as these academic and management changes should be developed, tested and packaged somewhat differently than such technological innovations as computers. These institutions did not buy finished products and just plug them in. They took an idea, a few guidelines, some practical tips on what works and what needs avoiding, some evidence to convince local skeptics, and then constructed their own innovation to fit their own institutions. Were I to package an academic innovation for adaptation elsewhere, therefore, I would put it together as raw materials for local development, as useful evidence and suggestions, rather than as *The Way* it must be done. Several Social Interaction factors, however, did apply. It helped that these models came from credible sources. The University of Michigan was a more impressive source of the Bachelor of General Studies to South Carolina faculty than the Union of Experimenting Colleges and Universities was regarding University Without Walls. Goddardites were not very credible to Hartwickians. Credible, however, did not necessarily mean the most prestigious colleges and universities by traditional measures. Messiah faculty were persuaded of the viability of calendar options being tried at nearby small colleges not much different from their own school. Homophily, Rodgers would call it. That place is like ours, and if they like this innovation and think it works for them, we ought to consider it seriously. Were I to fund the development of innovative models, therefore, I would look both to traditionally prestigious institutions and to similar and respectable institutions for the broader audience I have in mind.

It also seemed to help that each innovation was at base a fairly simple idea: a one-month term, an individualized degree or course, a merger of classroom and dormitory, support for teaching improvement, joint

A general strategy for change which omits the development of model innovations for adaptation elsewhere would ignore the evidence of these cases.

224

decision-making, an orientation to higher learning for new students. Elaborate and confusing packages such as the Hartwick vice president's proposals, the Experimental College at South Carolina, New Directions at Mountain College and the Messiah dean's 1-3-1-3-1 calendar were too much for faculty to handle at once. Were I to develop innovative models, therefore, I would create proposals simple to understand and adapt. Complexity may follow within the adapting institution as local people flesh out and test their adaptation, but initially large and complex models are awfully hard to swallow whole. Note also that most of these innovations could be tried out as small pilot projects before most faculty had to make a commitment of their own time and resources. Let the few volunteers do it on their own time and with soft money. We then will evaluate the pilot for more permanent status. The Bachelor of General Studies, Contemporary University, University 101, University Without Walls, Opportunity Scholars, Man in Focus, special freshman advising, 4-1-4: each began as a small pilot program under close faculty scrutiny. When respected faculty evaluators told their colleagues that Bachelor of General Studies had merit, the critics calmed down. Were I to seek to begin an innovative program in a college or university, therefore, I would propose a small "pilot" program to be evaluated by faculty opinion leaders.

Divisibility, another Social Interaction factor, also played its part. Once the Hartwick vice president's elaborate plan for student development was put in sequence so that a small freshman advising project could be taken as a first step, it passed. Once the sweeping Collegium was trimmed to be just a faculty planning council, it passed. When Individualized Educational Planning was proposed for adoption in easy stages, it passed. The same went for 4-1-4 at Messiah. Of course, stage two is often difficult to reach, for it usually must involve more people than the initial volunteers, but at least the divisibility of innovations gets a foot in the door.

I would worry about compatibility as well. The University Without Walls at South Carolina was made as incompatible with traditional academic values as its leader could manage, while the same program at Mountain College was presented as a good match with the personal concern for students of that college. The Experimental College was opposed as a separate and potentially competing operation but accepted as one part of an existing college whose mission seemed to fit the proposal. Hartwick faculty found non-traditional models too much at odds with their background, structure and students; but faculty development to improve traditional teaching was almost eagerly accepted. The Collegium proposed there not only was too much change to take at once but was also incompatible with existing governance structures. Pared down to a Planning Council which fit those structures, it passed. The cluster college concept made sense to Commuter Private faculty members who wanted to aid and encourage academic diversity, but that idea was quite incompatible with the values of a new president and senior faculty who wanted a more uniformly traditional model of excellence. Were I developing an innovative model, therefore, I would aim to make it fit my audience's values, structures and behaviors as much as possible short of sacrificing

Were I to seek to begin an innovative program in a college or university, therefore, I would propose a small "pilot" program to be evaluated by faculty opinion leaders.

225

Were I developing an innovative model, therefore, I would aim to make it fit my audience's values, structures and behaviors as much as possible short of sacrificing the integrity of the innovation itself.

the integrity of the innovation itself.

"What's the advantage of this new way over our old way?" faculty members ask of innovative models. The examples in these cases were hard pressed to demonstrate powerful advantages. The evidence that a semester's independent study, an individualized degree, a living-learning program, a new advising system on a short term really make a difference in learning, prestige or income for the student or the institution was not impressive. It may be the Achilles heal of academic innovations that evidence of their impact is hard to produce, often low in credibility because it comes from educational research or measures non-traditional outcomes and often is not gathered with much seriousness. It may make the innovator feel better to note that existing programs have no better evidence of their advantages, but that point is not going to win over anyone ensconced in the *status quo*. Change is hard, threatening work. Why risk it if the new is no more impressive than the old and is less secure? Were I to develop an innovative model, therefore, I would make every effort to seek evidence credible to my audience that the thing produces results desirable to that audience. At the same time, I would recognize that the audience probably will have to test out the new idea itself, using its own ways to evaluate worth and its own credible evaluators. As I just mentioned, small pilot projects evaluated by esteemed colleagues, the approach used at South Carolina to learn the relative advantages of the Bachelor of General Studies, Contemporary University and University 101 appear to be a good way to go concerning innovative models whose evidence of relative advantages is controversial.

In summary, development of innovative models for adaptation elsewhere is an important part of a general planned change strategy concerning such human interaction innovations as changes in curriculum, teaching and evaluation. But such models should not be packaged and sold as finished products. They should be presented as basic ideas and handy tips for local development. They should come from credible sources and should be offered as simple pilot projects or implemented in easy stages. They should be designed to fit existing values, interests, structures and behaviors as much as they can stand, and they should be as easy to test and observe as possible. The strongest possible evidence of relative advantages of a kind persuasive to the chosen audience should be generated. That is a conservative formula. It almost guarantees that innovations will start out as only small deviations from the *status quo*. If the power lies in the *status quo*, however, that small beginning is probably the best you can get. Whether it grows depends on tactics I will discuss more specifically in the rest of this book.

DIFFUSION CHANNELS AND METHODS

Once we have some innovations worth adapting, then what? How does anyone else get the message? Consistently, a few local administrators well-connected to the currents of innovation introduced new ideas. The president of South Carolina, the dean of Messiah, the provost of Quaker Academic, the president of Mountain College: each had external contacts with innovative persons, institutions or literature. Less frequently, a

226

faculty member such as the chairperson of the Faculty Advisory Committee at South Carolina and the assistant professor of economics at Commuter Private would introduce innovations which they had experienced in other institutions. These persons looked outside their local institution or recently had come from institutions with innovative programs. For the most part, they also were well-linked to local authority structures, usually administrative leadership, but occasionally faculty governance. They held formal office or had personal contacts with local leaders. In sociological parlance, they were "cosmopolitan-locals,"[1] both cosmopolitan in external contacts and local in internal access to authority. Were I to attempt to strengthen planned change in an organization, therefore, I would make sure the local cosmopolitans were well-connected to local leaders and the local leaders well-linked to innovative models beyond the institution.

In most cases, the contact was a personal one. The South Carolina president talked with Joe Rhodes, and out of this contact came Contemporary University. The Educational Policies Committee at Commuter Private interacted with Arthur Chickering and Tim Pitkin as well as individuals from other innovative institutions, and out of this came Individualized Educational Planning. Gary Quehl, then president of the College Center for the Finger Lakes, met consultants Bill Bergquist and Jack Noonan and out of that came that consortium's faculty development project. The president of Mountain College interned with Jim Dixon, president of innovative Antioch College, and out of that came New Directions. The president of Messiah talked with a consultant to Mennonite colleges, and a satellite campus was born. These local persons and their institutions of course had a strong hand in developing these innovations, and I mean to emphasize rather than de-emphasize the importance of local development. But the initial stimulus most often was personal contact with a respected consultant or colleague elsewhere.

In addition, books such as Gaff's *The Cluster College*, the Carnegie Comission's *Less Time, More Options*, Jerome's *Culture Out of Anarchy*, Chickering's *Education and Identity* and Katz's *No Time for Youth*[2] also spurred local persons to innovate. Ideas such as living-learning, freshman seminars and contract learning made connections through conference presentations. Journal articles may have provided some stimulation as well, although interviewees rarely mentioned them. The main channel for innovative news, however, was personal interaction, mainly between local administrators and external consultants or colleagues. The Strategies project itself is an example. Every institution in it joined because a high-level administrator knew Arthur Chickering or knew of him.

Were I to strengthen local planned change, therefore, I would take every opportunity to connect local leaders with outside individuals either expert about innovative developments or actually immersed in those developments. I would not neglect connections with books and journals and conference presentations as channels for innovation diffusion. But I would stress personal interaction, as indeed Social Interaction theory does. Incidentally, I would not assume that because administrators are most likely to have such contacts that there is something inherently

I would make sure the local cosmopolitans were well-connected to local leaders and the local leaders well-linked to innovative models beyond the institution.

227

I would pay particular attention to the connection of faculty opinion leaders to such outside channels of educational innovation.

administrative about links to outside sources of academic innovation. Rather, it verifies that most sources of innovation in teaching, curriculum and evaluation are aimed at administrators, and most local colleges and universities primarily encourage administrators to read pertinent books and journals, to attend pertinent conferences and to meet higher education innovators and consultants. Because faculty members usually do not trust innovations introduced to them by administrators as much as they do new ideas offered by esteemed colleagues, and because they have much leeway concerning educational practices, I would pay particular attention to the connection of faculty opinion leaders to such outside channels of educational innovation. Especially important would be senior "gatekeepers" of major academic committees, the persons who, if in close contact with bearers of innovative news, might become key sponsors of change, as did the biology chairperson at Hartwick and the distinguished professors of economics and government at South Carolina. I also would seek to introduce new teaching-learning ideas through the channels to which faculty members already are well-linked, namely the journals, conferences and leaders of their academic and professional associations.

In most Strategies cases, innovative models were not intentionally diffused beyond conference presentations and publications. A systematic network of personal interaction was not developed, except in the case of the University Without Walls. Rather, models appeared to be developed primarily for use in the local institution, with conference publications and articles produced as much for personal and institutional status as for diffusion of our neat idea. The University of Michigan had no careful plan for diffusing the Bachelor of General Studies. Empire State College and Ottawa University had no intentional network and process for disseminating contract learning. Rough attempts at cluster colleges, field experience and professional development associations for supporting and spreading these innovations have appeared; but I would suggest they have not thought very thoroughly about how to disseminate their ideas beyond the usual conferences, publications and interactions primarily directed to the innovators themselves. Were I to diffuse an academic innovation, therefore, I would take seriously the learnings of Social Interaction theory, which Strategies cases generally support, and build a dissemination process which emphasizes personal interaction with credible, trusted colleagues over time; which moves from innovators to cosmopolitan opinion leaders (credible consultants or local leaders) to the more cautious and skeptical in their institutions; which also moves intentionally from raising awareness to personal persuasion to local trial; and which presents innovations as credibly, simply, divisibly, compatibly and advantageously as possible. I would begin thinking about who is the appropriate audience for this innovation and how best can that audience be stimulated to give the innovation a try even before I begin developing the innovation itself. As I propose below, development of the innovation itself may be one of the most critical stages in broader dissemination.

Development of the innovation itself may be one of the most critical stages in broader dissemination.

A NEED TO CHANGE

In every case in Section II, local organizational innovation began with an initiative by an executive administrator, or, in some cases, a faculty member who felt a need to introduce some change in institutional practices. The business dean at South Carolina needed to get the university to find another way to handle low achieving students than to drive them toward the business school. The president of that university felt a need to make undergraduate education more responsive to average or below average students in all their diversity of motivations, skills and learning styles. The chairperson of the Faculty Advisory Committee felt a need to increase faculty voice in planning the university's future. At Hartwick, the president saw the writing on the wall that a traditional liberal arts college was going to have a hard time in the face of rising costs and increasing competition for fewer potential students unless it demonstrated impressive value added to student lives by their experience in that college. The provost of Quaker Academic felt that better ways must be found to create effective problem-solvers, and the president of that college saw a need to create a distinctive institutional image in order to succeed in the same, highly competitive future seen by the Hartwick president. At Messiah, the dean came to believe that teaching must be made more flexible and learning more diverse and independent.

In every instance, certain kinds of knowledge resources strengthened this need to change. Executive administrators in particular felt the pressures of economic, political and social trends. If Hartwick, Commuter Private, Quaker Academic, Black Cooperative and Mountain College were to survive, felt their executives, distinctively new and effective changes must be made. Institutional survival and prosperity is particularly an executive administrator's assignment, so it is understandable that these officials were the first to feel this pressure. Also, information about political, social and economic trends relevant to college survival flow primarily to the executive administration through such channels as legislative committees, state commissions, meetings of the American Council on Education, *The Chronicle of Higher Education*, foundations and federal agencies, boards of trustees and worried executives in other institutions. The disciplinary channels to which faculty are connected will deal with trends influencing the prosperity of that discipline, but faculty radar concerning general institutional survival is not as finely tuned as the administration's. When enrollments dramatically drop, faculty know they have a problem. But when the president, with trend information in hand, tells faculty that enrollment will drop dramatically within the next decade unless we act now, faculty are unimpressed. In consequence, it is an executive who is most likely first to feel from political-social-economic information the pressure to change.

Two practical tactics for planned change are implied by this tendency. One is to be sure executive administrators *are* well-connected to the latest socio-economic and political trends affecting the institution. That is a familiar approach. The second is to do all you can to get faculty opinion leaders who care about the college linked to the same information. Get them subscriptions to the *Chronicle* and *Washington Reports*. Send them to ACE meetings. Have them join executives and trustees in discussing the latest budget crunch. As Hartwick and Quaker Academic did, send them out with the admissions staff to find out what potential students really want these days and what the competition is offering. Hold special workshops and seminars on these subjects. Leaders of participative planning committees often discover that faculty and student leaders are just as capable as administrators of seeing a need for action in such information, even the same action administrators see, if effectively exposed to it. Were I to strengthen institutional capacity for self-renewal, therefore, I would expose as many local leaders as possible to the latest information regarding external trends likely to exert pressure on the organization.

Other kinds of information spurred the need to change as well. One was evidence of internal problems. The Messiah dean and several faculty members agreed with the *Experience of College Questionnaire* evidence that learning was too passive. The Quaker Academic provost and the few faculty members who came to his house saw in the *College Student Questionnaire* data a need to design educational practices to suit socially liberal and independent students. The president of the University of South Carolina saw in the very low *Institutional Functioning Inventory* score for "Concern for Undergraduate Learning" a need to create much more university interest in undergraduate students, while those who attended the *Institutional Goals Inventory* workshops at South Carolina agreed that they must improve their ability to develop students intellectually and personally as well as their ability to work together in a community of respect, trust and openness. Several leaders at Commuter Private agreed with interview feedback that there were serious "Faculty Misconnections with Students" that must be remedied.

This evidence did not create need. Rather, it drew attention to problems, catalyzed discussion of them, gave vague concerns some clarity, confirmed that many people besides me feel the same concern and motivated some people to do more than simply lament the problems. When communicated effectively, such internal evidence on goals and practices did lead to action. Were I to build my organization's planned change capacity, therefore, I would do all I could to generate persuasive evidence regarding local goals, practices and outcomes, and I would learn how to present that information in ways which create openness to its perhaps disturbing messages rather than defensiveness.

I have discussed a third kind of information which stimulates a need to change. That is news of promising innovations. In several cases, local action was initiated by someone who not only saw a local problem but already had discovered a promising solution. The Messiah dean had a 1-3-1-3-1 calendar in mind when he set up a calendar committee. The president of South Carolina already had Contemporary University, University Without Walls, freshman seminars and media centers in mind when he started institutional action to adopt such practices. Need perhaps came before solution in these individuals' minds (the need-solution sequence is one I could not determine in these cases), but the motivation to get the institution to act was partially encouraged by discovery of the solution as well as the need.

It was interesting to me that campus members rarely mentioned basic research and theory as the root of their motivation to change. No one

---

I would expose as many local leaders as possible to the latest information regarding external trends likely to exert pressure on the organization.

230

When communicated effectively, such internal evidence on goals and practices did lead to action.

initially talked about Newman and Ortega y Gasset, Piaget and Dewey, Tannenbaum and Etzioni, Havelock and Rodgers or any other theorists one might name for their relevance to college and university practices. Some applied research and theory was mentioned. The Messiah dean's reading of Katz, the South Carolina president's reading of Chickering and the Wild Card Committee's reading of Gaff are examples. A few persons such as the associate provost at Commuter Private were students of learning and higher education. For the most part, however, planned change was not a move from basic research and scholarship to local action. Despite the academic background of college administrators and faculty members, they do not turn to the library or to basic research projects to find motivation to change. That does not mean it is pointless to produce and publish research and theory pertinent to the functioning of these organizations. After all, cluster colleges, competency programs, contract and field experience learning, personalized instruction, planning bodies and professional development are grounded in basic and applied research and theory. The point is that between theory and a motivation to change, something must happen to make the message more practically useful and urgent. One intermediate step is the discussion of practical applications of theory, as the Katz and Chickering books do and as the Center for Research on Learning and Teaching's *Memo to Faculty* does very nicely. Another is to support development and testing of innovations based on such theory, as I discussed earlier. It is easier to adapt contract or field experience programs than it is to design applications of progressive education theory from scratch. It is easier to adapt personalized instruction than it is to begin with reinforcement theory in the abstract.

In an earlier essay on academic innovation,[3] I discussed several levels and kinds of motivation to change or not change in a complex organization. Burns and Stalker's study of innovation in English organizations dramatizes how concern about change occurs at the individual level (how will this new thing affect me?), at the sub-group level (what impact will this innovation have on my department?) and at the broad organizational level (will it help or hinder our college or university?).[4] Maslow reminds us that there probably are seven somewhat distinct kinds of motivation as well.[5] Before I do anything else, I must breathe, receive nourishment and tend to other bodily needs. My department or college first must survive. Then I worry about how safe I am from danger. Who is after my job? I worry that my department or college may suffer attack from the cutthroat competition out there. Once safe, I'd like to become secure. Tenure comes to mind. Getting my department or new program on a firm, annual budget becomes an important mission. Building up our endowment seems worth doing. With these matters in hand, I turn toward gaining acceptance of myself, my group and my organization among those whose acceptance I value (including me). Once accepted, I seek high status for myself, my department, my university. Not satisfied just with formal or informal status, I seek esteem, self-esteem and the esteem of valued others. Finally, all these worries met, I turn to those lofty "metagrumbles" which are expressed so nobly in the frontispiece of the college catalog and in the president's fine speeches: the pursuit of truth, beauty and justice. Figure 10

The point is that between theory and a motivation to change, something must happen to make the message more practically useful and urgent.

231

FIGURE 10
LEVELS AND KINDS OF NEEDS

	Individual	Sub-group	Organization
Survival			
Safety			
Security			
Acceptance			
Status			
Esteem			
Truth Beauty Justice			

232

depicts these levels and kinds of need to change or to thwart it.

Now, where in that grid were the motivations regarding change in Strategies institutions? We certainly saw some worry about organizational survival, safety and security, the lower left corner. The presidents of Commuter Private, Hartwick, Quaker Academic and Mountain College all felt a strong need to change in order to keep their institutions afloat. Not that these leaders did not have "higher" motivations. Each had a vision of quality education, the far right end of the matrix, and the route to survival became articulated as the route to "excellence" or "pragmatic idealists" or "value added" or "personalized-learning." Some leaders, those fortunate enough to be in reasonably secure institutions, focused particularly on what Maslow would call the "self-actualization" of their institution and its students. The presidents of South Carolina and Hartwick and the dean of Messiah were consistently concerned, it was my impression, to find better ways to make undergraduate education realize its goals, its potential. But the other kinds and levels of need intermingled in every case. The Arts and Sciences dean at South Carolina fought University Without Walls and the Experimental College in part because they threatened the security of his college and his own status as the dean of innovative liberal education programs. In several cases, innovations were opposed because they were not "accepted" forms of education or not of high status and esteem among traditional academics. The desire to be "distinctive" which colored the rhetoric of several institutional leaders was a call to seek status and esteem as well as to get a bit closer to truth, beauty and justice. This range of needs was visible among individual change leaders, followers and resistors as well. Concern for impact on departments and faculty were as much a part of the equation as the literature in Chapter One indicated it would be. The lower right corner of Figure 10, institutional goals, was as far away from most people's prime concerns as that grid suggests.

The more kinds and levels of need met by a proposed change, the more likely its full implementation. Ideally, a comprehensive strategy for change should pay heed to all the boxes in Figure 10. It seems safe to say, however, that the changes proposed in Strategies institutions did not meet many of these kinds of motivation to change at any level for more than a few initial advocates. Few people thought of Man in Focus or Individualized Educational Planning or New Directions as directly relevant to immediate survival or a secure future, as bringing their institutions any closer to fulfilling any higher goals than those currently being attempted. How, then, can such changes come into being?

SLIPPING THROUGH THE GATE

It is not enough that a few administrators and professionals feel a need to change. Someone must be moved to do something. We all are familiar with the old saw that everybody complains about the bad weather in our institution, but nobody does anything about it. Getting up the gumption to change one's own attitudes or behavior is hard enough, but to effect organizational change, one must take on the authorities. That is pretty risky business for people whose brainstorms may irritate the powers that be. Small wonder that the persons who articulated general needs into specific "demands" for campus action in Strategies cases were either authorities themselves or individuals with easy access to authority. Presidents and deans took the first step, for the most part. The few faculty members who proposed innovations were the young economics professor who had a pipe-line to the associate provost at Commuter Private, the English professor at Mountain College who found herself on the academic planning committee and the chairperson of the Faculty Advisory Committee and the Tuesday discussion group at South Carolina, both of which were well-linked to the Faculty Senate. The persons who made demands for organizational action, in brief, either were "gatekeepers" to the political system or had access to them and encouragement from them. That pattern strongly suggests two things helpful to a self-renewing organization. One already has been mentioned: top authorities well-connected to information concerning external pressures, innovative models and internal practices and who are willing to take risks. The other is easy access of innovators and innovative proposals to the centers of authority. Innovative persons at South Carolina and Hartwick, for instance, felt encouraged by their president to go ahead and propose new things. So they did. For a while, the Black Cooperative task force could not get rolling in part

The more kinds and levels of need met by a proposed change, the more likely its full implementation.

233

The persons who made demands for organizational action, in brief, either were "gatekeepers" to the political system or had access to them and encouragement from them.

because members suspected that the president and dean were not supportive of their effort. An organization's leaders would do well to ask independent evaluators to inquire of faculty how open they think those leaders are
to various kinds of change ideas; professional and organizational development might focus on improving such sense of openness. "Leaders" in
this sense should include all those who sit at the gates of governance:
committee and department chairpersons, deans, vice presidents, the
president.

INTO COMMITTEE OR PRESIDENTIAL FIAT

Once a demand for college or university action attracted some
gatekeeper's ear, one of two things happened in Strategies cases. In a few
instances, the president just went ahead and launched the innovation with
minimal faculty involvement. So the University Without Walls came into
being at South Carolina and Mountain College. Much more frequently,
however, the demand was assigned to a committee, usually an *ad hoc*,
administratively appointed body. The South Carolina Deans' Council set
up a special committee to study the problem of what to do with upper
division but marginal students, after which the president set up the special
Experimental College committee. He also set up a special committee to
study ways to improve the freshman year, out of which came University
101. The Hartwick president set up the *ad hoc* committee to study value-
added by the college. The Messiah dean and president established the
special Calendar Committee. The Mountain College president established
a temporary self-study and planning group and so forth.

On the surface, presidential fiat seems much faster and cleaner than
committees. You get what you want right away. Or do you? The presidential decisions to act without much faculty involvement concerned
small projects run by volunteers and financed by grants. No president
simply told the faculty as a whole that they all, or even a significant
minority of them, would teach differently next year. Also, these administrative acts raised the hackles of faculty members who believed academic
change was their business. University Without Walls and Contemporary
University drew close scrutiny and almost immediate skepticism from
faculty. Two years after their implementation, South Carolina's University Without Walls was gone, while Contemporary University was reduced in size. Only Mountain College's University Without Walls, with
its steadily increasing income for the college (a clear relative advantage)
and its leader's efforts to reduce faculty resistance, managed to grow. If an
innovation seems particularly worth doing, unlikely to gain initial faculty
favor but able to be operated by volunteers on soft money, presidential
fiat may be the only way to give it a chance. I would make every effort,
however, to do everything possible during implementation to persuade
faculty leaders of its educational worthiness and its compatibility with
their own interests.

As for the familiar committee process of studying problems and
designing solutions, the cases are most instructive. Several Strategies
committees were constituted to be politically representative and were not
given very clear charges regarding problems of much concern to those

On the surface, presidential fiat seems much faster and cleaner than committees. You get what you want right away. Or do you?

234

members. The Commuter Private, Hartwick and South Carolina task forces fit that pattern, and they went nowhere. Mostly, their members canceled each other out in rather unenjoyable debates. Each committee was then reconstituted to include a few persons with a common concern, among whom were innovative young faculty members, respected links to faculty and administrative centers of influence and staff to carry work forward between meetings when regular duties overwhelmed other members. The Messiah task force used that membership approach from the first, while still attempting to represent various points of view. The Quaker Academic group which began Man in Focus was composed of eager young faculty, interested and respected senior faculty and the provost, who added administrative clout. The Experimental College committee and the Tuesday discussion group combined the innovators and a few (probably too few at first) opinion leaders; the Wild Card Committee got the innovators but forgot the opinion leaders. Committee membership is in essence an implementation of Social Interaction findings. Innovators provide initial ideas and advocacy but must be joined to the persons others turn to for advice before their messages carry much weight with the rest of the institution.

Most committees did their work in isolation. They read articles about pertinent theory or models elsewhere, they looked at research data, they interacted with persons doing relevant innovations, they argued and discussed among themselves, they quibbled over the wording of proposals and finally they came out with innovations: an Experimental College, cluster colleges, a year-round calendar, a Collegium, an individualized degree. None were approved. Other people had not been through that learning experience. They had not slowly moved through study and interaction to the conclusion that this proposal is the best solution to a real problem. All they experienced was a quick reading of a final proposal and a brief critique of it in committee, senate or faculty assembly. As one Hartwick veteran of special committees finally saw, faculty critics only needed to find one loose brick, and the whole edifice would come crashing down.

A few groups learned in the course of the Strategies project alternative ways to study problems and develop proposals. Messiah provides the best example. The Calendar Committee presented early drafts to faculty meetings broken into small discussion groups. It asked J B Lon Hefferlin to meet with faculty members to broaden their awareness of various calendar forms. Its own members made personal visits to colleges with alternative calendars and reported back to the faculty. Questionnaires were circulated to learn faculty preferences. And faculty advice was heeded. The Committee revised its own thinking after faculty response. Such participation paid off in extensive initial adoption. The Quaker Academic leaders turned to a similar process for Individualized Educational Planning. They also used small groups crossing disciplines, meetings with enough time to move beyond debate, an *ad hoc* group to follow through on the recommendations of these "mini-retreats," direct contact with another college which had tried such an innovation and persistent advocacy. The South Carolina Strategies task force did not propose the

Innovators provide initial ideas and advocacy but must be joined to the persons others turn to for advice before their messages carry much weight with the rest of the institution.

235

Institutional Goals Study out of thin air. It familiarized the Academic Forward Planning Committee with the idea, got that group to try out the instrument and had these leaders then introduce the idea to the Faculty Senate. The task force summarized results but left interpretation, analysis, synthesis and evaluation to these groups and then, later, to volunteers in workshops using small groups. In each case, key administrative and faculty leaders were involved, although administrators intentionally tried to avoid becoming the focal advocates of change. In short, collaboration was attempted throughout study and formulation. These proposals passed into implementation. Collaboration was not the only factor in the favor of these innovative projects, but participants said it certainly helped.

Were I to create an effective committee process, therefore, I would include several ingredients: personal exposure to outside practitioners and experts, early and continuous sharing of thinking and background information with review bodies, small groups rather than large forums to encourage friendly interaction among many rather than tense debate by a few, opinion questionnaires (kept very brief and given after interest is raised), extended meetings or workshops to explore the subject in depth and continuous leadership by a group of committed advocates and open opinion leaders among both faculty and administration. I also would provide training for these activities and for the difficult business of making a committee both personally rewarding and effective at its task. Groups such as the Committee on Institutional Research at Hartwick and the *ad hoc* group which attended the AAHE workshop from Quaker Academic found much more personally enjoyable and potentially useful ways of behaving after the intervention of professional development or process consultants. As the back home frustrations of Quaker Academic group revealed, however, such aid needs to be continued long enough to take hold. One shot consultation raises expectations but may not raise skills sufficiently to fulfill those hopes.

SUPPORT FOR IMPLEMENTATION

Several Strategies innovations attracted grant support for implementation. Contemporary University, University 101, Man in Focus, Opportunity Scholars, University Without Walls, Individualized Educational Planning, faculty development at Hartwick, Messiah and South Carolina, and several innovations at Black Cooperative obtained "soft" money on which to begin the program. Rarely was such money available for any other part of the planned change process. Apparently, foundations agree with RD&D notions that the critical phase to fund is the "demonstration project," the testing of a new idea. How institutions identify problems, clarify goals, formulate solutions, raise support and reduce resistance is their business. Once they have a novel solution ready to launch or already begun (which shows commitment, they say), then they might help. Perhaps the most obvious way to see the weakness of this tactic is to hear the way funders speak of "institutions." "South Carolina wants to implement Contemporary University" means, we saw, that "the president and a handful of innovators want to implement Contemporary University." This applies to every other innovation funded by foundations and federal

Collaboration was not the only factor in the favor of these innovative projects, but participants said it certainly helped.

236

One shot consultation raises expectations but may not raise skills sufficiently to fulfill those hopes.

agencies. This is, we have seen, a naive view of an academic institution; this is, moreover, a considerable underestimation of the need to help advocates of innovation build local support and reduce local resistance prior to and during implementation. I daresay that persuading organization members that there is real need for change and that this innovation is a promising solution is at least as needful of special support as is implementation itself. The assumption that initial trial will demonstrate the innovation's merits without considerable advance involvement by the cautious and skeptical and without an intentional plan of persuasion during implementation is a grave error in trusting the power of formal authorities, the evidence of educational research and the rumor mill. Those who came to respect these experiments were almost exclusively their participants, close observers and the initially attracted few. None had very many active participants among faculty and administration well into implementation, despite this soft money. That broader acceptance is the real challenge facing foundations and other encouragers of innovation.

Certain kinds of support for implementation, however, did appear to make a difference. Faculty members who went through the two-week training for University 101 said it gave them new teaching tools and some support for the difficulties faced when teaching students instead of disciplinary content. The planning periods interspersed during Man in Focus enabled that program's faculty to make re-adjustments in response to student criticism, although thorough training to teach problem-solving never became part of the program. Coordinators of several of these programs were supported for the length of the grant, although few were then shifted to institutional funds. Except for the faculty development coordinators at Hartwick and Messiah, those without prior experience in their roles did not receive needed training. The vice president for institutional research at Hartwick, the dean in charge of the Bachelor of General Studies and the University Without Walls director at South Carolina, the coordinators of Man in Focus and Individualized Educational Planning at Quaker Academic all were competent people, but none had any background in guiding the implementation of academic innovations. They could have used it.

Several programs did benefit from thoughtful early evaluations, which calmed the critics of Contemporary University, University 101, the Bachelor of General Studies, the 4-1-3 calendar and University Without Walls at Mountain College, while directing appropriate criticism at South Carolina's University Without Walls. Some evidence was used in a formative way as well. The three-member Bachelor of General Studies committees were reduced to two when evidence of logistical problems grew. Man in Focus faculty changed that depressing lecture on contemporary problems to smaller discussion sections on the basis of student feedback. Messiah moved into faculty development in part because of evidence that 4-1-3 in itself was not stimulating sufficient change in teaching-learning practices. Unfortunately, the evidence regarding South Carolina's University Without Walls came too late to guide revision and improvement of that program despite the evaluator's belief that many promising things were occurring.

I daresay that persuading organization members that there is real need for change and that this innovation is a promising solution is at least as needful of special support as is implementation itself.

237

That broader acceptance is the real challenge facing foundations and other encouragers of innovation.

Another key
support for
implementation,
perhaps **the** key, is
an appropriate
system of rewards.

Another key support for implementation, perhaps *the* key, is an appropriate system of rewards. The freshman advising experiment at Hartwick gave no special time realignment or professional rewards for faculty, and initially committed professors could not carry through. The Bachelor of General Studies program provided time and rewards for its general studies coordinators but not for the faculty participants in other schools, and the brunt of its implementation shifted to those coordinators. Personnel policies and procedures were not altered to fit the new demands of innovation, and I became increasingly aware in the course of the Strategies project that personnel decisions were seriously neglected as targets of change activity. New criteria, standards and indicators of professional performance must be developed if innovation is going to become more a blessing than a burden.

Some of these innovations were intentionally supported for dissemination into the broader institution of higher education once their worth was demonstrated. The Union for Experimenting Colleges and Universities kept on seeking new homes for University Without Walls units. Formal evaluations of Opportunity Scholars and University 101 were bound and distributed outside the institution. Those close to the Bachelor of General Studies program became involved in organizing a national meeting for general studies leaders. Hartwick's approach to faculty development was spread around the country by its originators. But none of these "demonstrations" were supported for major dissemination along RD&D lines, with much money and highly sophisticated dissemination tactics and leaders. These innovations, indeed, fit the higher education norm. New programs are developed primarily for local use (and use only by a small part of the local institution at that). A paper, a brief brochure or a more elaborate soft-bound description, perhaps a conference presentation or two and some sharing with our own personal network of colleagues: this is dissemination of innovations as practiced in Strategies cases. Small wonder diffusion is a trickle rather than a torrent.

238

Were I to attempt to implement and spread innovations, I would intentionally orient and train faculty members and administrators for their new roles. I would take time out for planning. I would gather information early and use it both to defend the program and to improve it. I would keep outside opinion leaders and authorities well-informed, even involved, so that the innovation continues increasing support and reducing resistance rather than sinking into isolation and rumor. I would involve outsiders in the program as one part of a broad-range strategy of dissemination. I would provide special funds not so much to pay implementors but to build their skills and to increase support for the innovation before the decision to implement it, during initial implementation and throughout wider internal and external dissemination. I would continue outside consultation concerning both the process and the content of implementation.

COMMENTARY

I have outlined a rather full planned change agenda: developing innovative models for adaptation rather than adoption, strengthening diffusion channels and linking local leaders personally to them, concentrating on thorough diagnosis of local goals and needs, opening political gates to demands for change, involving organization members not only in these earlier parts of the process but in the thinking and formulation of proposals, supporting the orientation and training of innovation implementors and leaders, providing solid time, material and facilities, conducting both formative and summative evaluation, rewarding those who involve themselves in innovation and intentionally disseminating the innovation internally and externally. It is a strategy which joins RD&D, Social Interaction, Human Problem-Solving, and Political models. The cases give solid support to this approach, and they offer some detailed examples of how to do it.

A simple recitation of these stages of adaptive development, however, fails to express the implications of the concept for change theory and change leadership; it does not make clear that people will bring both reason and emotion to the consideration of change and that a leader must recognize and be skillful in handling both kinds of response. It is not easy for those in R&D or systems management to appreciate, let alone emulate, those psychologically oriented people who recognize the critical role that unspoken feelings play in change. By the same token, many process consultants appear to underestimate the importance of clear thinking, solid evidence, systematic organization and logical discourse. Especially in colleges and universities, those who will have to generate and implement change value cognitive rationality and often are very good at it. Sometimes this is a way of avoiding emotional issues, certainly; but it also reflects a genuine need to evaluate proposed changes in a "hard-minded" way through systematic scholarship, empirical research and logical argument. Those who think of the planned change process in political ways, in turn, are sensitive to the drive toward power and self interest. Those tendencies were easily apparent in the cases and were mediated by the familiar political process of coalition formation, compromise and use of formal authority or informal influence. But also apparent were concerns to improve the common good of one's academic community, to do what made rational sense, to act humanely toward colleagues and students, to seek open consensus through collaboration. The politically-oriented leader would say these are secondary to power and self-interest and therefore might neglect to attend to more noble motivations and processes. Interaction with both the change advocates and their opposition in Strategies institutions lead me to believe that such neglect was a serious underestimation of how academic people sometimes do, and often would like to, approach change.

As for those in the middle of the planned change process, the Social Interactionists, they also seem to me to be in the middle on rational-emotional-political scales as well. Theirs is an empirical approach to the process of innovation. They recognize psychological differences between such types as early adopters and entrenched laggards. Such factors as complexity, compatibility, divisibility and "trialability" include dimensions which relate to emotional as well as rational needs. "Relative advantages" include not just empirical evidence of effectiveness but evidence of

A simple recitation of these stages of adaptive development, however, fails to express the implications of the concept for change theory and change leadership.

239

which alternative might be better than another in its ability to provide security, status, power, material goods or whatever else is valued by those considering the change. Their sensitivity to the need to move through opinion leaders into reference groups reflects an awareness of the role of social and political influence as well as social and political group identity. But this model does not offer effective ways to build sound change messages, to get at hidden psychological defenses or to move within a formal political system. It touches the other strategies but needs their depth.

ADAPTIVE DEVELOPMENT FACTORS

I have described a process by which innovation or reform can be effected in colleges and universities; contained within that description are a number of important elements. But are there general, underlying factors? Five factors do stand out as critical ingredients in any attempt to introduce change in the practices of complex organizations: (1) interpersonal and informational *Linkage*; (2) active *Openness*; (3) initiating, guiding, involving and influential *Leadership*; (4) *Ownership* and (5) material and psychic *Rewards*. Unfortunately, the first letters of these words do not spell a memorable acronym, but they deserve to be repeated often by persons engaged in the planning and implementing of new behaviors.

In case after case, we saw the importance of bringing people together. Consultants interacting with college leaders, faculty and students and administration working together, members of one department or institution meeting with members of other units: it was this human contact across formal boundaries which helped stimulate change in several Strategies institutions. Committees with cross-group membership, task force meetings with other groups, workshops and retreats, conferences and consultant visits, bag lunches: these were some of the particular occasions which brought people out of their narrow confines and into interaction with a diversity of ideas and individuals. This kind of *linkage* was not just a matter of people getting together. There were several abysmal meetings in the Strategies cases in which people simply advanced old arguments or shared collective ignorance. Linkage to new information, new perspectives, new ideas and concerns made the difference. Research on local goals and practices, presentation of innovations from elsewhere, evidence of external pressures or internal problems, simply the chance to hear first-hand how students and the Chemistry department really are feeling about current practices and policies: these pieces of information new to their recipients opened their eyes to change needs and possibilities.

It is one thing to be linked to people and information beyond one's self and one's primary group. It is quite another to seek that linkage actively. This kind of *Openness*—not passive waiting but active searching, really hearing instead of politely listening, going to that other campus or office instead of saying "After all, my door was open if they wanted to see me"—was the characteristic that marked more successful change leaders or task forces in the Strategies cases. Most people feel uncomfortable when they leave secure ground (their own notions, their own information, their own cohorts) and open themselves to people and information which might challenge their view of what needs to be done and can be done. But that is

Five factors do stand out as critical ingredients in any attempt to introduce change in the practices of complex organizations.

240

Most people feel uncomfortable when they leave secure ground (their own notions, their own information, their own cohorts) and open themselves to people and information which might challenge their view of what needs to be done and can be done. But that is what it takes to make needed changes.

what it takes to make needed changes. Social Interaction theory is well-substantiated by the cases in suggesting that, except for folks who are actively open by nature, new information is most readily accepted if it travels person to person, from opinion leader to potential followers. Small groups and one-to-one contacts resulted in a flow of ideas from those who have new information through those who are sought out on their campuses for sound advice into their local groups.

Leadership was included within Havelock's "Capacity" factor, but the cases indicate that the skill, time and influence of leaders was an essential factor in accomplishing any change activity. This factor deserves central billing. Leadership, however, was not the kind traditionally associated with a strong, authoritarian father figure. No leader succeeded in telling largely autonomous professionals how to educate; no leader succeeded in making directions stick if those professionals were not in agreement with the leader's instructions. Rather, the approach to leadership which made a difference was a combination of initiating change activities, structuring and guiding and pushing and supporting the planned change process, linking ideas to people and money to ideas and involving both the influentials and the implementors in the whole process. The traditional leader roles of Expert and Influential or Authority were combined with the roles of the open Collaborator, the Linking Agent and the Facilitator. Leaders needed to combine change strategies just as adaptive development combines change models.

Ownership was a notion that rang true to Strategies leaders from the first. In order for anyone, and especially a professional, to give the time, energy and skill necessary to pull off organizational or personal change, that person needs to feel that this is a change she had a part in making. R&D makes the critical error of assuming that people will change their own behavior because someone else sees the need, develops the solution and directs them or encourages them to do it. That solution may be fine for you, but it does not fit my goals and needs, my setting, my skills, my students. A change process which involves throughout the persons whose understanding, acceptance, time and skills are needed to carry out the change has a far greater chance of success than an approach which ignores them at any point along the way.

Nobody does anything which is unrewarding for very long unless forced. In the Strategies cases, change often took excessive time and money, involved dull and tedious committees, got innovators in trouble with traditional promotion and tenure committees and did not seem to improve institutional practices and outcomes anyway. There were few *Rewards* to be found. The time and costs of beginning a project may be high, but leaders need to find ways to make innovations as soon as possible no more time-consuming and expensive than traditional practices. They need to learn how to make committee work and other components of planned change valuable experiences for their participants in terms of enjoyment, status and esteem. They need to make the development and implementation of new practices a high priority in promotion, salary and tenure decisions. They need to gather evidence on the impact of innovations and demonstrate for one and all the positive benefits of these

241

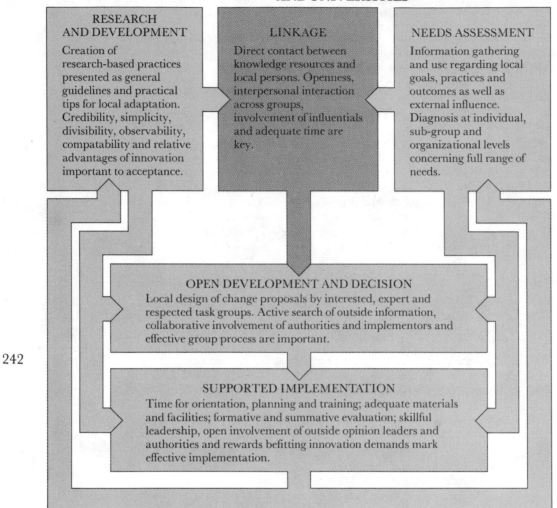

FIGURE 11
PROCESS AND FACTORS OF PLANNED CHANGE IN COLLEGES AND UNIVERSITIES

RESEARCH AND DEVELOPMENT
Creation of research-based practices presented as general guidelines and practical tips for local adaptation. Credibility, simplicity, divisibility, observability, compatability and relative advantages of innovation important to acceptance.

LINKAGE
Direct contact between knowledge resources and local persons. Openness, interpersonal interaction across groups, involvement of influentials and adequate time are key.

NEEDS ASSESSMENT
Information gathering and use regarding local goals, practices and outcomes as well as external influence. Diagnosis at individual, sub-group and organizational levels concerning full range of needs.

OPEN DEVELOPMENT AND DECISION
Local design of change proposals by interested, expert and respected task groups. Active search of outside information, collaborative involvement of authorities and implementors and effective group process are important.

SUPPORTED IMPLEMENTATION
Time for orientation, planning and training; adequate materials and facilities; formative and summative evaluation; skillful leadership, open involvement of outside opinion leaders and authorities and rewards befitting innovation demands mark effective implementation.

242

Leaders often forget even the least expensive forms of reward: "I really appreciate what you're trying to accomplish."

new ventures. Leaders often forget even the least expensive forms of reward: "I really appreciate what you're trying to accomplish." Even august professionals need a few "strokes" from time to time.

Linkage, openness, leadership, ownership, and rewards: these five factors can make the difference between an expensive lesson in frustration and a planned change process which actually gets somewhere. They are not frequently found in normal change activities, as the Strategies cases demonstrate, so they will require alterations in the ways institutions now plan, decide and implement change. As Strategies cases which incorporated these factors also testify, such alterations are well worth the effort.

SUMMARY

Emergent from the Strategies cases and prior literature on change is a general innovation or renewal process containing several key factors. Figure Eight summarizes them. Research and development of new practices and the assessment of local goals, practices, outcomes and problems form the knowledge base for planned change. This information informs every step of the process, as the dotted lines suggest, although R&D and needs assessment are logically and traditionally diagramed only at the front end of the problem-solving cycle. A rough sequence does commence with linkage of influential local people to information which stimulates a need to change. Then a local developmental process open to outside knowledge and influence takes place and a decision which represents authority and implementor commitment is reached. Implementation, and indeed the whole process, is strengthened by orientation, planning and training; by skillful leadership; by adequate materials and facilities; by evaluation and feedback as the innovation emerges; by appropriate rewards; and by continued persuasion of outsiders and their involvement in a dissemination process—which in essence starts the whole cycle all over again. Key to success of each stage is interpersonal and informational linkage, active openness, facilitating as well as initiating leadership, ownership by those who can make implementation happen and rewards both material and psychic.

Adaptive development as a whole is an ideal state, not a normal expectation. Every attempt at change will have factors beyond the change agent's control (which may make Figure 11 seem an impossible dream). The cases suggest, however, that any movement toward that ideal can make a difference. You are better off giving it a try than throwing up your hands. The next chapter describes more specifically what giving a try might entail.

243

10 Implementing Adaptive Development

INTRODUCTION

From conceptual model to actual practice is no easy journey. Even though we saw various aspects of adaptive development in the case histories, none of them "put it all together." We cannot turn to one institution or another, one leader or another, and say *there* is adaptive development at work. Although Figure Eight may seem ideal in the abstract, John Holt's question is still before us: "What Do I Do Monday?" Furthermore, Argyris and Schoen[1] offer us convincing argument and evidence that there is often a considerable gap between the way we think we behave and the way we do behave; we may think we're integrating change strategies when we actually are operating under primarily political or rational or human relations assumptions.

In this final chapter, therefore, I will try to spell out some of the personal roles and skills which seem necessary to carry out adaptive development as an organizational leader, member or consultant. I also will describe some of the organizational structures and activities which will enable a college or university to maintain vigorous attention to renewal and innovation. These recommendations are no more than a synthesis of prior research and the Strategies for Change cases. They need rigorous testing in organizational practice. Still, I find them helpful enough in my own work that I recommend your adapting them to your own teaching, counseling, consulting or leadership activities.

CHANGE AGENT ROLES

Anyone seeking to instill new knowledge, skills, attitudes or behavior in others is a change agent, although the term rubs some people the wrong way. A president, a department head, a salesperson, a professor, a counselor, a social worker or a parent hopes to be an effective agent for the development in others of new and hopefully better ways of being. We noted in Chapter One that some persons approach this task with a rational change model in mind, while others emphasize the social or human problem-solving or political strategies. The cases emphasize, however, that none of these approaches is adequate in itself. When faced with a complex, decentralized organization in which staff roles are defined as much by individuals and their professional associations as by institutional regulations but in which conservative defense of the *status quo* is strong, change agents can not simply dictate their expert solutions or exercise their formal authority. Their expertise will be challenged and their control limited.

245

We may think we're integrating change strategies when we actually are operating under primarily political or rational or human relations assumptions.

The solution most often used by the leaders of Strategies institutions was a combination of their own initiatives with increasing attempts to involve participants in setting their own goals, studying and deciding among themselves what needed changing, formulating and deciding their own solutions, and involving themselves in implementation and evaluation. Some leaders, such as the president at Mountain College and the provost at Commuter Private, gave over planned change to faculty without continuing to provide initiative and guidance. Wheels spun and, in the former case, the president grabbed back the reins and shifted to the authoritarian act of setting New Directions herself. That did not work either. Other leaders, such as the presidents of South Carolina, Hartwick and Quaker Academic and the dean of Messiah sought a middle ground in which they entered into collaborative planned change processes with faculty. These innovators were impatient with this slower method. They saw change needs and solutions before most faculty and wanted to get on with it. When they went ahead and set up innovative projects, however, they found only a few equally innovative faculty members ready to implement them. They recognized that they could not force most faculty to teach differently or to accept major changes in curricular structure and requirements. Even at Messiah, faculty members had too much collegial autonomy to be coerced into significant changes in behavior; in no case could basic attitudes toward education be dictated from above. The leaders' task, therefore, was to combine their own initiatives with efforts to raise interest and commitment among faculty.

Each leader had a somewhat different strategy for combining initiative with involvement. The South Carolina president turned from simply dictating new projects to routing them through faculty governance. He spurred on that process in the case of the Bachelor of General Studies and Experimental College proposals by initiating *ad hoc* committees to formulate suggestions, by encouraging the Tuesday discussion group, by working with the provost on an alternate proposal when things got bogged down, by shifting administrative assignments to get a strong leader in charge of implementation and then by holding that leader in check when he attempted to push through certain policies which riled the faculty senate. He sat with the new Academic Forward Planning Committee and found financial support for its major goals study and workshops. He routed the University 101 freshman seminar program through that same committee, although impatiently, and used that program to introduce many influential faculty members and administrators to new teaching approaches. He acted as entrepreneur to get the Ford Venture funds, Contemporary University and University Without Walls, and although he launched these programs on his own, he shifted toward support for faculty involvement in their implementation and evaluation. He never became, in personal style, particularly collaborative. His dominating personality and impatience to see new ideas tried made collaboration difficult for him, as he recognized. His successor was more effective at involving faculty, especially senior and traditionalist faculty; but would the new president take the initiatives and create the fireworks which did at least get small innovations started?

The leaders' task, therefore, was to combine their own initiatives with efforts to raise interest and commitment among faculty.

246

At Hartwick, the president took the role not of innovation entrepreneur but of gadfly and catalyst. He kept the college focused on the future and on what it might have to do to be successful in the years to come. He was too often redundant in his message that ordinary liberal education would have a hard time meeting competition and costs in the future, but over several years his concern became the concern of many faculty. Instead of launching particular innovations, he set up a Committee and Office for Institutional Research as a forum to study and discuss college needs. He also protected innovative faculty members when they ran the promotion and tenure gauntlet. He supported the faculty development project as a way to give faculty a first-hand taste of innovation and to develop skillful planned change facilitators. He backed the new planning committee as well as other attempts to democratize governance. He brought in an associate dean for off-campus learning, supported consortial programs which extended Hartwick's offerings, gave strong support to the building of a new arts center and, after enduring an unworkable relationship for several years, encouraged his conservative dean to leave. In short, he was far from a passive leader, but he did entrust major development of academic reform to the faculty, and they very slowly but surely took up the challenge.

At Messiah, the dean and the Strategies task force took three new approaches to what had been a planned change process of administrative initiative and cursory faculty review. First, faculty members were much more involved than before in knowledge utilization; they studied data on themselves and their students and learned about alternate approaches tried elsewhere. Second, task forces in charge of developing changes frequently interacted with the faculty so that their learning could spread and that people outside the committee could have a say before being forced to make a decision. Third, the governance structure was reorganized to get around a conservative bottleneck caused by a few senior division chairpersons. A planning council was set up as an alternate route for sending proposals to the full faculty; then a departmental structure was established to diffuse further the division chairperson's control. The dean did not give over to faculty his strong leadership; rather, strong faculty involvement was added to his own.

At Quaker Academic, the same strategy was developed but not sustained. The president and provost found that they could not budge a highly collegial faculty by focusing change discussion on their *own* ideas. In order to gain approval of Man in Focus, therefore, the provost invited interested faculty members to his home to discuss college needs, and that group proposed the program to the faculty. In the case of Individualized Educational Planning, a series of mini-retreats in which small faculty groups collaborated with these executives led to that faculty proposal. Administrators initiated and guided both projects, but it was a group of faculty which formulated the ideas for change. After approval, the executives acted as entrepreneurs to gain implementation grants, but in both cases they failed to generate strong faculty involvement in implementation. That case stands as a reminder that both leadership initiative and faculty involvement are as important after a decision to change as before.

247

The dean did not give over to faculty his strong leadership; rather, strong faculty involvement was added to his own.

All Strategies leaders were not executive administrators. Two faculty members at Messiah, the director of institutional research and the biology chairperson at Hartwick, the professors of economics, political science and psychology at South Carolina, the economics professor at Commuter Private, the director of research and ombudsman at Quaker Academic all attempted to influence their institutions toward undergraduate innovation. So did several other professors in these institutions. What characteristics did they have and what strategies did they use? First, like the executives, they saw a need for change before most other faculty members and were open to innovative experiments. They tended to be either "innovators" or "early adopters." They were either new to the institution or were in groups such as planning committees and Strategies task forces which studied matters relating to change, or both. Thus they were in a position to bring new information to bear on the local situation. Those who were effective in persuading other faculty either were senior opinion leaders of high esteem such as the biology chairperson at Hartwick and the political science and economics professors at South Carolina, or they were skillful at involving such senior leaders (including top administrators), a tactic used by the mathematics professor at Messiah, the psychology professor at South Carolina and the director of institutional research at Hartwick. A major strategy and personal characteristic of most of these leaders was persistence and creativity. Involving reluctant faculty was slow, difficult business. When the few leaders let up, involvement let up. When, as at Messiah, South Carolina and Hartwick, faculty leaders were given official responsibility and reward for this leadership, they could sustain planned change not as an overload but as part of a manageable workload.

I find it helpful to picture every leadership act in terms of two problem-solving cycles, the one the leader's or change agent's and the other the follower's or client's.

CHANGE MODELS AND LEADER ROLES

I find it helpful to picture every leadership act in terms of two problem-solving cycles, the one the leader's or change agent's and the other the follower's or client's. Figure 12 illustrates that roughly sequential (but usually interactive and repetitive) cycle. In any particular situation, both parties are going to diagnose needs and objectives. Both will cast about for alternate solutions and both will pick from those alternatives what seems to be a promising solution, which will be formulated as a change proposal. Each will attend to the reduction of resistance and increase of support for this proposal in one's self and others, each will come to a decision and each will be affected by the consequences of the decision. As Havelock's Linkage model depicts, these two problem-solving sequences will interact with each other. The essential question for leadership, however, is which problem-solving cycle is primary. That question separates R&D from Social Interaction and separates both from adaptive development.

One leadership model regards the leader's problem-solving process as the key. That is the Rational Planning as well as the political perspective. The leader decides what must be done and how to do it, then persuades or otherwise influences others to adopt that view. Professors who regard their job as dispensing their expertise and judging student performance in their field operate under these assumptions. Presidents who decide what the institution must do and then evaluate performance against their own standards fit this model. A committee which goes off to develop an innovation on its own, then attempts to persuade others to "buy" it, are behaving in this manner. Such change agents may give some attention to the needs and ideas of the person or group they hope to change, but the main locus of problem-solving is in their minds and emotions. This is the standard approach to teaching, administration and much change agentry (except perhaps clinical counseling). We have witnessed its inadequacies in the Strategies cases. Quite simply, it grievously underestimates the importance of the problem-solving activities of students, faculty and administration. And when one party does not dominate the other in expertise or other sources of power, this approach degenerates into a clash of adversaries. Students may feel their ideas are as good as their professors'; members of a committee may ignore the thinking of others while vigorously arguing their own case; and faculty and administration may line up across a bargaining table. Organizations with considerable autonomy and expertise among staff members have a hard time operating with leaders who assume an authoritarian role.

A second leader role is that of the collaborator. The assumption here is that groups of people have as much to contribute to solving a problem or developing an innovation as the leader does. We must work together, sharing our perspectives on goals, needs and solutions, decide by consensus or at least majority rule and accept equal obligation for implementation and evaluation. In several of the cases, collaboration between either administrators and faculty or committee and institution were both desired and effective. Collaboration requires openness. I cannot work with you if I do not listen to your ideas and explore their usefulness, just as I must share my own thinking.

A somewhat different change agent or leader role, although it too is part of the Problem-Solving perspective, is that of the facilitator. Here, the key problem-solving responsibility lies not with the leader but with the led. You must decide what your goals and problems are. You must come up with your own solution, make your own decision, carry it out yourself and act as principle judge of your deeds. The professor or president or change team will help you clarify your goals and needs, search out solutions, reduce resistance, arrive at open decisions and prepare for implementation and evaluation, but your ownership of all this is key to effective change. I can be no more than a facilitator of your change process.

The facilitator need not be a passive reactor. The provocateur who challenges us to become all we can be, to live up to our goals and fulfill our potential, is a stimulator and catalyst of our own problem-solving, not an expert telling us what to do or even a collaborator joining his problem-solving efforts to our own. This is the role both the Hartwick president and biology chairperson played. This is the role the Strategies task force played at South Carolina by encouraging institutional members to look at institutional goals and needs. Some provocateurs, like the presidents of Quaker Academic, Mountain College and Commuter Private, also had answers to offer. You folks should solve the institution's problems yourselves my way, comes the mixed message, and if you don't I am liable to

Organizations with considerable autonomy and expertise among staff members have a hard time operating with leaders who assume an authoritarian role.

249

In essence, the linker learns what the client's thinking is, then attempts to open that thinking to other approaches to that goal or problem.

250

impose it on you. That approach pretends, perhaps even intends, to facilitate institutional problem-solving by institutional members but in fact is the traditional role thinly disguised. Faculty are likely to suspect an expert lurking beneath the cloak of a facilitator anyway, as the Hartwick president learned. It is wise to anticipate that suspicion and be frank about which role is being played.

A fourth basic leader role is that of the linker. These professors or consultants or administrators bring students or faculty and outside resources together, while neither developing solutions themselves nor facilitating student or institutional problem-solving. In essence, the linker learns what the client's thinking is, then attempts to open that thinking to other approaches to that goal or problem. Such a leader needs to be a cosmopolitan in the areas pertinent to institutional practices, and several leaders involved in the Strategies project played this role by bringing to their institution fresh ideas from elsewhere and by continuing contacts with books, journals, conferences, consultants and innovative colleagues. These leaders introduced new ideas in speeches, by circulating articles, by personal contact with local innovators and opinion leaders. The president of South Carolina and the provost of Quaker Academic are excellent examples of innovation linkers. These persons also were entrepreneurs. They brought new ideas, interested people and funds together. Both presidents actively pursued grants for innovative programs. They did not claim to be the experts about these matters, but they did use their influence to gain institutional adoption. The linker, we see, is not necessarily any more passive and reactive than the facilitator.

Figure 12 illustrates each of these leader-follower emphases. A review of Chapter One will indicate the quite different assumptions each makes about what is the most useful role for a leader or change agent. My own experience is that leaders often do not know which role they primarily play. Some teachers or administrators who think themselves quite collaborative or facilitative turn out to rely much more heavily on their own problem-solving than on others'. A useful exercise is to video tape or audio tape an interaction (either role played or real) between a leader and a follower concerning any issue which might arise. Ask two observers to record who defines the problem, who sets the objectives, who suggests alternate actions, who proposes the action eventually accepted, who decides, who plans follow-through on decisions and who makes the evaluative judgments which are accepted. At the end of twenty minutes, ask the leader to indicate who actually solved each step of the problem. Then ask the follower. Then have the observers and tape present a perhaps more detached view, one which often will be quite a surprise to participants. My bet is that the authority role will mark most leaders, although they (and even their followers) may feel they were more collaborative and facilitative than the evidence reveals. Often good leader rapport is mistaken for collaboration or facilitation when in fact the leader calls most of the shots. This same kind of evidence can be gained by watching leaders as they interact over time in regular classes, committees and one-to-one contacts. It would be a rare leader who would let himself be followed around that way, but such observation could be most enlightening.

FIGURE 12
LEADERSHIP ROLES DEPENDING ON
WHO SOLVES THE PROBLEM

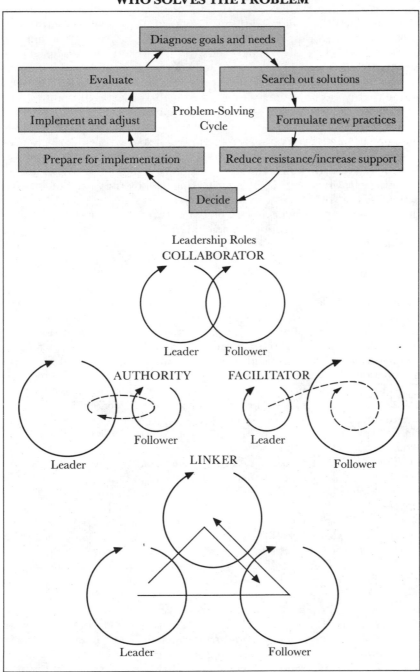

251

252

Adaptive development tells us that the collaborative, linking and facilitative change agent roles are especially pertinent to planned change under circumstances in which the change agent is not demonstrably more expert concerning local needs and conditions nor more influential over implementation than the client. Eventually, students or staff members or departments or institutions must solve their own problems, aided but not controlled by external agents of change. That does not mean expert advice, Research and Development activities and use of formal authority should be discarded. More authoritarian individuals and organizations will naturally have a tendency to depend on outside experts or authorities and will not, at first, be able to develop without strong external guidance. Besides, specialized experts in research and development, working full-time on such activities, can generate approaches to problems which local adapters do not have the time, the knowledge nor the skill to produce. Instead of discarding the authority role, adaptive development calls for its use *where appropriate* and *in addition to* linking, collaborative and facilitative activities. It also calls for transfer of all these roles and attendant skills to the client so that future development, whether individual or organizational, does not remain dependent upon external guidance. Well-developed organizations, like well-developed persons, should be able to solve their own problems, continue improving on their own, with stimulus and aid but not direction from change agents.

What knowledge and skills does this combination of change agent roles demand? Certainly one needs expertise in the organization's functions, in the goods and services which the organization produces. For colleges, knowledge of learning theory and research, of various academic fields, of teaching, research and administration would be needed. The change agent also needs knowledge of planned change strategies and organizational dynamics, the topics touched on in Chapters One and Two. Beyond this foundation knowledge, the effective adaptive developer should have various skills not normally found in academia (nor anywhere else, for that matter). Change agents need to be able *to help others diagnose needs and goals*. They need to be able *to present information clearly and persuasively*, especially in person but also in writing and other media. They need to be able *to design planned change activities* or facilitate design by others. They need to be able *to listen*, to open themselves to the information, needs and opinions of others. They need to be able *to facilitate or collaborate rather than direct the problem-solving of others*, whether this activity is carried out by the whole organization, a committee or an individual. They need to be able *to link problem-solvers to useful resources outside themselves*. They need to be able *to evaluate and to enable others to evaluate* both formatively and summatively. They need to be able *to use political influence and social networks* to gain acceptance and support for proposed changes.

All this knowledge and skill is not gained overnight. Indeed, some roles may be difficult for certain persons ever to attain. The facilitative role, for instance, is extremely hard for an aggressively independent or authoritarian person to play; non-directive persons have a hard time being authoritative. Elaborate training programs are available for each of these roles. Professional schools focus particularly on gaining appropriate knowledge to conduct various change agent roles. In postsecondary education, for instance, education, business and agriculture schools, psychology, sociology and political science all offer courses and institutes which provide background knowledge for leading organizational change efforts. Clinical psychology or social work and agencies such as the National Training Laboratory Institute for Applied Behavioral Science and University Associates' Intern program train people in the collaborative and facilitative skills needed to help individuals, groups or organizations solve their own problems. In postsecondary education, the new Professional and Organizational Development Network and various administrative and faculty development centers are beginning to train people in the knowledge and skills needed to be an effective collaborator or facilitator or linking agent. Although no professional development program yet attempts to train people in the full range of knowledge and skills demanded by adaptive development's combination of strategies, such programs are beginning to emerge. Until there are consultants and organizational leaders able to integrate rational, social, political and human problem-solving strategies with an emphasis on implementor-owned changes, a fair test of adaptive development is not possible. A major contribution to higher education would be the establishment of training programs to impart this combination of knowledge and skills.

Until there are consultants and organizational leaders able to integrate rational, social, political and human problem-solving strategies with an emphasis on implementor-owned changes, a fair test of adaptive development is not possible.

ADAPTIVE DEVELOPMENT SERVICES

Katz and Kahn[2] stress the importance of "adaptive subsystems" for the ability of organizations to achieve their goals in the face of changing conditions. The notion is at base a simple one. If all the organization's energy and skill is put into implementation of existing policies and programs, that is what the organization is going to do, even if the resulting *status quo* is not working. Some parts of the system must devote significant time and skills to assessing organizational needs and goals, to searching and retrieving promising alternatives to current ways of meeting those needs, to formulating and deciding changes, to the development of the professional skill and materials resources necessary to implement current and new programs and to formative and summative evaluation.

Institutional research and planning, policy and program formulation and decision-making, professional and organizational development, and experimental units are some of the adaptive development services which can focus professional skill and time on renewal, reform and innovation. Small organizations might devote no more than half of one professional's time to *each* adaptive service, as Hartwick and Messiah do. An adaptive development team of such individuals can pool efforts to aid the entire planned change process, while at the same time supporting each other. Large institutions will need full-time staffs in *each* area if they are really serious about increasing their effectiveness. These staffs might be integrated in a general adaptive development services center.

The remainder of this chapter will suggest the four kinds of services which might be needed. Two cautions, however, should be sounded. First, these services bear familiar names. You will see as I describe each that I do not think most existing institutional research offices or faculty development centers integrate planned change strategies; the evidence indicates that they should. Second, I do not think anybody, no matter how trained and skilled, can do these functions in her spare time. Faculty members and administrators now attempt planned change in the few moments they can get free from current policy and program implementation. The powerful inertia of the *status quo* cannot be overcome with such feeble efforts. There is no lack of sad evidence to support that statement.

FIGURE 13
ADAPTIVE DEVELOPMENT SERVICES

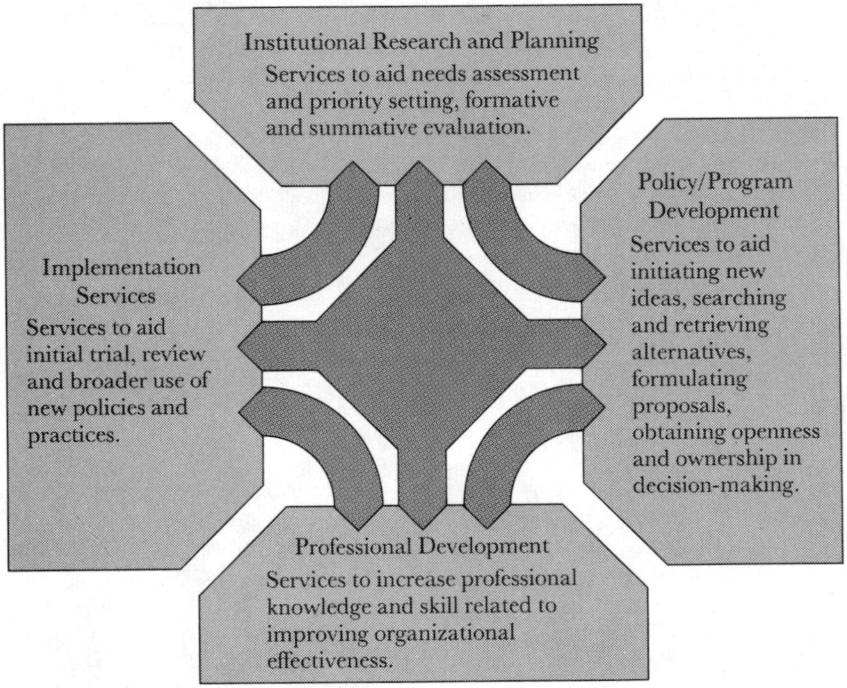

Institutional Research and Planning
Services to aid needs assessment and priority setting, formative and summative evaluation.

Policy/Program Development
Services to aid initiating new ideas, searching and retrieving alternatives, formulating proposals, obtaining openness and ownership in decision-making.

Implementation Services
Services to aid initial trial, review and broader use of new policies and practices.

Professional Development
Services to increase professional knowledge and skill related to improving organizational effectiveness.

INSTITUTIONAL RESEARCH AND PLANNING

How are we doing? What should we be stressing in the near future? These are the questions which should be the primary concerns of some service unit. In some colleges and universities, there are institutional research and planning staffs to help the decision makers answer these questions, but they often are ineffective. Many efforts relate mainly to top management, as if collegial governance and de-centralization of decision making into departments and individual professionals did not exist. Many use only the rational tools of psychometric research, management by objectives and dissemination through formal administrative channels and print. Many are isolated from program development, professional development and implementation units. Many gather bits and pieces of information, often on "unit costs," and base plans on them instead of conducting longitudinal research into program effectiveness and emerging external needs and demands.

Adaptive development requires several modifications of the traditional institutional research and planning strategies. Research should focus on organizational "inputs," "throughputs" and "outputs," as the systems theorists call what comes into an organization, what happens in the organization and what comes out. (Perhaps this unfortunate language was invented by a frustrated shotputter.) Longitudinal studies using multiple methodologies along lines modeled by the Program Effectiveness and Related Costs project[3] would replace scattergun approaches to self-study. Moreover, what gets studied, how, and for what purpose would not be decided only by the researchers and their administrative supervisors but by these individuals in collaboration with key governance units and opinion leaders in the organization as a whole, especially in collaboration with institutional planning committees. Institutional researchers would serve in a staff capacity on program, policy and professional development groups so that they have a solid information base on which to act. The research and planning staff would link decision makers not just to their own studies but to broader research and theory. Furthermore, they would serve as process consultants to help organization members confront and use information which reveals problems such as weaknesses in interpersonal relations or conflicts between sub-groups. This organizational development role is rarely played by research services, and that may be a major reason research ends up on shelves rather than institutional action. Institutional research should help planners set priorities which fit the information and which have sufficient agreement among organization members that those priorities can be implemented.

In essence, this service would combine research and planning expertise with skills in linking together people and research, in helping planners confront and use disturbing research and in helping planners build consensus. Such a service would need the autonomy of an organizational development consultant, for its credibility and effectiveness would collapse if any executive could control information generation and use, especially when the information disturbs the executive. In an organization as complex and decentralized as a college, bureaucratic ownership must be shared if the information and priorities which emerge are to be trusted and followed by semi-autonomous departments and professionals as well as by executives.

POLICY AND PROGRAM DEVELOPMENT SERVICES

If new policies and programs are to happen, someone needs to help the organization encourage and support the initiation of new ideas. Key gatekeeping units and persons need to be helped to become actively open. Proposal formulation groups need to be linked to a wide range of alternate solutions to their problem. They need help in working together as an effective and enjoyable team instead of a plodding, frustrating committee. They need help in involving various organizational influentials and experts so that resulting proposals are sound and accepted. They need help in ways to create open consideration of their idea in review bodies.

Adaptive development requires several modifications of the traditional institutional research and planning strategies.

255

All these functions can be played by a policy and program development staff or by a team such as the Strategies for Change teams at South Carolina, Messiah and Hartwick. If a team is used, however, released time and training will be necessary. Policy and program development would also be helped if certain structural changes were made in governance. Initial advocates of a change, or subcommittees charged with formulation of proposals for change, for instance, probably become on that issue the most expert and committed organization members. Rather than disband such groups once a proposal is made, they might be charged with helping each level of review understand and appreciate their idea; they might have the same charge of educating implementors if their proposal gets approved. Such energy and expertise too often is lost in the shuffle. Also, governance can be streamlined by joining collegial and bureaucratic structures in forms of shared goverence[4] and by reducing the overlap among various committees and offices. Other structural adjustments are possible and are the typical solutions to governance problems. Adaptive development suggests, however, that it is the planned change skill and behavior of organization members more than the structures within which they operate which make the most difference. I recommend a policy and program development service, therefore, as more needed than structural tinkering.

256

PROFESSIONAL DEVELOPMENT

Many businesses and industries now have elaborate, long-term programs to help administrations and staff develop and renew their skills. Colleges and universities have had support for sabbaticals, conference attendance and colloquia for some time, but only recently have they established formal programs to aid ongoing staff development.[5] Most of these programs focus on faculty, not administrative, development. Few stress the improvement of interpersonal relations and the resolution of conflict which Zaltman observes is crucial to organizational innovation.[6] Some aid personal growth, career advancement and scholarly attainment, but the emphasis of most programs is on teaching improvement.[7] Although one can see rational planning, social interaction, human problem-solving and political strategies at work in these programs, I suspect few intentionally combine these strategies.[8]

Professional development for adaptive development would integrate functions and strategies. Both administrators and staff would be served. Attention would be given to improving various professional functions, including interpersonal relations and conflict management. Research and theory would be presented, professionals would be exposed to innovative practices, individual problem-solving would receive expert counsel and political supports for professional improvements (time, promotions, higher salary, personal or group approval) would be sought. Professional development would be integrated closely with institutional research, planning and program development. Once again, this scenario requires that service staff themselves learn new roles (or add them in the form of new staff or new team members). Those expert in instructional development, for instance, usually approach change according to the rational planning model. They would need to learn (or add) human problem-solving knowledge and skills to their efforts. Those trained in clinical counseling or organizational development would need to learn (or add) instructional development. And both would need to take some lessons from communication of innovations specialists and political experts. In postsecondary education, a major strength of the new Professional and Organizational Development Network is that it contains adherents to each change strategy. If each learns from the others, adaptive development can emerge.

PROGRAM IMPLEMENTATION

In profit-making organizations, there are R&D units whose job is to research, develop and test new products. Non-profit organizations often do not have comparable functions. Colleges and universities have some "experimental" programs, but for the most part these units are busy implementing one innovative program, not researching and developing, testing and disseminating one after another. They often have technological services to aid implementation, such as computer and media centers, but rarely do they have developmental services directed at new program implementation. It may not be financially or politically realistic to expect colleges and universities to support RD&D units regarding their own functions (although universities partially subsidize such centers and institutes concerning other people's business). It is realistic, however, to expect them to provide expert aids to the initial implementation of new programs.

Such services would include aid in helping implementors design programs which probably were only generally described in their proposals. It would include aid in recruiting and selecting appropriate leaders and staff. It would include help in developing and garnering funds for an adequate budget and help in obtaining adequate facilities and materials. It would include help in the orientation, training and interpersonal effectiveness of implementors, in cooperation with professional development. It would include linking implementors to similar programs elsewhere in cooperation with program development. It would include aid in formative and summative evaluation in cooperation with institutional research. A major function would be to help initial implementors share their new model with others in the organization and beyond so that it obtains as wide use as its effectiveness warrants. The idea in general is that initial implementation and broader dissemination of new programs is too crucial a part of planned change to be left unattended by persons skilled in this process. Implementors themselves will be too busy trying to implement to be able to give necessary time and skill to all the supporting services which make actual change occur. Recent research such as that of Gross[9] and Berman and McLaughlin[10] demonstrate that innovations often fail not because they were not promising or accepted, but because they did not get properly implemented.

SUMMARY

Planned change does not just happen. It takes the integration of several

257

The idea in general is that initial implementation and broader dissemination of new programs is too crucial a part of planned change to be left unattended by persons skilled in this process.

strategies for change, the combination of several roles and skills, the establishment of various services. Expertise and authority must be joined to the skills of the linking agent, the open collaborator and the problem-solving facilitator. Services are needed to make research and planning, policy and program development, professional and organizational development and the implementation of new practices actually occur. These services may take the form of change agent teams or formal offices and centers or both. In general, their charge is to bring to life the planned change process and factors presented in Chapter Nine. Prior theory and the Strategies cases strongly suggest that without such an integration of strategies for change, knowledge, skills and services, internally-controlled reform and innovation in organizations such as colleges and universities are unlikely. Organization members stand helpless between organizational inertia and external pressures unless they take a serious grip on planned change. As colleges such as Empire State mount developmental services,[11] and as theory and training continue to move toward a combination of change strategies, such helplessness should become less common. The members of such institutions, and the clients they serve, surely deserve the attempt.

258

Postscript

There is another step beyond this book. If adaptive development makes as much sense to you as it does to me, how does one learn to do it? How can you adapt this innovation to yourself and to your organization? Certain practical manuals are a help. Havelock's *Guide to Innovation in Education*[1] is one such book. Forthcoming volumes titled *Designing Teaching Improvement Programs*[2] and *Developing the Curriculum: A Handbook for Faculty and Administrators*[3] contain practical tactics and instruments for adaptive development in colleges and universities. The Kellogg Use of Innovations Project is producing handbook materials and conducting training workshops for external consultants and internal facilitators of adaptive development. And, of course, you can approach the learning of adaptive development the way a student must approach most college curriculums: read the rational planning, communication of innovations, applied behavioral science and political process books. Attend the separate training programs in each. Then do your own integrating and synthesizing.

However you go at it, good luck. Our ability to renew and improve our institutions is vital, and our record is not very good. Our students need your help.

Our ability to renew and improve our institutions is vital, and our record is not very good. Our students need your help.

259

Notes

Chapter 1

[1]Ronald Havelock and others, *Planning for Innovation Through the Dissemination and Utilization of Scientific Knowledge* (Ann Arbor: Institute for Social Research, 1971).

[2]Goodwin Watson, "Resistance to Change," in Gerald Zaltman, Philip Kotler, and Ira Kaufman, eds., *Creating Social Change* (New York: Holt, 1972), pp. 610-618.

[3]David Clark and Egon Guba, "An Examination of Potential Change Roles in Education" (paper delivered at Symposium on Innovation in Planning School Curricula, Airlie House, Virginia, October 1965).

[4]Guba, "Development, Diffusion, and Evaluation," in Terry L. Eidell and Joanne M. Kitchel, eds., *Knowledge Production and Utilization in Educational Administration* (Eugene, Oregon: University Council on Educational Administration and Center for Advanced Study of Educational Administration, 1968), pp. 37-63.

[5]Havelock, *Planning for Innovation*, Chapter 11, p. 5.

[6]Talcott Parsons and Gerald Platt, *The American University* (Cambridge: Harvard University Press, 1973).

[7]Barry Richman and Richard Farmer, *Leadership, Goals, and Power in Higher Education* (San Francisco: Jossey-Bass, 1974).

[8]Neal Gross, Joseph Giacquinla and Marilyn Bernstein, *Implementing Organizational Innovations* (New York: Harper and Row, 1963).

[9]Gerald Zaltman, Robert Duncan and Jonny Holbeck, *Innovations and Organizations* (New York: Wiley, 1973); and Paul Berman and Milbrey McLaughlin, *Federal Programs Supporting Educational Change: The Findings in Review* (Washington, D.C.: HEW, R-1589/4, April, 1975).

[10]Everett M. Rogers, Rehka Agarwala-Rogers and Chin Chuan Lee, *Diffussion of IMPACT Innovations to University Professors* (New York: Exxon Foundation, 1975); and Rogers and F. Floyd Shoemaker, *Communication of Innovations* (New York: Free Press, 1971).

[11]Ralph Rosnow and Edward Robinson, *Experiments in Persuasion* (New York: Academic Press, 1967), p. 25.

[12]John D. Lindquist, "Political Life in the State University: A Systems and Community Power Analysis." Unpublished doctoral dissertation (Ann Arbor: University of Michigan, 1972).

[13]"Stability and Change in the American University," *Daedalus*, 103 (1974), 271.

[14] Everett Hagen, "The Predictive Power of Social Change Theory," (1970), 2, p. 17.

[15] Watson, "Resistance to Change," *Creating Social Change*.

[16] Robert Blake and Jane Mouton, *Grid Organization Analysis* (Reading, Mass.: Addison Wesley, 1969).

[17] Walter Sikes, Lawrence Schlesinger and Charles Seashore, *Renewing Higher Education from Within: A Guide for Campus Change Agents* (San Francisco: Jossey-Bass, 1974).

[18] Ronald Boyer and Campbell Crockett, "Introduction, Special Issue on Organization Development in Higher Education," *Journal of Higher Education*, 44 (1973), 339-351.

[19] Paul Lawrence and Jay Lorsch, *Developing Organizations: Diagnosis and Action*, (Reading, Mass.: Addison-Wesley, 1969).

[20] Warren Bennis, *Organization Development: Its Nature, Origin, and Prospects* (Reading, Mass.: Addison-Wesley, 1969).

[21] David Bowers, "OD Techniques and Their Results in Twenty Three Organizations: The Michigan ICL Study," *Journal of Applied Behavioral Science*, 9 (1973), 31-34.

[22] Havelock, *Planning for Innovation*, Chapter 11, p. 13.

[23] David Easton, *A System Analysis of Political Life* (New York: Wiley, 1965).

[24] Ronald Lippett, Goodwin Watson and Bruce Westley, *The Dynamics of Planned Change* (New York: Harcourt, Brace and World, 1958).

[25] William Gamson, *Power and Discontent* (Homewood, Ill.: Dorsey Press, 1968).

[26] J. Victor Baldridge, *Power and Conflict in the University* (New York: Wiley, 1971), p. 96.

[27] Havelock, *Planning for Innovation*, p. 11.

[28] Lindquist, "Political Linkage: The Academic Innovation Process," *Journal of Higher Education*, 45 (1974), 323-343; and Lindquist, "Institutional Services for Teaching Improvement: Combine Your Change Assumptions," in Clifford Steward and Thomas Harvey, eds., *Strategies for Significant Survival* (San Francisco: Jossey-Bass, 1975).

[29] Berman and McLaughlin, *Federal Programs Supporting Educaitonal Change*.

[30] Havelock, *A Guide to Innovation in Education*, (Ann Arbor, Mich.: Institute for Social Research, 1972).

[31] Zaltman, Duncan, and Holbek, *Innovations and Organizations*.

Chapter 2

[1] George Bonham, "Academic Reform: Still a Pseudo-Science," *Change Magazine*, 7 (1975), 11-12, 65.

[2] Warren B. Martin, *Conformity: Standards and Change in Higher Education* (San Francisco: Jossey-Bass, 1969).

[3] J B Hefferlin, *The Dynamics of Academic Reform* (San Francisco: Jossey-Bass, 1969).

[4] Dwight Ladd, *Change in Educational Policy: Self-Studies in Selected Colleges and Universities* (Hightstown, New Jersey: McGraw-Hill, 1970).

[5]Richard I. Evans, *Resistance to Innovation in Higher Education* (San Francisco: Jossey-Bass, 1970).

[6]Frank House, *The Politics of Educational Innovation* (Berkeley: McCutchan, 1974).

[7]John D. Lindquist, "Political Life in the State University." Unpublished doctoral dissertation (Ann Arbor: University of Michigan, 1972).

[8]Gary L. Harmon, "Academic Policy Making: A Study of Organization and Decision Makers in a Liberal Arts College." Unpublished doctoral dissertation (Bloomington: Indiana University, 1966).

[9]Walter Sikes, Lawrence Schlesinger and Charles Seashore, *Renewing Higher Education from Within* (San Francisco: Jossey-Bass, 1974).

[10]Sebastian V. Martorana and Eileen Kuhns, *Managing Academic Change* (San Francisco: Jossey-Bass, 1975); Barry Richman and Richard N. Farmer, *Leadership, Goals, and Power in Higher Education* (San Francisco: Jossey-Bass, 1974); Robert E. Lahti, *Innovative College Management* (San Francisco: Jossey-Bass, 1973); and Frederick Balderston, *Managing Today's University* (San Francisco: Jossey-Bass, 1974).

[11]Arthur Levine and John Weingart, *Reform of Undergraduate Education* (San Francisco: Jossey-Bass, 1973); David Riesman and Verne Stadtman, eds., *Academic Transformation; Seventeen Institutions under Pressure* (New York: McGraw-Hill, 1973); and Riesman, Joseph Gusfiel and Zelda Gamson, *Academic Value and Mass Education* (Garden City, New York: Doubleday, 1970).

[12]Lawrence Kohlberg and Rochelle Mayer, "Development as the Aim of Education," *Harvard Educational Review*, 42 (1972).

[13]Kenneth A. Feldman and Theodore M. Newcomb, *The Impact of College on Students* (San Francisco: Jossey-Bass, 1969).

[14]James G. March and Herbert A. Simon, *Organizations* (New York: Wiley, 1958).

[15]Tom Burns and G. M. Stalker, *The Management of Innovation* (London: Tavistock, 1961).

[16]Rensis Likert, *The Human Organization: Its Management and Value* (New York: McGraw-Hill, 1967).

[17]Ernest G. Palola and William Padgett, *Planning for Self-Renewal; A New Approach to Planned Organizational Change* (Berkeley: Center for Research and Development in Higher Education, University of California, 1971).

[18]Jerald Hage and Michael Aiken, *Social Change in Complex Organizations* (New York: Random House, 1970).

[19]Gerald Zaltman, Robert Duncan and Jonny Holbek, *Innovations and Organizations* (New York: Wiley, 1973).

[20]Burton R. Clark, "The Organizational Saga in Higher Education," *Administrative Science Quarterly*, 17 (1972), 178-184; Lindquist, "Political Life in the State University" (1972); and Lindquist, "Institutional Sources for Teaching Improvements," in Clifford Stewart and Tom Harvey, eds., *Strategies for Significant Survival* (San Francisco: Jossey-Bass, 1975).

[21]Edward Harvey and Russell Mills, "Patterns of Organizational Adaptation: A Political Perspective," in Mayer N. Gold, ed., *Power in Organizations* (Nashville, Tenn.: Vanderbilt Univ. Pr., 1970).

[22]Martin, *Conformity* (1969); Hefferlin, *The Dynamics of Academic Reform* (1969); and Ladd, *Change in Educational Policy* (1970).

[23]David Easton, *A Systems Analysis of Political Life* (New York: Wiley, 1965).

[24]Victor J. Baldridge, *Organizational Change Processes: A Bibliography with Commentary* (Palo Alto: Stanford Univ. Pr., 1972).

[25]Ruth E. Eckert, "The Share of the Teaching Faculty in the University Policy-Making," *AAUP Bulletin* (1975), 346-351; Eckert, "Participation in University Governance: A Second Look," unpublished manuscript reported by T. R. McConnell, "Faculty Government," in Harold Hodgkinson and L. Richard Meeth, eds., *Power and Authority: Transformation of Campus Governance* (San Francisco: Jossey-Bass, 1971); McConnell, "Faculty Government," in Hodgkinson and Meeth, eds., *Power and Authority* (1971); and Lindquist and Robert Blackburn, "Middlegrove: The Locus of Campus Power in a State University," *AAUP Bulletin* (1974), 367-378.

[26]Rue Bucher, "Social Process and Power in a Medical School," a paper presented at the first Annual Vanderbilt Sociology Conference on Power and Organizations, March 27-28, 1969.

[27]Gerald M. Platt and Talcott Parsons, "Decision-Making in the Academic System: Influence and Power Exchange," in Carlos E. Kruyttosch and Sheldon L. Messinger, eds., *State of the University: Authority and Change* (Beverly Hills, Sage, 1970), p. 174.

[28]William A. Gamson, *Power and Discontent* (Homewood, Ill.: Dorsey, 1968), p. 24.

[29]Archie Dykes, "Faculty Participation in Academic Decision-Making," *Liberal Education*, 54 (1968), 394-408.

[30]Lindquist, "Political Life in the State University" (1972).

[31]Douglas McGregor, *The Human Side of Enterprise* (New York: McGraw-Hill, 1960); Likert, *The Human Organization* (1967); and Robert Blake and Jane Mouton, *Building a Dynamic Corporation Through Grid Organizational Development* (Reading, Mass.: Addison-Wesley, 1969).

[32]Chris Argyris and Donald Schoen, *Increasing Professional Effectiveness: Theory and Practice* (San Francisco: Jossey-Bass, 1974).

[33]Peter M. Blau, *Exchange and Power in Social Life* (New York: Wiley, 1964).

[34]Riesman, *Constraint and Variety in American Education* (Lincoln: Univ. of Nebraska Pr., 1956).

[35]Blau, *The Organization of Academic Work* (New York: John Wiley, 1973); and Parsons and Platt, *The American University* (Cambridge, Mass.: Harvard Univ. Pr., 1973).

[36]Edward Gross and Paul Grambsch, *University Goals and Academic Power* (Washington, D.C.: American Council on Education, 1968), p. 31.

[37]Martin, *Conformity* (1969), pp. 210, 221.

[38]Richard Peterson, *Goals for California Higher Education: A Survey of 116 College Communities* (Berkeley: Educational Testing Service, 1973); Gross and Grambsch, *Changes in University Organization: 1964-1971* (New York: McGraw-Hill, 1974); and Robert Wilson, Jerry Gaff and others, *College Professors and their Impact on Students* (New York: Wiley, 1975).

[39]Hefferlin, *The Dynamics of Academic Reform* (1969), p. 145.

[40]Clark Kerr, *The Uses of the University* (Cambridge, Mass.: Harvard Univ. Pr., 1963); Robert M. Hutchins, *The Higher Learning in America* (New Haven: Yale Univ. Pr., 1936).

[41]William Gamson, *Power and Discontent* (1968), p. 242.

[42]Lindquist, "Political Life in the State University" (1972).

[43]Robert Lipsett and Everett Ladd, Jr., "The Divided Professoriate," *Change*, 3 (1971), 54-60.

[44]Zelda Gamson, "Performance and Personalism in Student Faculty Relations," *Sociology of Education*, 40, (1967), 279-301.

[45]Theodore M. Newcomb and Everett K. Wilson, eds., *College Peer Groups* (Chicago: Aldine, 1966).

[46]Norma Anderson, "A Clique Analysis of the Effect of Proximity upon Communication Structure and Interpersonal Relationships for Permanent and Non-Permanent College Staff Members." Unpublished Ed.D. dissertation. (Bloomington: University of Illinois, 1966); Richard L. Case, "An Analysis of the Communication Structure of a University Administrative and Instructional Unit." Unpublished Ph.D. dissertation (Bloomington: University of Illinois, 1969).

[47]Max Heirich, The *Spiral of Conflict: Berkeley, 1964* (New York: Columbia, 1971).

[48]Willis D. Hawley and Frederick M. Wirt, eds., *The Search for Community Power* (Englewood Cliffs, N.J.: Prentice-Hall, 1968), p. 309.

[49]Peterson, *Goals for California Higher Education* (1973).

[50]George Weathersby, *Closing the Loop* (Cambridge, Mass.: Harvard Graduate School of Education, 1974).

[51]Daniel Katz and Robert Kahn, *The Social Psychology of Organizations* (New York: Wiley, 1967).

[52]Lindquist, "Political Life in the State University" (1972).

[53]Eckert, "The Share of the Teaching Faculty in the University Policy-Making," *AAUP Bulletin* (1975); and Eckert, "Participation in University Governance: A Second Look," (1971).

[54]McConnell, "Faculty Government," in Hodgkinson and Meeth, *Power and Authority* (1971).

[55]Floyd Hunter, *Community Power Structure* (Garden City, N.J.: Anchor, 1963).

[56]Chester R. Hastings, "The Influence Structure Within a State-Supported Four-Year College." Unpublished Ph.D. dissertation (Austin: Univ. of Texas, 1964).

[57]Harmon, "Academic Policy Making" (1966).

[58]Richard M. Merelman, "On the Neo-Elitist Critique of Community Power," *American Political Science Review*, 42 (1960), 451-460.

[59]Nicholas J. Demerath, Richard W. Stephans and Robb R. Taylor, *Power, Presidents and Professors* (New York: Basic Books, 1967).

[60]Marvin Peterson, "An Organizational Study of University Departments: Openness and Structural Complexity." Unpublished Ph.D. dissertation (Ann Arbor: University of Michigan, 1968); and Blau, *The Organization of Academic Work* (1973).

[61]Lindquist, "Political Life in the State University" (1972).

265

[62]Lindquist and Blackburn, "Middlegrove," *AAUP Bulletin* (1974).
[63]Hefferlin, *The Dynamics of Academic Reform* (1969), p. 146.
[64]Martin, *Conformity* (1969).
[65]Riesman, Gusfield and Gamson, *Academic Values and Mass Education* (1970), p. 285.
[66]Lindquist, "Political Life in the State University" (1972).
[67]Ladd, *Change in Educational Policy* (1970), p. 9.
[68]Michael D. Cohen and James G. March, *Leadership and Ambiguity: The American College President* (New York: McGraw-Hill, 1974).

Chapter 3

[1]Robert Pace, *College and University Environment Scales: Technical Manual* (Princeton, Educational Testing Service, 1969).
[2]Arthur Chickering and James McDowell, *Experience of College Questionnaire* (available from Chickering, Empire State College, 28 Union Avenue, Saratoga Springs, New York 12866).
[3]Wilbert J. McKeachie, *Teaching Tips; a Guidebook for the Beginning College Teacher* (Lexington, Mass.: Heath, 1969); and Stanford Erickson, *Motivation for Learning* (Ann Arbor: Univ. of Michigan Pr., 1974).
[4]John Dewey, *Experience and Education* (New York: Macmillan, 1938).
[5]Joseph Axelrod, *The University Teacher as Artist* (San Francisco: Jossey-Bass, 1973); and Richard Mann, *The College Classroom: Conflict, Change and Learning* (New York: Wiley, 1970).
[6]Mann, *The College Classroom* (1970).
[7]Robert Wilson, Jerry Gaff and others, *College Professors and their Impact on Students* (New York: Wiley, 1975).
[8]Chickering, *Education and Identity* (San Francisco: Jossey-Bass, 1969).
[10]Matthew Miles, "Planned Change and Organizational Health: Figure and Ground," in F. Carver and T. Sergiovanni, eds., *Organizations and Human Behavior: Focus on Schools* (New York: McGraw-Hill, 1969).
[11]Ronald Havelock, *Planning for Innovation through Disemination and Utilization of Knowledge* (Ann Arbor: Institute for Social Research, 1971).
[12]Richard Peterson, John Centra, Rodney Hartnett and Robert Linn, *Institutional Functioning Inventory: Preliminary Manual* (Princeton: Educational Testing Service, 1970).

Chapter 4

[1]Neal Gross, Joseph Giacquinla and Marilyn Bernstein, *Implementing Organizational Innovations* (New York: Harper and Row, 1963).

Section II

[1]Michael D. Cohen and James G. March, *Leadership and Ambiguity: The American College President* (New York: McGraw-Hill, 1974).

Chapter 5

[1]John Gardner, *Self-Renewal: The Individual and the Innovative Society* (New York: Harper and Row, 1963).

[2]David Katz and Robert Kahn, *The Social Psychology of Organizations* (New York: Wiley, 1967).

[3]Arthur Chickering, *Education and Identity* (San Francisco: Jossey-Bass, 1969).

[4]Esther Raushenbush, *The Student and His Studies* (Middleton, Conn.: Wesleyan University Press, 1964).

Chapter 6

[1]Alexander Astin, *The Invisible Colleges* (New York: McGraw-Hill, 1971).

[2]Michael Cohen and James March, *Leadership and Ambiguity: The American College President* (New York: McGraw-Hill, 1974).

[3]Walter Sikes, Lawrence Schlesinger, and Charles Seashore, *Renewing Higher Education from Within* (San Francisco: Jossey-Bass, 1974).

Chapter 7

[1]Frank Newman, *Report on Higher Education* (Washington, D.C.: HEW, March, 1971; Jerry Gaff, *The Cluster College* (San Francisco: Jossey-Bass, 1970); and David Riesman, Joseph Gusfield and Zelda Gamson, *Academic Values and Mass Education* (Garden City, N.J.: Doubleday, 1970).

[2]Paul Heist, *The Creative College Student: An Unmet Challenge* (San Francisco: Jossey-Bass, 1968).

[3]Judson Jerome, *Culture Out of Anarchy: The Reconstruction of American Higher Learning* (New York: Herder and Herder, 1971).

267

Chapter 8

[1]Edward Stevens, "Evaluation of the 4-1-4/Modular Term," (paper presented at the Association for Innovation in Higher Education Conference, March, 1973).

Chapter 9

[1]Andrew J. Grimes and Phillip K. Berger, "Cosmopolitan-Local: Evaluation of the Construct," *Administrative Science Quarterly*, 15 (1970), 407-416.

[2]Jerry Gaff, *The Cluster College* (San Francisco: Jossey-Bass, 1970); Carnegie Commission, *Less Time, More Options* (New York: McGraw-Hill, 1971); Judson Jerome, *Culture Out of Anarchy: The Reconstruction of American Higher Learning* (New York: Herder and Herder, 1971); Arthur Chickering, *Education and Identity* (San Francisco: Jossey-Bass, 1969); Joseph Katz, *No Time for Youth* (San Francisco: Jossey-Bass, 1968).

[3]Jack Lindquist, "Political Linkage: The Academic Innovation Process," *Journal of Higher Education*, 1974, 323-343.

[4]Tom Burns and George Macpherson Stalker, *The Management of Innovation (London: Tavistock, 1961)*.

[5]Abraham Maslow, *The Farther Reaches of Human Nature* (New York: Viking, 1972).

Chapter 10

[1]Chris Argyris and Donald Schon, *Improving Professional Effectiveness: Theory and Practice* (San Francisco: Jossey-Bass, 1974).

[2]Daniel Katz and Robert Kahn, *The Social Psychology of Organizations (New York: Wiley, 1967)*.

[3]Ernest Palola, Paul Bradley, Richard Debus and Timothy Lehmann, *Handbook on Program Effectiveness and Related Costs* (Saratoga Springs, N.Y.: Empire State College, 1975).

[4]Morris Keeton, *Shared Authority on Campus* (Washington, D.C.: American Association for Higher Education, 1971).

[5]Jerry Gaff, *Toward Faculty Renewal* (San Francisco: Jossey-Bass, 1975).

[6]Gerald Zaltman, Robert Duncan and Jonny Holbek, *Innovations and Organizations* (New York: Wiley, 1973).

[7]Gaff, *Toward Faculty Renewal;* and Albert B. Smith, *Faculty Development and Evaluation in Higher Education* (Washington, D.C.: American Association for Higher Education, 1976).

[8]Jack Lindquist, "Institutional Services for Teaching Improvement: Combine Your Change Assumptions," in Clifford Stewart and Thomas Harvey, eds., *Strategies for Significant Survival* (San Francisco: Jossey-Bass, 1974).

[9]Neal Gross, Joseph Giacquinla and Marilyn Bernstein, *Implementing Organizational Innovations* (New York: Harper and Row, 1963).

[10]Paul Berman and Milbrey McLaughlin, *The Findings in Review: Federal Programs Supporting Educational Change* (Washington, D.C.: HEW, R-1589/4, April, 1975).

[11]Jack Lindquist, "Can There Be An Experimenting College?", in William Bergquist and William Shoemaker, eds., *A Comprehensive Approach to Institutional Development* (San Francisco: Jossey-Bass, 1976).

Postscript

[1]Ronald Havelock, *A Guide to Innovation in Education* (Ann Arbor, Mich.: Institute for Social Research, 1972).

[2]Jack Lindquist, William Bergquist, Lance Buhl, Chester Case, Thomas Clark and Claude Mathis, *Designing to Improve College Teaching Programs* (Berkeley, Calif.: Pacific Soundings Press, forthcoming).

[3]Arthur Chickering, David Halliburton, Bergquist and Lindquist, *Developing the Curriculum: A Handbook for Faculty and Administration* (forthcoming)

DATE DUE

WITHDRAWN

DEMCO 38-296

Please remember that this is a library book,
and that it belongs only temporarily to each
person who uses it. Be considerate. Do
not write in this, or any, library book.